Developing Multicultural
Teacher Education Curricula

SUNY Series, The Social Context of Education
Christine E. Sleeter, editor
and
SUNY Series, Teacher Preparation and Development
Alan R. Tom, editor

Developing Multicultural Teacher Education Curricula

edited by

Joseph M. Larkin and Christine E. Sleeter

State University of New York Press

Published by
State University of New York Press, Albany

© 1995 State University of New York

For information, address the State University of New York Press,
State University Plaza, Albany, NY 12246

Production by Christine Lynch
Marketing by Theresa Abad Swierzowski

Library of Congress Cataloging-in-Publication Data
Developing multicultural teacher education curricula / edited by
    Joseph M. Larkin and Christine E. Sleeter.
        p.   cm. — (SUNY series, the social context of education)
    (SUNY series, teacher preparation and development)
      Includes bibliographical references and index.
      ISBN 0-7914-2593-2 (CH : acid-free paper). — ISBN 0-7914-2594-0
    (PB : acid-free paper)
        1. Teachers—Training of—United States—Curricula. 2. Curriculum
    change—United States. 3. Multiculturalism—United States.
    I. Larkin, Joseph M., 1947– . II. Sleeter, Christine E., 1948–
    . III. Series: SUNY series, social context of education.
    IV. Series: SUNY series in teacher preparation and development.
    LB1715.D48—1995
    370'.7.320973—dc20   94-38173
                                                               CIP

10 9 8 7 6 5 4 3 2 1

CONTENTS

JOSEPH M. LARKIN AND CHRISTINE E. SLEETER _____

INTRODUCTION

It has been nearly thirty years since our nation first turned its attention to the task of providing meaningful and equitable educational opportunities for all of our children. Over the course of these years, the struggle to develop the political will, the resources, and the educational strategies required to meet this challenge has been, at best, only partially successful. While it is possible to point to improvements in both access and outcomes for segments of the youth population whose educational needs previously had simply been ignored, the overpowering fact is that our system of education continues to distribute benefits inequitably among its students. And the interactions of such factors as social class, race, ethnicity, gender, language, and disability remain powerful predictors of the types of educational benefits children are likely to derive from their school experiences.

This book has been developed in response to the need for teacher education programs to reconsider how they prepare beginning teachers to contribute more affirmatively to this continuing struggle for educational equity in the schools. The role which teacher education should or even can play in confronting the problems of poverty, discrimination, and exclusion in school settings has never been clear (Weiner 1993), and this book makes no pretense of offering a comprehensive resolution to that important debate. Rather, the more limited purpose of this book is to explore ways of redesigning teacher education coursework to better prepare preservice students to respond to the diverse array of students they are likely to work with in the schools and to examine critically relationships among diverse sociocultural groups in the broader society.

In recent years, both scholarly journals and the mass media have devoted considerable attention to the rapidly increasing cultural diversity and escalating poverty among the school-aged population in our country. These demographic profiles are commonly associated with predictions of tremendous growth in the social costs and taxes that can be expected unless the schools find ways to effectively provide educational success for far more students than they currently do. Regardless of the questionable legitimacy of the expectation that the schools should be primarily responsible for addressing this change, there is little question that this scenario has created renewed interest among teacher education programs in developing new strategies to prepare teachers to work with culturally diverse students. This interest has been reflected both in the popularity of "diversity" as a conference theme across the country and in the recent publication of several books relating cultural diversity to various aspects of teacher preparation (Dilworth 1992; Grant and Gomez, in press; Kennedy 1991; O'Hair and Odell 1993).

While the focus of this book is on developing multicultural curricula in teacher education, we feel it is important to express our belief that this is only one of a number of fundamental changes that will be needed if programs are to prepare beginning teachers to work with the poor and students of color in urban or isolated rural school districts. For example, given the rather weak track record of university programs in affecting the attitudes and beliefs of mainstream teacher education students, it should be a priority for programs to recruit aggressively preservice teachers of color and others with cross-cultural life experience and a positive orientation to working in culturally diverse settings. Likewise, as many teacher education faculty, themselves, have weak affiliations with oppressed populations and communities, faculty recruitment and faculty development are other areas that need to be addressed.

Beyond revising curricula and course syllabi, it is also likely that programs will need to undertake more fundamental program restructuring efforts. If programs are to equip new teachers realistically to work in urban, multicultural settings, it seems clear to us that the locus of that preparation will need to shift away from the isolation of the campus toward greater interaction and collaboration with the schools and other agencies which know and serve urban communities. These same cooperative mechanisms will be needed to provide teacher candidates with the experiential opportunity to develop the cross-cultural knowledge which is required for multicultural teaching. Rarely do the time and scheduling restrictions of traditional university-based courses and school-based field experiences allow for the type or degree of collaboration which is probably necessary.

Moreover, these types of changes in professional preparation programs cannot be considered apart from the context of the broader university or college in which they are located. Indeed, the programmatic changes being suggested here would hardly be possible without the leadership and strong support of institutional administrators willing to discuss alterations in such basic issues as faculty teaching loads, faculty reward structures, and student graduation requirements. And, it must be kept in mind that teacher candidates obtain a majority of their credits and academic content knowledge from faculty in the liberal arts and sciences. Therefore, it will be difficult to establish a credible multicultural teacher education program or curriculum if most of the students' education is conducted within a narrow dominant-culture perspective.

The curriculum revisions discussed in this book are not intended to provide an alternative to these other fundamental changes. Rather, they are offered with an awareness that curricular issues are part of a broader agenda that must be addressed by teacher education programs willing to face the challenges of cultural diversity and educational equity. At the same time, with this acknowledgment we certainly do not want to diminish the significance of developing multicultural teacher education curricula. Regardless of the progress programs make in these other areas, we believe that the curriculum activities presented in this volume represent a type of change that is both possible and necessary.

In this book we conceptualize multicultural education as an approach to school reform which attempts to support, build on, and adapt to the strengths and aspirations of various oppressed social groups. Multicultural education can be conceptualized in different ways (Sleeter and Grant 1993), and the chapters in this volume vary somewhat in the main concepts they emphasize. While some authors emphasize building congruence between classroom instruction and children's cultural backgrounds, others stress the teaching of skills in social critique and social action. While some chapters focus mainly on racial and ethnic culture, others speak also to gender, social class, and/or disability. Nevertheless, authors in this volume agree that, unlike more traditional efforts to repress, remediate, or compensate for cultural differences which students bring to school, multicultural education works to accommodate those differences in cultural patterns and life experiences through adaptations in curricula, instructional activities, communication styles, and other educational components. Following from this definition, therefore, the goal of a multicultural teacher education curriculum should be to develop in preservice students the knowledge, skills, and dispositions needed to teach within the framework of multicultural education.

The concept of multicultural education is certainly not new and most teacher education programs have already incorporated at least some of its tenets into their curricula. But, the typical means of doing so has been to add on to the traditional program a discrete and usually isolated course with a title such as "Teaching the Culturally Different," "Bilingual Education," or "Multicultural Education." However, we believe that this approach trivializes and marginalizes multicultural education and does little to prepare beginning teachers to move beyond traditional approaches to teaching culturally diverse students.

Rather than viewing it as content to be covered in a course, this book has been developed on the assumption that multicultural education represents a basic reconceptualization of the process of preparing teachers. As such, it has implications for all components of a program, including those identified above. Moreover, it requires that the principles and practices of multicultural education be infused throughout all courses in the curriculum.

Over the past twenty years, significant research on the influence of culture on cognition and on the teaching-learning process has led to important developments in K–12 education in such areas as goal setting, instructional activities, assessment, and the preparation of multicultural curriculum materials. Ironically, however, this research has not had the same influence on the development of or on the literature relating to curriculum in teacher education. One consequence of this fact is that university professors wishing to redesign their coursework within a multicultural perspective have limited literature to draw upon which is directly related to their work.

This book is intended to address that problem. In chapters which follow, teacher educators working in a wide array of curricular areas describe and explain some of the curriculum modifications and pedagogical activities they have implemented in order to bring a multicultural perspective to their skill or content area. Rather than focusing on theoretical issues or literature review, the emphasis in these chapters is on illustrations of concrete practice drawn from the authors' own teaching experiences. It is our hope that sharing these ideas and strategies will provide some guidance to other teacher educators and will stimulate further development and discussion of multicultural teacher education curricula.

The opening chapter provides a brief overview of the literature on multicultural teacher education. Its purpose is to identify common themes and issues contained within that literature and, in so doing, to offer an intellectual framework within which the following chapters might be considered. One of the themes discussed in this chapter concerns the pressing challenge for teacher education programs to help teacher candidates grapple with and understand such things as prejudice, institutional discrimination, and the alternative life experiences and perspectives of oppressed peoples, all of which are fundamental to our concept of multicultural education. Thus, in chapters two to six the authors discuss ways in which they approach these complex issues. Most of the authors work within what are traditionally considered to be the sociocultural and psychological foundations areas, and they relate a variety of university activities and community-based field experiences which they employ in their courses.

Just as the language skills of speaking, reading, and writing are a central part of culture, so too are they rightfully considered basic to education and the school experience. For this reason, the ability to work with and build on cultural diversity in literacy development is an important part of multicultural teaching. In chapters seven and eight, the authors present strategies which they use to foster multiculturalism in coursework which focuses on literature and on reading and language arts methods. These are supplemented by chapter nine in which the authors report on a research effort to assess the impact of various approaches to multicultural literature on elementary preservice teachers. In chapter ten, the author discusses some of the issues faced in trying to develop a secondary English methods course within a multicultural framework.

Multicultural teacher education attempts to help prospective teachers, not only to develop a variety of teaching styles and methods, but also to develop a multicultural knowledge base in the academic subject areas they will be teaching. In chapters eleven through sixteen, therefore, education methods instructors describe both pedagogical exercises they have used and ways in which they have expanded or modified academic content in the subject areas of social studies, science, mathematics, technology, fine arts, and health. Chapter seventeen describes an introductory course on exceptional education, and it provides a good illustration of how reconceptualizing an academic discipline within a multicultural framework may well lead to nontraditional approaches to course organization and pedagogy.

In most teacher education programs, student teaching serves as a transitional experience between preparation and professional practice. It is an experience which provides a significant opportunity to help teacher candidates bring together the various components of their training into a more holistic teaching performance and gain some insight into the types of orientations the candidates are likely to bring to their work as teachers. Thus, student teaching is a crucial part of any program which is attempting to establish a teaching paradigm which differs from the deeply rooted patterns of traditional practice. In chapter eighteen, the authors discuss ways in which teacher education programs can enhance the likelihood that student teaching will strengthen and reinforce, rather than undermine, the preparation of multicultural educators.

None of the chapters claims to offer the definitive formula for restructuring the curriculum. Indeed, we believe there is no single way that a multicultural curriculum should look. Rather, the authors share ideas, struggles, and experiences, as well as syntheses of research literature, in order to provide departure points for teacher educators in the quest for developing their own multicultural curricula.

REFERENCES

Dilworth, M. E., ed. (1992). *Diversity in teacher education.* San Francisco: Jossey-Bass.

Grant, C. A., and Gomez, M. L., eds. (in press). *Campus and classroom: Making schools multicultural.* New York: Macmillan.

Kennedy, M. M., ed. (1991). *Teaching academic subjects to diverse learners.* New York: Teachers College Press.

O'Hair, M. J., and Odell, S. J., eds. (1993). *Diversity and teaching.* Orlando, FL: Harcourt Brace Jovanovich.

Sleeter, C. E., and Grant, C. A. (1993). *Making choices for multicultural education,* second edition. Columbus, OH: Merrill.

Weiner, L. (1993). *Preparing teachers for urban schools.* New York: Teachers College Press.

1

JOSEPH M. LARKIN_____

Curriculum Themes and Issues in Multicultural Teacher Education Programs

As teacher preparation programs attempt to respond to the increasing cultural diversity of our society, the traditional preservice teacher education curriculum is one of a number of areas that will need to be broadly reconsidered. What types of knowledge, skills, and attitudes or dispositions might better equip preservice educators to work constructively with the challenges and opportunities of cultural diversity which they will face in the schools? Most of the chapters in this book address this question from the perspective of a rather specific course, content area, or component within the wider curriculum.

This chapter, however, will provide an overview of the professional literature pertaining to the knowledge, skills, and attitudes which ought to be included in the preparation of educators for multicultural teaching. This literature is far from uniform in its recommendations, and no attempt is made here to exhaustively review all the points of disagreement which might distinguish scholars working in the area. Rather, the purpose will be to identify and discuss the common curricular themes which clearly run throughout this literature and to identify issues which I feel are either raised or left unresolved by these widely shared prescriptions.

The literature on multicultural teacher education, albeit under different labels, may date its origins within the mainstream of educational literature (AACTE 1973; Baker 1977; Klassen and Gollnick 1977; Smith 1969) to roughly the same period when the profession was beginning to acknowledge the unique problems associated with poverty and racism in urban schools across the country. Yet, compared to the significant attention given to urban, multicultural school issues over the last few decades, the initial preparation of teachers to work in such settings has not been accorded the same degree of rigorous attention or status within the field of teacher education (Grant and Secada 1990). Until recently, according to Kenneth Zeichner, much of the work in this area could only be found in the "fugitive educational literature" (1992, 3) of less accessible journals, conference papers, or unpublished reports. This observation is supported by the fact that the major teacher education reform proposals of the 1980s gave very little attention to the particular challenges of preparing educators for multicultural or urban schools (Haberman 1987).

Due in part to this neglect, and to the fact that program or action research in the complex human services rarely yields clear or unambiguous conclusions, the available literature on multicultural teacher education provides little empirical evidence on the types of preservice programs which might effectively prepare teachers for cultural diversity. Indeed, the research which is available on both preservice and inservice professional development in this area suggests that commonly used training strategies often fail to achieve either meaningful or lasting results (Grant and Secada 1990; McDiarmid 1992; McDiarmid and Price 1993). In the absence of consistent research findings, most of the literature reviewed in this chapter is largely propositional in nature, derived from the reasoning and varied experiences of scholars long involved with urban, multicultural schools and teacher education.

While a more extensive examination of the literature could well address a broader and more detailed set of factors, the summary overview which follows will be limited in a couple of ways. First, although issues relating to gender, disability, and sexual orientation are frequently and legitimately considered under the canopy of multicultural education, the concept of culture in this chapter focuses primarily on the dimensions of race, ethnicity, and social class. Then, within this narrowed purview, consideration will be further limited to four areas which I believe serve to organize and focus the curricular themes and issues in the discussion of multicultural teacher education. These areas will include program ideology and orientation, dispositions toward multicultural teaching, cultural knowledge, and classroom practice.

PROGRAM IDEOLOGY AND ORIENTATION

Although it appears not to be widely reflected in practice, there is nearly universal agreement among theorists that attention to cultural diversity needs to be woven throughout all components of the teacher education curriculum, rather than treated only in an isolated course or in fragments scattered across a program (Grant and Koskela 1986). Multiculturalism, that is, ought to be understood, not as an addition to traditional teacher education, but rather as an alternative way of conducting teacher education. This understanding, in turn, will require teacher educators to move toward "rethinking the overall goals and structures of both their programs and the curricula that define them" (Hixson 1993, 2). Yet, I would suggest that, as soon as such programs begin moving from the easy rhetoric of cultural pluralism toward achieving the type of consensus, cohesion, and thematic unity which characterize any quality professional education program (Goodlad 1990; Howey and Zimpher 1989), they must face some very basic and difficult issues.

Such concepts as "cultural diversity" and "multicultural education," by themselves, are sufficiently broad and diluted to engender widespread support among teacher educators, but they are inadequate as organizing principles capable of giving direction to program development. Indeed, Christine Sleeter and Carl Grant (1988) have described and documented the wide variety of theo retical and programmatic orientations to multicultural education; and conflicting assumptions, goals, and strategies abound within this universe of activities joined by little more than a common label. Thus, teacher educators in a particular program need to operationally define their orientation to multicultural teacher education. That is, they need to define the nature of the work for which they will attempt to prepare their students.

The difficult and inherently political nature of this task can be illustrated with just a few alternatives. One fairly common rationalization for infusing multiculturalism into preservice teacher preparation grows out of a recognition that the cultural diversity of the population and the rates of cross-cultural interaction, both domestically and globally, are increasing dramatically. According to this perspective on growing global interconnectedness, all preservice programs need to adopt multicultural teacher education as a means of preparing all future teachers to help all children and youth develop the sensitivities and skills which this type of society and world will require (Garcia and Pugh 1992; Hixson 1993; Zimpher and Ashburn 1992).

This orientation to multicultural education as an effort to help all students "act as responsible members of the world community" (Polites 1993, 54) is quite appealing because it easily, and, I think, intentionally, generates images of teachers going forth into the schools of suburban and small town America to extol the liberal values of respect, tolerance, cooperation, and democratic citizenship. Moreover, while this orientation does encompass domestic cultural diversity, its broader international framework removes multicultural education from the political problem of being viewed as just "a minority thing" (Garcia and Pugh 1992, 215).

However, the problem with this definition is that it provides a weak and inadequate paradigm for understanding and action within culturally diverse settings as they actually exist within the United States. In the central cities and some rural areas of this country, cultural differences are inextricably tied to racial segregation, economic oppression, and political powerlessness; the consequences and human dynamics produced by these forces must be considered integral to any meaningful conception of multicultural education. Indeed, urban multicultural schools can hardly be understood apart from the poverty which fuels and sustains the context in which they are located. And generic efforts to prepare teachers to promote cross-cultural awareness and sensitivity in all schools will not prepare teachers for this reality in urban schools (Haberman 1987).

Yet, acceptance of the argument that the forces and consequences of social inequality are central to multicultural teaching still leaves open the question of the nature of the work for which preservice educators are to be prepared. Perhaps the most logical, or at least the purest, extension of this line of reasoning is offered by the critical theorists and the social reconstructionists who use such concepts as empowerment, emancipatory pedagogy and change agent as ways of broadly defining the range of roles appropriately to be expected of urban multicultural educators (Gordon 1985; Sleeter 1991; Sleeter and Grant 1988). In this orientation, multicultural teacher education needs to ground itself in an ideology focused on social justice and programmatically "strengthen its connections with those social movements that are attempting to reconstruct American society" (Sleeter 1991, 217). Among its many role implications for teachers, this perspective calls for preparing educators who can design and implement learning activities which develop simultaneously the students' academic skills and their capacities to critique and act on the structures of oppression which impose on their daily lives (Bigelow 1990; Shor 1980).

Despite the moral persuasiveness of the reconstructionist argument, the ideology which, at least implicitly, undergirds most of the multicultural teacher education literature seems to accept social inequality as an inherent consequence of our competitive society, values education as a means of equalizing competition, and acknowledges the severe limitations of the school as an agency to redress society's broader structural problems (Weiner 1989). Philosophically, moreover, although aggressively promoting the principles and conditions required by our espoused commitment to democracy (Liston and Zeichner 1990), this liberal perspective questions the appropriateness of a teacher education curriculum which attempts to impose a particular ideology on its students (King, Bay and Hare 1993). As Lois Weiner articulated this concern,

> Fusing the teachers' roles as educator and as activist against social injustice destroys the capacity of each role to inform and check the other. Further, it damages our credibility with parents and students who may have political ideas different from our own and ignores our responsibility to develop students' ability to critique all points of view, including the one we advocate. (1989, 154)

The challenge of developing a cohesive program orientation or philosophy is complicated by the dual needs of creating a curriculum which does more than merely legitimize and perpetuate the hierarchical structure of our society (Gordon 1985) and of establishing a program which realistically relates to the backgrounds most teacher candidates are coming from and the nature of the schools into which most of them will be going. The difficulty of this task was reflected in one alternative teacher education program which attempted to prepare nontraditional students for multicultural teaching around the organizing themes of critical inquiry and action for social justice. Not surprisingly, the program experienced some tensions between its efforts to prepare the students for the classroom "as it should be" and the students' desire to develop the skills which would give them credibility and success in the classroom "as it is" in the schools in which they were working (Anoka-Hennepin School District and St. Cloud State University 1992, 33).

The ideological tensions conveyed by this illustration need to be confronted collectively by teacher education program faculty. Maintaining credibility among preservice students and school personnel, as alluded to above, is a very real concern, yet it is a concern which tends to reinforce fairly traditional conceptions of the teacher's role and modes of practice. Establishing credibility with oppressed urban families and communities, on the other hand, might well require the type of social reconstructionist paradigm for teacher education that is advocated in this volume by Sleeter and by William Armadine and Kathleen Farber, among others. Having spent considerable time attempting to work through these issues within our own program, we have learned that, while reaching a detailed consensus at a philosophical level is very difficult, the debate of these issues can lead to an agreement at a programmatic level within which concerted and meaningful change can occur.

For preservice programs attempting to restructure for multicultural education, these issues of orientation and ideology present more than an academic exercise. They are fundamental to defining the framework within which the program will not only plan curriculum but also will set standards for admission and graduation, select field sites and cooperating teachers, design field experiences, and hire faculty. However, in what follows, the discussion will be limited primarily to curricular issues.

DISPOSITIONS TOWARD MULTICULTURAL TEACHING

At least at one level, there appears to be a fairly broad consensus among scholars concerning the types of attitudes which education programs should attempt to develop in those preparing to teach in urban, multicultural schools. At a minimum, students need to understand and personally value the goals and philosophy of cultural pluralism as a basic tenet of multicultural teaching, and they need to genuinely respect the behavioral expressions of cultural diversity (Baker 1977; Bennett 1979; McDiarmid 1992; Zimpher and Ashburn 1992). Students need to understand and positively reject the manifestations and the consequences of prejudice, racism, sexism, and other group-debilitating forces (Gay 1977; Gollnick 1992; Nelson-Barber and Mitchell 1992). Moreover, students must develop a willingness to explore honestly and discuss openly their own feelings, values, and attitudes relating to race, class, gender, and other difficult dimensions of multicultural teaching (Ladson-Billings 1991).

Beyond the frame of mind reflected by the above, however, students must also develop an "attitudinal infrastructure" (Hixson 1993, 7) which more directly expresses a positive disposition toward teaching and working in urban, multicultural schools. Such an infrastructure might begin with an acknowledgment that poverty, cultural differences, and public bureaucracy often make urban teaching more difficult than teaching in other settings (Brown 1992; Haberman 1987; Montero-Sieburth 1989). In spite of this, it includes the choice or the willingness to work in urban schools and the ability to be comfortable among diverse learners (Pasch et. al. 1993). And, perhaps most importantly, this disposition includes genuinely held high expectations for all students and a commitment to the flexibility and perseverance required of teachers to realize these expectations (Tippeconnic 1983; Haberman 1993; Zeichner 1992). At their very best, efforts to assist students to develop this positive disposition toward multicultural teaching would move them from the stage of tolerance for cultural differences to a point where they could truly embrace what Maxine Greene so powerfully describes as "the passions of pluralism" (1993, 13).

Affecting the formation of or changes in the types of attitudes and dispositions identified here is very difficult, and including these in its curriculum will present a teacher education program with no small challenge. Indeed, Martin Haberman has argued, reflecting his opinion that universities and teacher education faculty are ill-suited for this task, that "the obvious implication, for me, is that if these traits are truly crucial, then selection is far more important than training" (1993, 84). And the available evidence on the success of developmental efforts to influence these deeply seated attitudes in either preservice or experienced educators offers little reason to contradict Haberman's judgment (Grant and Secada 1990; Haberman and Post 1992; McDiarmid and Price 1993; Sleeter 1992). This evidence strongly suggests that, in addition to the curriculum modifications discussed in this book, programs will also need to place a priority on recruiting a diverse array of prospective teachers who already possess both a positive orientation to cultural pluralism and a "cultural solidarity" (Foster 1994) with urban students.

However, at least for the near future, it is likely that many teacher education programs will continue to work, not with students who are aggressively recruited or carefully selected, but with those students who, for their own reasons, choose to become teachers and meet the admissions standards, which typically have little to do with either attitudes or dispositions (Pugach 1984). And, the composition and teaching aspirations of this self-selected corps of prospective teachers will further complicate the challenge facing programs which are attempting to prepare educators for urban, multicultural teaching. In their summary of the data on preservice teachers, Nancy Zimpher and Elizabeth Ashburn wrote,

> These findings from a random sample of teacher education programs stratified by institutional type show that the average preservice student is typically a white female from a small town or suburban community who matriculates into a college less than one hundred miles away from home and intends to return to small town America to teach middle-income children of average intelligence in traditionally organized schools. (1992, 41)

As programs experiment with strategies to encourage these students to develop the dispositions required for constructive urban teaching, it will clearly be necessary to go beyond the superficial courses and the standard reading, writing, and field assignments normally employed for this purpose. By this point in their educational careers, most students are quite capable of producing whatever academic responses are required to "get their multicultural tickets punched"

(Garcia and Pugh 1992, 216). Thus, it will be necessary to reach through the knowledge base of multicultural education and, as Sheryl Santo challenges us, to "enter the very private and delicate world of the affective domain" (1986, 21). This is not to suggest the need for a resurgence of touchy-feely encounter sessions; it is to emphasize the importance of building into programs opportunities for the open, honest, tough, and respectful exchange of ideas and attitudes which matter in multicultural teaching.

CULTURAL KNOWLEDGE

Educators have always realized, at least in some fashion, that teaching entails teaching something to someone and that good teaching, therefore, requires knowledge of both the subject matter and the students (Kennedy 1992, viii). In recent decades, however, this simple framework has been extended and complicated by recognition of the fact that teachers, students, and subject matter interact within multiple, layered contexts which profoundly influence both the actors and the subject matter in the teaching-learning process (Cazden and Mehan 1989). It follows, therefore, that effective teaching is now understood to require knowledge not only of subject matter and students but also of the contextual fabric within which they meet.

In situations of cross-cultural teaching, as when the preservice teachers profiled above work with poor children or students of color in urban or multicultural communities, developing knowledge of unfamiliar cultures will be indispensable to a teacher's need to make sense of the subject matter, the students, or the contextual forces. This cultural knowledge is at the heart of multicultural education, and proposals to include this component in teacher education programs serve as a constant thread running through the literature (Baker 1977; Gay 1977; Grant 1991; Zeicher 1992).

Addressing this task, however, is more complicated than simply offering ethnic study courses in which preservice students learn about African, Asian, or Hispanic Americans. Rather, from my reading of the literature, I would suggest that this broad area of cultural knowledge might be divided into three categories: (1) knowledge of the nature, functions, and processes of culture itself; (2) knowledge of the cultural foundations of schools, teaching, learning, and subject matter; and (3) content, language, and process knowledge relating to particular cultural groups. I will briefly explain each of these below.

If programs hope to get their students to make a genuine and lasting commitment to cultural pluralism or multiculturalism, a commitment which will withstand the forces of monoculturalism which pervade our society and many of its schools (Santos 1986), then it will be necessary to provide them with an understanding of culture and diversity of cultural patterns which go far deeper than the slogans and superficial political debates which currently dominate much campus discourse on culture (Price 1992). They will need to understand the components which comprise culture, that each of these components is a variable, that these variables can and do combine into a staggering array of patterns, and that patterns are evolving, changing arrangements which respond to both external forces and members' needs.

This knowledge of culture and cultural pluralism cannot be transmitted to or received by the students as subject matter to be stored and eventually lost. Rather, the goal needs to be to fundamentally establish a cultural framework within the students' cognitive structures, to create a "multicultural mind-set" (Polites 1993, 54) which students will habitually use to interpret, analyze, and make sense of their life experiences. This anthropological mind-set will not only help students understand and appreciate the legitimacy of the cultural differences they will encounter in the schools, but, more basically, it will also help our white, middle class, dominant culture students to see their own taken-for-granted values and styles and the institutional arrangements with which they are so familiar as simply illustrations of "culture in action" (Brown 1992, 11), rather than continuing to perceive these as divinely ordained definitions of how things are supposed to be. And liberating the dominant culture from its ethnocentrism is the first step toward providing real opportunities to those who are "culturally different."

In addition to this multicultural frame of mind, programs secondly will need to assist students in developing broader knowledge about the cultural foundations of education and schooling. Most teacher education students have detailed knowledge about schools that is grounded directly in their particular and personal experiences, and this experiential knowledge base provides a very limited perspective from which to analyze and understand much that goes on in and around urban, multicultural schools. Cultural foundations knowledge should enable preservice students to comprehend social diversity, not only in terms of individual differences, but also in terms of the power differential between social groups based on race, class, language, and gender (Grant and Koskela 1986; Ross and Smith 1992). Moreover, it should move students beyond their common habit of thinking about schools as just familiar places toward an understanding of schools as social institutions with embedded structures, norms, and recurrent practices which can and do systematically obstruct the educational development of some groups of students (Liston and Zeichner 1990). And, very importantly, this foundations knowledge should help prospective teachers understand how culture and language influence the processes of cognition, learning, communication, and interaction styles which so powerfully and immediately affect classroom climate and teaching-learning activities (Cazden and Mehan 1989; Garcia 1988; Shade 1989).

As students prepare to go to work in culturally diverse, and often unfamiliar settings, they need to develop a broad array of concepts, knowledge, and explanatory formulations if they are to make sense of the preservice and teaching experiences they will have. History, anthropology, sociology, linguistics, psychology, philosophy, and political-economics all have important perspectives to contribute to this learning process. Such knowledge will not only help students understand the contextual factors which influence teaching and learning within the classroom and school, but it will also lead to a greater awareness of those forces in the broader community, state, and national contexts which impinge on the educational process.

The third, and the most difficult, category in this area which students need to learn about relates to knowledge of particular cultural groups which differ from their own. From the early stages of the multicultural education movement, theorists have argued that teacher preparation programs need to employ a wide range of strategies to assist educators in developing cross-cultural content knowledge (Banks 1981; Gay 1977), with some suggesting that students should be allowed to focus on or specialize in the study of one particular group in order to better grasp the depth and richness of cultural patterns (Gay 1993). And prescriptions of this nature remain common throughout the literature.

More recently, however, scholars have begun to emphatically warn against the harmful paradox in which cultural group studies transmit superficial and often inaccurate generalizations about particular racial, ethnic, or gender groups for the purpose of getting educators not to generalize about their students based upon their group memberships (Grant 1991; McDiarmid, 1992). Noting the impossibility of teaching preservice educators cultural content knowledge about all the possible groups they might encounter in their schools, Courtney Cazden and Hugh Mehan have cited some of the problems that can result from such efforts.

> The dangers come from the likelihood that such knowledge will contribute only stereotyped categories and labels that then become barriers to understanding the behavior of a particular child working on a particular task, and contribute to lowered expectations about the child's possible achievement. (1989, 54)

The conclusion to be drawn from these warnings is not that we should use only "individual difference" theories to explain diversity, as was discussed above, nor that providing students with any information about group histories, struggles, or their perceptions and definitions of their experiences and events will necessarily be harmful. Rather, it suggests the need to prepare educators to use their knowledge about individuals, groups, and contexts as tools to help them critically analyze, interpret, and understand particular students and events within their classrooms. Thus, in addition to scholarly ethnic studies content, students also should develop the skills to question and observe cross-cultural phenomena, or to interrogate diversity, as Marilyn Cochran-Smith and Susan Lytle (1992) have described it, so that they learn how to learn from their own students about the cultural traits and patterns which have significance in their own particular schools (Noordhoff and Kleinfeld 1991).

Many writers on multicultural teacher education have suggested that having preservice students study or examine their own cultural identities and group patterns is a useful way to begin developing the skills to explore other cultures (Ladson-Billings 1991). Others have pointed out that such works as autobiographies, fiction, poetry, music, drama, and film by and about persons of color provide effective means for gaining knowledge and insight across cultural boundaries (Gay 1977 ; Green 1993; Jackson, this volume). Most scholars argue, however, that programs do need to provide preservice students with early, frequent, and carefully supervised direct experiences with members of other cultures (Pasch et. al. 1993). And, increasingly, it is being suggested that these direct experiences need to occur, not just in schools, but also in other community agencies and settings where prospective teachers are likely to get a fuller picture of the depth, richness, and strengths of the cultural patterns of their students (Brown 1992; Irvine 1992; Ladson-Billings 1991; Montero-Sieburth 1989; Tellez et al., this volume).

CLASSROOM PRACTICE

The question frequently can be heard from persons not familiar with urban schools, particularly from educators, whether teaching culturally diverse students is really that different from teaching in other kinds of schools. After all, the question goes, isn't good teaching just good teaching, regardless of where or with whom? And, by implication, wouldn't a quality teacher education program prepare students to succeed in any type of school? Putting aside for a second the answer to be drawn clearly from the preceding sections, that generic teaching models are neither appropriate nor adequate for work in multicultural schools, this question deserves to be addressed more directly. The literature suggests that both "yes" and "no" are possible answers, depending upon the level at which the question is asked.

It is at the level of articulating general types of classroom practices or pedagogical skills that one could reasonably respond affirmatively to the proposition that good teaching is just good teaching. The terms and labels used to describe, for example, the repertoire of instructional practices, classroom management techniques, or motivation strategies needed by effective teachers apply equally in suburban, rural, and urban schools (Irvine 1992; Stallings and Quinn 1991), as well as in both English-speaking and multilingual schools (Garcia 1988; Lucas, Henze, and Donato 1990). Urban, multicultural educators do not have their own unique or secret vocabulary or set of pedagogical skills which radically demarcate their professional domain from that of other professional teachers. In fact, as Hilliard has argued, "there is no special pedagogy for at-risk students....Further, at-risk students fail to achieve because appropriate regular pedagogy has not been provided them." (in Irvine 1992, 81).

Thus, in terms of the tools of the trade, it would seem to make sense to talk about school teaching as a set of common and transferable classroom skills. Yet, at a deeper level, any meaningful discussion of the competencies needed for effective teaching can hardly ignore the students with whom and the contexts in which these tools will be used. Teaching is an interactive and context-dependent activity, and good educators are ones who can adapt their teaching skills to the environment in which they are working (Burstein and Cabello 1989; Montero-Sieburth 1989). And, it is these contextual differences which significantly distinguish teaching mainstream culture children in small town or suburban schools from teaching in urban, multicultural schools. The dispositions and types of cultural knowledge identified above represent parts of the preparation for multicultural teaching which are often not addressed in traditional preservice programs. If and when they are, however, it will remain for preparation programs to help educators learn how to use these to adapt their classroom practices to the lives and cultural realities of their students. While this sounds almost like a cliché, it warrants careful consideration; for, adapting education to fit the students, rather than the reverse, represents a radical reconceptualization of the traditional education process. Yet, the need to do so, if we genuinely hope to provide real educational opportunities to all students, is sounded throughout the literature.

Whether it is described as scaffolding (Zeicher 1992), cultural context teaching (Gay 1993) or responsive teaching (Bowers and Flinders 1990), it is a common theme which provides a holistic philosophy of teaching in multicultural education. As Judson Hixson described it,

> A multicultural approach to instruction requires that teachers learn how to assess and build on the personal, cultural, and social strengths, skills, and competencies that students bring to the classrooms; on their prior knowledge and experience; that they help students build on those strengths, rather than replace them; and, that they help students see connections between curricular content, their current realities, and their future possibilities. (1993, 10)

Thus, culturally responsive teaching is not a particular method to be added to a teacher's collection of techniques. Rather, it is a comprehensive approach to the teaching role which informs and guides all aspects of classroom practice. Grant and Sleeter (1989), for example, have illustrated in great detail how the lesson planning process can be adapted to the immediate lives of a culturally diverse student population. Numerous writers have discussed procedures for locating, selecting, adapting, and developing curriculum materials for multicultural education (Gay 1990; Hernandez 1989). Several others have described or proposed ways in which teachers can more effectively respond to the variety of styles of communication, behavior, and interaction often exhibited in heterogeneous classrooms (Bowers and Flinders 1990; Shade and New 1993). And still other scholars have provided accounts of successful efforts to consciously adapt school and classroom practices to reflect the family values and cultural patterns with which students are already accustomed (Abi-Nader 1993; Comer 1988; Foster 1994; Vogt, Jordon, and Tharp 1987). Moreover, the bilingual education literature provides many insights into how teachers can be prepared to respond educationally to the language and cultural diversity present in a growing number of public schools (Chu and Levy 1988; McLeod 1994), including the educational advantages to be derived from English-speaking teachers learning to communicate at some level in the languages of their language-minority students (Lucas, Henze, and Donato 1990).

Now, clearly, preparing preservice educators with the dispositions, cultural knowledge, and competencies to adapt their curriculum and instructional skills for culturally responsive classroom practice reintroduces the issue of preparing teachers either for schools as they should be or for schools as they are. Even though, I would argue, the K–12 schools are further ahead on these issues than most teacher training programs, it is still evident that culturally responsive teaching is not widely practiced in the public schools of this country, including the urban, multicultural public schools. And this poses the potential risk, should we succeed in the preparation efforts proposed here, of training new teachers to engage in a form of practice which may well be devalued or more actively frustrated by the prevailing norms and professional expectations in their school assignments.

However, while acknowledging this as a legitimate concern, particularly when it is raised by preservice students themselves, the issue needs to be considered in perspective. Both justice and national self-interest demand that we change our traditional approaches to education in our multicultural, urban centers. This process of change will be neither quick, nor smooth, nor well-coordinated among the various educational agencies. Teacher education institutions and the K–12 schools will continue to push and pull one another, to alternately support and restrain each other's efforts. Within this context, teachers prepared for the complexities of multicultural education will be able to adjust their professional practice to whatever institutional demands they may encounter, including the demands of traditional, monocultural schools. Some may even induce changes in institutional practices which do not deserve compliance. By contrast, however, years of experiential evidence demonstrate that traditionally trained teachers cannot readily adapt their conventional paradigms and professional practices to the challenges and opportunities contained in the approaches to multicultural education discussed in this chapter.

REFERENCES

Abi-Nader, J. (1993). Meeting the needs of multicultural classrooms: Family values and the motivation of minority students. In *Diversity and teaching*, ed. M. J. O'Hair and S. J. Odell, 212–228. Orlando, FL: Harcourt Brace Jovanovich.

American Association of Colleges for Teacher Education (AACTE). (1973). No one model American. *Journal of Teacher Education*, 24(4):264–265.

Anoka-Hennepin School District and St. Cloud State University. (1992). *Preparing teachers for diversity: An alternative preparation for teacher licensure program.* (Report).

Baker, G. C. (1977). Multicultural imperatives for curriculum development in teacher education. *Journal of Research and Development in Education* 2(1):70–83.

Banks, J. A. (1981). *Multiethnic education: Theory and practice.* Boston: Allyn and Bacon.

Bennett, C. T. (1979). The preparation of preservice secondary social studies teachers in multiethnic education. *The High School Journal* February:232–237.

Bigelow, W. (1990). Inside the classroom: Social vision and critical pedagogy. *Teachers College Record* 91(3):437–448.

Bowers, C. A., and D. J. Flinders. (1990). *Responsive teaching: An ecological approach to classroom patterns of language, culture, and thought.* New York: Teachers College Press.

Brown, C. E. (1992). Restructuring for a new America. In *Diversity in teacher education,* ed. M. E. Dilworth, 1–22. San Francisco: Jossey-Bass.

Burstein, N. D., and B. Cabello. (1989). Preparing teachers to work with culturally diverse students: A teacher education model. *Journal of Teacher Education* 40(5): 9–16.

Cazden, C. B., and H. Mehan. (1989). Principles from sociology and anthropology: Context, code, classroom, and culture. In *Knowledge base for the beginning teacher,* ed. M. C. Reynolds, 47–57. New York: Pergamon Press.

Chu, H., and J. Levy. (1988). Multicultural skills for bilingual teachers: Training for competency development. *NABE Journal* 12(2):153–169.

Cochran-Smith, M., and S. L. Lytle. (1992). Interrogating cultural diversity: Inquiry and action. *Journal of Teacher Education,* 43(2):104–115.

Comer, J. P. (1988). Educating poor minority children. *Scientific American* 259:42–48.

Foster, M. (1994). Effective black teachers: A literature review. In *Teaching diverse populations: Formulating a knowledge base,* ed. E. R. Hollins, J. E. King, and W. Hayman, 225–242. Albany, NY: SUNY Press.

Garcia, E. E. (1988). Attributes of effective schools for language minority students. *Education and Urban Society* 20(4):387–398.

Garcia, J., and S. L. Pugh. (1992). Multicultural education in teacher preparation programs: A political or educational concept? *Phi Delta Kappan* 74(3):214–219.

Gay, G. (1977). Curriculum for multicultural teacher education. In *Pluralism and the American teacher,* ed. F. H. Klassen and D. M. Gollnick, 31–62. Washington, DC: AACTE.

———. (1990). Achieving educational equity through curriculum desegregation. *Phi Delta Kappan* 72(1):56–62.

———. (1993). Building cultural bridges: A bold proposal for teacher education. *Education and Urban Society* 25(3):285–299.

Gollnick, D. M. (1992). Understanding the dynamics of race, class, and gender. In *Diversity in teacher education,* ed. M. E. Dilworth, 63–78. San Francisco: Jossey-Bass.

Goodlad, J. I. (1990). *Teachers for our nation's schools.* San Francisco: Jossey-Bass.

Gordon, B. M. (1985). Teaching teachers: "Nation at risk" and the issue of knowledge in teacher education. *The Urban Review* 17(1):33–46.

Grant, C. A. (1991). Culture and teaching: What do teachers need to know? In *Teaching academic subjects to diverse learners*, ed. M. M. Kennedy, 237–256. New York: Teachers College Press.

Grant, C. A., and R. A. Koskela. (1986). Education that is multicultural and the relationship between preservice campus learning and field experiences. *Journal of Educational Research* 79(4):197–203.

Grant, C. A., and W. G. Secada. (1990). Preparing teachers for diversity. In *Handbook of research on teacher education*, ed. W. R. Houston, 403–422. New York: Macmillan.

Grant, C. A., and C. E. Sleeter. (1989). *Turning on learning*. Columbus, OH: Merrill.

Green, M. (1993). The passions of pluralism: Multiculturalism and the expanding community. *Educational Researcher* 22(1):13–18.

Haberman, M. (1987). *Recruiting and selecting teachers for urban schools*. New York: ERIC Clearinghouse on Urban Education.

———. (1993). Contexts: Implications and reflections. In *Diversity and teaching*, ed. M. J. O'Hair and S. J. Odell, 84–89. Orlando, FL: Harcourt Brace Jovanovich.

Haberman, M., and L. Post. (1992). Does direct experience change education students' perceptions of low-income minority children? *The Midwestern Educational Researcher* 5(2):29–31.

Hernandez, H. (1989). *Multicultural education: A teacher's guide to content and process*. Columbus, OH: Merrill.

Hixson, J. (March 19, 1993). *Multicultural issues in teacher education: Meeting the challenge of student diversity*. Paper presented at the Conference on the Career-Long Education of Wisconsin Teachers, Wisconsin Dells, WI.

Howey, K. R., and N. L. Zimpher. (1989). *Profiles of preservice teacher education*. Albany, NY: SUNY Press.

Irvine, J. J. (1992). Making teacher education culturally responsive. In *Diversity in teacher education*, ed. M. E. Dilworth, 79–92. San Francisco: Jossey-Bass.

Kennedy, M. M., ed. (1991). *Teaching academic subjects to diverse learners*. New York: Teachers College Press.

King, S. J., M. Bay, and V. C. Hare. (Feb. 25, 1993). *Preparing the next generation of urban teachers: Sharing the lessons we've learned*. Paper presented at the annual conference of the American Association of Colleges for Teacher Education, San Diego, CA.

Klassen, F. J., and D. M. Gollnick, eds. (1977). *Pluralism and the American teacher*. Washington, DC: AACTE.

Ladson-Billings, G. (1991). Coping with multicultural illiteracy: A teacher education response. *Social Education* 55(3):186–194.

Liston, D. P., and K. M. Zeichner. (1990). Teacher education and the social context of schooling: Issues for curriculum development. *American Educational Research Journal* 27(4):610–636.

Lucas, T., R. Henze, and R. Donato. (1990). Promoting the success of Latino language-minority students: An exploratory study of six high schools. *Harvard Educational Review* 60(3):315–340.

McDiarmid, G. W. (1992). What to do about differences? A study of multicultural education for teacher trainees in the Los Angeles Unified School District. *Journal of Teacher Education* 43(2):83–93.

McDiarmid, G. W., and J. Price. (1993). Preparing teachers for diversity: A study of student teachers in a multicultural program. In *Diversity and teaching*, ed. M. J. O'Hair and S. J. Odell, 31–59. Orlando, FL: Harcourt Brace Jovanovich.

McLeod, B., ed. (1994). *Language and learning: Educating linguistically diverse students.* Albany, NY: SUNY Press.

Montero-Sieburth, M. (1989). Restructuring teachers' knowledge for urban settings. *Journal of Negro Education* 58(3):332–344.

Nelson-Barber, S., and J. Mitchell. (1992). Restructuring for diversity: Five regional portraits. In *Diversity in teacher education*, ed. M. E. Dilworth, 229–262. San Francisco: Jossey-Bass.

Noordhoff, K., and J. Kleinfeld. (1991). *Preparing teachers for multicultural classrooms: A case study in rural Alaska.* Paper presented at the annual meeting of the American Educational Research Association in Chicago.

Pasch, S., M. Pasch, R. Johnson, S. Ilmer, J. Snyder, E. Stapleton, A. Hamilton, and P. Mooradian. (1993). Reflections of urban education: A tale of three cities. In *Diversity and teaching*, ed. M. J. O'Hair and S. J. Odell, 9–30. Orlando, FL: Harcourt Brace Jovanovich.

Polites, G. R. (1993). Developing a multicultural mind-set. *Equity and Choice* 9(2): 54–58.

Price, H. B. (1992). Multiculturalism: Myths and realities. *Phi Delta Kappan* 74(3): 208–213.

Pugach, M. C. (1984). The role of selective admissions policies in the teacher education process. In *Advances in teacher education*, ed. L. G. Katz and J. D. Raths, 1: 145–169, Norwood, NJ: Ablex.

Ross, D. D., and Smith, W. (1992). Understanding preservice teachers' perspectives on diversity. *Journal of Teacher Education* 43(2):94–103.

Santos, S. L. (1986). Promoting intercultural understanding through multicultural teacher training. *Action in Teacher Education* 8(1):19–25.

Shade, B. J. R., ed. (1989). *Culture, style, and the educative process.* Springfield, IL: Charles C. Thomas.

Shade, B. J. R., and C. A. New. (1993). Cultural influences on learning: Teaching implications. In *Multicultural education,* ed. J. A. Banks and C. A. Banks, 317–331. Boston: Allyn and Bacon.

Shor, I. (1980). *Critical teaching and everyday life.* Boston: South End Press.

Sleeter, C. E., ed. (1991). *Empowerment through multicultural education.* Albany, NY: SUNY Press.

Sleeter, C. E. (1992). *Keepers of the American dream.* Washington, DC: The Falmer Press.

Sleeter, C. E., and C. A. Grant. (1988). *Making choices for multicultural education.* Columbus, OH: Merrill.

Smith, B. O. (1969). *Teachers for the real world.* Washington, DC: AACTE.

Stallings, J. A., and L. F. Quinn. (1991). Learning how to teach in the inner city. *Educational Leadership* 49(3):25–27.

Tippeconnic III, J. W. (1983). Training teachers for American Indian students. *Peabody Journal of Education* 21(3):6–15.

Vogt, L. A., C. Jordon, and R. G. Tharp. (1987). Explaining school failure, producing school success: Two cases. *Anthropology and Education Quarterly* 18(4):276–268.

Weiner, L. (1989). Asking the right questions: An analytic framework for reform of urban teacher education. *The Urban Review* 21(3):151–161.

Zeichner, K. M. (1992). *Educating teachers for cultural diversity.* East Lansing, MI: Michigan State University, National Center for Research on Teacher Learning.

Zimpher, N. L., and E. A. Ashburn. (1992). Countering parochialism in teacher candidates. In *Diversity in teacher education,* ed. M. E. Dilworth, 40–62. San Francisco: Jossey-Bass.

2

CHRISTINE E. SLEETER

White Preservice Students and Multicultural Education Coursework

Over the years as I have taught predominantly White groups of preservice students and in-service teachers, I have found myself repeatedly puzzled. Why do so many accept as "normal" low achievement levels on the part of children of color and/or from low-income backgrounds? Why do many continue to view multicultural curriculum as consisting of information about customs in other countries, despite coursework and exposure to curricular materials that frame it very differently? Why do many argue vehemently that bilingual education is wrong, in spite of research evidence that good bilingual programs tend to raise academic achievement and teach English more effectively than English-only programs (Cummins 1989)?

In this chapter I will argue that, whether it takes the form of a discrete course or some other form, teacher education programs need to plan for and address directly a clash between the worldview of most White teachers and that under-girding multicultural education. Regardless of how little White preservice and in service teachers believe they know about cultural diversity, I have come to realize that they bring a well-developed world view about the nature of society and inequality which is based on their life experiences and interpreted through dominant modes of thought. Their world view provides guidance as they make decisions about how and what to teach; and it serves as a filter as they interpret multicultural content. Hence, the persistence of patterns such as those above. The following analysis of points of conflict between multicultural education and the world view of most White teachers suggests implications for teacher education.

MULTICULTURAL EDUCATION AND WHITE TEACHERS: DIVERGENT VIEWPOINTS

Ask your students to jot down answers to the following: 1) What is the relative economic position of Mexican Americans (or another racial minority group) and Anglo-Americans (e.g., average earnings, unemployment rate)? 2) What have you learned about history that would explain why there is an economic discrepancy? and 3) List the stereotypes you have learned about Mexican Americans, regardless of whether you believe them or not.

Typically, students who are not Mexican American are somewhat aware that Anglos fare better but can rarely write more than one or two sentences of historical information about why an economic gap exists. However, they have all learned stereotypes, and the list any given class generates is long and largely negative. In the absence of a convincing alternative explanation for gaps between Mexican Americans and Anglos—or other "haves nots" and "haves"—most of us tacitly accept the stereotypes we learned. Critiquing stereotypes by itself, however, does not change this; we only adopt or create new ones because we need ways of interpreting what we see.

This class exercise points to fundamental differences between the world view embodied in multicultural education and that of most White people. Multicultural education is rooted in a concern about inequality among groups; scholars explain inequalities primarily with respect to historic as well as contemporary institutional discrimination, such as the Jim Crow laws of the past, and discriminatory patterns today in schools and the job market. They view oppressed groups primarily in terms of strengths, such as their cultural resources, coping abilities, and persistent struggles against oppression.

Most teachers bring a mainstream viewpoint that is diametrically opposed. They view social institutions as largely fair and open to those who try. Even obvious historic contradictions to fairness, such as slavery, are interpreted as temporary aberations that have been corrected. Inequality is explained largely in terms of what "have not" groups lack. This viewpoint historically maintained that non-Westerners lacked civilization and the genetic capacity for advanced culture; today, arguments focus on lack of education, motivation, effort, language, morals, and family support.

In this chapter I will discuss four interconnected concepts spinning out of these different viewpoints that most White preservice students find very difficult to grasp. I will then suggest teaching processes and experiences that can help to some degree. Although I have separated these issues for discussion here, it is important to recognize that they are interconnected and must be addressed as such. Prospective teachers of color probably also need to address issues and concepts discussed below (Montecinos in press), but usually in my experience they grasp the concepts much more readily than White prospective teachers because these concepts mesh with their life experiences.

Historic Roots of Racist Opportunity Structures

Whites often describe the United States (U.S.) as a nation of immigrants, but describing it in this way minimizes very important distinctions in groups' historic experiences with opportunity. John Ogbu argues that how a group became a part of the U.S. defines the trajectory for the group's subsequent experiences and perspectives. European ethnic groups, as well as Asian and some Latino groups, voluntarily immigrated to North America in search of better opportunities, expecting to endure some hardships and discrimination initially. African Americans, indigenous Native people, Puerto Ricans, and Mexican Americans, on the other hand, whom he refers to as "involuntary minorities…were brought into their present society through slavery, conquest or colonization" (1991, 9). Rather than seeking voluntarily to affiliate with the dominant society to gain opportunities, they were forced to become part of it and, in the process, lost vast amounts of freedom, land, and economic resources. European groups developed an opportunity structure that allowed for individual upward mobility (a process that did involve considerable conflict among European groups) but until 1954 legally barred groups of color from participating in that structure. These very different histories generated present life conditions and perspectives that diverge to a much greater degree than most White teachers grasp.

White people in general find it very difficult to appreciate the impact of colonization and slavery on oppressed groups as well as Whites; they tend to prefer to regard everyone as descendents of immigrants. I believe Whites retreat from confronting the profound impact of conquest and slavery because doing so calls into question the legitimacy of the very foundation of much of White peoples' lives. The economic legacy of conquest is that Whites are indebted to Indian, Mexican, Puerto Rican, and Hawaiian people for the land we inhabit, as well as gold and other resources our ancestors extracted from the land to build industries (Weatherford 1988); the economic legacy of slavery is that Whites owe African Americans about three hundred years of back wages, money that Whites used instead to build profits and profit-generating industries. Economic disparities today are legacies of history (Roediger 1991).

However, the idea that the U.S. is a nation of voluntary immigrants is consistent with the family histories of Euro-Americans and affirms the desire of Whites to believe that our ancestors earned fairly what we have inherited. Generally when acknowledging conquest and slavery, Euro-Americans bracket these off as historic incidents that have little bearing on today. Typical White responses to this history are: "I didn't do it; why punish me?" "My family worked for what they got; we didn't have anything to do with slavery," and "That was a long time ago; can't we just forget all that?" Also, typically, White preservice students have only a sketchy idea of the histories of diverse American groups and do not situate current issues in a historic context (Lauderdale and Deaton 1993).

The Nature and Impact of Discrimination

Oppressed groups experience discrimination daily in relationship to individuals and in interaction with institutions; its impacts are psychological as well as restrictive of opportunities. This is true of voluntary non-White immigrants (such as Korean Americans), as well as indigenous minority groups, poor Whites, women, and gays and lesbians. While immigrants often attribute discrimination they experience to their foreign ways (Ogbu 1991), American minority group members, particularly African Americans, see systematic racial discrimination as a deep and ongoing problem (Kluegel and Smith 1986).

Most White teachers greatly minimize the extent and impact of racial (as well as other forms of) discrimination, viewing it as isolated incidents that hurt a person's feelings. Americans, in general, attribute differences in wealth, income, and lifestyle to individual effort on a playing field we assume to be even, particularly with passage of civil rights legislation (Kluegel and Smith 1986). In fact, many White students regard legislation such as affirmative action as giving groups of color an unfair advantage, racial discrimination itself having been largely eliminated.

The view that discrimination has minimal impact was illustrated to me in how one of my White students interpreted an exercise. She spent an hour at the mall with a Black friend, then with a White friend, in order to compare the treatment they received. She reported that when she was with the Black friend, two sales clerks seemed more rude than sales clerks normally are to her; aside from these two clerks, she saw no difference in treatment. Her initial conclusion was that discrimination does not happen very often, although when it does, it makes people feel bad. I suggested to her that a different way of viewing this is that her Black friend probably faces some negative treatment every time he goes to the mall, as well as other places; she had not considered it that way and had some difficulty doing so.

Further, discrimination restricts opportunities, an impact that extends far beyond hurt feelings. For example, racial housing patterns result partially from housing discrimination, which still occurs on a very wide scale despite open housing laws (Schuman and Bobo 1988). Through case studies of communities in Missouri, Gregory Weiher (1991) argues that political boundaries segregating people on the basis of race and social class are created through complementary processes of exclusion of those whom residents of a community do not want and recruitment of residents similar to themselves, people with the most resources having the greatest power to create the most desirable communities for themselves. Where people live affects access to jobs and schools, which, in turn, affects access to income; exclusionary barriers are interconnected and have a huge impact on living conditions. The impact of systematic and persistent discrimination is a very difficult concept for most White teachers to grasp, since they do not experience racial discrimination themselves.

Women experience sex discrimination, however, and seem more likely to acknowledge the presence of other forms of discrimination than men. For example, some of my female students draw parallels between discouraging remarks made to girls and to students of color, between stereotypes of girls in texts and stereotypes of groups of color. However, most have not engaged in a systematic study of patriarchy and often resist examining how their own lives have been shaped by it. When they draw parallels between race and sex discrimination, many appear to conclude that young people need to learn to ignore it, to "tough it out." For example, a White female teacher discussed both race and sex discrimination with me, arguing that the main reason girls do not compete well is that we do not teach them to ignore discrimination and persist anyway:

Enabling people to make excuses, we do too much of that, this [girls in athletics] is an example. We have to be tough, here are the norms, here is how we have to act.

In their own experience, many White women have learned to ignore or overcome overt sex discrimination and wonder why groups of color do not seem to be trying to do the same.

Because they conceptualize discrimination as consisting of isolated acts by prejudiced individuals, most teachers do not explain inequality in terms of systemic discrimination. Mark Ginsburg interviewed seventy-five preservice students (75 percent female, 85 percent White) to find out how they interpret inequalities in achievement (in both schools and the larger society) and what implications their interpretations had for teaching. A small minority "emphasized the school's role in reproducing inequalities," contextualizing children within a stratified and unjust social structure (1988, 167). A much larger second group viewed individuals as freely choosing their own destinies and degree of social mobility and schools as neutrally facilitating mobility for everyone. A third group also viewed individuals as freely choosing their own destinies but believed that people are hindered by individual attitudes and prejudice.

If discrimination consists largely of one-on-one acts by overtly prejudiced people, then the solution must be to be open-minded and accept everyone. If I as a teacher adopt an open attitude, I am not part of a problem. This line of thinking denies a need to learn much of what is described in this book, but it is a common view.

The Significance of Group Membership

The dominant ideology of the U.S. is strongly individualistic, a perspective that teachers commonly share. Americans commonly learn that the U.S. is a nation in which affiliations are voluntary and people participate in the public arena as individuals. For example, Bloom wrote that, in the American political system, "Class, race, religion, national origin or culture all disappear or become dim when bathed in the light of natural rights, which give men common interests and make them truly brothers" (1989, 27). The purpose of schooling is to cultivate reason so that citizens can rise above their own particular circumstances and participate as individuals in a common culture. Similarly, Arthur Schlesinger describes the U.S. as a nation in which people "escape from origins" (1992, 15) and go about "casting off the foreign skin" (112) in order to rise or fall on their own merit and effort as individuals, rather than as members of ascribed groups. This ideology suggests that Americans should not identify themselves with any ascribed group for purposes of public participation and that it is possible and meaningful to ignore ascribed group memberships of other people, treating them as individuals.

Historically for Whites, the significance of ethnic membership has indeed diminished; the ideology above fits family histories. When Europeans immigrated to the U.S., ethnicity structured many aspects of their lives, such as choice of spouse, job, and location of residence. However, today, with a few exceptions, European ethnicity is unrelated to life chances and choices (Alba 1990).

The problem is that, while European ethnic group membership no longer structures opportunity to a significant degree, other forms of ascribed group membership are still very significant. Insisting on the individual as the main unit of analysis deflects attention away from examination of social responses to visible differences. I believe White teachers resist examining the significance of group membership to social structure and opportunity because doing so becomes threatening.

Most Whites profess to be colorblind. But, in doing so, Whites cover over the meanings they attach to race, rather than actually dissociating race from meaning. If one conceives of the U.S. as a nation of voluntary immigrants and the rules of society as essentially fair (with some isolated instances of discrimination still occurring), then why do some groups fare better than others? Typically, most Americans explain group differences in terms of characteristics and desires of group members themselves: for example, women choose low-paying jobs, Mexicans do not want to learn English, low-income people lack the desire to work or keep their homes up. If one asks a White audience to jot down all the negatives they have heard associated with another racial group, then all the positives, the list of negatives is usually much longer. Trying to be colorblind means trying to suppress the application of those largely negative associations to individual children one is teaching.

Trying to be colorblind also means denying the existence of racial boundaries Whites usually do not cross. If one asks a White audience how many of them have ever chosen to live in a neighborhood or attend a school or church in which the majority of the people are not White, few hands go up. Whites do see and adhere to racial boundaries, and most feel very uncomfortable when in the minority. But Whites with at least modest income have many choices (such as where to live, whom to associate with) within White-dominated terrain, and can exercise many options without crossing racial boundaries. This does not mean that Whites do not see the boundaries, however.

In addition to explaining inequalities in terms of negative characteristics of "have not" groups, most White teachers simply do not know very much about non-White groups, nor can most conceptualize poor White homes and neighborhoods in terms of cultural strengths or sensible behavior. If we assume that the context in which people live is fair and neutral, and that they live in segregated areas that afford little firsthand contact with the homes and communities of other groups, we draw on media images, hearsay, stereotypes, and suppositions to explain differences that we see. For example, it is difficult to conceptualize how an extended family structure may be highly functional if one has limited contact with close extended families, and if extended family structures seem more prevalent in poor families than middle-class families.

Recently in class, students were discussing whether children's socioeconomic background matters. Some students took the position that children generally become adults of the same social class as their parents because of home-related influences; they regarded their observations about lower class homes as statements of fact rather than prejudice. If this is true, I asked, is our social system open to mobility? Some argued that it is, but home or culture usually hold people back. Others argued that their peers were verbalizing prejudices that will affect how they teach and that will act as self-fulfilling prophecies.

Part of the difficulty for teachers—or for anyone—is confronting the possibility that what one believes to be true may be prejudice. But assumptions that "have not" groups are pathological also protect one's privileged position, which is even more difficult to confront. For example, in most political arenas, such as city and state governments, Whites constitute the majority of officeholders. White citizens can feel fairly safe that lawmakers will not compromise our racial privileges and status. This was precisely the political issue that Lani Guinier questioned, which made her a threat to Whites. Ultimately, examining the social significance of group membership means questioning the legitimacy of unequal statuses of groups in American society and the institutional structures that maintain inequality. People are very reluctant to question institutional structures that protect what they have.

Nature of Culture

Multicultural education is very often reduced to folksongs and folktales, food fairs, holiday celebrations, and information about famous people. Even when teachers are shown more substantive examples of multicultural practice, many still revert to superficial renditions of cultural differences.

There is a pattern to how White teachers often conceptualize culture that is rooted in European immigrant backgrounds. In his study of European ethnic identity, Richard Alba (1990) found that the most salient expression of ethnic culture among Euro-Americans is eating ethnic foods; Euro-Americans also experience "culture" by using words or phrases of an ancestral language, attending ethnic festivals, and practicing "Old World" holiday customs. Ethnic culture consists of remnants of Old World practices that are celebrated, and often shared across ethnic groups, at particular times. Alba's description of Euro-Americans' expressions of ethnicity correspond very well to much multicultural education as White teachers construct it.

Rosaldo connects the myth of immigration with what he terms "cultural stripping," in which Euro-Americans believe that immigrants brought culture but lost it as they assimilated. "Social analysts sat at the 'postcultural' top of a stratified world and looked down the 'cultural' rungs to its 'precultural' bottom" (1989, 209). In this conception, "primitive" people lack culture; immigrants brought culture from another country and era; and mainstream Americans have surpassed the need for culture through technological development.

This is a very different notion of culture from that advocated in multicultural education. The term *culture* was probably adopted in response to the myth of "cultural deprivation" that was popularized during the early 1960s. By "culture," groups of color generally mean the totality of the group's experience: its history, literature, language, philosophy, religion, and so forth. While my teacher education students can usually grasp this idea intellectually, most have so little knowledge of the culture of any group other than that into which they were born and into which schools have been inducting them since kindergarten—which they regard not as culture but as given—that they simply do not realize the complexity and degree of sophistication of any other group. Without some depth of knowledge of at least one other cultural group, teachers will probably continue to greatly oversimplify the meaning of "culture."

IMPLICATIONS FOR TEACHER EDUCATION

What experiences can be built into a teacher education program that specifically address the kinds of issues discussed above? The suggestions that follow are intended to accompany other processes described throughout this volume. I will highlight some processes I use with students in two sequential, required multicultural education courses; elsewhere I have described my own coursework in more detail (Sleeter, in press).

A helpful departure point for multicultural education is teaching history as experienced and viewed by an "involuntary minority group" and connections between history and current conditions. An entire course in the history of one oppressed group would be very helpful. But even time spent, for example, showing and discussing the documentary *Eyes on the Prize* is very illuminating. William Lauderdale and William Deaton (1993) found preservice students to react strongly to this series because it provides information about legalized racial discrimination in recent history, depicts a level of White racism and Black struggle and persistence that students had not been taught about, and gives them a sense of very different historical experiences between Blacks and Whites. Providing background information about Indian treaties and U.S. government-Indian relations is also very helpful; typically, students have only a very sketchy idea about treaty issues. At the same time, it is also helpful to have students develop a profile of their own family histories and to compare these histories with each other and/or with those of groups different from their own. Teaching the history of a group such as African Americans does not deny the validity or importance of students' European ethnic immigrant histories. Allowing students to explore and compare their own histories illustrates the wide variability in groups' experiences. For example, when a student whose ancestry is largely Norwegian places his or her family history (or a biography) beside another student who is Ojibway, they see limits to the generalizability of the European immigrant paradigm.

Rather than teaching separate units about group cultures, for the reasons mentioned by Joseph Larkin in chapter 1, I focus on group relations, particularly differential access to resources. I also involve students as much as possible in constructing ideas from guided experiences rather than bombarding them with information myself. Central concepts that structure my courses are institutional discrimination, racism, sexism, power, and knowledge construction; I also try to teach students to learn for themselves using ethnographic skills. Kathleen Farber and William Armaline, in chapter 4, discuss their use of similar central concepts in social foundations coursework.

I begin with the book *The Education of a WASP* (Stalvey 1988), which gives an autobiographical account of a White woman's learning about White racism during the 1960s. After having students read the book, I have them generate a list of all the ways Lois Stalvey found that African Americans were denied full access to resources such as housing and jobs; I also have students identify beliefs Whites used to justify their actions and ways in which the media reinforced White beliefs. Excerpts from *Eyes on the Prize* help develop the book's historic context.

Then I have students generate questions they could investigate about racism here and now, as a whole class and with my help. The main guidelines are that they are not investigating characteristics of groups but rather comparing at least two groups' access to society's resources, such as housing or health care; or they can investigate media images that help shape our belief systems. Further, students should think critically about the degree to which they can generalize from single investigations. We generate questions in a class discussion and also discuss methods for gathering information. Students have two or three weeks to collect their data; they share their findings during class sessions in which the students assume the role of teacher.

Everytime I have done this, most of the students' data illustrate various forms of racial discrimination that students had believed no longer exist. For example, students have interviewed realtors, analyzed the racial and gender composition of jobs in their workplaces (grocery stores are popular), and analyzed movies. Not every student brings examples of racism; some bring solutions. In one class, a student brought personnel data from a company that has a strong affirmative action policy, while another brought similar data from another company that does not; this provided a very useful discussion about the difference affirmative action can make. Over the semester, I use a similar process of having students generate questions and bring data to class regarding poverty and sexism.

These student investigations help illustrate current forms of inequality in a much more believable fashion than I could through lecture, since skeptical students are the ones bringing the examples. Further, their examples help students gain a sense of what institutional discrimination is and how it impacts on life circumstances. For example, one student wondered how many people of color had served on the local city council; I suggested he also look into the school board and county board of supervisors. At the time, the city was about 89 percent White, with African Americans and Latinos making up the two largest minority and rapidly growing groups. He was surprised to find out that all officeholders had been White until two African Americans were elected to the city council a year previously. This led to a consideration of aldermanic districts and racial housing patterns, as well as effects of local political power on city, county, and school policies.

Others have reported having students conduct mini-ethnographies of schools and classrooms to help them understand how institutions reproduce inequality (Gottlieb and Cornbleth 1988; Teitelbaum and Britzman 1991). Such activities are similar to those I use in that they involve students in collecting data and constructing patterns collectively and require guidance that will direct students toward institutional processes rather than characteristics of groups.

I supplement students' investigations with readings, films, and speakers. For example, a book of readings that helps to frame students' investigations is *Oppression and Social Justice* (Andrzejewski 1994). Speakers on housing discrimination usually jolt students, since most of them have sought housing, and most assume that the housing market is fair and open. I usually begin media analyses by having students examine magazine ads for gender images. I begin with this because the biases are so glaring and students can easily detect (when asked to notice) how narrow and stereotyped images of each sex are. At first, students try to dismiss the sexist images as inconsequential, but a consideration of the advertising industry indicates that advertisers deliberately choose images to which the public responds. If we regard ads and other media images as reflections of what we respond to, then media can serve as a lens for viewing our own beliefs and biases.

These activities raise awareness that institutional and individual discrimination exist. They do not, however, drive home to students the impact of persistent, daily discrimination. What I hope students gain is a disposition to listen to, rather than dismiss, other peoples' discussions of discrimination, as well as sensitivity to their own behaviors and beliefs. One indication that this begins to happen is when students bring newspaper and magazine articles to class to share with me.

Kip Tellez and colleagues in chapter 5 discuss the strong importance of community-based field experiences in multicultural teacher education programs. I regard extended contact with another group on its own "turf" as essential in the education of White teachers. In my own life, this has certainly been the case. In the courses I teach, prior to community-based field experiences students tend to comprehend material at an intellectual level only, and their discussions are often rather sterile. After spending some time in a community setting dominated by another sociocultural group, students begin to confront their own fears, misconceptions, and ignorance.

In one of my courses, I have connected such a field experience with other investigative assignments. One set of assignments involves mini-ethnographies in which students are to interview or observe people in their field placement, choosing from an array of nineteen investigation activities. For example, they can interview a community center director about the purpose and activities of the center; I provide questions to get them started. Typically, this interview sensitizes students to the active self-help role of many community organizations, as well as problems and needs in the communities, calling into question the assumption many make that poor communities and communities of color do not try to help themselves.

For another assignment, students are to pose a "why?" question involving a racial, language, social class, or gender issue they do not understand and that relates to their community-based field experience. They are to seek answers from at least six sources. Before they begin, we spend time in class discussing potential differences between in-group and out-group perspectives (such as how language minority people might view questions about language differently from native English speakers) and difference in perspective one might get from children, adults in the community, or scholars who have studied the issue. Their six sources should include at least one interview and at least one scholarly article or book. They should attempt to find out a perspective shared by members of a group of which the student is not a member. So, for example, male students investigating gender issues may seek the perspectives of males but must also seek perspectives of females.

With few exceptions, these investigations have been very enlightening. For example, in one class four White women wondered why African American males have difficulty in school; their conclusions explored the fears of White female teachers, cutbacks in job opportunities and economic resources in poor Black neighborhoods, the indifference of White society, and so forth. Their information came largely from Black male adults and articles published in various Black journals and magazines. One of the main insights students seem to gain from this assignment is how little they knew about accessing another group's perspective. For example, few are aware of any publications by groups of color with the exception of *Ebony*; until this assignment, most students had never sought a journal or book written by someone of a different race. Following the assignment last semester, a White student told me that he will start consulting *Journal of Negro Education* periodically because he learned so much reading it for this assignment.

This field experience, combined with concurrent classwork, helps to penetrate students' perceptions to some degree. Students must admit that they are not colorblind when they have to grapple with their feelings about entering the placement site for the first time. The mini-ethnographic assignments guide students in learning first-hand about children's cultural patterns and life experiences to use as resources in teaching. For example, one assignment guides students in listening for dialect patterns; this coordinates with a class session about Black English. Students who have completed this assignment express some amazement that they can now hear patterns they had not been aware of before. Another assignment is to walk around the neighborhood and observe, then think of twelve ways to link what they saw with academic content. This assignment attempts to help students to connect culture with everyday life and to view daily life as a teaching resource.

I cannot claim that these assignments and activities penetrate deeply the difficulties outlined in the first part of this chapter. However, I believe that they provide a beginning. About twenty-two years ago, I occupied the same conceptual space as the White students I now teach. In retrospect, two of the most important lessons I learned—and learning them took a great deal of time and work—were to ask the right questions and to seek answers from people I had been socialized to ignore or look down upon. I believe that it is reasonable, as well as imperative, to start our preservice students to doing this.

REFERENCES

Alba, R. D. (1990). *Ethnic identity: The transformation of White America.* New Haven, CT: Yale University Press.

Andrzejewski, J., ed. (1994). *Oppression and social justice: Critical frameworks.* Needham Heights, MA: Ginn Press.

Bloom, A. C. (1989). *The closing of the American mind.* New York: Simon and Schuster.

Cummins, J. (1989). *Empowering minority students.* Sacramento, CA: California Association of Bilingual Education.

Ginsburg, M. B. (1988). *Contradictions in teacher education and society: A critical analysis.* London: The Falmer Press.

Gottlieb, E., and C. Cornbleth. (1988). Toward reflective social studies teaching. *Teaching Education* 2(1):60–63.

Kluegel, J. R., and E. R. Smith. (1986). *Beliefs about inequality: Americans' views of what is and what ought to be.* New York: Aldine de Gruyter.

Lauderdale, W. B., and W. L. Deaton. (1993). Future teachers react to past racism. *The Educational Forum* 57(3):266–276.

Montecinos, C. (in press). Culture as on-going dialogue: Implications for multicultural teacher education. In *Multicultural education, critical pedagogy, and the politics of difference,* ed. C. E. Sleeter and P. McLaren. Albany, NY: SUNY Press.

Ogbu, J. U. (1991). Immigrant and involuntary minorities in comparative perspective. In *Minority status and schooling,* ed. M. A. Gibson and J. U. Ogbu, 3–33. New York: Garland.

Roediger, D. R. (1991). *The wages of whiteness.* London: Verso.

Rosaldo, R. (1989). *Culture and truth.* Boston: Beacon Press.

Schlesinger Jr., A. M. (1992). *The disuniting of America.* New York: Norton.

Schuman, H., and L. Bobo. (1988). Survey based experiments on White racial attitudes toward residential segregation. *American Journal of Sociology* 94:273–299.

Sleeter, C. E. (in press). Teaching Whites about racism. In *Practicing what we teach,* ed. R. J. Martin. Albany, NY: SUNY Press.

Stalvey, L. M. (1988). *The education of a WASP*. Madison: University of Wisconsin Press.

Teitelbaum, K., and D. P. Britzman. (1991). Reading and doing ethnography: Teacher education and reflective practice. In *Issues and practices in inquiry-oriented teacher education*, ed. B. R. Tabachnick and K. Zeichner, 186–202. Bristol, PA :Falmer Press.

Weatherford, J. (1988). *Indian givers*. New York: Fawcett Columbine.

Weiher, G. R. (1991). *The fractured metropolis*. Albany, NY: SUNY Press.

3

Sandra Jackson

Autobiography: Pivot Points for Engaging Lives in Multicultural Contexts

Introduction

Preservice teachers will be faced with the awesome responsibility of teaching other people's children and youth. When they enter the classroom, they will be taking with them values, beliefs, dispositions, and practices which will influence their ability to work with students effectively. Their knowledge, awareness, understanding, and attitudes towards students—especially those who are ethnically and culturally different from themselves—will necessarily influence the teaching and learning dynamic. Individuals who have reflected upon their own experiences, who have experienced being the "other," and have examined the implications for education will hopefully be challenged to develop ways of teaching which empower themselves as well as their students.

In this chapter I discuss autobiography and its potential to create contexts for multicultural engagement. I describe two courses which I have taught using autobiography and personal narrative as powerful media for the study of self and the posing of critical questions regarding the study of difference and diversity in ways which empower teachers and students.

Why autobiography? There is power in personal narratives. Within the context of multiple voices, reflection and critical discourse can challenge preconceived notions about others who are different and lay a foundation for change in attitudes, beliefs, and practices. For these reasons, the study of autobiography and personal accounts is a viable and compelling way to engage preservice teachers in discourse about differences and about their impact on individuals and their lived experiences. The study of autobiography provides concrete contexts in which to experience difference, for the subjects are real persons to whom one can respond and relate.

By its very nature, autobiography is a medium through which individuals speak as subjects, in their own voices, and represent themselves and their stories from their own perspectives. (Allender 1991). The study of autobiography from a multicultural approach, which legitimizes the voices and experiences of diverse people, provides occasions to bring these experiences to the center of discourse—foregrounded in bold relief. Through studying autobiography in this manner,

31

preservice teachers experience an approach to teaching which they, in turn, can practice and model. They can be challenged to critique traditional approaches to education and teaching which have alienated, marginalized, and silenced students, excluded rather than included, attempted to homogenize instead of diversify…and have been complicit in the reproduction of inequalities. Preservice teachers who have gained insight about the meanings of individual and institutional responses to difference which have been dysfunctional in teaching and learning will hopefully be motivated to teach in ways that reaffirm, challenge, and empower.

EXPERIENCING DIFFERENCE, SUBJECTS AND SUBJECTIVITIES

What is it about autobiography which provides occasions for the critical examination and experience of difference? Autobiography (and biography) is an art (Novarr 1986; Rampersand 1989) which transcends mere truth telling and divulgence of "facts" about a person's life; it is interpretation. Autobiography is "also history—individual and collective—for it recreates a past shared with others, one which has actually happened and not [been] only imagined" (Stone 1982, 3). This nonfictional writing, by and about the self—both as subject and object, can represent a life in a variety of modes: memoir, reminiscence, confession, apology, testament, case history, diary, journal, novel, experimental form, or mock (Stone, 2).

Reading individual lives as texts enables one to situate herself or himself in the subjectivities of others…and to vicariously reexperience events which have influenced an individual's growth and development, perceptions of self, values, philosophy, personality, and feelings. "What makes a [life story] worthwhile…is the discovery of a life [as it] develops, opens up to new horizons, and unfolds… potentialities" (Rampersand 1989, 212). And, as with the viewing of a flower blossoming, as captured by time-lapse photography, the reader of a life story becomes both a participant and an observer in witnessing a self in the process of becoming.

As one relives another's experience, one engages in opportunities to reflect upon the meanings of experiences—especially if these are unfamiliar or in contrast to one's own way of being in the world. Diverse prose portraits of individuals of different racial and ethnic groups, cultures, and classes—female and male—capture meanings of what it has meant to be within particular historical periods: female and working class in the early 1900s; Black, male, and urban in the 1960s; White, male, protestant, and privileged; Mexican American female and Catholic; Asian American female and second generation; Native American male in the 1990s.

As readers of autobiography, we revisit scenes from the lives of individuals as reflected upon and recreated by the subjects themselves. Through these revisitings, readers have opportunities to be in someone else's place…space and "consider similarities and differences to the reader's own life" (Felski 1989, 93). Herein lie a multitude of opportunities to reexamine one's perceptions of others and one's own responses to the differences they present in these autobiographical encounters. Can we understand? Can we empathize? Can we appreciate other points of view? Can we accept the differences? Can we negotiate our encounters with tensions which emerge? Do these recreated experiences resonate with those which we have when we encounter others who are different in our own daily lived experiences? The reading of life stories promises to encourage reflection about ourselves in relationships with others as we contemplate seeing ourselves in them: mirrors of otherness.

What are the possibilities of studying autobiography? Consider that auto-biography as a genre developed out of the tradition of religious confession and self-analysis grounded in exploration of intimacy, emotion, self-understanding, and individualism. When we then consider the experiences of oppressed and exploited groups in terms of race, class, and gender, we confront subjugated subjectivities which have been inscribed in struggles and resistance. According to Rita Felski (1989, 104), autobiographical writing by oppressed groups is infused with contradictions which can make such writing a liberatory process and/or one which is anxiety and guilt producing as one negotiates the space between self-affirmation and self-denial in the telling of one's life story. As readers, we can be participants in reaffirming the valuing of differences as we experience and examine the challenges involved with defying categorization of others as deviant, inferior, and exotic. Consider studying the autobiography of people of color and the particular case of African Americans.

According to Arnold Rampersand (1983, 3), autobiography of African Americans is defined as the "formal, detailed life story of a Black individual told by herself /himself" (or, in the case of biography, by a fellow Black). Given the historic experience of African Americans in America, a number of themes become the leitmotifs inscribed in life stories of Black people: the desire for polit-ical freedom; obsession with the notion of justice; concern for community; and integration of the place of the Black individual in the modern world (1983, 13–15). Within this context, the life stories of Maria Stewart, Frederick Douglass, Ida B. Wells, Richard Wright, Malcolm X, W. E. B. Du Bois, Septima Clark, Martin Luther King, Maya Angelou, Angela Davis, Lorene Cary, Thurgood Marshall, Charlayne Hunter-Gault, and Fannie Lou Hamer come to mind. Each addresses issues of identity, struggle, resistance, and negotiations of places to be within the larger society.

As we negate essentializing the experiences of African Americans and acknowledge the problematic of gender and its intersection with race and class, we must reckon with the reality that Black women's life stories are, at once, similar to and different from those of Black men. The study of Black women's participation in the literary genre of autobiography reveals much about the ways in which the experience of racial and gender difference influences the develop-ment of identity and the sense one makes of one's experiences. "Black women's autobiography presents occasions for viewing the female individual in relation-ship to those others [her community and family] with whom she shares emotional, philosophical, spiritual affinities, as well as political realities" (Braxton 1989, 9).

The voices of Black women necessarily represent self and the articulation of experiences in tenors and textures different from those of Black men given experiences with patriarchy and sexism as well as racism.

There is another axis of difference in the representations of life stories regarding gender, race, and class. When a reader juxtaposes the experiences of Black women as told through personal narratives, such as *Our Nig, Dust Tracks on the Road, Incidents in the Life of a Slave Girl*, and *A Taste of Power*, with that of the prevailing model of womanhood, one learns of the contrasts in life experiences as well as differences in values and priorities (Fox-Genovese, 1987, 176). The differences about what it means to be a woman within Black and White communities become manifest; the same applies to differences inscribed in what it means to be a woman from and within other communities: Mexican, Vietnamese, Japanese, Puerto Rican, Native American, Thai, Iranian.

Autobiographical writing inspired by the women's movement differs from the traditional autobiography of the bourgeois individual (primarily European and male) which presents itself as the record of an exemplary, universal life, often heroic in proportion. Instead, women often write about ordinary lived experiences. When we shift our attention to the articulation of women's experiences in juxtaposition to those of men, readers come to understand that feminist autobiography, often in the form of confession, seeks to confirm female experiences which have often been repressed and rendered invisible. (Jelnick 1986; Felski 1989). These confessional narratives are often presented in nontraditional ways, capturing ambivalence and the sometimes tentative nature of lived experiences in episodic, fragmented, and nonlinear ways. Readers experience multivocal representations of self. Speaking about women's lived experiences in everyday life with attention to intimate details and writing them into existence has given women voice and the ability to name those things which have silenced, oppressed, marginalized, and trivialized them. Women have empowered themselves by telling their own stories in their own voices.

In a similar vein, the stories of people of color highlight the problematic of difference(s) regarding race and ethnicity and culture vis-à-vis the experiences of individuals and groups. Autobiographical works by individuals from cultures in which humility and the avoidance of drawing attention to oneself are valued introduce readers to approaches to telling life stories inscribed with a different ethos (Swann and Krupat 1987) and provide insight into ways of self-representation which are not grounded in individualism and narcissism. Through reading these life stories, we have opportunities to understand why others behave differently and develop traditions and norms rooted in different values and ethics. Reading autobiographical material of people from various cultures introduces us to the complexities of the human experience and reaffirms multiple perspectives and world views about interpretations of life experiences.

Autobiography (and biography) is a "leveler" (Rampersand 1989, 195); it makes the lives of persons ordinary and extraordinary—with their strengths, limitations, and eccentricities—accessible to a multitude of readers. For people of color, as well as all women, this means that their lives—those not previously deemed worthy of the autobiographical/biographical project—can be read and reflected upon. No longer is it the singular, great man who commands attention because of his exploits and achievements; housewives, sharecroppers, office workers, persons with disabilities, survivors of child abuse, artists and entertainers, gays and lesbians, politicians, and heads of state can share their stories from which readers can learn. This means that people of color are no longer limited to reading about great (white) men and heroic women who have often been privileged. Instead, we can read about people much like ourselves and their commonplace, yet unique, lives.

And yet, the reading of autobiography by individuals of color and women can present a contradiction. For when we focus upon the life of an individual and what it means, we are confronted with the reality that "the dividing line between represessive stereotype and empowering symbol of cultural identity is often a very narrow one" (Felski 1989, 119). To avoid such pitfalls and limitations, readers should contextualize and historicize autobiographical experiences and not reduce particular life stories to emblems which represent whole groups. Instead, particular life stories should be approached as prisms through which one can view the human condition from different angles of refraction. Classroom discourse about the meanings of lives studied—at once unique and representative—can enable students to begin to appreciate the multifaceted nature of human experiences. In this regard, the telling of an individual life is just that—a recount of a particular woman or a man from a particular cultural, ethnic group, and class, who cannot be regarded as a template for others from the same community.

Reading and examining autobiography from a multicultural and gendered perspective promises opportunities for learning through growth, development, and reflection. In this regard, James Stone (1982, 5–7) offers some thoughts about the power of the personal narrative.

> If one begins with the aim of trying to understand how a single life becomes at once distinctive and representative as the result of narrative reconstruction...one can appreciate autobiography as a rich cultural medium for examining the necessary interplay between the particular and the genera....As a more or less trustworthy linguistic bridge between oneself or society and others...autobiography recreates a model of literary culture itself and the social circumstances in which an individual personality is discovered, asserted and confirmed (or denied) and community potentially established.

Autobiography as mirror, as process, an opportunity to juxtapose one's own experiences with those of others, reflect, and engage in an I-to-I encounter with another, telling his and her own stories, in their own voices, representing themselves as they see fit, invites the reader to reexperience a life and discern the meanings within multiple contexts.

AUTOBIOGRAPHY, MULTICULTURALISM AND TEACHER EDUCATION

> I am convinced that educational biography is a
> valuable, indeed powerful but unfortunately
> neglected instrument in the preparation of
> teachers and other professionals in education.
>
> (Gutek 1991, preface)

In my quest to discover and create meaningful contexts in which to engage students in examination and reflection about teaching, I have experimented with using autobiographical occasions as ways of addressing multiculturalism in theory and practice. In two elective courses which I teach, we start with self because it is palpable and concrete. We honor the powerful ideas and feelings related to identity and their implications for teaching and learning because, when we enter the classroom, these things will be manifest and will necessarily have profound effects upon what happens. I also want to confront the notion that multi-cultural issues are not "out there" apart from us, but are within our own class-rooms. In the two courses, we read and examine diverse autobiographies, and we write personal narratives which we use as pivot points for discussion and reflec-tion about identity, attitudes, beliefs, and actions in an effort to become self-conscious agents of our own development in working with others.

The two relevant courses are "Social Justice: Multiculturalism, Valuing Diversity," and "Education and Literature: Autobiography and Journeys to Self." They have provided me with insights about how the study of autobiography and the writing of personal narratives present opportunities for preservice teachers to experience the lives of others, reflect upon their own development, and then engage in processes which are grounded in affirmation of the capacity to feel, empathize with, know, and change. In addressing basic questions related to a person's development, we focus upon, not only why, but also how (Rampersand 1983) one negotiates becoming; and, through dialogue about the meanings of these experiences juxtaposed with those of the readers, we are able to draw atten-tion to, and critically examine issues of, the curriculum and responses to diver-sity. While reading various texts (Sleeter 1991: Peshkin 1991: Weis 1988), as well as supplementary articles about issues of multiculturalism, empowerment, and change, students write personal narratives about issues which emerge.

In the course on multiculturalism, the emphasis is upon *personal reflection and understanding self.* The objectives are to engage students in deliberation about identity as a multifaceted social construction and reflect upon their own identity; provide opportunities for students to examine their own attitudes, beliefs, and practices towards others who are different; study culture as a broad category which encompasses a range of variables which mark individuals and groups as the other; address issues of voice, representation, and agency in terms of education and schooling; and examine implications of multiculturalism and empowerment in a range of spheres in public life. There are five major assignments—four of which require personal narrative and reflection. The fifth involves a group project—a media critique regarding the representation of women and men of different cultural and ethnic groups. The topics of the essay assignments are as follows:

(1) Personal Reflection: Identity and Community. Students are to discuss how they see themselves in terms of ethnicity, gender, language, culture, and class affiliations. Then they are to situate themselves within the context of the community(ies) with which they identify and comment on how their concept of self and community has influenced their attitudes and practices towards individuals and groups who are culturally and ethnically different.

(2) Ethnic and Cultural Differences: Teaching and Learning. Students are to write an essay in which they discuss how their cultural and ethnic identity has influenced their educational experiences. They may juxtapose personal experiences with material in assigned readings.

(3) Gender, Class, and School Experiences. For this assignment, students are to select a quote or an issue from an article read in class and discuss how it has been a catalyst for their reflections about their own awareness of how gender and class have affected their own personal experiences in education.

(4) Multiculturalism and Education: Taking a Stand. Students have options regarding this assignment. They may critically review an article about multiculturalism and share their own views; they may discuss changes in their own attitudes and beliefs towards others who are different; or they may relate multiculturalism to settings other than schools and reflect upon their own values and thoughts in this regard.

In this series of writings, students begin by articulating what Patricia Hill Collins calls self-defined standpoints. Essays are shared in class in small groups, and then students select ones to share with the whole group. Papers are read aloud, and the issues which emerge are discussed. Through this process, we invoke validation of individual experiences and then juxtapose them with material read in class which includes research and articles on difference and diversity. We use "dialogue as a way of ascertaining truth, valuing an ethic of care based upon individual uniqueness, expressiveness and empathy; holding individuals accountable for attitudes, beliefs as well as facts and theories they produce" (Collins 1991, 373).

In classes in which there is apparent homogeneity regarding the issues of race, there are still likely to be differences regarding class, gender, ethnicity, and religion. These are starting points for the study and examination of multiple perspectives and differences. What happens in the context of a course with students from a diversity of ethnic, social, and cultural backgrounds is that their personal narratives are used as pivot points for engagement in discourse about the problematics of difference. For example, in a given class, we necessarily transcend dichotomous thinking about race and gender, given the range of standpoints which are articulated. Women from different ethnic and cultural groups, as well as different social classes, experience both similarities and differences with other women; at times, one is privileged, at others, one is subjugated, and, at still other times, one is simultaneously privileged and put at disadvantage given one's race, class, or age. Women also understand that, at times, they have shared interests with men of the same class and/or ethnic group. Men likewise find that they share experiences with women based upon class and race and/or status, and gays and lesbians experience discrimination akin to that which people of color experience as the other. Through the writing of autobiographical pieces, we have rich opportunities to discuss multiple perspectives, without privileging one over the other, and we examine structures of domination and oppression in various manifestations which resonate with individual and group experiences. We discover that, at one time or another, we have each been the "other" to someone else; these experiences expand the parameters of difference and add texture to the complexities.

The first essay in the series establishes a tone and invites students to share their own views and insights candidly. From the very beginning students engage in building a community of trust and creating a climate in which we explore the similarities as well as the differences in their experiences as women, men, individuals from various cultural, ethnic, and language groups, and classes. In the subsequent assignments, students again are invited to reflect upon a theme related to difference, by drawing upon personal experiences. These writings, done in conjunction with readings about the educational experiences of individuals and groups of diverse backgrounds, provide opportunities to engage in circumspect examination of institutional responses to difference. We interrogate the notion of the Black experience, the Native American experience, the Asian American experience, the woman's experience, the immigrant experience…and we negate totalizing experiences of others as artifacts and constructs. Throughout this course, we talk about the implications for curriculum and pedagogy, given what we come to understand about voice, representation, cultural politics, power, and knowledge. The discussions and conversations we have lay a foundation for critical examination of the cognitive and affective aspects of teaching and learning and developing understandings about how these things influence student attitudes towards school, learning, performance, and achievement. We also consider teacher attitudes and behaviors in terms of expectations of students and relationships with them in terms of communication, motivation, classroom management and discipline, grades, advising, and mentoring.

For the media review project, students select a television program series, a film, or a video of a commercial movie which they critically evaluate in terms of representation of gender, ethnicity/race, and culture. Who is represented? How are they represented, and what are the identifying images? What is the treatment, texture, and use of nuance? Are there caricatures and stereotypes? Who is the targeted audience? What is the usefulness of this medium as a teaching tool to address issues related to diversity and empowerment? Student groups make presentations and are responsible for discussion and problem-posing about the media, popular culture, and the construction of images about individuals and groups.

For the culminating experience, students are invited to reflect upon their own personal journey and growth in terms of knowledge and awareness, as well as attitudes and behaviors towards individuals and groups who are different. Again, the personal and the concrete are validated from multiple self-defined standpoints. These sessions invoke powerful responses and commentary about learning, challenges, responsibilities, accountability, and possibilities. Students speak of change and growth. They also speak of having many more questions. They comment on insights gained about the complexities of individual and group experiences and relate these things to understandings about what happens to children and youth in schools, their responses to institutions and curricula, and approaches to teaching. Students find their voices and become more comfortable in naming the things which have affected their own lives and marked them as different. They remark about having journeyed to the edge of their comfort zones, having to look critically at themselves and reexamine their own thoughts and values, and being moved to consider what they can do as agents of change. They have looked in the mirror and seen themselves in others. Our classroom discourse becomes textured, multilayered, and nuanced as each individual articulates his/her own position(s). We bring the experiences of historically marginalized groups and women to the center and create spaces in which individuals can express themselves, see connections between individuals and groups, reflect upon personal experiences, critique theories and research, and engage in critical pedagogy which empowers.

The other course under discussion, "Education and Literature," provides another angle for the use of autobiography and personal narratives in teacher education programs. In this course, the emphasis is upon *understanding others* through critical reflection upon the life stories of individuals in which issues related to education figure prominently. Through a multicultural approach with attention to race, class, and gender and their intersections, we examine what it means to become educated from a diversity of perspectives. As a result of careful reading and critical examination, students develop a comparative framework of how individuals from different cultures come to terms with who they are and struggle to reconcile the differences between self and others. We draw attention to a number of issues as they relate to the goals of education, its purposes and functions. Of primary concern is the development of an understanding of how the political, social, and economic dimensions of education impinge upon the lives of individuals, groups, and their communities.

The assigned readings for the course have included the following titles: *The Struggle That Must Be*, Harry Edwards; *Hunger of Memory*, Richard Rodriguez; *Woman Warrior*, Maxine Hong Kingston; *A Voice from the South*, Anna Julia Cooper; *Double Yoke*, Buchi Emecheta; *When the Legends Die* (a fictionalized biography), Hal Borland; and *Jane Addams on Education*, Elizabeth C. Langemann. Students are also required to read an additional autobiography of their choice. Supplementary readings include articles by Rampersand, Felski, Elizabeth Fox-Genovese and Joanne Braxton on autobiography of African Americans, African-American women, and women; literary criticism about autobiography as a genre; and Lawrence Kohlberg's, Erik Erikson's, Abraham Maslow's, and Carol Gilligan's theories on human development.

Regarding written assignments, students must write an essay upon completion of reading and discussion of each assigned text. We examine such themes and topics as follows as they relate to individuals read about: personal reflection upon a woman or man's own education—formal and informal within another society or culture; an articulation of a particular individual's philosophical orientation about education and the embedded values; an examination of how race, class, gender, and other dimensions of difference have affected access to education, choices, and quality of life; comparison-contrast of students' own experiences with education and schooling and that of a person read about from another country; the purposes of writing one's autobiography; and analysis of style and voice in representation.

The culminating assignment for this course is that students write on one of two topics. The first option is to write their own autobiographical account in which they in some way address education as broadly defined. Students are invited to be creative in their approach to narrating their life stories, and they may experiment with form and treatment. The second option is to write about an autobiography or biography of their choice in light of a compelling issue or idea as their controlling purpose.

What I have experienced in this course is that through studying the experiences of diverse individuals from different historical periods, countries, ethnic/racial groups, and cultures, students develop an enriched knowledge base about others. The comparative approach provides multiple contexts in which to engage in reflection about others and how they come to be. Encounters with real people, from diverse backgrounds, provide occasions for preservice teachers to examine issues and ideas which they may face when they enter the classroom.

Upon completion of this course, students volunteer comments about how much they have been challenged through encounters and confrontations with difference as articulated through self-defined standpoints. They have been engaged in critical reflection through vicarious experiences which have invoked empathy and a willingness to see things differently. They have been moved to understand others as subjects and not objects through autobiographical encounters.

This ability to critically reflect upon self in relationship to others, and create ways of educating which include rather than exclude and cross boundaries, is at the core of a multicultural approach to teaching and learning. For the teacher herself/himself must be able and willing to model attitudes, beliefs, and practices which respect and acknowledge difference at the center of the curriculum and pedagogy. Students in the two courses I have briefly described leave with a greater awareness of themselves and others. They articulate a realization that they need to learn even more…and they speak of commitments to be more open, to examine assumptions, images, stereotypes of others, and a need to develop a repertoire of ways to teach students who have different ways of knowing, cultural knowledge, interests, and abilities.

Through autobiographical encounters and immersion in the study of another's life, students can learn that "the path to the fuller understanding of the individual lies through the group, and that understanding the groups lies through understanding the individual" (Stone 1982, 27). Understanding another person as both symbol and unique entity can mediate against stereotyping and totalizing notions about communities of others. Furthermore, when students examine, not only the lives of others, but also their own, they have opportunities to engage in dialogue about the meanings of human experiences; as they study someone else's personal journey to selfhood, they also engage in thinking about their own journeys as they are confronted with differences in a myriad of manifestations. The studies in contrasts as well as similarities present occasions for reconceptualizing oneself in relationship to and with others who are different. Contextualizing the developments of difference and the meanings inscribed call to question facile explanations about how and why women, men, individuals of different cultural, and ethnic groups have become what they are through the exercise of agency. An understanding of identity as a social construction and insight into how different individuals have negotiated their experiences and made decisions, provides opportunities for students to think critically about the idea that "identity is not destiny, but a choice…a self-creation in ground not freely chosen, but laid out by history" (Felski 120). What the study of autobiography can do in this regard, is to provide powerful case studies through which one reexperiences the lives of others and has opportunities to consider contradictions, conflicts, and differences as articulated from others as subjects, self defined.

Using autobiography in teacher education as a way to provide pivot points for engaging lives in multicultural contexts reaffirms the importance of reflection on self and self in relationship to others. This approach necessitates a paradigm shift in ways of conceptualizing and rationalizing curriculum and determining what is legitimate knowledge, in making decisions about what to teach and how, multiple perspectives and multiple voices become integral to this approach to teaching and learning. What this approach requires of teacher education is that teachers be prepared to be reflective practitioners who first examine themselves—their knowledge base, their attitudes, beliefs and practices—and then develop approaches to teaching and learning which challenge and empower. This project will entail deconstructing canons and challenging the authority of traditional approaches to curriculum development and teaching which have privileged the experiences of particular groups. For educators, this will mean redefining what is important to know by legitimizing the experiences of a diversity of people in terms of race, gender, class, and culture and demonstrating through our pedagogical practices our commitments to multicultural education rooted in ethical, intellectual, and asethetic values of inclusiveness (Hogan 1992) in pursuit of understanding truths about human experiences.

In the two courses which I have described, preservice teachers must first confront themselves—their own views of others and the world. They must also engage in critical reflection about difference in terms of journeying to selfhood. It is my belief that engagement in autobiographical encounters—the study and the examination of the lives of others, and the writing of narratives rooted in personal experience—create occasions for reflection about difference and implications for teaching and learning. When we become the other, we perceive realities within the context of the authority of experiences, self-defined. The other in us looks back, and we are challenged to reckon with being both similar and different.

When I first developed the two courses described in this chapter which focus on autobiography, my intent was to experiment with the autobiographical encounter as a pivot point for conversations about difference. By design, the material addressed in these courses is multicultural and gendered. Student responses to the content and processes of each course, as well as the assigned writings, have reaffirmed my belief that reexperiencing the lives of others and engaging in discourse about difference promises to be a thought-provoking enterprise through which the study and experience of multiculturalism augurs well for individuals planning to enter the teaching profession with commitments to social justice and empowerment, predisposed to face and embrace the challenges of difference in teaching and learning and not shrink from them.

REFERENCES

Allender, J. (1991). *Imagery in teaching and learning: An autobiography of research in four world views*. New York: Praeger.

Anson, R. S. (1987). *Best intentions: The education and killing of Edmund Perry*. New York: Random House.

Birkerts, S. (1992). Prior use. *Transitions* 55:168–172.

Borland, H. (1963). *When the legends die*. New York: Bantam Books.

Braxton, J. M. (1989). *Black women writing autobiography: A tradition within a tradition*. Philadelphia: Temple University Press.

Brown, E. (1992). *A taste of power: A Black woman's story*. New York: Pantheon Books.

Cary, L. (1991). *Black ice*. New York: Alfred A. Knopf.

Coles, R. (1990). *The call of stories: Teaching and the moral imagination.* Boston: Houghton Mifflin.

Collins, P. H. (1991). On our own terms: Self-defined standpoints and curriculum transformation. *NWSA Journal* 3(3):367–381.

Edwards, H. (1980). *The struggle that must be.* New York: Macmillan.

Emecheta, B. (1982). *Double yoke.* New York: George Braziller.

Erickson, P. (1992). What multiculturalism means. *Transition* 55:105–114.

Felski, R. (1989). *Feminist literature and social change.* Cambridge: Harvard University Press.

Fox-Genovese, E. (1987). To write myself: The autobiography of African American women. In *Feminist issues in literary scholarship*, ed. S. Benstock, 161–190. Bloomington, IN: Indiana University Press.

Gagnier, R. (1991). Feminist autobiography in the 1980s: A review essay. *Feminist Studies* 17(1):135–148.

Gay, G. (1977). Curriculum design for multicultural education: Some concerns about a neglected dimension of research on teaching. *Contemporary Education* 46:183–188.

———. (1983). Multiethnic education, historical development and future prospects. *Phi Delta Kappan* 64:560–563.

Gutek, G. (1991). *Cultural foundations of education: A biographical introduction.* New York: Macmillan.

Heilbrun, C. (1988). *Writing a woman's life.* New York: Ballantine.

Hogan, P. C. (1992). Mo' better canons: What's wrong and what's right with mandatory diversity. *College English* 54(2):182–191.

Hutchinson, L. D. (1981). *Anna J. Cooper: A voice from the south.* Washington, DC: Smithsonian Institute Press.

Jelinek, E. C. (1986). *The tradition of women's autobiography from antiquity to the present.* Boston: Twayne Publishers.

Kingston, M. H. (1989). *The woman warrior.* New York: Vintage International.

Langemann, E. C., ed. (1985). *Jane Addams on education.* Classics in Education No. 51. New York: Teachers College, Columbia University.

Novarr, D. (1986). *The lines of life: Theories of biography 1880–1970.* West Layfayette, IN: Purdue University Press.

Penelton, B. S. (1991). Preparing teachers to be effective multicultural educators. In *Multicultural education*, ed. J. Q. Adams et al. Board of Governors of State Colleges, 71–79. IL: Western Illinois University Foundation.

Peshkin. A. (1991). *The color of strangers: The color of friends*. Chicago: University of Chicago Press.

Rampersand, A. (1983). Biography, autobiography and Afro-American culture. *The Yale Review* 73:1–16.

———. (1989). Biography and Afro-American culture. In *Afro-American literary studies of the 1990s*, ed. H. Baker Jr. and P. Redmond, 194–224. Chicago: University of Chicago Press.

Rodriguez, R. (1982). *Hunger of memory: The education of Richard Rodriguez*. New York: Bantam Books.

Schon, D. (1991). *The reflective turn: Case studies in and on educational practice*. New York: Teachers College Press.

Schubert, W. A., and W. C. Ayers, eds. (1992). *Teacher lore: Learning from our own experiences*. New York: Longman.

Shor, I., and P. Freire. (1987). *A pedagogy for liberation*. Cambridge, MA: Bergin and Garvey Publishers.

Sleeter, C. E., ed. (1991). *Empowerment through multicultural education*. New York: SUNY Press.

Stone, A. E. (1982). *Autobiographical occasions and original acts*. Philadelphia: Pennsylvania Press.

Swann, B., and A. Krupat, eds. (1987). *I tell you now: Autobiographical essays by Native American writers*. Lincoln, NE: University of Nebraska Press.

Weiler, K. (1988). *Women teaching for change: Gender, class, and power*. Cambridge, MA: Bergin and Garvey.

Weis, L. (1988). *Race, class and gender in American education*. Albany, NY: SUNY Press.

4

WILLIAM D. ARMALINE AND KATHLEEN S. FARBER

Developing Social and Cultural Foundations from a Multicultural Perspective

In this chapter we address teaching preservice teachers about social and cultural dynamics as they might affect teaching and learning in schools from a multicultural perspective. Key considerations in developing such a social and cultural foundations component in teacher education include: (1) an understanding of the role and functioning of culture and ideology in schooling, and (2) the reciprocal relationship between power and knowledge as they interact over time, both in the unfolding history of schooling in the United States and in the social construction of individual identities and the resulting manifestations of oppression (e.g., racism, sexism, homophobia, and class bias) as they play themselves out in and through schooling.

We begin the chapter with a brief overview of our pedagogical orientation and purposes for engaging students in a reflective journey through concepts and content in social and cultural foundations of education. We then discuss and illustrate core concepts such as culture, ideology, power, and knowledge that frame our pedagogical efforts, coupled with a discussion of an introductory set of activities and an assignment that can be used to initiate reflection on critical issues related to schooling and its purposes. Having established a starting point, we then move to a discussion of particular activities and assignments that focus in greater depth on how socially constructed categories such as gender, social class, race, and sexual orientation might relate to the interplay of ideology, power, and knowledge production as found in schools. Throughout the chapter, we depend on student writing to illustrate the ways in which students are constructing their understanding of the concepts and to point to places where we might wish to engender further reflection.[1] We end the chapter with our own reflections on teaching about issues of diversity in the education of preservice teachers.

PEDAGOGY AND PURPOSE

Our pedagogical approach is based on principles of teaching and learning rooted in the social construction of knowledge (Berger and Luckmann 1967) and reflective thinking (Dewey 1933; Farber 1994). To view knowledge as being socially constructed suggests that learners are actively configuring and reconfiguring meaning as a function of their own experience in transaction with their environmental context. Since other people form a significant part of that context, learning can be facilitated and enriched by interacting with others and drawing from their experiences, as well. Dewey's notion of reflective thinking provides a vehicle for constructing problematic situations or learning opportunities for and with our students such that we might tap into shared experience and elaborate, extend, and reconstruct that experience reflectively through the content that we are attempting to teach in our courses.

We design our courses, therefore, to link the biographies of class participants (both our own biographies and those of our students) with writing on the social and cultural foundations of schooling. This literature is vast, so obviously we engage in a highly selective process regarding course readings and activities. Our judgments about curriculum, and about classroom activities and other pedagogical elements, are based on a number of concerns. First, we want our students to develop a feel for the complexity surrounding and within schooling. Second, we want diverse cultural experiences represented in the readings and reflected in activities, discussions, and assignments throughout the course. Third, we want our students to engage in a critical analysis of schooling, at the level of both theory and practice, and to see how the two are intimately and unavoidably linked. Fourth, we want our students to become sensitive to the ways in which power, ideology, culture, and knowledge interact conceptually to frame the educative endeavor. Fifth and finally, we want our students to become conscious of the decisions that teachers must make regarding representation in the curriculum and in classroom activities and to become aware of the results of those choices on student knowledge and identity construction.

This final concern is addressed, in part, by focusing with our students on the pedagogical choices we make in our own courses and the effects of those choices on the meanings they (and we) make. Further, we explore with students how our courses may, indeed, be foundational for pedagogical study. In other words, we are concerned ultimately with how our courses inform instruction.

CORE CONCEPTS

Given the comments regarding purpose and orientation, we need to discuss the major ideas and concepts that frame our exploration of social and cultural foundations of schooling with preservice teachers. As stated in the introduction, understanding the interplay of culture and ideology is crucial to our purposes, and we work with students on these notions throughout the term. In addition, the relationship between occupying positions of relative power and privilege and the production of knowledge in terms of the knowledge that is taught as official curriculum, the knowledge that is omitted, and the knowledge that is gained in and through attending schools is a central theme. Further, elements of culture related to one's race, ethnicity, gender, social class, and sexual orientation are discussed and explored as they relate to power, knowledge, and ideology.

As we explore the web of relationships among various cultural memberships, power relations, knowledge production, and ideology, a second tier of concepts come into play. These include notions of hegemony, cultural capital, hier-archical positioning, privilege, production/reproduction (of culture, economic struc-tures and relations, and the like), equality of educational and economic opportunity, and marginalization, to name a few. Further, in the course of discussing specific cultural memberships, such as race or class or gender, these second tier concepts serve as common themes that show the intimate connections that exist among cultural memberships. In other words, it is pointless, indeed inappropriate, to speak of race or class or gender as distinct and separate from one another. Rather, through our activities, discussions, and readings we come to recognize their interrelatedness and their mutual effect on knowledge and identity constructions.

While it would be constructive to engage in a theoretical and conceptual discussion of each of these notions and how they relate to one another, that is not the purpose of this chapter. Yet, we do need to make clear how we use the terms in class and how our students come to understand them. We attempt to do this somewhat inductively using class writing assignments, discussions, and other activities, as this method of explication parallels our pedagogy. We begin by discussing how we initially engage students in a reflective process as a means to understanding social and cultural dynamics relative to schooling.

BEGINNINGS

The class meetings over the first few weeks are crucial in terms of creating the conditions and context for bringing to consciousness beliefs and ideological constructs related to the role and functioning of schooling in our society. We often begin a history and philosophy of education or a sociology of education class with a discussion of the current state of schooling, using accounts in the popular press and the Gallup Poll that appears each fall in *Kappan*. Discussions center first on students' views of what schools are supposed to do, how well schools perform their various social roles, and the major problems faced in and by schools. Next, we compare their views with those found in the media and Gallup Poll. What is apparent from these discussions is that both our students and the general public see schools failing in many ways. They see a number of social problems such as drugs, violence, crime, and unemployment influencing schooling experience and effectiveness. At the same time they see the schools as sites for addressing those very same problems. Invariably, students are struck by the myriad purposes that schools are expected to serve and by the woefully inad-equate results of schooling efforts, at least in terms of their own reports and accounts in the media.

In the context of a sociology of education class, these discussions lead to a critical assessment of the social role of schooling in a democratic society from multiple theoretical perspectives. In a history and philosophy of education class we move to a discussion of how, historically, schools came to serve all of these functions, accompanied by a discussion of competing educational ideals. In both cases, we are trying to create a connection between what we want to teach throughout the course and the lived experience of students relative to schooling, as gleaned from their own reflections, the media, and public opinion polls. In the process, we can together begin to approach our overall purposes of helping students to appreciate the complexity of social and historical forces at work in the development of the institution of schooling, the varied cultural experiences that have been brought together in schools, the relationships between beliefs and ideals and the practices of teaching and schooling, and the effects of these practices on students of varying backgrounds.

In addition to and concurrent with in-class discussions and assigned readings, students write on a number of topics related to the above concerns. These writings are incorporated into class discussions, in that students can interject ideas or problems from their paper drafts during class. As an early writing assignment in a history and philosophy of education context, we ask students to develop a short reflection paper over the first three weeks of the term. During the first two weeks of class, while they are reading from works such as Joel Spring's *The American School, 1642–1993* (1993) and Mary Wollstonecraft's *A Vindication of the Rights of Woman* (1792, 1985), they are to reflect on and write about their own education and schooling, as well as the education and schooling of a parent, grandparent, or ancestor. In their educational "family history," we ask them to discuss what major purposes schooling seems to serve in their lives, how it relates to their lives, to their personal fulfillment, and to the various social roles that they have taken or will take. We also ask them to discuss how their ancestor or family member might respond to the same questions. By the third week of the term, we ask that they extend the paper to make connections between their personal and family educational histories and readings and discussions, focusing only on what they deem most important and instructive.

We introduce student narratives here to illustrate how this introductory set of activities gives us text and information to inspect major course concepts in greater detail. In addition, it provides a glimpse into the actual process of student reflection. We ask that these reflections be read with an eye toward the pedagogical opportunities that they offer us. For example, what is in these narratives, or what is *not* in the narratives, that we might use to organize class discussions or activities to facilitate a deeper understanding of course concepts?

Most of the students suggest that purposes for schooling include creating an educated citizenry and providing a means to upward social mobility. Further, this is seen to be the case across generations. In this regard a female from rural working class roots who returned to school after her own children began elementary school wrote:

> My parents…possessed a strong work ethic. This meant I viewed any education almost as a civic duty. The goal was to be a productive citizen and not drain on societal resources. The individual was to prepare him/herself to give back at least as much as he/she had been given, if not more. It was the way to

show gratitude and allegiance to a nation that had provided for and guarded the rights and freedoms of its citizens. (LC)

While giving testimony to the espoused role of schooling in our democracy, most students also highlighted some problem or issue relative to the actual functioning of schooling in their lives and the lives of their ancestors. LC goes on to remark:

> Just an interesting note on the value of education for women of my parents' generation: out of the five boys and one girl in my mother's family, four boys completed four year degrees with three of them going on to become physicians. These were not options open to my mother.
>
> An interesting contrast appears when considering the maternal educational ancestry of my husband. The influence of an urban setting and the higher social standing of the men involved dictated a different educational path…(T)he goal of education for my mother-in-law was far different than for my mother. She was educated in the fine arts and groomed to move in the higher social circles. (LC)

A working class male observed:

> From the crowd I hung out with in school, I seemed to be a gem in the rough….I graduated with academic honors and stayed out of trouble. Some of it had to do with luck…the staying out of trouble part, that is. My friends had a hard time staying out of jail let alone staying in school and graduating. I think the schooling system of my time emphasizes being disciplined over that of pulling good grades. At my high school severe punishments were dealt to students who would misbehave or not follow orders. Very little concern was shown for students failing academically….Social class is probably a major factor as to the value of discipline over that of academic success at my high school. An overwhelming majority of students' parents are of the working class….On the other hand, if a student were to follow in the footsteps of his/her parents into the upper aristocratic class, then academic success would be important. These people must be able to think for themselves and make crucial decisions. (RH)

A White female noted:

> As an American woman, I shudder with indignation at the system which deprived so many women in the past of the access to knowledge. Not only in the institution of public schooling, but also in the socialization which teaches us our roles in society, have (we) generally pushed women toward a subservient position in society. I am quite interested in the advancements women have gained and the prices paid for such progress….An important implication of Wollstonecraft's work is that a society which suppresses large portions of its population simply cannot function at the same level possible if all members enjoyed liberty. (MB)

Among the most complex and intertwined set of problems and contradictions arose in a paper written by a female African-American student. Seeing in rap music a reflection of the lived experience of Black working-class youth, she wrote that schools did little more than solidify members of her group into their oppressed conditions. Citing the effects of tracking and differential expectations, she articulated the feelings of abandonment and her reactions, which resulted in a somewhat antagonistic resolve to do what she had been told she could not do.

> It was almost as though both the teachers and the curriculum had given up hope on us. It was assumed that we would graduate high school and go straight into the workforce. I had become so disappointed with my schooling that it gave me the motivation to attend college. After senior year, the parting words from my English teacher were as follows: "Best wishes in the future. Remember to put a hundred percent behind everything you do. Years from now, even if you guys turn out to be janitors, be the best janitors that you can be!" From that point on, I made it my business to always strive for excellence....
>
> It is now 2:30 AM, and I may as well go to bed questioning my aspiration of becoming a teacher. I was not very happy with any schooling experience. I am beginning to agree that...one major purpose is submission to authority; and for some reason, I have a problem with that. I am not the only one who is unhappy:

> "Ice Cube wishes to acknowledge the failure of the public school system to teach all of its students about the major contributions made by our African American scientists, inventors, artists, scholars, and leaders (with all due respect for your lectures on the planet). Without its role in the conspiracy, the *Predator* album might not have been made." (Ice Cube, Acknowledgment on the *Predator* album)

> Education in colonial New England must be understood in the context of a group of people struggling for survival in an unknown wilderness....; I could not have said it better! (PG)

What was accomplished through this assignment and the resultant class discussions of these personal and family histories? First, students began to discuss how history is constructed by selecting, representing, and interpreting the experiences of some and not others. The history of education in the United States, for example, has been defined largely by texts that speak differentially to human experiences and that ignore or gloss over the experiences of marginalized groups, as reflected in the family histories many students constructed. This selective representation often leads to the creation of ideological structures that obscure, mystify, and distort the lived experience of many who attend and believe in schools. Second, this assignment provided an introduction to the ways in which race, class, ethnicity, and gender interact with the knowledge/power dynamic relative to the production of knowledge in and through school. Seeing the experience of being a woman translated into less educational opportunity (LC) and into decreased access to certain knowledge deemed important (MB) is significant and eye-opening. Seeing social class (RH) and race (PG) as factors that influence teacher expectations and student access to knowledge also speaks to educational and economic opportunity. Further, this introduction is accomplished largely through the experiences and words of the students themselves. Third, the conditions were set for us to pursue with our students details of their constructions in ways that might challenge them to rethink, deepen, and refine those constructions in light of experience beyond their own. In other words, we can engage them in reflectively incorporating the experiences of their classmates, as well as the experiences distilled in assigned texts, into their existing knowledge structures. For example, we might ask students to read one anothers' papers with an eye toward how they construct their understandings in light of varying lived experience. In this way, they can begin to see their own writings as text that, due to the diversity represented in their experience, might add richness to the course and enhance learning for all.

This kind of early writing assignment can be used in almost any foundations class. The idea is to get students to reflect on the espoused purposes of schooling in light of and often in contrast to what they actually live in schools. This lived experience is influenced by cultural memberships such as race, class, and gender, as evidenced by our students' own words. As a result, we have the pedagogical opportunity to inspect these memberships more carefully and directly. We can begin to investigate, describe, and analyze issues of diversity and culture as they influence schooling experience. Additionally, the early set of activities and assignments establishes a pattern that we tend to follow, with minor alterations, throughout the course. We engage students in exploration of their own experiences along a number of fronts, expose them to video and literary treatments of social issues, assign various types of readings which connect those issues to schooling, and employ reflective discussion and writing exercises which ask students to explore and connect all of the above.

Extended Explorations and Student Knowledge Construction

Two of the first deviations from the role of schooling in the American Dream as represented by student writing above have to do with gender and class. LC noted that her mother did not have the same educational advantages as her male siblings. Gender was also a concern of MB, in terms of women not being represented in the curriculum. In addition, LC stated that a working-class position may have played a role in her mother's experience, in contrast with her more affluent mother-in-law. RH interjected class as a variable in his experience, as well. If we are fortunate enough to have students of color (such as PG) in our classes, we also may get student writing that positions race as a critical variable in schooling experience. Given that most of our students are White and that Whites generally do not have to focus on being racialized (Sleeter 1994), such is often not the case, however. How can we extend our students' understandings of how cultural memberships such as gender, class, and race influence schooling experience?

We employ a wide array of activities to encourage students to explore and inspect their own experience as it influences their construction of self in terms of gender, class, and race. One activity that explores how one's gendered identity is formed in terms of social and cultural expectations is also described by us else-where (Farber and Armaline 1992). We begin by drawing male and female symbols on the board and ask what attributes or descriptors are brought to mind by such symbols. Next, we ask where and in what ways these various traits are valued by society. What students begin to bring to awareness is that the character traits expected of and developed in women differ from those expected of men and tend to be those not valued, at least in terms of social and economic benefits. Further, when women try to develop the "male" traits in an effort at realizing the American Dream of economic self-sufficiency, they are not only not given the same rewards as men, they are often devalued even further. In like fashion, men who display "feminine" traits are viewed and treated as less than "real men." Further, in both cases of "gender crossing," intimations of homophobia often arise, giving us the opportunity to explore the social constructions of sexual iden-tities with our students.

We discuss with students how, while both sexes are diminished by such socially determined genderized traits, the effect on a woman is far more imme-diate and disastrous, in that her ability to live and support herself and her family is materially affected. Yet both males and females suffer, in that they are prevented from constructing a fully mature identity that blends the male and the female traits so necessary for healthy and productive lives.

We often pair such an activity with videos that explore various aspects of gender in society. For example, in the video "Still Killing Us Softly," Jane Kilbourne (1987) explores gender and advertising. She links the devaluing and objectifying of women in the media to various breakdowns in human relationships and, ultimately, to violence against women. In another video, "Dreamworlds " (Jhally 1990), the violence against women as an outcropping of objectification is explored by juxtaposing MTV videos with clips from the rape scene in the film, "The Accused." In both of these videos, students can begin to link their own expe-riences as men and women with popular cultural images that permeate our daily experience and thereby influence how we define and construct ourselves.

We also often ask students in a free write to discuss a time or situation when they were (first) made aware of their gender.[2] This in-class activity can be done, obviously, using any number of other cultural memberships such as race, ethnicity, class, or sexual orientation. It is generally quite instructive in terms of the situations and experiences that are generated. It is also useful because, while women in the class typically have little difficulty coming up with illustrations relative to gender, men will often be quite perplexed. This is an excellent oppor-tunity to discuss the nature of privilege and power, not merely in terms of overt advantage, but also in terms of more subtle forms of advantage emanating from defining what is "normal" and accepted. Living one's life not having to think about one's gender, class, race, or sexual orientation, in other words, is a form of privilege.

At some point connections need to be made directly to schooling. It is here that research on gender discrimination in schools, such as the report by the American Association of University Women titled "How Schools Shortchange Girls" (1992) becomes very important. Often, when only the research is discussed, it is resisted and dismissed through various forms of denial, trivialization, rationalization, and distortion. However, given the cultural context that is established through the discussion of lived experience and popular cultural images, the data on male versus female treatment in schools as it relates to schooling success and achievement make more sense and are more difficult to dismiss. Further, the complexity of the matter is emphasized in that students can begin to see this literature, not merely as the reflection of malicious and/or inadequate teachers, but rather as an extension of how we live. As such, we hope that they will be more likely to inspect how the way that we live our lives influences our assumptions about life and our behavior as students and teachers in schools.

As stated above, both LC and RH saw class as an important variable in schooling experience also. One way to get students to talk about social class is to discuss the various factors that distinguish students in schools by asking them about the social groups that students form. In a chapter on the formation and effects of youth culture, Kathleen Bennett and Margaret LeCompte suggest just such an activity (1990, 111). They ask students to think about the various groups that students formed, the ways that the groups distinguished themselves from one another, what they called themselves (and we add what they were called by others), and how teachers and administrators related to each of the groups. Students typically generate numerous groups using a variety of names with varying degrees of humor and, at times, ridicule. As we discuss the factors that separate the groups, social class background always emerges as prominent, usually in combination with race and gender. Further, when students reflect on the ways that others, especially adults, related to the groups, they find that groups with higher class standing are generally viewed more positively than those with lower class standing. Additionally, this hierarchical ordering is mediated by other factors, such as race and gender.

This discussion and the earlier gender activity create the conditions to explore why it is that some are valued more than others. We can examine such related notions as cultural capital, cultural production and reproduction, and hegemony relative to the ways in which schooling might *not* actually provide for personal affirmation or for upward social mobility. In addition to the Bennett and LeCompte text, one piece that has been especially useful in this regard is Jean Anyon's "Social Class and the Hidden Curriculum of Work" (1980). Here Anyon describes the differing schooling experiences for students of differing social classes. Our students' discussions generally resonate with elements of her work, and it provides a backdrop for a number of additional class activities that encourage students to reflect on social class as it affects students' schooling experience.

The concept of class is quite complex, of course, and students need time and opportunity to begin to move beyond merely viewing class in terms of earned income and parental status. Course readings on class such as those found in Bennett and LeCompte (1990) extend class to include parental occupations and educational levels; sets of shared behaviors, aspirations, and beliefs; power; status; and various configurations of cultural capital. These extensions of the concept of class, combined with the experiences generated in the students' own writings, help to engender deeper insights into class and its effects on educational and economic opportunity. Further, the role of teacher, given such insights, begins to be recast. We are especially interested in how our students can begin to think in terms of the cultural capital that their students will be bringing to their class-rooms as added resources, as an expanded base from which to select a diversity of experiences that can enhance and enrich the experiences of all class members. This is one way that content and concepts from social and cultural foundations can inform instruction. Cultural capital is, not only a generative concept for discussions of social class, but also for other cultural memberships, including race and ethnicity.

We often begin our discussion of race and ethnicity with a short free write on our students' perceptions of racial and ethnic relations on campus. Do we have problems? If so, what are the most serious ones, and why do you think those prob-lems exist? If not, why do you suppose that we are experiencing harmonious rela-tions among the various racial and ethnic groups on campus? Typically, White students from the dominant culture see campus life as relatively harmonious with few serious incidents of racial and ethnic tension. Students of color are more likely to cite points of tension, but, since they are often in the extreme minority in teacher education classrooms, serious discussion of these incidents as anything more than individual isolated experiences is quite difficult.

To get at a more in-depth analysis of racial and ethnic relations on campus, we often follow a brief discussion of the students' responses on the above free write with a video such as "Racism 101." This video depicts incidents of racial tension and violence taking place on campuses across the country in the late 1980s. The scenes range from violence that resulted from the World Series victory of the New York Mets over the Boston Red Sox, to hate mail and threats made to African Americans on predominantly White campuses over perceptions of differential treatment and "reverse discrimination," to a depiction of the campaign against many faculty and students at Dartmouth University by *The Dartmouth Review*, a conservative local newspaper. Students are asked to reflect on (1) what they think and feel as they watch the video, (2) what major issues were raised, (3) how they might explain the actions of the various participants in the video, and (4) how the situations depicted in the video match their own expe-riences. Further, they are asked to reflect on the notion of "equality of educational opportunity" in light of the video.

The incidents strike home in that they take place on campuses in many ways very similar to where we teach. Therefore, student denial that there exists much racial and ethnic tension is called into question, whether there are persons of color in the room or not. In addition, many of the rationalizations for racial/ethnic tension which entail victim blaming, such as the claim of reverse discrimination, can be inspected carefully. An especially useful piece in this regard is Julie Andrzejewski's "The Myth of Reverse Discrimination" (1993, 93) in which she examines the concept in light of its use to counter attempts by oppressed groups to press for social and political change.

"Racism 101" is a very powerful video, but there are risks involved in its use. So many issues arise that one can easily get overwhelmed, and resulting discussion may not be sufficient for any of the issues raised. Further, if there are persons of color in the room, they may be unfairly put "on the spot" and treated as spokespersons for "the race." This can be avoided by using other videos, such as "A Class Divided," which is a retrospective look after fourteen years at participants in the blue-eye/brown-eye activity done with elementary school students in "Eye of the Storm." In this activity, over a two-day period elementary school students were placed both in positions of subordination and of superiority based on eye color and then asked to discuss the effects on their behavior, thoughts, and feelings about themselves and others who differed from them by eye color. In either of these videos students can witness the effects of discrimination in a less volatile way.

We also use selections from the "Eyes on the Prize" series to complement students' understandings of the ongoing Civil Rights Movement. Some paper assignments focus on race specifically, as does the assignment above relative to analyzing the schooling experiences of marginalized populations. The discussion of racial and ethnic tension is important in and of itself, just as are discussions of sexism and class bias. Two texts that have been especially useful in stimulating discussion and writing on the current and historical roles of education for African American students are Richard Wright's *Black Boy* and W. E. B. DuBois' *The Souls of Black Folks*. Each of these texts places the education of African American students at its center and seats the schooling process in a complex social, historical, and cultural context revolving around race. But we also extend the discussion of racism, class bias, homophobia, and sexism to address the concept of "equality of educational opportunity," as we suggested earlier. Here, again, we draw from student narratives to illustrate the meanings they make relative to the above and to examine where, pedagogically, we might go with those meanings.

IN STUDENTS' WORDS

One writing assignment asks students to discuss the "experiences" over time of women, African Americans, working-class people, or any other marginalized group in the schooling system from the perspective of their being teachers or students (or both). How have these groups negotiated schooling in an effort at defining themselves, at constructing their individual and collective identities?

A White, working-class male began his essay with the following:

> Men, how many times have you heard or said yourself that a woman's place is
> at home with the kids, making dinner and cleaning house?!...Women have
> been brought up to believe the domestic life to be their only possible profes-
> sion due to their natural skills in this field. This patriarchal view of domestic
> women is echoed in the schooling system. The values and characteristics
> imposed on females in school are miseducative because they have "the effect
> of arresting or distorting the growth of further experience." (Dewey 1938, 25)
> (RH)

He continued by discussing women's learned passivity through schooling and
family life and recognized it as miseducative in that it impedes women's success
in the world of work. Further, he saw the conceptual connecting of passivity and
femininity as both destructive and socially constructed.

> As Ann Lane states in her introduction for Gilman's *Herland*, "men long had
> the power to create their own kind of woman—fragile, dependent, passive,
> timid—by not marrying those who deviated" (1979, xiii). Thus, femininity is
> of man's creation serving to satisfy him. (RH)

He ended on an optimistic note, however, suggesting that in the United States
there is opportunity for change in the status and position of women. A question
we might place before him as a White male in this society, or use as a point for
group discussion, is what is his responsibility in the process of social change, as
a male teacher, spouse, friend, potential parent?

The next response reflects a student who is able to imagine the intersection
of multiple cultural memberships, weaving together race, gender, class, age, and
sexual orientation. At the same time, he seems to retreat to an ideological position rooted in the belief that these differences and the unequal power relations that
emanate from them are natural and not socially constructed. How can we use,
pedagogically, what he knows as well as what he does not know?

> Our experience is not hermetically sealed off from the rest of the human race,
> but instead is an ever-interacting part of it....John Dewey put it: "Experience
> does not go on simply inside a person. It does go on there, for it influences the
> formation of attitudes of desire and purpose. Every genuine experience has an
> active side which changes in some degree the objective conditions under which
> experiences are had" (1938, 39).
>
> So, when someone like Audre Lorde makes the claim that she is a "forty-
> nine-year-old Black lesbian socialist feminist mother of two and a member of
> an interracial couple" (1991, 213), using Dewey's line of thought we can
> assume that Ms. Lorde is affecting the world around her in such a manner to
> advance the ideals or goals that a "forty-nine-year-old Black lesbian socialist
> feminist mother of two and a member of an interracial couple" might hold....
>
> The adjustments that Ms. Lorde wants made are in the nature of domi-
> nant/subordinate relationships which she feels exist in society. She feels that
> we live in a society that has distorted and emphasized the differences of
> marginalized groups from the mainstream. She states, "We have all been

programmed to respond to the human differences between us with fear and loathing and to handle that difference in one of three ways: ignore it, and if that is not possible, copy it if we think it is dominant, or destroy it if we think it is subordinate" (1992, 214).

The experience of the African-American female in our society then becomes an interesting one. How much can she choose to ignore? How often is she subjected to a greater societal force than her own? Is this at all relevant, and could she move beyond societal effects on her?...

Her experience would not even be the same as a White female because, as Lorde points out, "white women ignore the built-in privilege of whiteness and define *woman* in terms of their own experience alone, then women of Colour become 'other,' the outsider whose experience and the tradition is too alien to comprehend" (1992, 216). (RJ)

He concluded that education and social justice require attention to difference that results from such factors as race and gender, not just individually, but also in combination.

I don't believe the dominant/subordinate relationship that exists between so many marginalized groups and the dominant culture in this country can ever truly be eradicated. Man or woman, Black or White, one group will always have the upper hand. It is just the nature of things that, given two forces, one is usually more powerful than the other. The thing we can do through education is try to recognize these differences, see the pitfalls that the marginalized groups fall in, eliminate them, and work hard to negate the advantage of the dominant group. (RJ)

Again, we see a respect for complexity, yet it is operating concurrently with a retreat to the mystification of ideology, seeing in socially determined divisions and constructions "the nature of things." He also, however, came close to articulating a transformative role and function for schooling, a role concerned with striving toward social justice. These points, along with others in the earlier excerpts, became opportunities to investigate and question student thinking about issues of diversity relative to schooling and educational ideals.

We end this section with writing from two African American students on the roles and functioning of schooling in the United States. Both students reflect on very negative schooling experiences that raise questions of teacher responsibility and ethical practice. They wonder whether they really do want to teach, given what we have discussed, and whether teachers can truly be transformative. Yet these narratives are not only expressions of despair. They also point to possibilities that help all of us construct images of transformative practice.

An African American female began her essay by quoting her own reflections on schools and society.

What good shall my education do? Throughout my schooling experience, I have often heard my Black counterparts telling me, "You of all people, Pamela, have to apply yourself." But what for? Why is it going to be that much harder for me to succeed? My teachers told me that my credibility would be doubted. Why? Is this a Black thing? (PG)

She then discussed the "academic discouragement" experienced by African Americans in our schools, coupled with a grim employment outlook, largely as a function of race. In preparation for her paper she actually talked with school children about their perceptions of the future.

> I was in total amazement with the negative attitudes of the children that I had spoken with. Where did they get such negative attitudes? Whether intentional or not, are these types of attitudes being implicitly taught and unconsciously learned in the classroom? I was equally astonished to sit and listen to these students speak of their future; they did not believe that they had one, and they attributed that belief to their blackness....I can remember one kid saying, "O.K. So what if I go to school and get straight A's. What good is that gonna do ME?" The problem is that many African Americans truly believe that school and good grades will get them nothing, for they are Black, and being Black will get you nowhere. (PG)

She found somewhat different versions of the above when she considered gender, with Black females giving more positive predictions of their futures than Black males, should they finish school and go to college. She used these differing perspectives to suggest in her paper that, should visitors arrive from Gilman's Herland, they would get very different images of our schooling, depending upon what schools they visited and what students they interviewed and observed.

Finally, PG commented on representation and the curriculum in schools, suggesting that the experience of African Americans is absent and that what "is presented is somewhat one-sided, and somewhat sugar coated." This paper, in the context of others that she wrote, suggests a student grappling with some very difficult issues, not only relative to understanding schooling, teaching, and learning, but also to her chosen career. She actively struggled with what it means to teach in the public schools and with the promises and pitfalls of such a choice relative to her own goals. These are all serious issues that we explore with our students. She also raised questions about "equality of educational opportunity," perhaps *the* ideological hallmark of schooling in the United States.

Students writing on equality of educational opportunity indicate that they understand legal guarantees to access to schooling facilities, providing for people to have the same chance to receive an education. They have a great deal of difficulty, however, recognizing that equality does not necessarily mean providing everyone with the *same* education in terms of curriculum, teaching methods, resources, and the like. Fairness and justice may actually require *difference* relative to many facets of the schooling experience. We try to work out ways to vary curriculum and instruction in light of student background experiences, interests, and abilities to increase the likelihood that students will be able to exercise their rights of access in meaningful ways, thereby working toward equality of educational opportunity in terms of the outcomes of schooling. We do this in our own classes with our students and expect that they will learn to do the same as they move through the teacher education program. This, of course, is not always a warranted assumption. So, we attempt to extend our foundations classes into the realm of methodology, discussing with students how pedagogy might change to be more culturally sensitive and inclusive without falling into the trap of intellectual relativism.

A final set of excerpts by an African American male begins to address a struggle to understand some of the complexities involved in such pedagogy.

> When I was in kindergarten and first grade, I attended a school that was predominately Black. My growth and confidence as a student and person were coming along very nicely, and being that most of the teachers were (Black), I had no concept of the negative views some Whites had of Blacks....At the end of my first grade year, it was decided by the school board that it was in the best interest of the students to bus us to various schools (predominantly White schools) in order to create racially balanced schools. When we arrived at our new school the following academic year, the parents of our new classmates were unhappy with our arrival. Many of these parents were at the bus stop with picket signs voicing their opposition to bussing. This was one of the first times that I realized that I was different and that this difference did not place me in an advantaged position. The teachers helped magnify these feelings by treating us like we had a sub-par education before we walked into their school. (KM)

He then discussed the negative effects of tracking and ability grouping, which he saw separating students "on the basis of race and economic background." He also reacted strongly to the ideology of "cultural deprivation" undergirding much of the early compensatory education legislation. He stated:

> I commend many of the federal and state programs that focused on financial disadvantages, such as the...program that gives hot lunches to students who can neither afford to buy or bring lunches to school. (However) I am strongly offended by the "Cultural Deprivation" programs designed to give poor minority children "culture." An example of this is the yearly trips to the symphony that are made by elementary school children. Though there is nothing wrong with the children attending the symphony, but by not allowing the minority children to share their own cultural experiences (African poetry reading, Gospel choir concerts, etc.), it can give the impression that their cultural experiences are inferior.
>
> Consequently, it is no wonder that there are generation upon generation of children who feed into these inferior attitudes and eventually fulfill the negative views society holds of them....Schools are just a portion of society and society continues to withhold opportunity from certain segments of it. Educators are participators in (the) larger society, therefore they bring (the) larger society's views into the classroom. (KM)

Using KM's experience of exclusion in conjunction with the realization that his cultural background is indeed rich, we can begin to discuss with our students how his cultural experience can be used, not only to connect him to the classes and curriculum we wish to teach, but also enrich the educational experiences of all in our classes who differ from him by, in this case, race. Further, we can begin to link this kind of pedagogical practice to the ethics of teaching in a multicultural democracy.

ENDING THOUGHTS AND NAGGING QUESTIONS

The primary reason for our writing this piece is to inspect how we have multi-culturalized our own pedagogy and the potential effects of that effort. We have discussed our approach to social and cultural foundations content, and we have included excerpts from our students' writing to illustrate their knowledge constructions, both in terms of their insights and limitations, relative to what we teach. We would like now to raise some issues that arise and remain unresolved in our pedagogical efforts. First, how can we understand what our students leave out of their writings, those aspects of our pedagogical content that they do not "get?" How can we better understand the limits to student insight and under-standing? From a modernist, enlightenment perspective, we might assume that students have not been exposed to the "right" knowledge in the "right" ways. Their shortcomings, therefore, suggest a need merely to be exposed to new knowledge of multiculturalism in better, more seductive, and meaningful ways, and then they will increasingly understand issues of multicultural education. However, we do not find this to be the case. Shoshana Felman, in her essay "Psychoanalysis and Education: Teaching Terminable and Interminable," suggests that equating ignorance with a lack of knowledge is too simplistic. Using psychoanalytic insights from Sigmund Freud and Jacques Lacan, she sees in ignorance the active resistance to knowledge. She states:

> Ignorance…is not a passive state of absence, a simple lack of information: it is an active dynamic of negation, an active refusal of information….Teaching, like analysis, has to deal not so much with lack of knowledge as with resistance to knowledge. Ignorance, suggests Lacan, is a passion. Inasmuch as traditional pedagogy postulated a desire for knowledge, an analytically informed peda-gogy has to reckon with "the passion for ignorance…." Ignorance, in other words is nothing other than a *desire to ignore*: its nature is less cognitive than performative. As in the case of Sophocles' nuanced representation of the igno-rance of Oedipus, it is not a simple lack of information but the incapacity—or the refusal—to acknowledge one's own implication in the information.
>
> The new pedagogical lesson of psychoanalysis is not subsumed, however, by the revelation of the dynamic nature, and of the irreducibility, of ignorance. The truly revolutionary insight…consists in showing the ways in which igno-rance itself can teach us something, becoming itself instructive. (1987, 79)

Perhaps, using a psychoanalytic metaphor, the silences and gaps in student understanding are instructive in that they point to the location of resistance, the ideological structures that affect knowledge construction. If we were to begin to understand the origins of the resistance, the conceptual constructs that organize and structure knowledge, we might have some insight into why it is that students maintain a particular intellectual direction. In other words, we must become a student of our students' knowledge and/or passion for not knowing.

One way we may do this is by drawing from Foucault's notion of "conceptual needs" (1982, cited in Britzman 1993). Let us return to statements made by RJ concerning education as a remedy for social injustice and oppression to illustrate. He alluded to effects of racism, sexism, and heterosexism in our society, but, at the same time, he did not seem to see the systematic and institutionalized nature of these forms of oppression. He was holding to a belief that schooling can be the vehicle for eradicating the negative effects of difference. He stated: "The thing we can do through education is try to recognize these differences, see the pitfalls that marginalized groups fall in, eliminate them, and work hard to negate the advantage of the dominant group" (RJ). While we recognize his insights relative to the possibility of developing a transformative pedagogy, we also might view his conclusion that we can rectify an oppressive system through that very same system absent a radical transformation as reflective of a conceptual need. Our problem becomes how to understand and identify these conceptual needs, this tendency toward "stable and non-contradictory knowledge" (Britzman 1993, 127). Students' current state of knowledge seemingly creates a content in which they select and reject new knowledge based largely on its concurrence with what they currently believe and hold dear.

This problem of understanding how students' conceptual needs are reflected in their writing and understanding has led us to another issue revolving around the question, What content is, indeed, foundational or necessary for preservice teachers studying the social and cultural dynamics of schooling? An imbedded question prior even to this one is, How are we using the term "cultural?" According to Deborah Britzman, the traditional view has been from "anthropological and sociological models of the culture as the sum of inherited rituals and roles that actors take up to function in everyday life" (1993, 128–9). With this view of culture operative, knowledge from these disciplines relative to rituals, roles, and positions of actors from various cultures becomes the basis for what is "foundational." Yet this knowledge often fails to be situated in a context where the historical meanings of the concepts relative to the lives of people are actively and consciously considered. In terms of how that content relates to the conceptual needs of our students, it appears to suggest categories such as race, class, gender, and sexuality that become essentialized constructs and play into their desire for stability and certainty. It might be that this content actually functions as a set of constructions that works to obscure the very complexities of representation and identity that we are trying to uncover and inspect relative to cultural difference.

We suggest that Britzman is correct in asserting that, in the present context, culture ought to be "likened to a complex and contradictory array of discursive meanings and social practices vying for the performative attention of its actors even as it conditions possibilities for new forms of conduct and for the emergence of new identities" (1993, 129). This shift in meaning of "culture" would lead us to focus, for instance, on the actual practice of meaning making employed by our students, including the knowledge they bring to class, the knowledge they make, and the knowledge they ignore, as well as the effects of their sets of constructions on social action. In other words, the discursive practices and narratives of our students become relevant foundational texts for us and for them. These texts are foundational for us in that they help us to understand the dynamics of culture and conceptual needs relative to our students' educative endeavor, and they are foundational for our students because they point to ways that they might reflect on their students' discursive practices and narratives as they develop their own multicultural pedagogy.

NOTES

1. We wish to thank our students for their willingness for us to use their writings in our efforts at developing and articulating a social and cultural foundations component for multicultural teacher education.

2. We would like to thank Renee Martin for her creativity in designing this activity.

REFERENCES

ABC News. (1970). Eye of the storm. New York: ABC News.

Anyon, J. (1980). Social class and the hidden curriculum of work. *Journal of Education* 162(1):67–92.

American Association of University Women (AAUW). (1992). How schools shortchange girls: Executive summary. Washington, DC: AAUW Education Foundation.

Andrzejewski, J. (1993). The myth of reverse discrimination. In *Oppression and Social Justice*, ed. J. Andrzejewski. Needham Heights, MA: Ginn Press.

Bennett, K., and M. LeCompte. (1990). *The way schools work.* New York: Longman.

Berger, P., and T. Luckmann. (1967). *The social construction of reality.* New York: Doubleday.

Britzman, D. (1993). The ordeal of knowledge: Rethinking the possibilities of multicultural education. *Review of Education* 15(2):123–135.

Dewey, J. (1933). *How we think.* Lexington, MA: D. C. Heath.

———. (1938). *Experience and education.* New York: Macmillan.

DuBois, W. E. B. (1903, 1961). *The souls of Black folk.* Greenwich, CT: Fawcett.

Farber, K. (1994). Teaching about diversity through reflectivity: Sites of uncertainty, risk, and possibility. In *Practicing What We Teach: Confronting Diversity in Teacher Education*, ed. R. Martin. Albany, NY: SUNY Press.

Farber, K., and W. Armaline. (1992). Unlearning how to teach: Restructuring the teaching of pedagogy. *Teaching education* 5(1):99–111.

Felman, S. (1987). *Jacques Lacan and the adventure of insight: Psychoanalysis in contemporary culture.* Cambridge, MA: Harvard University Press.

Foucault, M. (1982). Afterward: The subject and power. In *Michel Foucault: Beyond Structuralism and Hermeneutics*, ed. H. Dreyfus & P. Rabinow, 2nd ed., 208–226. Chicago: University of Chicago Press, 1983.

Gilman, C. (1915, 1979). *Herland.* New York: Pantheon Books.

Jhally, S. (1990). Dreamworlds. Northampton, MA: Foundation for Educational Media.

Kilbourne, J. (1987). Still killing us softly. Cambridge, MA: Cambridge Documentary Films.

Lorde, A. (1992). Age, race, class, and sex: Women redefining difference. In *Ethics: A feminist reader*, ed. E. Frazer, J. Hornsby, and S. Lovibond. Oxford: Blackwell.

Public Broadcasting Corporation. (1986). Eyes on the prize. New York: Public Broadcasting Corporation.

Public Broadcasting Stations. (1985). A class divided. New York: PBS/Frontline.

Public Broadcasting Stations. (1988). Racism 101. New York: PBS/Frontline.

Sleeter, C. (1994). Teaching Whites about racism. In *Practicing what we teach: Confronting diversity in teacher education*, ed. R. Martin. Albany, NY: SUNY Press.

Spring, J. (1990). *The American school: 1642–1990.* New York: Longman.

Wollstonecraft, M. (1792, 1985). *Vindication of the Rights of Woman.* New York: Penguin Books.

Wright, R. (1937, 1966). *Black Boy.* New York: Harper and Row.

5

KIP TELLEZ, PETER S. HLEBOWITSH, MYRNA COHEN,
AND PAMELA NORWOOD

Social Service Field Experiences and Teacher Education

> Education is a regulation of the process
> of coming to share in the social con-
> sciousness.
>
> *John Dewey*

Think of the way that the world looks to many beginning educators working in the urban centers of our society. Children often go to school in neighborhoods with rising homicide rates; they come from families victimized by sinking wages, a lack of job opportunities, and curtailed government assistance. Some of them are homeless, many are in despair. For all, a prevailing sense of social disaffection combined with drug abuse and violent crime provide the admixture for a fearful and hopeless street climate. Significantly, these children of poverty and violence are, more often than not, also children of color.

Now think of the way that the world is presented in many teacher education programs in the United States. Popular references to time-on-task, to various preset models, taxonomies, and generic teaching strategies, to recipelike discipline and management techniques, to narrow conceptions of lesson plan design, and to a general mentality of matching learning behaviors with prefashioned learning objectives (Ginsburg 1988) still dominate, underscoring the fact that teacher education is still removed from broader socioeconomic considerations.

There are, of course, many thinkers who have sought to broaden the analytical sights of teacher education and who have brought the causes of justice and equality to the forefront of educational studies, particularly and quite appropriately, to teacher education. The work of educators such as Ira Shor (1983), whose experience with working-class students in New York, provides a positive direction for teacher education; Paulo Freire's (1970) well-known achievements with oppressed workers in South America are also paramount. Yet, for many educational theorists and the students they teach, the notion of cultural diversity, social disaffection, and poverty is rarely informed by the hard realities of life in our cities. Educational thinkers who confuse rhetoric for active social amelioration may not

65

be promoting the kind of teacher who will work in the interests of culturally diverse and low-income youth. Similarly, those who promote "reflective" teacher education also hope for teachers who will look broadly at the profession of teaching and at the social consequences of the teacher's influence. We maintain, however, that deep reflection can only occur when students have something meaningful upon which to reflect. Landon Beyer (1984) reminds teacher educators that reflection is method, not a curricular theme, and that reflection, in and of itself, promises nothing.

We suggest that preservice teachers can best broaden their view by discussing issues of race, class, and gender and by working in the interests of disenfranchised, inner-city youth in a community-based field experience. We hope that students, through classroom discussions and firsthand experiences with diverse students and their families, will come to find joy in helping those students in most despair and will, as a result, commit themselves to teaching in urban settings, instead of opting for suburban teaching positions. Our views are confirmed by teacher educators such as Martin Haberman (1992) who maintains that urban teachers must receive their professional preparation in the urban environment (although we do not share his faith in alternative certification). To this end, we have sought to recover the socio-civic and multicultural ground of teaching at the University of Houston by placing our preservice teachers in social service activities throughout our city.

Being There

Fall of 1991 was the inaugural semester of our newly developed teacher education program. It was marked by a series of stops and starts, questions about the worth of various assignments, and an unfulfilled sense of what was really appropriate for beginning teacher education students. Like most other teacher educators, we were saddled with far too many students, shrinking budgets and resources, and students who had already been bruised by the bureaucracy of a large public university. Our course in the teacher education program, which would best be considered an introduction to teaching and education, and is a junior-level undergraduate course, is the first in the University of Houston's eighteen credit-hour professional development sequence. In the second semester, students take specialized methods courses; the third and final semester consists entirely of student teaching.

Like most other teacher educators, we require our students to observe and student teach in local public schools. In initially trying to deal with issues of social consciousness, we added a cultural dimension to their school experience by placing students in schools where the population is comprised primarily of low-income students of color. However, we grew dissatisfied with this experience as the single engagement with diverse students and their families. We found, with a few outstanding exceptions, that the teachers with whom our students were placed did not represent culturally sensitive teaching. Thus, it became clear to us that simply working in diverse schools was not enough. We then asked our students to conduct a community study of a neighborhood school that integrated what we believed to be central questions of race, diversity, ethnicity, and socioeconomics. We had hoped that such an assignment would provide our students with an emerging sense of an ethnography as conducted by a participant-observer, but the results were disappointing. To wit, many students wrote passages that showed little insight into the conditions of those they saw and often observed from the distance of their car windows.

In thinking back on our "mini-ethnography" assignment, we had expected that our students would come to understand better and appreciate the multicultural richness of Houston's neighborhoods and that they would later incorporate what they learned into their teaching. Other teacher educators have employed the ethnographic method with the hope that their students would show the depth of understanding of the anthropologist who conducts such investigations routinely.

Our lack of success with student ethnographies could not be attributed to familiar and routine locales. The majority of the neighborhoods surrounding the University of Houston, a truly urban university, are decaying parts of the inner-city. One area in particular is known as Freedman's Town, where many African Americans settled after the Emancipation Proclamation. In fact, many of the brick streets and old clapboard homes are used today. Unfortunately, poverty is also far too common. Another neighborhood, to the east, known as Denver Harbor, is predominantly Latino. Owing to its proximity to the Port of Houston, Denver Harbor's residents are largely the working poor. However, the high labor force participation in the area does not eliminate extreme poverty, violence, and social disaffection.

The rich ethnic life of these neighborhoods gave us a unique opportunity for our student ethnographics. Yet, even when placed in these settings, our students had trouble taking hold of the assignment. Whether it was owing to our inability to communicate ethnographic methods to our students or the nature of the assignment, many wrote papers that showed little understanding of the conditions they saw. Part of the problem, we surmise, was due to our students' wariness of such neighborhoods. We were the first to admit that many of the neighborhoods in which our students observed were potentially dangerous.

We acknowledge the complexity and sophistication of ethnographic work and wonder whether it can be successfully managed in an introductory course. Indeed, it might be considered pedagogical arrogance to believe that our instructional and motivational skills were so developed as to enrich our students' understanding of professional anthropology. Many of the finest social minds of the day struggle with ethnographic methods. As an example, the superb work of Jose Limon draws attention to the complexity of the ethnography. In his rich work on the subjugation of Mexican American men in south Texas, he writes:

> In the construction of our own ethnographic narratives, we are inevitably faced
> with the problem of rhetorically managing what we are pleased to call "the

data." How much is enough to persuade and not bore or overwhelm? And, where do we place it in the structural development of our own text? What is the proper relationship between the data and our interpretive analysis, recognizing full well that the selection and organization of the data have already taken us a long way toward our understanding of it? (1989, 472–473).

Even if teacher educators were able to develop ethnographic expertise in their students, such an assignment cannot act as a substitute for *interacting* with people who represent diverse cultures. Ethnographic methods certainly have their place in multicultural teacher education field experiences, but overemphasizing method may tend to obscure the important issues of where such experiences take place and with whom. We are very much concerned with the process by which our students report their experience, but we are more concerned with our students' active, cultural acquisition and the natural learning situations that emerge as a result.

Our early assignments served to increase our dissatisfaction with the ethnography, and we searched for a new way for our students to feel and appreciate the lived experience of inner-city youth and to understand better the social context of inner-city problems.

We knew of other so-called multicultural methods we did not want. Suggestions to expand our reading list, while important, struck us as a typically institutional and ineffective response, as a bookish attempt to transmit information about diversity and other provocative themes. Our previous experience with readings about diversity led us to believe that there were diminishing returns associated with such assignments; a few readings were effective, but adding more did little to increase our students' cultural awareness or sensitivity. The work of other teacher educators, like Mary Louise Gomez (1991), who staked her hopes on using a reading list that included pieces like Richard Rodriguez's (1983) *Hunger for Memory*, reinforced in our minds the proclivity among well-intentioned teacher educators to talk about students and their families rather than to talk with them. We were also influenced by our intuitions, which were corroborated by the results of Michigan State University's *National Center for Research on Teacher Learning* report on learning to teach (1992). The report suggested that providing teachers with knowledge about various cultural groups simply did not make them better able to teach children of color. More talk about our problems and about the children of Houston clearly failed to fulfill the need for our students to talk *with* our city's children and their families. In our deliberations, we recalled the work of Florence Kluckhorn, whose early work on the participant-observer technique in a New Mexico village led her to admit, "...I think I gained more than I lost by...lapses of cold objectivity" (1940, 343). We were also reminded of Ruth Landes's admonishment that "separateness from the objects of discussion forfeits the experience that words should mirror" (1965, 64).

In this manner, we became convinced that there was simply no substitute for experience. If a teacher education program claimed, as we hoped ours could, to speak for the social needs of teaching, then its students and instructors would have to become participants in the public sphere. All too often we felt that the voice of the oppressed had been taken up by others who stretch credulity in speaking from distant and comfortable places. For our own part, we recognized that, in spite of our firsthand experience with urban persons of color, we could not speak for them; rather, we wanted our students to speak with them and to discover for themselves the problems associated with urban life. We wanted our students to listen and to develop a commitment to public engagement. Immersion in culture through social service in a community-based project represented, in essence, our best chance at developing a more socially enlightened generation of teachers.

THE COMMUNITY-BASED PROJECT

Houston is the fourth largest city in the country, replete with most of the problems facing other major cities. The extraordinary diversity of our city is reflected in the ethnicity of the largest school district in the metropolitan area. The Houston Independent School District's student population represents Latino (46.5 percent), African American (37 percent), White (13.6 percent), and Asian (2.7 percent) students. Like California, the public school population in Texas recently became a "majority minority." The diversity of our city suggested to us that we could help to engage our students in the development of their social consciousness by asking them to participate in community service.

After contacting our university's volunteer program, we discovered that our institution already had in place a vehicle for placing students in social service agencies. We then chose those agencies that we thought would be most effective in helping our students understand diversity and assisted in making the necessary contacts. Students were given a list of our selected agencies from which to choose. However, if students wished to find a community-based project on their own (i.e., one not on our list) that fit the objectives of the study, they were given the opportunity to work in those sites. To avoid potential legal challenges or liabilities, we did give our students the option of a library-based, local history research project. However, very few students chose this assignment.

The agencies which our students chose were wide-ranging. Several chose to work in the schools attended by the children of battered women. Others worked at a Salvation Army evening "English as a Second Language" program. Still others chose to work as volunteers at Chicano Family Centers, urban YMCA after-school programs, community health centers, Big Brothers/Big Sisters, homeless shelters, or homes for mothers addicted to crack cocaine and their children, to name a few.

However, the true success of this venture was to be revealed in the students' reactions to their experiences. In their community-based report, we invited them to address a few questions, such as "What can schools do to address the kinds of social problems that you saw during your community-based experience? What surprised you, and why? Would schools be different places if all educators shared in your community-based experience?"

What Our Students Said

In general, we were overwhelmed by our students' responses. For example, a student who volunteered in a school for the children of undocumented workers, whose parents were either in jail, dead, or missing, wrote that "those who claim that we do not have a responsibility to educate these children have not seen them." Another student maintained that she now saw the connection between teaching and social service. She wrote that teachers have "to act as a caseworker many times to try to find out what is really going on in that child's life." She continued, "most people need to spend a couple of weeks in the trenches and get their hands dirty and see that life isn't as peachy for everyone else."

Another student volunteered at a Houston food bank, where he loaded trucks with donated goods. In addition to serving the community, he worked with court-sentenced traffic offenders (mostly those who had outstanding traffic tickets who were given community service as part of their sentence) who taught him "street talk" in Spanish and Vietnamese. He, in turn, taught them how to say the equivalent words in English. Learning "the talk" may not seem important or meaningful, but we would argue it is indicative of cultural participation and a sense of social understanding, precisely the kind of experience we were seeking. And in his paper, he wrote, "We talked about our backgrounds, our lives, our different and separate communities and all the while we were working with one common goal to help the hungry and needy of Houston."

Another student who worked at a Latino Family Center wrote, "I realized that it was not so much that their fathers were drunks or that their mothers preferred welfare, it was just that society did not prepare itself for the multitude of people who were willing to work to have a better life, who happened to be a darker color and speak a different language. I learned some new things about life and myself." A student who volunteered in a shelter for battered women suggested that "so many schools stress academics without considering the children's personal situations."

Many of our students reported dramatic personal revelations regarding race and ethnicity and class. As an example, one student volunteered at a clothing bank serving a large Latino neighborhood. She was surprised that the people who came to the clothing bank were part of strong family units and admitted that her early misconceptions, which were not firsthand, were formed largely by the media and the dominant culture. She noted that frequently whole families, often with six or seven children, came together to the bank. She realized that poor English skills and the lack of education, rather than fragmented family units, prevented economic success for this population. She reflected on the culture uniting her clients and concluded that, although most of them were Latino, it was more a culture of poverty that was common to those she met than a specific ethnic culture. She observed that the volunteers themselves were poor and extremely committed, reporting that her experience caused her to gain great respect for this culture. It also showed her that, within the culture of poverty, people were generous and committed to helping one another.

Perhaps the best example of the community-based assignment came from a young woman who admitted in her paper that her life had been somewhat sheltered. Her community-based work at Houston's Salvation Army "English as a Second Language" Center introduced her to a family who recently arrived in the U.S. from Mexico. Nina[2] expected to expand her knowledge about Latino culture from her tutee, Maria, but was surprised by the extent of her misconceptions about that culture. Nina explained that prior to her work with Maria she had held many beliefs about Latinos commonly accepted among educators. These beliefs were dispelled by what Nina learned about Maria and Maria's family.

For example, many teachers in Maria's school assumed that students like Maria were not succeeding because they were not interested in learning. Yet, as Nina got to know Maria better, it became evident that Maria was more sincere about learning than any of her teachers realized. In fact, Maria felt that her teachers were more interested in grades than in real teaching and real learning. She thought that her teachers cared less about her desire to speak English like a native speaker than they did about her passing exams.

Nina's acquaintance with Maria's family further contradicted her notion that Latino students typically do not succeed in school because they do not value education. Nina saw that education was of paramount importance to Maria's family. Her father worked very hard to learn English and was promoted due to his language improvement. This reinforced the family belief that education is the key to success. Moreover, when Nina met Maria's younger siblings, she asked the typical question, "What do you want to be when you grow up?" Nina admitted that she was surprised by their high aspirations. Their responses included veterinarian, lawyer, and teacher.

Nina was also surprised by how much the family respected teachers and the school system. For instance, just prior to Nina's visit with the family, the middle school attended by Maria's sister had been criticized in the media. Maria's sister was outraged at the bad press given to her school and kept emphasizing to Nina all of its positive aspects. Nina concluded that "teachers don't know how much they are respected." She had not anticipated so much school pride from Maria's sister.

The same misconception surfaced in regard to Maria's mother and her attitude toward school. The teachers were under the impression that Maria's mother was not interested in the education of her children because she was not involved in the school. Nina described her amazement at the magnitude of this misconception. In actuality, the mother did not talk to the teachers because she was ashamed of her limited English skills and relied on her children for school communication. Yet, Maria's mother devoted countless hours a week driving her children to various school activities and then waiting in parking lots for them to finish. Nina explained that the teachers were upset that they were not getting parent participation, and yet "they didn't realize how much participation they were getting."

Nina's relationship with Maria also taught her to interpret events from a cultural perspective. For example, during the time that Nina was tutoring Maria, Maria's mother decided to get a job cleaning offices. At first Nina considered the turmoil that this decision cast on the family to be stereotypical. She later understood that this incident thrust the family into a basic questioning of values and roles that comes about when people adopt a new culture. The whole family began to reevaluate the role of the mother and to compare it in terms of Latino versus European-American norms.

Nina also viewed Maria's choice of boyfriends through a cultural lens. She was choosing between one young man of Latino descent who believed that married women should stay at home after marriage and a young European American man from school who encouraged Maria to continue on to higher education. Nina claimed that superficially Maria's conflict was between two young men, but on a deeper level they represented her own cultural conflict. Nina came to be part of Maria's family, joining them for dinner and spending many hours in conversation. Nina is now learning Spanish, and there are plans to go to Mexico with the family next summer.

Students easily connected their community-based experiences to their observations of public school classes, also required during the semester. When students conducted ethnographies, they had great difficulty applying what they had learned to the world of schools. For example, several students felt that the teachers at their assigned observation schools were divorced from the problems they encountered at their community-based sites. Many felt that teachers were mainly caught up in trying to get their standard work done and remained focused only on academic aspects of their jobs. In particular, one student wished that the teachers would concentrate more on the children. As she stated, "If they (the students) know you and trust you, they will talk to you, and you can help them out. If kids are falling asleep in class, find out why, don't just assume that they're bad kids trying to get you mad. Maybe they're hungry. Don't assume that they're bad kids trying to give you a hard time. Think about other reasons." Back in the school setting, she was stunned to find that the teachers at her school were apathetic about what she had learned during her community-based experience.

On the other hand, the teachers at another student's site were very impressed by and interested in her community-based work. Yet, she observed situations at the school which she criticized in light of her experience. She stated, "I've seen instances in schools where teachers screamed at the children with behavioral problems. If they had seen what I saw, the real situation the child has to live in everyday, they wouldn't yell and scream and treat them so badly." She continued, "Anytime that a child is acting out, it's for a reason, and you need to find what that reason is. I know teachers are there to teach all the content areas and all that which is a lot of work, but they're also there for the child's psychological benefit. A lot of people choose to ignore that. They don't want to be involved."

The interviews we conducted suggested to us that the students had, indeed, internalized a dedication to working with urban youth. One student who projected herself into her future as an urban teacher reported that what she had seen in her community-based experience would influence her teaching, suggesting that the community-based experience "helps you understand them (students) better." Another student communicated to us the spirit of the community-based project, noting the impact her work had had on her both personally and professionally: "I can't help but think that if I'm a better person I'll be a better instructor."

Many of our students reported that they will continue to volunteer even after the course is over. We are hopeful that the community-based experience will encourage the unique leadership abilities that result when one first serves others (Devle & Rice 1990). In addition, we are confident that the community-based experience will encourage our students to redefine their values (Schultz 1990), perhaps creating teachers who will encourage their students to conduct community service.

Although we are pleased with the impact of the community-based project, we are mindful that much more needs to be done to prepare our students for the urban classroom. For example, we have recently established several urban professional development schools where teachers-to-be work with exemplary urban teachers. The experienced teachers, in turn, work with university faculty to improve the urban educational experience. Our initial results suggest that the teachers who have been prepared in the urban professional development schools are more successful with diverse students than those who have been educated in the traditional program.

However, our efforts at improving the preparation of teachers are still hampered by state regulations and mandates. In 1987, the Texas Higher Education Coordinating Board, responding to legislative pressure to eliminate so-called unnecessary education courses, reduced the number of teacher education professional development courses to a maximum of eighteen credit hours, six of which are student teaching. The course in which we require the community-based field experience is three credit hours. But this class also requires a minimum of forty-five hours of classroom observation (another state requirement, yet we require more hours of observation). The curriculum includes multicultural issues but must also deal with instructional issues, classroom management, and other curricula that must be explored before students take methods classes. This legislation will "sunset" in 1994, but it remains to be seen what type of courses will be approved.

ESTABLISHING A COMMUNITY-BASED FIELD EXPERIENCE

As teacher educators, we hope to educate future teachers who will resist formulaic approaches to instruction and who will see their profession as one that has strong ties to the improvement of society. At the University of Houston, we want our students to understand the relationships among dominant culture ideology, the disaffection among people of color, and the disenfranchisement of those for whom poverty is a way of life. The insights our students have made as a result of their community-based experience have led us to the conclusion that teacher education programs might benefit from a course requirement like our social service experience. We share Joseph Larkin's (1993) view that such an experience can enhance preservice teachers' ability and willingness to serve urban students.

A good starting point for other teacher educators interested in this idea would be to contact either their institution's volunteer program or other volunteer agencies within their city. Or, perhaps teacher education faculty can develop a list of minority community centers and projects sponsored by organizations such as the National Association for the Advancement of Colored People (NAACP) or the Urban League.

It is important to point out that teacher educators must be involved in organizing these activities and model the commitment they expect of the students. In our program, faculty make as many visits as possible to community-based project sites and engage in projects of their own. For example, the lead author, located at an urban professional development school, works with several elementary school students from a large apartment complex who have shown signs of gang affiliation. Pamela Norwood conducts parent training programs at a multiservice school where teacher education students work in the interests of poor African American students side-by-side with graduate students in social work. Our own work in the community not only makes us better teachers but also adds to our credibility with students. If teacher education faculty assign students to a community-based field experience about which they have little knowledge, students will take notice and make the same claim they do now about field experiences in the school: that the university faculty is out of touch. Significantly, universities rarely reward faculty for this type of community work, but we have come to recognize the importance of our projects and argue that faculty must make a serious commitment to the socio-civic orientation.

Our community-based field experience is unique to our institution and city, but we are willing to share our insights on the implementation of this project with others who are interested in developing a similar program. While we invite personal inquiries, a few initial suggestions follow. To begin, we would like to point out that multicultural teacher education must take place in distinctly urban and ethnically diverse locations and that both school and community multicultural field experiences must be an ongoing programmatic focus. The community-based project is only one piece of our overall program. For instance, students are placed in schools where a majority of the pupils are of color and on free or reduced lunch. We do not allow a student to observe or student teach in a school that does not fit these requirements (the diversity of the Houston area, however, makes this an easy task).

We would also suggest that such placements be long term. Cultural learning cannot be reduced to a field trip. Forays into the urban and culturally diverse world for a week or a month may serve only to reinforce dangerous stereotypes, a point which leads to another suggestion. Teacher educators must let the experience do the teaching. Of course, it is very important to discuss and debrief with students about their community-based field experiences, but, if teacher educators must continually "teach" students about societal inequality and "talk them out" of their initial and sometimes intolerant views of low-income, culturally diverse students and families, then the experience is not sufficiently expansive. A fear may exist among teacher educators that students' initial, and often racist, views will become more entrenched as a result of a community-based experience. We argue that a student who continues to "blame the victim" in spite of striking evidence to the contrary may not be fit to teach and should perhaps be counseled out of the profession. Teacher educators must be willing to go to great lengths to ensure that future teachers embody the aims of a democratic and diverse society. We also recognize that multicultural learning involves moral learning, and moral learning, as Aristotle pointed out, is learned best through experience.

Teacher educators of color who have experiences with culturally diverse students are crucial for multicultural teacher education. What message is sent to students when multicultural education is a curricular priority, yet none or very few of the faculty who teach in that program represent persons of color with experience in culturally diverse settings?

We suggest that the community-based field experience be attached to a three to five credit-hour class that includes a concurrent placement in diverse schools settings. The class should deal with specific instructional issues, such as lesson planning, and integrate these topics into the overall theme. Such integration helps students to see how issues of race, class, and gender are incorporated into the daily life of teaching. For instance, when faculty discuss various models of instruction, which includes alternative "models" such as critical pedagogy, students are asked to think about which of these methods might be most sensitive to the learners they have encountered in their field work. After experience in their community-based projects, the inadequacies of the seven-step lesson, for example, are evident to students.

Another critical activity is to evaluate the community sites yearly. We send out surveys to each of our students and ask them to report on their community-based experience. We have found that a positive site one year can become a very dissatisfying experience the next. Of course, our students cannot help but share their experiences in class, and we use those reactions in our planning as well. While we have found at least a dozen sites where students consistently come away with precisely the experience we hope for (a Chicano family center is one that comes to mind), we continue to look for additional placements. And placements come looking for us. Schools that maintain after-school tutoring programs, in particular, seek our students as volunteers. It is often difficult to explain to the schools that the focus of our program is to place students "outside" the school walls. We have not quite arrived at the best way to deal with such inquiries, but we have not compromised our requirement that their community-based learning activity be completed in the community.

We ask our students to commit a total of twenty hours to their community-based field experience, which we would increase if we were able to provide additional credit hours to the course. However, the state of Texas does not allow additional certification courses or credit hours.

CONCLUSION

While we place great hope in our teacher education program, it remains a singular voice in an otherwise hostile landscape. The state of Texas continues to address the statewide, urban teacher shortage with quick fix "alternative certification" programs and heavy recruitment of newly certified teachers from other states, who are often educated in middle-class, White communities. Whereas neither of these strategies is fundamentally inconsistent with multicultural teacher education, we have some very serious concerns regarding these trends.

Modern educators tend to view the past as both pristine and barbaric. Our nostalgia is tempered by reminders of many of the nation's early educators who, for instance, thought that separate but equal schools served the interests of a democracy. At the same time, we may long for elements of the Progressive movement and the important innovations it introduced. We survey the past and both long for it and are repulsed by it. We wonder about our legacy.

We wonder what the heritage of contemporary teacher education will be. Perhaps our era will be viewed by future teacher educators as one that offered vital insight. Perhaps our current efforts at a multicultural teacher education will be remembered as a turning point in the history of American schools, a new awakening for equality in education. Our legacy will have everything to do with whether our theory lives as practice.

Unfortunately, our era will likely be remembered as the generation that failed to recruit additional persons of color into education. This trend is unequivocal, and, for the moment at least, it is irreversible. A multicultural teacher education without persons of color cannot be considered truly multicultural.

Our work today will one day be thought of as teacher education at the turn of the century—the twenty-first century. Will our rhetoric be the mark of our day, or will we be thought of as visioned professionals who took their civic responsibility to educate all children seriously?

In 1991, University of Houston president Dr. Marguerite Ross Barnett died from a sudden illness. Her legacy for our university, however, lives on in our teacher preparation program. As an African American, she was particularly clear in shaping the mission of the university in terms of service to society, especially in relation to those who are most in need. Higher education, in her words, had a social responsibility to help "solve society's conundrums." We remember Dr.

Barnett and her ambitions. We hope our students will remember her as well; we believe that she would be proud of them.

NOTES

1. Portions of this chapter are reprinted from an article in Tellez, K. and Hlebo-witsch, P. S. (1993). Being there: Social service and teacher education at the University of Houston. *Innovative Higher Education* 18(1):87–94.

2. All names are pseudonyms.

REFERENCES

Beyer, L. E. (1984). Field experience, ideology, and the development of critical reflec-tivity. *Journal of Teacher Education* 35(3):36–41.

Dewey, J. (1916). *Democracy and education.* New York: The Free Press.

Delve, C. I., and K. L. Rice. (1990). The integration of service learning into leadership and campus activities. In *Community service as values education*, ed. C. Delve, S. Mintz, and G. Stewart, 55–64. San Francisco: Jossey-Bass.

Freire, P. (1970). *Pedagogy of the oppressed.* New York: Continuum.

Ginsburg, M. (1988). *Contradictions in teacher education and society: A critical analysis.* London : The Falmer Press.

Gomez, M. L. (1991). Teaching a language of opportunity in a language arts methods course: Teaching for David, Albert, and Darlene. In *Issues and practices in inquiry-oriented education*, ed. B. R. Tabachnick and K. M. Zeichner. London: The Falmer Press.

Haberman, M. (1992). Alternative certification: Can the problems of urban education be resolved by traditional teacher education? *Teacher Education and Practice* 8(1):13–28.

Kluckhorn, F. (1940). The participant observer technique in small communities. *American Journal of Sociology* 46:331–343.

Landes, R. (1965). *Culture in American education: Anthropological approaches to minority and dominant groups in the schools.* New York: Wiley.

Larkin, J. (1993). The case for community experience in urban, multicultural teacher education. Unpublished manuscript.

Limon, J. (1989). Carne, carnales, and carnivalesque: Bakhtinian batos, disorder, and narrative discourses. *American Ethnologist*, 471–486.

National Center for Research on Teacher Learning. (1992). *Findings on learning to teach.* East Lansing, MI: National Center for Research on Teacher Learning.

Rodriguez, R. (1983). *Hunger of memory.* New York: Bantam Books.

Schultz, S. (1990). From isolation to commitment: The role of the community in values education. In *Community service as values education*, ed. C. Delve, S. Mintz and G. Stewart, 91–100. San Francisco: Jossey-Bass.

Shor, I. (1987). *Critical teaching and everyday life*. Chicago: University of Chicago Press.

6

Francisco A. Ríos and Gerardo M. González_____

Psychological and Developmental Perspectives in a Multicultural Framework: Exploring Some Possibilities[1]

Many teacher education programs in the United States (U.S.) require their preservice teachers to take course work in psychological and developmental foundations as they relate to teaching and learning. The research base in the fields of educational and developmental psychology has *traditionally* focused on the inner processes (thinking, behaving, and feeling) of the individual as they develop over time (Lee 1994). Because most of this research is conducted in the U.S., because of the traditional focus on inner processes, and because textbooks in the field are limited in their coverage of multicultural issues, it is easy for teacher educators to present a monocultural perspective of psychological and developmental foundations (Moss 1986). This is unfortunate, since discussion of cultural differences and the cultural context in which individuals grow and learn can enrich course content and, more importantly, prepare preservice teachers to teach students from diverse cultural backgrounds. Fortunately, provocative scholarship is being conducted (especially in cross-cultural psychology and in an emerging critical tradition in psychology) that can inform teacher educators of critical cultural differences.[2]

Beyond these curriculum concerns lie issues revolving around how these courses are taught. Indeed, the teaching methods become part of the implicit curriculum (Eisner 1985). The implicit curriculum socializes students into the values that are acceptable in that particular classroom and school. Thus, by the structure of the course and the teacher's behavior, the teacher can potentially affect preservice teachers' values with respect to compliance or initiative, competition or cooperation, mindlessness or critical reflection, homogeneity or diversity, inequality or social justice. How you teach becomes, in short, another opportunity to teach.

This chapter will begin by identifying a theme and resultant goals that guide our own[3] thinking and behavior with respect to an *introductory* educational psychology course that has a multicultural focus. We will then share some of the critical issues we struggle with as we strive to infuse multicultural education into the explicit and implicit curriculum. Next, we will highlight some critical components of the multicultural educational psychology curriculum. Finally, we will focus on several features of the course structure we have used for addressing

79

issues of diversity, while simultaneously socializing preservice teachers to value initiative, cooperation, critical reflection, diversity, and, ultimately, social justice.

We have chosen to describe what might be done when attempting to operate within the traditional psychology framework. We acknowledge, however, the work of Valerie Walkerdine, Michael Sampson, Constance Gergen, James Wertsch, and Michael O'Loughlin, to name a few, who question traditional psychological frameworks (e.g., O'Loughlin, 1992a, questions Piagetian "constructivism" since it does not necessarily call into question unjust power relations and is, thus, not emancipatory; for its implications to teacher training, see O'Loughlin 1992b); instead, the focus is on anthropological and cultural frameworks to address issues of race, class, gender, and schooling more inclusively. By doing so, this alternative advances an entire reconceptualization of the field since "psychology and an emancipatory cultural focus are fundamentally at odds" (O'Loughlin, personal communication, August 1993). We welcome the efforts along this line of inquiry; we also recognize that the decision to follow one path or the other is, ultimately, a matter of values.

THEMES AND GOALS

One broad theme guides the way we think about teacher education: We aim to prepare individuals to teach in culturally and linguistically diverse classrooms by modeling good practice for diversity. This theme is made explicit at the beginning of the course, is addressed early on in the class, is restated throughout the course, and is discussed as models of practice are presented. Having one theme and stressing it in multiple places sends a message to preservice teachers about our vision of the course and our vision of education.

Several goals support this theme. The first goal is to have preservice teachers share our belief that ALL students can learn (Edmonds 1979). Many preservice teachers regard student failure as a product of the students' personal or cultural deficiency. Deficiency, we suggest, is the result of attempts to take away a student's language and culture. We also suggest that if teachers, schools, and society so desire, schools can be set up for success for broader groups of students (Cuban 1989).

A second goal is to model an empowering education for our preservice teachers, though this is not always easy (Ellsworth 1989). This goal is partially addressed by discussion of ways in which teachers are disempowered (Nieto 1992).

A third goal is to make explicit the role of prejudice and racism in how teachers teach and how students learn. We feel that preservice teachers need to see a connection between prejudices and the academic outcomes of their students.

Our final goal is having preservice teachers connect their learning about issues of diversity to actual experiences in the field. Though the presentation of issues of diversity and the modeling of instruction for diversity are critical, preservice teachers need actual experiences in the classroom to make connections. Thus, we strive to make continuous, repeated connections between theory and practice. These connections are critical, in our opinion, for developing multicultural competency among preservice teachers.

This theme and these goals guide our vision of a multicultural educational psychology course. Their actual implementation will be, we hope, evident in our discussion of content and process. However, they have presented us with some provocative issues which we continually struggle to resolve.

ISSUES

Rather than taking a monolithic theory and applying it to all groups, educational psychology is exploring culture-specific models that best explain and understand the interests, styles, and behaviors of ethnic minority students (see, for example, Bilingual Education Office 1986 and Goodchilds 1991 for an exemplary collection of articles on culture-specific models). The ongoing development of these models has increased the chances of preparing teachers for successfully teaching ethnically diverse students. However, these multicultural psychological models are relatively unknown. Thus, there is minimal application in many classrooms.

The following issues relate to teaching a multicultural educational psychology course to preservice teachers. The questions concern how psychology (generally), which has an emphasis on inner processes, can add to our understanding of teaching and learning in multicultural contexts (Laosa 1977). We believe that preservice teachers need to understand the link between internal processes and external contexts, especially when we think about redefining psychological processes as socioculturally situated and contextual specific (Resnick 1987). The following questions arise in the process of attempting to prepare multiculturally competent educators via the educational psychology course. These questions move from specific concerns to broader issues.

(1) *How does one cope with the depth versus breadth dichotomy when teaching about issues of diversity? What role can "others" play in resolving this dilemma?*

Ideally, a multicultural educational psychology course should be both broad and deep in its coverage of critical teaching and learning issues in diverse contexts. Preservice teachers who work in multicultural contexts need to understand psychological processes of students as they relate to issues such as the motivational, identity, and developmental differences of ethnically diverse students.

This "depth and breadth" approach immediately raises a critical issue: the impact of comprehensively addressing diversity issues in an already information-loaded class. We realize that, to cover aspects of diversity, the instructor may have to deemphasize other material for the course because of time constraints. One factor that helps us with this dilemma is our knowledge that there are other courses and other faculty members in the College who teach from a multicultural focus. Thus, a multicultural perspective of teaching and learning is best served when it is integrated in a program-wide curriculum with the goal of preparing all preservice teachers to be multiculturally competent. Communication across disciplines with all faculty who work with preservice teachers is critical in this regard. A concomitant result of this cross-discipline discussion would be a collaboration among various faculty toward strengthening the theory and application of multicultural perspectives. For students, a positive outcome of this effort would be a better understanding of contextual teaching and learning.

(2) *Should issues of diversity be infused throughout the course or taught separately?*

The use of "mainstream" methods (didactic) and content (research on Euro-Americans) in educational psychology has not proven effective for preparing preservice teachers to work with ethnically diverse students. Approaches to overcome this dilemma involve either the infusion of issues of diversity throughout the course *or* separation of issues of diversity into a unit within the course. There are advantages and disadvantages to using either method.

A combination of infusion *and* separation in the curriculum of issues of diversity is the approach we prefer since we believe it is more powerful for our Euro-American preservice teachers whose knowledge and experiences with diversity is (generally) limited. Thus, we take time to deal with issues of diversity explicitly and exclusively, while infusing issues of diversity throughout the curriculum. This presupposes that the instructor is competent and committed to issues of diversity.

(3) *Who is teaching the multicultural educational psychology course?*

There remains an underrepresentation of ethnically diverse scholars in psychology (generally) and in educational psychology (specifically). This lack of role models in psychological and developmental foundations courses sends a disturbing, implicit message about who psychology (and teaching) is for and about. It is incumbent upon the disciplines to work to increase the number of scholars of color.

Importantly, a multicultural educational psychology class can contribute indirectly to an increase in the ethnic diversification in the psychology and education fields. For example, by discussing cultural issues in education and in psychology, by noting career interests in the field of educational psychology, and by fostering the development of a professional identification, preservice teachers of color may feel valued in their press to enter the teaching field (and perhaps later, academia). This should not suggest, however, that Euro-American educational psychologists should not teach this class. In fact, the race or ethnicity of the instructor is less important than having the interests, skills, and knowledge associated with teaching in diverse classrooms. Nonetheless, we are cognizant of the research demonstrating that diverse models may make a difference in academic retention and persistence of students of color (González and Thomson 1993).

(4) *Can an entire teacher education program, let alone one course, make a difference in preparing individuals to teach in multicultural contexts?*

Educators teach in the fashion that they were originally taught (Lortie 1975). Thus, university professors probably teach teacher education courses, including the educational psychology course, in the ways taught to them. In short, we often perpetuate mainstream teaching methods unintentionally. These habits are difficult to change. Therefore, all of teacher education, including educational psychology, needs to take a hard look at ways to break the mold, especially if we desire to model effective approaches to teaching a diverse student body.

A multicultural educational psychology course has the added burden of trying to make a difference in how preservice teachers think about teaching and learning, since this is a big part of the explicit curriculum. The current literature, however, is relatively limited in what it can tell us about teaching students from diverse cultural and linguistic backgrounds (Krashen 1981; Ladson-Billings 1992). Educational and psychological researchers need to continue addressing the following substantive questions: What are the effective methods or techniques of teaching in diverse classrooms? How do we assess that efficacy? What difference does a teacher preparation program make in how individuals teach students from diverse cultural and linguistic backgrounds? And, finally, what difference can be made by a multicultural educational psychology course?

CONTENT

In 1977, Luis Laosa wrote an article titled "Multicultural education: How psychology can help." At the time the article was written, the dominant contribution psychology could offer to teaching in multicultural contexts, according to Laosa, was research on the nature of culture and cognitive style. Much important work has been conducted since then in a variety of subdisciplines within the field of psychology to move us beyond the narrow scope of cognitive-style research. In this section, we will detail some of the concepts we have gleaned from psychology that have important implications for teaching, learning, and development. We begin with describing the way we make explicit our focus on issues of diversity in the course. We follow that with a general description of issues we address, issues that might be addressed, and include one critical component in each of three areas of the course: learning, teaching, and development.

Diversity

By the second or third class meeting, we provide a short description of our nation's changing demographics and point out that jobs are located where the largest number of ethnically diverse students are schooled. In addition, we use the series of articles which appeared in the December 1991/January 1992 issue of *Educational Leadership* by Sara Bullard (4–7), Diane Ravitch (8–11), Asa Hilliard III (12–16), and James Banks (32–36). We think that these articles provide sufficient basis to begin the "diversity" conversation. The conversation begins in small groups, then moves to a whole class discussion of the ideas shared in the small groups and in the articles.

We think it is critical to discuss issues of diversity in this course, since preservice teachers may have little or no exposure to questions of diversity. Our goal is to get preservice teachers thinking about issues of diversity (such as the existence of multiple perspectives about diversity, about implications for curriculum, instruction, school policy, society, etc.) in explicit ways. Discussing issues of diversity in an educational psychology course also sends as strong a message about our vision of the importance of diversity as what it is we discuss!

Learning

When we focus on issues related to learning in this course, we find that some topics are especially relevant to our multicultural curriculum. These topics include stylistic differences (especially cognitive and learning styles), schema theory, and motivation (table 6.1). Other topics which might be included are intelligence and the nature-nurture controversy as it effects ethnically diverse students (Garcia 1981; Mercer 1979) and the nature of knowledge (Banks 1993).

Of particular focus during our discussion of learning theories is social learning theory (Bandura 1977) as a lead-in to the work of Lev Vygotsky (1978), Barbara Rogoff (1981), and Carla Childs and Patricia Greenfield (1982) on social cognition. Following Vygotsky's conceptualizations, learning comes from one's culture. It then serves as the context from which form and function of learning emerge. Since the first mediators of learning are the primary care givers, building bridges from that context to the school context, requiring authentic home-school collaboration, is critical. This theory is useful for demonstrating the ways in which culture and cognition are taught. It provides a description of how thinking is a product of social and historical conditions (Cole & Scribner 1974). It is particularly powerful in suggesting that learning is not a function of ability or the absence of essential cognitive processes; rather, the functions and content of thinking are different and are influenced by culture (Barnow 1985; Cole and Scribner 1974; Luria 1971; Price-Williams 1980).

It's important when discussing the theoretical to connect to the practical. With respect to social learning theory, it is rich in suggesting ways that teachers act as social mediators of knowledge (Rogoff and Morelli 1989) and learning skills, that students need a kind of social help that will allow them to perform tasks (including the use of "instructional conversations"; Tharp and Gallimore 1991), and that students will gradually integrate that help and perform the task on their own as they operate within and through their "zone of proximal development" (Cole 1981). We use this as an opportunity to illustrate the importance of heterogeneous grouping.

Teaching

Issues central to multicultural education and teaching that we attempt to address include the role of teacher expectations (including expectations based on the teachers' stereotypes and prejudicial viewpoints) and their relation to student achievement, the role of intercultural communication in the classroom (sociolinguistics), and the importance of teaching thinking and learning strategies to

Table 6.1 – Curriculum Topics with Multicultural Perspectives – Learning

Topic & Definition	Concepts Relevant to Multicultural Education (With Related References)
Stylistic Differences - *How students' thinking and learning styles affect their academic achievement.*	• Cognitive Style, with special focus on field dependence-field independence (Barnow 1985; Berry 1976, 1979; Kogan 1976; Messick 1970; Witkin 1967) (for a review, see Messick 1970) • Other stylistic differences include conceptual tempo (reflective-impulsive), locus of control (internal-external), scanning (ability to perceive experience vividly and with great awareness), breadth of categorizing (narrow-broad), conceptualizing style (thematic-analytic), cognitive complexity versus simplicity (amount of multidimensionality and discrimination in construing the world), leveling versus sharpening (ability to have distinct memories), constricted versus flexible control (differences in distractibility), tolerance for unrealistic experiences (degree that feelings of self-worth are tied to accomplishments) (Ausubel 1968) • Cognitive styles are encouraged in a particular cultural, ecological, and ecocultural environment; they are, in short, adaptive to their environments (Price-Williams 1980) • Cognitive sytles show the power of culture (Hilliard 1976; Ramirez & Castaneda 1974; Shade 1989) • Strong connection between cognitive style and learning style (Anderson 1988; Castaneda & Gray 1974; Dunn & Dunn 1978; More 1987); learning style differences exist in environmental conditions, psychological conditions, affective conditions, etc. (Dunn & Dunn 1978) yet only 6 to 14 of these stylistic factors are salient for any one individual (Dunn 1984; • Implications for classroom instruction (Shade & New 1993; Smith & Renzulli 1984) • In practice, it is a relatively messy construct to deal with (Bloomers 1970; Cazden & Leggett 1981); for example, with respect to cognitive styles, tests are not reliable (Briesel & Richter 1987), replication of findings is weak and do not generalize across tasks, confounds include protein intake, hormone balance, neurological factors, socialization practices, levels of education, wage employment, rural-suburban differences, population density, etc. (Berry 1979); no consistent pattern of success when students and teachers match (Cronbach & Snow 1977) and little connection to academic achievement (Ladson-Billings 1992) • Thus, hard to generalize to any cultural group; need to avoid promoting stereotypes about groups of individuals *continued*

Table 6.1 *continued*

Topic & Definition	Concepts Relevant to Multicultural Education (With Related References)
Schema Theory - *How cognitive structures impact on how students understand and organize incoming information.*	• Students have schema for people (including themselves), roles, events, objects and abstract concepts • Schemas are culturally dependent since schema is shaped largely by experience (Kearney 1984) and since cultural groups share many common experiences (Cole & Scribner 1974) • Students also have schema for language: words, sentence structure, forms of language and content (Adamson 1993) • Important to education since students' schema guide their perceptions, inferences, and memory (Rummelhart 1980); likewise, affect students' performance on tests (Adamson 1993) and language (i.e., reading/listening) proficiency (Goodman 1967) • Also have school schema (called scripts) which are culturally based (Saville-Troike & Kleifgen 1986) • Interesting debate about whether teachers need to know about schema theory (see Anderson 1989; Engleman 1989; Floden 1989)
Motivation - *What motivates students to perform well and persistently in the classroom.*	• Each culture plays a pivotal role in providing a predisposition to be motivated toward and by different things; often these include a difference in value orientation (Hofstede 1984; Kluckhohn & Strodtbeck 1961) • Differences exist, for example, in whether individuals from a particular cultural group are motivated by collective versus independent schemes (Anderson 1988; Hofstede 1984; Kluckhohn & Strodtbeck 1961; Moss 1986; Ramirez & Price-Williams 1976) • Differences have also been found in how individuals from different cultures define success, the criteria used for success, individual versus social evaluations of achievement, time perspective, etc. (for an excellent review of these and other factors, see, Kornadt, Eckensberger, & Emminghaus 1980)

ethnically diverse students (table 6.2). Additional topics that might be covered include the biases associated with standardized testing (Miller-Jones 1989), the use of alternative forms of assessment that are sensitive to the cultural and linguistic needs of ethnically diverse students (Fitchner, Peitzman, and Sasser 1991), and culturally responsive pedagogy (Ladson-Billings 1992; Molina 1994).

Part of instruction for diversity involves sharing with preservice teachers a variety of models (direct instruction, cooperative learning, presentation-discussion-recitation, group discussion, mastery learning, etc.) that might be employed depending upon the task and learning needs of the students (Louisell and Descamps 1992). Particular attention has been paid to the important role cooperative learning can play in serving culturally and linguistically diverse students (Kagan 1986).

More recent has been the introduction of models for instruction which provide enough "scaffolding" so that potentially English proficient students can learn both content and English language simultaneously. Obviously, linguistically diverse students have varying degrees of English language ability. Depending upon their level of English language ability, teachers need to use different techniques, since the students' ability to receive instruction and produce responses differs. A specific model, described in the English language development research, appropriate to *emerging* English speakers is called "specially designed academic instruction in English" or less formally is known as "sheltered teaching" (Northcutt and Watson 1986; Sasser and Winningham 1991). The goal is to provide comprehensible input of ideas in the students' second language, especially by way of using concrete contextual referents in a relatively stress-free environment (Krashen 1981). The features of a sheltered model lesson include the following:

1. *Develop schemata* - provide the necessary cultural, historical, scientific, etc., background knowledge.
2. *Establish set* - provide an overview, advanced organizer, and/or anticipatory set.
3. *Teach vocabulary* - provide basic English and content vocabulary to be used in the lesson using multiple modalities (visual via pictures/gestures; tactile via realia, etc.) until students demonstrate their understanding of the words via vocabulary logs, discussing experiences, categorizing/illustrating the words, etc.
4. *Teach the lesson* - use multiple modalities (aural, visual, and kinesthetic) and teach (or access) a learning strategy/study skill explicitly.
5. *Provide guided practice* - work via cooperative activities which require that students interact with the concepts, use higher order level questions, etc.
6. *Check for understanding* - have students demonstrate their understanding via oral summary, matching questions, creating drawings/illustrations, etc.

Table 6.2 – Curriculum Topics with Multicultural Perspectives – Teaching

Topic & Definition	Concepts Relevant to Multicultural Education (With Related References)
Teacher Expectations - *How teachers' expectations influence student academic achievement*	• Students are treated differently as a function of race, gender (Cazden 1986; Morine-Dershimer 1985; Sadker & Sadker 1985) • Some of the specific factors affecting differential treatment include: generation of presence in the U.S., dialect, foreign language fluency (Matute-Bianchi 1986), past academic performance, dress, and cleanliness (Rist 1979) • Differential treatment, then, partly a product of teacher expectations, a.k.a. self-fulfilling prophecy (Rist 1979; Rosenthal & Jacobson 1968) • Students begin to play out the expectations and stereotypes attributed to them (Snyder 1981) • We communicate our prejudices in different ways (Brislin 1988) • Teachers need to be keenly tuned to their own prejudices, biases, and stereotypes; also need to be aware of "ethnocentric pedagogy" (Cervantes 1984) • Also need to have high, realistic expectations for ethnic minority students (Wilson 1984) and present students with academically rigorous tasks (First & Crichlow 1989).
Sociolinguistics - *How communication is used in specific social contexts (home, school, stores, etc.).*	• Principle focus is on communication differences between home and school (Brice-Heath 1986; Cazden 1988) • Includes things like amount of wait-time (White & Tharp 1988), rhythm (Erickson & Mohatt 1982) and participation structures (Au & Mason 1981) • Critical concepts include notion that each group is lingua-centric, each way of using language is limited (including the way we use language in schools), teachers employ their own language patterns in the class, most often the pattern of language used in the school is compatible with Euro-American culture, conflict arises when the pattern of language use is inconsistent with a teacher's expectations, and the goal should be to teach ALL students a variety of language patterns (Brice-Heath 1986) • Same principles can be applied to nonverbal differences such as eye-contact, interpersonal distance, silence, etc. (Hall 1976; Kochman 1981)

continued

Table 6.2 – continued

Topic & Definition	Concepts Relevant to Multicultural Education (With Related References)
Teaching Thinking - *How teachers begin to help students learn how to learn, to think logically and critically.*	• Each culture has a particular world view that they pass from generation to generation (Jahoda & Lewis 1988; Kim 1988; Kraft 1978) • Though world view encompasses many concepts, critical to education is the notion that world view influences how you learn and what's important to know (Jahoda & Lewis 1988) • World view also impacts our metacognitive assumptions (how people think, think they know, and think they learn) as well as what types of activities are important for learning (Greeno 1989) • World views between students and schools may conflict, so need to teach students metacognitive skills associated with success in Western schools • These strategies are also critical for second-language learners, since they're trying to learn content and language at the same time (Chamot & O'Malley 1984)

7. *Assign independent practice* - reinforce the ideas and provide extended opportunity to interact with the concepts.

To keep stress levels low, students are allowed to use their primary language throughout and the teacher does not overtly correct grammar errors but rather models appropriate English language use (Krashen 1981).

Development

A third broad topic with implications to teaching for diversity is development. Of special relevance are questions of the development of first and second languages and the development of students' ethnic identity (table 6.3).

One goal associated with development is to counter the claim that stages of development are universal. For example, Piaget regarded cognition as biologically determined (Wadsworth 1971), whereas Vygotsky regarded development as a social process whereby children acquire cognitive abilities as a result of interacting with others in culturally defined situations (Dasen 1977; Jahoda and Lewis 1988).

With respect to this question, differences have been found in cognitive levels of development based on levels of literacy (Scribner and Cole 1981), familiarity with the testing stimuli (Pick 1980), amount of social and cognitive stimulation, nutrition (Berry 1976), levels of education (Rogoff 1981), urban-rural differences (Munroe and Munroe 1975), and the degree to which students have adapted to western values (Irvine 1970). Importantly, these differences are a product of the kinds of experiences that are critical to operating successfully in a particular ecological, social, and cultural environment. For example, Douglas Price-Williams, William Gordon, and Manuel Ramirez (1969) found that conservation performance increased with certain manual experiences (children whose parents were potters outperformed those whose parents were not potters on conservation tasks). Cultures provide unique patterns of experiences (Triandis and Brislin 1984) that impact cognitive development. These studies prove that development, like behavior, varies according to cultural context (Rogoff and Morelli 1989).

Charles Super and Sara Harkness (1986) have described these culturally relevant differences via the "developmental niche." For them, development is influenced by culture in three ways: in physical and social settings; in culturally regulated customs of care and rearing; and in the influence of significant others' cognitive and affective orientations. Piagetians themselves now recognize the need to take into account specific cultural factors when describing cognitive development. The current task is to fully understand the culture-specific contexts in which ethnically diverse students develop (Erickson and Mohatt 1982).

PROCESS

The following pedagogical issues concern the general processes involved in teaching a multicultural educational psychology course. Ultimately, we hope that preservice teachers will learn from both what and how we teach.

Table 6.3 – Curriculum Topics with Multicultural Perspectives – Development

Topic & Definition	Concepts Relevant to Multicultural Education (With Related References)
<u>Language Development</u> - *How students' acquire a second language and the stages of that acquisition.*	• Establish the link between cognition, culture, and language (Pick 1980) • Includes the value of bilingualism on cognitive development for cognitive flexibility, metalinguistic awareness, concept formation, creativity (Hakuta & Garcia 1989; Hakuta & Gold 1987) and divergent thinking (Price-Williams & Ramirez 1977) • Describe stages people go through in learning their primary language (L1): Silent period, prespeech, holophrases, telegraphic utterances, short sentences, complex sentences and adultlike utterances (Wood 1981) • Students learn a second language (L2) in the same order described above; called the natural order hypothesis (Krashen 1981) • An additional principle includes the notion that the amount of time it takes to learn a second language mirrors that of what it takes to learn your first language; that is, basic interpersonal language skills (BICS) in 2 years and cognitive-academic language proficiency skills (CALPS) in 5–7 years (Krashen 1981) • Developing your CALPS in your primary language helps you learn a second language (Cummins 1981)
<u>Ethnic Identity Development</u> - *How students, and in what stages, come to regard and understand what it means to be ethnic minority.*	• Minority students deal with their ethnic identity as part of their personal identity (Maldonado 1975) • Personal identity development is based on work of personality development described by Erickson (1963) and extended by Marcia (1966) • Scholars have extended Marcia's work to looking at ethnic identity (for an excellent review, see Tatum 1992) • Several models applicable to minority students include those developed by Arce (1981), Cross (1978), Kim (1981), and Phinney (1989) • Stages (based on Phinney 1989) include: Diffusion, foreclosure, crisis, exploration, and commitment

continued

Table 6.3 – *continued*

Topic & Definition	Concepts Relevant to Multicultural Education (With Related References)
Ethnic Identity Development - *continued*	• Findings suggest that ethnic identity is a salient feature for minority students (Phinney 1988; Phinney 1990; Phinney & Alpurria 1987); that Euro-American students generally don't deal with issues of their own ethnicity (Phinney 1989; Phinney & Alpurria 1987) though they may have to deal with the implications of being white and overcoming racism (Helms 1990); that Euro-Americans define "ethnicity" differently (Alba 1990); that academic achievement and positive affect for Euro-Americans increase as ethnic minority students reach the level of commitment (Watt 1987); that there's a connection between self-esteem and stage of ethnic identity (Phinney 1989); that which aspects of ethnicity are salient for one group (such as language) may not be for other groups (Phinney 1989); that acculturation, age, gender, and sociocultural context all affect identity (Phinney 1989); that biracial students have higher levels of identity conflict (Phinney 1988); and that ethnic identity resolution does not happen without some kind of intervention (Gay 1985; Phinney & Alpurria 1987) (see Gay 1985 for the kind of curricular intervention which may be constructive)
	• Alternately, one way to resolve the conflict is via becoming "raceless" (Fordham 1988)
	• Connection between cultural identity and definitions of literacy (Ferdman 1990)

Course Content

Empowering the preservice teachers who take our class has proven to be a powerful educational tool. Our preservice teachers see how learning can be empowering for students. The empowerment of students is challenging, since mainstream education stresses authority in the instructor and student conformity to this authority (O'Loughlin 1988). Through a process of empowerment, our preservice teachers learn to develop their voices in the construction of their own curriculum. One technique we have used to accomplish this goal is to start with preservice teachers' questions about teaching and learning, building the course around those questions. That is, we allow the students to make decisions on topics for course investigation and discussion (Shor 1992); this is a practice important with ethnically diverse students (First and Crichlow 1989). We begin by presenting the preservice teachers with the challenge of creating a course outline. The preservice teachers participate in a dialogue of their course interests, needs, and goals. Our responsibility is to generate material that meets the needs of the preservice teachers, while maintaining a focus on building competent multicultural educators.

Oral Presentations

Since we choose not to answer all the questions generated by the process described above, we invite the preservice teachers to join with several of their colleagues to research questions of importance to the class and present their findings to the class. The assignment asks the group to provide an overview of the issue(s), resources, unresolved questions, and implications for student diversity.

Preservice teachers must learn to be empowered in order to empower their own students. Teaching preservice teachers how it feels to be empowered is an important first step. Empowerment also involves a thinking about and an understanding of why instructors should seek to empower others. Once this purpose is understood, teachers will empower their own students (Freire 1972).

Written Assignments

Our practice of assigning written papers has proven useful for preservice teachers. This assignment provides preservice teachers with opportunities to develop and demonstrate their critical thinking processes, to construct knowledge, and to see how that knowledge is, ultimately, limited (Banks 1993). The rationale for the requirements is to instill a basic foundation for exploring and understanding multicultural issues through the analysis and synthesis of the material. The written and oral exercises emphasize the scholarly expression of preservice teachers' thoughts. The aims are to develop a firmer understanding of the material, as well as to enhance the preservice teachers' critical thinking skills. Either method can be successfully implemented via team collaboration on a group product.

More specifically, linking theory and practice, we ask our students to conduct critical reflection via "insight" papers on a variety of issues related to teaching and learning (socio-emotional climate, classroom management, motivation, instruction, and thinking and problem-solving content and process). Part of this reflection asks that preservice teachers participate in a dialogue about their own observations in the field and beliefs. Thus, we engage our students in an ongoing dialogue about teaching and learning in diverse contexts that allows for the kind of challenge that might produce change. We benefit from this dialogue by knowing what the preservice teacher is thinking; we can then make appropriate comments to the writer and adjustments to the class. The preservice teacher benefits from the dialogue by making his or her implicit beliefs explicit. The preservice teacher hears our challenge to think in different, more culturally responsive ways. These processes cultivate a mastery of critical reflection and dialogue among the preservice teachers.

We use two written assignments intended to explicitly guide the preservice teachers to focus on issues of diversity. One paper focuses on their observations of the classroom social context (Borich 1990). Preservice teachers are asked to focus on such factors as diversity, friction, and cliquishness, to connect observations to class discussions about the social context, and to present a synthesis of their own thinking about the kind of context they desire. A second paper used in this course requests that the preservice teachers write a case study of a student whose background is different from that of the preservice teacher's. The preservice teacher observes the student for a day and then interviews her. This project generally promotes empathy for students who may be out of the mainstream.

Classroom Discussion of Diversity

The classroom discussion about diversity issues early on in the course has been very helpful to the emphasis on culturally responsive teaching. The preservice teachers are provided with opportunities to respond to provocative material and to participate in a dialogue where they exercise their voice. The technique also provides preservice teachers with instances to evaluate one another. A preservice teacher will hear a public response to his or her arguments as other participants point out the strengths and weaknesses. Likewise, preservice teachers are compelled to synthesize the critical cross-cultural material. The aim is for preservice teachers to understand the challenging cross-cultural issues. This is an important first step in the process to generate reflective and sensitive professionals competent in dealing with multicultural student groups. Of note, we recognize the critical importance of fostering a climate for discussions where people demonstrate understanding of each others' ideas and unconditional acceptance of each other.

Supplementary Readings

Since there is still no ideal textbook or manual on multicultural perspectives for educational psychology, we have had to select supplementary readings on cultural diversity perspectives, since we carry the burden to provide material that will cover these important areas from a multicultural perspective. The topics in these readings focus on issues of diversity in areas of study traditionally under the domain of educational psychology (see starred "*" items in our references).

Modeling Good Practice

Finally, a significant pedagogical process is modeling a variety of teaching methods for preservice teachers. Importantly, we model these methods as we teach course content. One important objective is to impress upon preservice teachers the connections between using a variety of teaching techniques and student diversity (Moll 1988). Modeling these techniques, we believe, is the most suitable method for affecting change in the preservice teacher's vision of learning and teaching. Afterwards, we ask the student teachers to describe the benefits and costs of the modeled teaching method, including how it might affect students from diverse backgrounds. So far, we model direct instruction, presentation-recitation-discussion, mastery learning, and cooperative grouping, as well as strategies for conducting discussions, role playing, demonstrating, peer tutoring, and teaching thinking and problem solving. Our next goal is to model "sheltered instruction."

SUMMARY

An integral part of what preservice teachers need to know about multicultural issues can be presented in a multicultural educational psychology course. More important, however, is the support and commitment of a *program* that emphasizes multicultural perspectives.

Before we conclude, we want to emphasize the need to explore and expand the application of multicultural models in psychology and multicultural education. We need to continue to grapple with issues of depth and breadth of course content. We need to attain the endorsement and commitment of the whole teacher education program to make issues of diversity a primary focus. We need to continue pursuing research on the effectiveness of a multicultural educational psychology course and multicultural teacher education program. Finally, we need to bridge the dialogue between the fields of psychology and multicultural education. Indeed, psychology can contribute to multicultural education, and, as important for their mutual benefit, multicultural education has much to contribute to psychology.

NOTES

1. We wish to thank Cherry Ross Gooden (Texas Southern University) and Carol Robinson-Zañartu (San Diego State University) for their helpful comments on a draft of this chapter. We offer special thanks to Mary Lundeberg (University of Wisconsin-River Falls) and, especially, Michael O'Loughlin (Hofstra University) for their detailed feedback and dialogue.

2. While we realize the importance of preparing preservice teachers to be aware of diversity in gender, sexual orientation, class, etc., the focus in our course (and in this chapter) is on the salience of the ethnic diversity in our schools and communities.

3. While we are from different colleges and have never team taught this course, we choose to use the plural personal pronoun, since this chapter reflects our collective thinking and acting, and since we're both committed to multiculturalizing traditional psychology course work. Thus, ideas shared here (including teaching strategies) have been used by either of us or both of us.

REFERENCES

Adamson, H. D. (1933). *Academic competence*. White Plains, NY: Longman.

Alba, R. D. (1990). *Ethnic identity: The transformation of White America*. New Haven, CT: Yale University Press.

Anderson, A. B. (1991). Teaching children: What teachers need to know. In *Teaching academic subjects to diverse learners*, ed. M. Kennedy, 203–217. New York: Teachers College Press.

Anderson, J. A. (1988, January-February). Cognitive styles and multicultural populations. *Journal of Teacher Education*, 2–9.

Arce, C. (1981). A reconsideration of Chicano culture and identity. *Daedalus* 110(2): 172–192.

Au, K. H., and J. M. Mason. (1981). Social organizational factors in learning to read: The balance of rights hypothesis. *Reading Research Quarterly* 17(1):115–152.

Ausubel, D. (1968). *Educational psychology: A cognitive view*. New York: Holt, Rinehart & Winston.

Bandura, A. (1977). *Social learning theory*. Englewood Cliffs, NJ: Prentice-Hall.

Banks, J. A. (1991–92, December and January). Multicultural education: For freedom's sake. *Educational Leadership* 49(4):32–36.

————. (1993). The canon debate, knowledge construction, and multicultural education. *Educational Researcher* 22(5):4–14.

Barnow, V. (1985). *Culture and personality*. Homewood, IL: The Dorsey Press.

Berry, J. W. (1976). *Human ecology and cognitive style*. Halsted, NY: Sage Publications.

Berry, J. W. (1979). Culture and cognitive style. In *Perspectives on cross-cultural psychology*, ed. A. J. Marsells, R. G. Tharp, and T. J. Ciborowski, 117–135. New York: Academic Press.

Bloomers, P. (1970). Comments on Professor Messick's paper. In *The evaluation of instruction: Issues and problems*, ed. M. Wittrock & D. Wiley, 202–204. New York: Holt, Rinehart & Winston.

Borich, G. D. (1990). *Observation skills for effective teaching*. Columbus, OH: Merrill.

*Bilingual Education Office, California Department of Education (1986). *Beyond language: Social and cultural factors in schooling language minority students*. Los Angeles, CA: Evaluation, Dissemination and Assessment Center, CSU.

Brice-Heath, S. (1986). Sociocultural contexts of language development. In *Beyond language: Social and cultural factors in schooling language minority students*, ed. Bilingual Education Office, California Department of Education, 143–186. Los Angeles, CA: Evaluation, Dissemination and Assessment Center, CSU.

Brislin, R. W. (1988). Prejudice in intercultural communication. In *Intercultural communication: A reader*, ed. L. A. Samovar and R. E. Porter, 339–344. Belmont, CA: Wadsworth.

Bullard, S. (1991–92, December and January). Sorting through the multicultural rhetoric. *Educational Leadership* 49(4):4–7.

Cazden, C. B. (1986). Classroom discourse. In *Handbook of Research on Teaching*, ed. M. C. Wittrock, 3rd ed., 432–463. New York, NY: Macmillan Publishing Co.

Cazden, C. B. (1988). *Classroom discourse: the language of teaching and learning*. Portsmouth, NH: Heinemann.

Cazden, C. B., and E. L. Leggett. (1981). Culturally responsive education: Suggestions for achieving Lau remedies. In *Culture and the bilingual classroom: Studies in classroom ethnography*, ed. H. T. Trueba, G. P. Guthrie, and K. H. Au, 69–86. Rowley, MA: Newbury House.

Castaneda, A., and T. Gray. (1974). Bicognitive processes in multicultural education. *Educational Leadership* 32(3):203–07.

Cervantes, R. A. (1984). Ethnocentric pedagogy and minority student growth: Implications for the common school. *Education and Urban Society* 16(3):274–3.

Chamot, A. U., and J. M. O'Malley, (1984). *Using learning strategies to develop skills in English as a second language*, Focus 16. Rosslyn, VA: National Clearinghouse for Bilingual Education.

Childs, C. P., and P. M. Greenfield. (1982). Informal modes of learning and teaching: The case of the Zinacenteco weaving. In *Advances in cross-cultural psychology*, ed. N. Warren, vol. 2. London: Academic Press.

Ciborowski, T. J. (1979). Cross-cultural aspects of cognitive functioning: Culture and knowledge. In *Perspectives on cross-cultural psychology*, ed. A. J. Marsells, R. G. Tharp, and T. J. Ciborowski, 101–16. New York, NY: Academic Press.

Cole, M. (1981). *The zone of proximal development: Where culture and cognition create each other*, Report No. 106. San Diego, CA: University of California, Center for Human Information Processing.

Cole, M., J. Gay, J. A. Glick, and D. W. Sharp. (1971). *The cultural context of learning and thinking*. New York: Basic Books.

Cole M., and S. Scribner. (1974). *Culture and thought*. New York: Wiley.

Cronbach, C. J., and R. Snow. (1977). *Aptitudes and instructional methods*. New York: Irvington Press.

Cross Jr., W. E. (1978). The Cross and Thomas models of psychological nigrescence. *Journal of Black Psychology* 5(1):13–19.

Cuban, L. (1989). The "at-risk" label and the problem of urban school reform. *Phi Delta Kappan* 70(10):780–4.

*Cummins, J. (1981). The role of primary language development in promoting the educational success of language minority students. In *Schooling and Language Minority Students: A Theoretical Framework*, ed. Office of Bilingual Bicultural Education, California Department of Education, 3–50. Los Angeles, CA: Evaluation, Dissemination and Assessment Center, CSU.

Dasen, P. R. (1977). Are cognitive processes universal? A contribution to cross-cultural Piagetian psychology. In *Studies in cross-cultural psychology*, ed. N. Warren, vol. 1. London: Academic Press.

Delpit, L. (1986). Skills and other dilemmas of a progressive Black educator. *Harvard Educational Review* 56(4):379–85.

*Dunn, R. (1984). Learning styles: State of the science. *Theory Into Practice*: 23(1): 10–19.

Dunn, R., and K. Dunn. (1978). *Teaching students through their individual learning styles: A practical approach*. Reston, VA: Reston Publishing Co.

Edmonds, R. (1979). Some schools work and more can. *Social Policy* 9:28–32.

Eisner, E. (1985). *The educational imagination: On the design and evaluation of school programs*, 2nd ed. New York: Macmillan.

Ellsworth, E. (1989). Why doesn't this feel empowering? Working through the repressive myths of critical pedagogy. *Harvard Educational Review* 59(3):297–324.

Engelman, S. (1991). Teachers, schemata, and instruction. In *Teaching academic subjects to diverse learners*, ed. M. Kennedy, 218–234. New York: Teachers College Press.

Erickson, F., and G. Mohatt. (1982). The cultural organization of participation structures in two classrooms of Indian students. In *Doing the ethnography of schooling*, ed. G. Spindler, 132–174. New York: Holt, Rinehart & Winston.

Erikson, E. (1963). *Identity: Youth and crisis*. New York: Norton.

Ferdman, B. M. (1990). Literacy and cultural identity. *Harvard Educational Review* 60(2):181–203.

Fichtner, D., F. Peitzman, and L. Sasser. (1991). What's fair? Assessing subject matter knowledge of LEP students in sheltered classrooms. In *With different eyes*, ed. F. Peitzman and G. Gadda, 143–154. Los Angeles, CA: UCLA Publishing.

First, D., and W. Crichlow. (1989, February). Effective teachers knowledge and practice in working with "at-risk" students in an urban school district: A collaborative investigation by teachers and researchers. Paper presented at the 10th Annual Ethnography in Education Research Forum, University of Pennsylvania, Philadelphia, PA.

Floden, R. E. (1991). What teachers need to know about learning. In *Teaching academic subjects to diverse learners*, ed. M. Kennedy, 181–202. New York: Teachers College Press.

Fordham, S. (1988). Racelessness as a factor in Black students' school success: Pragmatic strategy or pyrrihic victory? *Harvard Educational Review* 58:54–84.

Freire, P. (1972). *Pedagogy of the oppressed.* New York: Continuum.

Gay, G. (1985). Implications of selected models of ethnic identity for educators. *Journal of Negro Education* 54:43–55.

Garcia, J. (1981). The logic and limits of mental aptitude testing. *American Psychologist* 36:1172–1180.

González, G. M., and G. Thomson. (1993). Precollege attitudes and college persistence among Chicano, African-American, and White students. *Association of Mexican American Educators Journal* 2:39–44.

Goodchilds, J. D. (1991). *Psychological perspectives on human diversity in America.* Washington, DC: American Psychological Association.

Goodman, K. (1967). Reading: A psycholinguistic guessing game. *Journal of the Reading Specialist* 4:126–135.

Greeno, J. (1989). A perspective on thinking. *American Psychologist* 44:134–141.

Griesel, R. D., and L. M. Richter. (1987). Cognitive performance and cognitive style amongst a group of young bushman children. In *Growth and progress in cross-cultural psychology*, ed. C. Kagit Cibasi, 286–292. Amsterdam: Swets & Zeitlinger B.V.

Hakuta, K., and C. E. Garcia. (1989). Bilingualism and education. *American Psychologist* 44(2):374–379.

Hakuta, K., and L. Gould. (1987). Synthesis of research on bilingual education. *Educational Leadership* 44(6):38–45.

Hall, E. (1976). *Beyond language.* New York: Doubleday.

Harrington, C. (1979). *Psychological anthropology and education: A delineation of a field of inquiry.* New York: Ams Press.

Helms, J. E., ed. (1990). *Black and White racial identity: Theory, research and practice.* Westport, CT: Greenwood Press.

Hilliard III, A. (1976). *Alternatives to IQ testing: An approach to the identification of gifted minority children.* Final Report to the California State Department of Education.

———. (1991–92, December and January). Why we must pluralize the curriculum. *Educational Leadership* 49(4):12–16.

Hofstede, G. (1984). *Culture's consequences*. Beverly Hills, CA: Sage Publications.

Jahoda, G., and I. M. Lewis. (1988). Introduction. In *Acquiring culture: Cross-cultural studies in child development*, ed. G. Jahoda and I. M. Lewis. London: Croom Helm.

*Kagan, S. (1986). Cooperative learning and sociocultural factors in schooling. In *Beyond Language: Social and Cultural Factors in Schooling Language Minority Students*, ed. Bilingual Education Office, California Department of Education, 231–298. Los Angeles, CA: Evaluation, Dissemination and Assessment Center, CSU.

Kearney, M. (1984). *World View*. Novato, CA: Chandler and Sharp.

Kim, J. (1981). The process of Asian-American identity development. Ph.D. dissertation, University of Massachusetts, Amherst, MA.

Kim, Y. Y. (1988). Communication and acculturation. In *Intercultural communication: A reader*, ed. L. A. Samovar & R. E. Porter, 344–354. Belmont, CA: Wadsworth.

Kluchhohn, F., and F. Strodtbeck. (1961). *Variations in value orientations*. Evanston, IL: Row, Peterson, & Co.

Kochman, T. (1981). *Black and White styles in conflict in communication*. Chicago, IL: University of Chicago Press.

Kogan, N. (1976). *Cognitive styles in infancy and early childhood*. Hillsdale, NJ: Lawrence Erlbaum Associates.

Kornadt, H. J., l. H. Eckensberger, and W. B. Emminghaus. (1980). Cross-cultural research on motivation and its contribution to a general theory of motivation. In *Handbook of cross-cultural psychology: Vol. 3. Basic processes*, ed. H. C. Triandis & W. Lonner, 223–321. Boston: Allyn and Bacon.

Kraft, C. H. (1978). Worldview in intercultural communication. In *International and intercultural communication*, ed. F. Casmir. Washington, DC: University Press of America.

*Krashen, S. D. (1981). Bilingual education and second language acquisition theory. In *Schooling and Language Minority Students: A Theoretical Framework*, ed. Bilingual Bicultural Education Office, California Department of Education, 51–82. Los Angeles, CA: Evaluation, Dissemination and Assessment Center, CSU.

*Ladson-Billings, G. (1992). Culturally relevant teaching: The key to making multicultural education work. In *Research and multicultural education*, ed. C. Grant, 106–121. London: The Falmer Press.

Laosa, L. (1977). Multicultural education: How psychology can help. *Journal of Teacher Education* 28(3):26–30.

Lee, Y. T. (1994). Why does American psychology have cultural limitations? *American Psychologist* 49(6):524.

Lortie, D. (1975). *Schoolteacher.* Chicago, IL: University of Chicago Press.

Louisell, R. D., and J. Descamps. (1992). *Developing a teaching style.* New York: Harper Collins.

Luria, A. R. (1971). Towards the problem of the historical nature of psychological processes. *International Journal of Psychology* 6:259–272.

Maldonado Jr., D. (1975). Ethnic identity and self understanding. *Social Casework* 56:618–622.

Marcia, J. (1966). Development and validation of ego-identity status. *Journal of Personality and Social Psychology* 3:551–558.

Matute-Bianchi, M. (1986). Ethnic identities and patterns of school success or failure among Mexican-decent and Japanese-American students in a California high school: An ethnographic analysis. *American Journal of Education* 95:233–255.

Mercer, J. R. (1979). In defense of racially and culturally nondiscriminatory assessment. *School Psychology Digest* 3:89–95.

Messick, S. (1970). The criterion problem in the evaluation of instruction: Assessing possible, not just intended, outcomes. In *The evaluation of instruction: Issues and problems,* ed. M. Wittrock and D. Wiley, 183–202. New York: Holt, Rinehart & Winston.

Miller-Jones, D. (1989). Culture and testing. *American Psychologist* 44(2):360–366.

Molina, H. (1994). Ways to empower the Second Language classroom: An introduction. In *Educating Americans in a Multi-Cultural Society,* ed. A. Nava, H. Molina, B. Cabello, B. De La Torre, and L. Vega Castaneda, 79–96. New York: McGraw-Hill.

Moll, L. (1988). Some key issues in teaching Latino students. *Language Arts* 65(5): 465–72.

More, A. J. (1987). Native American learning styles: A review of researchers and teachers. *Journal of American Indian Education* 27:17–29.

Morine-Dershimer, G. (1985). *Talking, listening, and learning in elementary classrooms.* New York: Longman.

Moss, R. (1986). Cross-cultural perspectives in the psychology curriculum. In *Unmasking culture: Cross-cultural perspectives in the social and behavioral sciences,* ed. L. Baskauskas, 57–74. Novato, CA: Chandler and Sharp.

Munroe, R. L., and R. H. Munroe. (1975). *Cross-cultural human development.* Monterey, CA: Brooks/Cole Publishing Co.

Nieto, S. (1992). *Affirming diversity: The sociopolitical context of multicultural education.* New York: Longman.

Northcutt, L. G., and D. Watson. (1986). *Sheltered English teaching handbook.* Carlsbad, CA: Gonzales and Gonzales.

102   *Ríos and González*

O'Loughlin, M. (1992a). Rethinking science education: Beyond Piagetian constructivism toward a sociocultural model of teaching and learning. *Journal of Research in Science Teaching* 29(8):791–820.

———. (1992b). Engaging teachers in emancipatory knowledge construction. *Journal of Teacher Education* 43(5):336–346.

Phinney, J. (1988, June). The development of ethnic identity in adolescents. Paper presented at the Utah State University workshop on identity formation, Logan, UT. ERIC 298 224.

———. (1989). Stages of ethnic identity in minority group adolescents. *Journal of Early Adolescence* 9:34–39.

———. (1990). Ethnic identity in adolescents and adults: Review of research. *Psychological Bulletin* 108(3):499–514.

Phinney, J., and L. Alipurria. (1990). Ethnic identity in older college students from four ethnic groups. *Journal of Adolescence* 13(2):171–83.

Pick, A. D. (1980). Cognition: Psychological perspectives. In *Handbook of Cross-cultural Psychology: Vol. 3, Basic Processes*, ed. H. C. Triandis & W. Lonner, 117–153. Boston, MA: Allyn and Bacon.

Price-Williams, D. R. (1980). Anthropological approaches to cognition and their relevance to psychology. In *Handbook of Cross-cultural Psychology: Vol. 3, Basic Processes*, ed. H. C. Triandis and W. Lonner, 155–184. Boston, MA: Allyn and Bacon.

Price-Williams, D. R., W. Gordon, and M. Ramirez. (1969). Skill and conservation: A study of pottery-making children. *Developmental Psychology* 1:769.

Price-Williams, D. R., and M. Ramirez. (1977). Divergent thinking, cultural differences, and bilingualism. *Journal of Social Psychology* 103:3–11.

Ramirez, M., and A. Castaneda. (1974). *Cultural democracy, bicognitive development, and education.* New York: Academic Press.

Ramirez, M., and D. R. Price-Williams. (1976). Achievement motivation in children of three ethnic groups in the United States. *Journal of Cross-Cultural Psychology* 7:49–60.

Ravitch, D. (1991–92, December and January). A culture in common. *Educational Leadership* 49(4):8–11.

Resnick, L. B. (1987). Learning in school and out. *Educational Researcher* (December): 13–20.

*Rist, R. C. (1970). Student social class and teacher expectations: The self-fulfilling prophecy in ghetto education. *Harvard Educational Review* 46(3):411–451.

Rogoff, B. (1981). Schooling and the development of cognitive skills. In *Handbook of cross-cultural psychology: Vol. 4., Developmental psychology*, ed. H. C. Triandis & A. Heron, 233–294. Boston, MA: Allyn and Bacon.

*Rogoff, B., and G. Morelli. (1989). Perspectives on children's development from cross-cultural psychology. *American Psychologist* 44(2):343–348.

Rosenthal, R., and L. Jacobson. (1968). *Pygmalion in the classroom.* New York: Holt, Rinehart & Winston.

Rummelhart, D. E. (1980). Schemata: The building blocks of cognition. In *Theoretical issues in reading comprehension*, ed. R. J. Spiro, B. C. Bruce, and W. F. Brewer, 33–58. Hillsdale, NJ: Erlbaum.

*Sadker, M. P., and D. M. Sadker. (1985). Sexism in the classroom: From grade school to graduate school. *Phi Delta Kappan* 67(7):512–515.

Saville-Troike, M., and J. Kleifgen. (1986). Scripts for school: Cross-cultural communication in the elementary classroom. *Text* 6(2):207221.

*Sasser, L., and B. Winningham. (1991). Sheltered instruction across the disciplines: Successful teachers at work. In *With different eyes*, ed. F. Peitzman and G. Gadda, 27–54. Los Angeles, CA: UCLA Publishing.

Scribner, S., and M. Cole. (1981). *The psychology of literacy.* Cambridge, MA: Harvard University Press.

Shade, B. (1989). *Culture, style and the educative process.* Springfield, IL: Charles C. Thomas.

*Shade, B., and C. A. New. (1993). Cultural influences on learning: Teaching implications. In *Multicultural education: Issues and perspectives*, ed. J. A. Banks and C. Banks, 317–331. Boston, MA: Allyn & Bacon.

Shor, I. (1992). *Empowering education.* Chicago, IL: University of Chicago Press.

Sims, W. E. (1983). Preparing teachers for multicultural classrooms. *Momentum* 14(1): 42–44.

*Smith, L. H., and J. Renzulli. (1984). Learning style preferences: A practical approach for classroom teachers. *Theory into Practice* 23(1):44–55.

*Snyder, M. (1981). Self-fulfilling stereotypes. In *Contexts of communication*, ed. J. Civikly, 153–160. New York: Holt, Rinehart & Winston.

Super, C. M., and S. Harkness. (1986). The developmental niche: A conceptualization at the interface of child and culture. *International Journal of Behavioral Development* 9:545–69.

Tatum, B. (1992). Talking about race, learning about racism: The application of racial identity development theory in the classroom. *Harvard Educational Review* 62(1): 1–24.

Tharp, R. G., and R. Gallimore. (1991). *The instructional conversation: Teaching and learning in social activity*, Research Report No. 2. Washington, DC: Office of Educational Research and Improvement.

*Triandis, H. C., and R. W. Brislin. (1984). Cross-cultural psychology. *American Psychologist* 39(9):1006–16.

Vygotsky, L. S. (1978). *Mind in society: The development of higher psychological processes*. Edited by M. Cole, V. John-Steiner, S. Scribner, & E. Souberman. Cambridge, MA: Harvard University Press.

Wadsworth, B. J. (1971). *Piaget's theory of cognitive development*. New York: Longman.

Watt, N. (1987). *A psychological study of educational attainment among Hispanics*. Denver, CO: Denver University. ERIC 298 198.

White, S., and R. G. Tharp. (1988, April). Questioning and wait-time: A cross-cultural analysis. Paper presented at the annual meeting of the American Educational Research Association, New Orleans, LA.

Wilson, L. S. (1983–84, December and January). Clark and Bell are both right. *Educational Leadership* 41:88–89.

Witkin, H. A. (1967). A cognitive style approach to cross-cultural research. *International Journal of Psychology* 2:233–50.

Wood, B. S. (1981). *Children and communication: Verbal and nonverbal language development*. Englewood Cliffs, NJ: Prentice-Hall.

*denotes supplemental reading suggestions for a multicultural educational psychology course.

7

CLARA A. NEW _____

Oral Histories: An Interactive Link
in Teaching Language Arts

A notable percentage of preservice teachers, particularly those who may tend to hold stereotypical beliefs about how language arts should be taught, may also institute practices which can interfere with children's communication proficiency in diverse classroom settings. They tend to conceptualize these beliefs in terms of single-dimension demonstrations of complex constructs such as the only or "correct" way to listen, speak, read, and write, without having adequate evidence of culturally diverse children's knowledge and/or experience in manipulating and making meaning in the classroom context.

The societal contingencies placed on language usage present ample opportunity for children who are linguistically and/or culturally different to feel vulnerable, isolated, and rejected in urban classrooms, and markedly so when their backgrounds and experiences are incompatible with that of the teacher. Christine Bennett (1989, 76), defines "worldview as the way a cultural group perceives people and events." She further notes that mutual misunderstandings based on differing "world views" frequently result in hostile conflict and impasse (1989, 77). Thus, it is imperative that preservice teachers learn more effective ways to entice children into teaching-learning processes in language arts, so that their own skills and abilities as future teachers are broadened to accommodate multiple modes of expression. This process can begin and be nurtured with preservice teachers in a language arts/children's literature course in the teacher preparation program.

Preparation of preservice teachers to work with students from diverse cultural backgrounds, including Anglo-American students, must begin at preservice teachers' demonstrated levels of readiness to comprehend, challenge, and apply concepts from multiple points of view. Planning and implementing natural social settings in the university class for preservice teachers to examine as they teach language arts lessons in the field is essential to helping them identify their own levels of comfort as monocultural learners in the classroom context.

A communication circle is a very effective vehicle to use through the school term, and it is especially meaningful to help preservice teachers identify diversity found in personal oral histories, for it signals a willingness for all to join in, take risks with learning, and learn more about self and others in the communication process. Additionally, it is very important to help preservice teachers demonstrate understanding of the concept that language arts emanate from the children they will be teaching and that everyone has a language he/she can use to tell a story in the classroom. Having preservice teachers assess "where they are," using personal oral histories, is a beginning. Using personal oral histories is a logical beginning, for it helps preservice teachers evaluate their status as thinkers, listeners, readers, and writers in the communication process.

It is essential, then, that a language arts/children's literature course models approaches that will enable preservice teachers to successfully meet the following objectives:

1. to teach language arts from multiple perspectives, which include cultural and racial diversity;
2. to use many examples to express and explain ideas while persisting to obtain understanding;
3. to take risks easily and frequently as a learner, giving generously of self, individually and in groups;
4. to gain a genuine appreciation for the numerous avenues of language expression that exist in urban classrooms; and
5. to learn to value the differing life experiences that children of color, as speakers, listeners, readers, and writers, bring to a language arts encounter.

These foci assume critical importance when preparing some White preservice teachers to guide children in settings where aspects of cultural learning style and patterns of communication may be minimally—or not—addressed. This article will discuss the use of personal oral histories as a critical, pivotal process for showing (1) how preservice teachers view language arts content (an integrated communication process or a series of discrete activities in the curriculum), and (2) the organization and implementation of approaches that assist preservice teachers in meeting the aforementioned course objectives.

THE POWER OF MULTIPLE PERSPECTIVES

The importance of oral language as the primary vehicle to communicate thoughts and ideas becomes integral to all dimensions of teaching and learning as teachers continuously seek to discover meaningful ways of eliciting oral and written responses from students whose language backgrounds may not be congruent with their own. Considering that an overwhelming percentage of time spent in communication involves the conveyance of personal feelings about what is momentarily taking place in a person's life, whether in the classroom context or in an antecedent happening, interpersonal aspects of classroom communication can hardly be ignored. According to Gerald Weinstein and Mario Fantini (1970), a sense of *identity, power and connectedness* occupy a place of dominant concern in the thoughts and feelings of most people. Being able to accurately assess through oral language experiences whether one's feelings, thoughts, and concerns have validity to significant others, particularly the teacher, is vital to initiating and maintaining communication in almost any context. Sandra Garrett, Myra Sadker, and David Sadker assert that interpersonal communication skills may be seen as "a series of specific verbal and nonverbal behaviors that stimulate personal inquiry between two or more persons—inquiry that leads to greater self-knowledge." (1990, 188) Teaching and learning are highly interpersonal endeavors dependent upon personal oral histories.

Initially, it was noted (by the author) that preservice teachers tend to generalize what they may be thinking to other students in the course: that is, they assume that they all share the same understanding about what constitutes a language arts experience and that they are adequately prepared to plan and teach language arts because they satisfy course prerequisites. It is through the personal oral history that each is obliged to share during the first class regarding how language arts have been essential to their academic/personal backgrounds that preservice teachers begin to discover that they have varying histories of language arts which result from variations and distinctions in culture, religion, race, ethnicity, gender, and other aspects of diversity. In other words, they experience first hand "the power of multiple perspectives" about language arts.

The innately sensitive and value-laden connotations placed on oral language presentation often obfuscate meaning. How a child or preservice teacher chooses and uses words may take precedence in the mind of the intended receiver (teacher and other students) over what is intended to be communicated. The hegemony supporting the disposition of conventional schooling involving how to speak, read, and write tends to exacerbate feelings of powerlessness in children who are immobilized by the "culture of power" found in American classrooms (Delpit 1988). Lisa Delpit's assertion regarding a culture of power suggests that a form of double jeopardy exists: How can expectations for consistent growth and achievement in listening, speaking, reading, and writing skills be satisfied, if the language used to convey such expectations cannot be decoded by the learners and, in fact, may be incongruent with the reality of their socialized experiences in using and manipulating language? Preservice teachers in the university class assumed that they possessed perfect, explicit understanding of each other's language, until they began to share the initial oral histories in the communication circle.

In culturally diverse classrooms where the "assumption of shared identity" (Jackson 1986, 26), does not prevail, the probability of error in interpretation is high, and the frequency, quantity, and quality of student-teacher interaction may be significantly reduced. Thus, a primary objective of interpersonal communication (in the classroom), learning about self and others, is minimalized or lost for both teacher and student. Sharing personal oral histories at the onset and throughout the course permits preservice teachers to observe that everyone has thoughts to share, that language arts emanate from the children that they will be teaching, and that "communication should be the foundation of the curriculum" (Hennings 1990, 10). More importantly, preservice teachers directly experience the need to investigate, test, and adopt philosophy, methodology, and pedagogy that facilitate the needs of an ever-increasing multicultural school population confronting them as teachers, beginning with their awareness of the diversity exhibited among their peers in the university course. Organizing and implementing in-class and field experience activities that bring preservice teachers closer to the children they will be teaching demands knowledge of their respective backgrounds and the levels of comfort that they exhibit. Personal oral histories can be utilized as relevant pivotal points—in formal and informal classroom settings—to achieve this objective.

HELPING PRESERVICE TEACHERS FIND THEIR LEVELS OF COMFORT

Chairs are placed in a large circle (the communication circle) so that no spaces occur between students. Preservice teachers need to experience the concept that meaningful communication is interpersonal and that the circle signifies a collective willingness to be actively involved. During the first session, preservice teachers are informed that the instructor (university professor) is also a member of the circle at all times, though he/she may be the initial leader, and that oral histories will form a natural basis for learning about each other in ways that might otherwise not be discovered, if the first approach was through formal writing. Impromptu writing about self does not always come easily for many children or adults upon request; furthermore, it cannot always be immediately amended to enhance or clarify subjective meaning, as is possible through oral presentation, which invariably includes nonverbal gestures and facial expressions that enhance communication. It is recognized that many children and preteachers do willingly and energetically participate in journal and other interpersonal forms of writing which can be utilized to develop and enhance communication skills; indeed, subsequent in-class writing such as small and total group creation and illustration of stories was a natural outgrowth and by-product of oral histories emanating from the communication circle. The initiative to create often superceded the agenda intended for class discussion on many occasions.

The immediate and long-term goals are for all preservice teachers in the course to have fun with aspects of communication and to help them continuously identify, study, and practice approaches that accommodate children's needs to comfortably express themselves in all areas of the curriculum. The communication circle is the vehicle used to demonstrate the expectation that every word to be spoken, read, written, or listened to by preservice teachers could be viewed with the same value as literature preserved in libraries, namely, as a sincere attempt to explain, clarify, deconstruct, or present ideas for others to consider. Therefore, every contribution, beginning with the oral histories during the first class session, would be considered integral to subsequent, ongoing diverse communication activities, with the probability that members of the class would discover similarities and differences in opinion and thinking, based on divergent cultural orientation and the prevailing values which cultures hold dear. Preservice teachers are reminded that this observation would be very important as we explored traditional and contemporary literature from persons of color and as we listened to oral histories during class sessions.

THE ORAL HISTORIES

Starting with the instructor, each member of the circle then tells the class about the role and influence of language arts in his/her professional and personal life. Preservice teachers are directed to note unfamiliar words and expressions used by the instructor and their peers so that these representations can be used as springboards for extending both oral and written communication, for example, teaching specific, designated skills such as identifying parts of a sentence, modifiers, idiomatic expressions ("aina," "I *know* that's right!") and the highly interrelated functions involved in all aspects of communication across the curriculum. Sharing ideas, informally, tends to produce the idiomatic expressions that are cultural in orientation and that lead to deeper and more extensive understanding of meaning.

This approach is consonant with the integrated whole language concept, which stresses oral language as the dimension of communication which unites listening, reading, writing, and speaking (Hennings 1990) across the curriculum. It involves preservice teachers in making meaning from the moment they enter the university class and facilitates their understanding of the level of trust they must also obtain from children they will be teaching. Trust is achieved as leadership in the discussions that follow the oral histories calmly shifts from the instructor to students and back, with preservice teachers noting that the personal language arts oral histories (stories) emphasize varying perspectives about the value of language arts curriculum and begin at different points in their lives, particularly for those for whom English is not the first language.

For example, preservice teachers are asked to recall how they learned to read, beginning with their earliest experiences. For the majority of students, this is the first opportunity that they have had to express their perceptions of and feelings about reading and other aspects of communication without apprehension of being personally evaluated. Some remember feeling inferior because they were identified as poor readers and writers, while others describe the difficulties they faced in transferring from the primary language spoken by parents and grandparents at home to the English expressions demanded in school. Also, some preservice teachers recall the joy of being read to and encouraged to tell and retell stories as well as recite poetry in elementary school. Leadership in these discussions is comfortably shifted as the instructor and preservice teachers affirm similar experiences, express differing opinions, seek additional information and clarification of language used by the participants, and add multiple ways of oral and written expression to their functional vocabularies. Further exhibition of preteachers' growth in multicultural communication is evident as they create *cinquains* and *haikus* later in the semester and as they spontaneously create story narratives to accompany pictures that they draw to illustrate story designs.

This revelation is especially meaningful in establishing the concept that language differences do not constitute language deficiencies, that all children come to school with proficiency in some language that they can use to make themselves understood to teachers or to significant others who possess multicultural communication ability. It also serves to initiate the awareness in preteachers that children, whose avenues of communication in the classroom expand to incorporate that of monocultural teachers, make the major adjustment that is essential to their survival in the typical classroom. It is imperative that preservice teachers be able to more accurately assess "who is moving toward whom" in the communication process to prevent distortions in what was said, rather than what was intended. Two-way disclosure in the classroom results in teacher and student(s) forging paths that lead them toward clarification, understanding, and mutual satisfaction. Each learns to identify the personal contribution made to affect the desired results, and wrestling with concepts, in oral conversation or writing, becomes a truly intellectual enterprise with delightful rewards.

To further illustrate this concept using a simple process, the word *boot* (or another choice) is written on the chalkboard, and each preservice teacher is given a moment to define it. The general response given by preservice teachers is that "boot" refers to a shoe that is ankle height. They are then decisively told to "put it in the boot," at which point they may tend to exhibit confusion. While this may appear surprising, if the assumption is that everyone knows what a/the "boot" means, the preteachers experienced the fact that the word "boot" means different things to different people, even in the university class. Mutual understanding could not be presumed. Comprehension and transference of this activity to a culturally diverse classroom setting is critical in providing an environment where children (and preservice teachers) feel free to express themselves without fear of personal evaluation and rejection. Other words such as "bubbler," "fountain," and "drinking/water fountain" produce equally provocative responses.

Another example given preservice teachers is that of some children of color entering the kindergarten and printing their names or "pet" names in capital letters because that is the way they have been taught at home or orally giving their pet names when introducing themselves during the first week of school. It is not uncommon that they are told that these representations are not their names and that they are wrong, rather than moving children toward understanding multiple ways of being addressed in speaking and writing, in formal and informal fashion. Such indignities that convey teacher insensitivity as well as ignorance of the multiple perspectives that children are exposed to prior to beginning kindergarten are more easily explored when preservice teachers are provided with corresponding experiences. An analogy can be drawn between this example and the names preservice teachers prefer to be used in class, regardless of the official names found on the university class roster. Undergirding each name preference appeared a personal oral history which reinforced preservice teachers' comprehension of the power of multiple perspectives in the classroom context.

Starting with preservice teachers "where they are" in the communication process is a prerequisite to moving them in the direction of becoming language facilitators in urban classrooms. Frequently, they do not know "where they are" on the continuum from being monocultural to multicultural in their views of teaching language arts. They may perceive one way to be the only correct way to listen (with eyes on the teacher at all times), to speak (in linear fashion), to write (using "correct" English), and to read (with standardized pronunciation). Course content begins with the experiences, background, and demonstrated levels of competence in communication that they bring with them, as portrayed through personal oral histories.

USING MULTICULTURAL LITERATURE TO BRIDGE COMMUNICATION GAPS

Preservice teachers need to see immediate relationships between objectives of the course and the initial oral history activity, and they are able to do so as the instructor records unique words and expressions used by each member on the chalkboard. The diverse nuances and meanings of these unfamiliar words and expressions are further defined and demonstrated through analogies and examples provided by the students contributing the word or expression, making language come alive and active, and through the use of traditional (folk) literature.

Of particular note is the perception that using literature from diverse cultural groups in a literature-based language arts program connotes that strenuous efforts in the classroom are being directed toward acceptance of, and belief in, the rewards of diversity that extend far beyond the level of tolerance. However, Rosalinda Barrera purports that "literature-based children's literacy programs usually lack cultural foundation on the part of the teachers providing the instruction" (1992, 227). To introduce preteachers to this critical dimension of providing multicultural encounters with language, an initial assignment consisted of selecting a story, etc., written by an author of color, explaining the main idea from the perspective of a person from the same or very similar culture, and using the language of that culture. Some of the preteachers were quick to point out the fact that they would have difficulty explaining something about which they knew little. The "Ah-Ha" experience helped them to see the cultural gaps in their backgrounds, as well as realize that an extensive bibliography of culturally diverse contributions does *not* a multicultural language arts program make.

Providing preservice teachers the opportunity to integrate theory and practice is accomplished through placements in field classrooms where they work with cooperating teachers to plan and teach three language arts lessons, using multicultural literature as the basis for questioning, explaining, clarifying, and enhancing concepts across the curriculum. They are concurrently assigned to work with the school librarian to (1) obtain an overview of how the librarian functions to supplement student learning in the classroom context, (2) compile an annotated bibliography of multicultural literature, and (3) assume direct responsibility for tasks delegated to them by the librarian, such as selecting appropriate literature for individual students and classes and learning the respective cataloging system used in the field schools. The three lessons to be taught would integrate the use of oral histories (talking) before, during, and in follow-up language arts activities. The topics and concepts chosen must be currently relevant to the daily lives of children in the field classroom.

For example, in preparation for this task, preservice students are given an African folk tale such as "Men of Different Colors" (1984, 305) to read during the second class meeting. This provocative tale presents an explanation, from an East African cultural perspective, of how men acquired different skin colors and provides references that are similar to and divergent from those held in Judeo-Christian, American society. Preservice teachers are directed to search for similarities and differences and to make comparisons between currently held ideologies about racial differences that prevail inside and outside school settings and the impact that these ideologies may have on teaching and learning processes. As they are helped to examine their own responses to what they read, they are invited to speculate about the responses that children from diverse cultures might have to a language arts curriculum that assumes a monolithic acceptance of how they came to be as they are, particularly content that marginalizes their existence as human beings. Some preservice teachers instantly grasp the implication inherent in the concept that what the reader brings to the page tends to be more influential than what is written on the page. In other words, learning as a personal construct becomes instantaneous for many preservice teachers. This understanding is further displayed, or not displayed, in the rationales that they form for selecting the literature that they will use to teach their field lessons and for creating K–8 language arts curricula.

Using another approach to helping preservice teachers connect language arts to children's everyday lives, themes from traditional literature and contemporary literature from persons of color are placed on time lines to see whether the complexities that arise from diversity of race, culture, and gender have received consistent attention in traditional and contemporary literature. If so, from which cultures or groups? For example, students need to be cognizant of the difference in perspective that American society has about "who" and "what" is considered feminine and the ways in which America's perceptions are substantiated in folk literature from other White, ethnic groups throughout the world. A multicultural approach to examining this concept is having students identify Cinderella themes from as many folk tales as they can find, record the adjectives used to describe the Cinderella character, categorize them according to least/highest level of social acceptability, determine whether current definitions of beauty are similar, and explore the implications for using such literature with children based on their race, culture, gender, exceptional condition(s), etc. Activities like that above are designed to help preservice teachers learn to conduct language arts activities that are meaningful to everyday life and to model instructional processes that move children to higher levels of reasoning and evaluation, particularly being more alert to what they read and see in the media, including textbooks and curriculum guides. Multicultural literature can be found that examines every aspect of the human condition, that facilitates preservice students in making teaching and learning more personal and connected.

Teaching specific language arts concepts such as the use and implied connotations of certain racial descriptors (adjectives), i.e., Black, White, Yellow, etc., to denote acceptable social class position in American society, and identifying various types of media styles (headlines) that perpetuate negative and unproven propaganda about individuals based on group membership should receive constant attention in a language arts/children's literature course. A continuing assignment is that of having preservice teachers identify and share newspaper headlines or other examples of visual media that perpetuate stereotypes of disenfranchised groups. Included in this exploration are titles from research literature, as well as any literary work which might be distorted by the reader, due to the reader's lack of experience with the content or concepts presented. Where titles in the media may state "Blacks…," it is observed that many preservice teachers tend to include all persons who happen to be dark skinned or to presume that "Whites…" also includes them, unless the article is decidedly negative. This blind categorizing interferes with the ability to perceive individual or specific group differences based on varying ways of socialization. As just one example, such stereotypes reinforce the generalized notion that exceptions to African Americans speaking "Black English" are indeed rare and are only found in the highest echelons of academe, like being the professor who teaches language arts methods.

To examine this vestige of prejudice, preservice teachers are helped to critique the form of English spoken by Scarlett O'Hara in *Gone With the Wind*. Many appear to have seen the movie, but not to have read the book, and are consequently shocked to discover that her on-screen oral expressions are not necessarily consistent with the lower-class usage found in the book. When asked to name characters who used "correct" versus Black English, preservice teachers recalled that Mammy and other African American characters used broken English and that Rhett used correct language. In reality, Scarlett's place and role in Southern society, as described in the book, were glamorized in the movie to the extent that her extremely limited educational level, three marriages, and multiple pregnancies before age twenty were of minimal significance. Investigation of Scarlett's oral histories helped preservice teachers reassess a timely American sociological perspective of White females and to begin to comprehend the objection that many White Southerners had to Margaret Mitchell's treatise. Preservice teachers learned that Scarlett's oral expressions were not indicative of her intelligence and that the same premise applies in culturally diverse classrooms. Ironically, a few had read the widely publicized sequel to the book and the movie and thought that Scarlett had always spoken proper English. This literary work made it easier for preservice teachers (all were White and female), in cooperative learning groups, to discuss social class differences among and between Whites based on culture, ethnicity, and socialization, and, like traditional literature, it helped them analyze current indices of self-worth for White females without personalizing. This process is used to guide preservice teachers in providing appropriate introduction to multicultural literature written in dialect, so that children see relationships (Brother, Bruh, Bro) and do not feel victimized in culturally diverse settings. Recognizing their own discomfort when confronted with the idiomatic language of Scarlett made many preteachers much more sensitive to the comfort level of students who may be culturally and linguistically different.

Using personal oral histories as the springboard to subsequent language arts activities in listening, speaking, reading, and writing, whether in the university class or the field classroom, can lessen the almost obsessive dependency that some teachers and preteachers have on curriculum guides, to the exclusion of student needs. Using multicultural literature to introduce, explain, clarify, and enhance different perspectives can make teaching and learning a thoroughly enriching, exciting, and meaningful experience for White and other preservice teachers and for children in culturally diverse classrooms.

REFERENCES

Barrera, R. B. (1992). The cultural gap in literature-based literacy instruction. *Education and Urban Society* 24(2):227–243.

Bennett, C. (1989). Teaching students as they would be taught the importance of cultural perspective. In *Culture, style and the educative process*, ed. B. J. R. Shade. Springfield, IL: Charles C. Thomas.

Delpit, L. (1988). Power and pedagogy in educating other people's children. *Harvard Educational Review* 58(3):280–298.

Garrett, S. S., M. Sadker, and D. Sadker. (1990). Interpersonal communication skills. In *Classroom teaching skills*, ed. J. A. Cooper, 4th ed. Lexington, MA: D. C. Heath and Company.

Hennings, D. D. (1990). *Communication in action: Teaching the language arts*, 4th ed. Boston, MA: Houghton Mifflin.

Jackson, P. W. (1986). *The practice of teaching*. New York: Teachers College Press.

Men of different colors. (1984). In *The Scott Foresman Anthology of Children's Literature*, ed. Z. Sutherland and M. C. Livingston. Glenview, IL: Scott, Foresman and Company.

Weinstein, G. A., and M. F. Fantini. (1970). *Toward humanistic education: A curriculum of affect*. New York: Praeger.

8

ROSE MARY SCOTT_____

Reading Methods Courses: A Multicultural Perspective

This chapter will discuss ways in which multicultural content and pedagogical strategies were infused into reading methods courses for predominatly White (only two Mexican Americans and two African Americans) preservice teachers who are preparing to teach in grades 1–9 and how these preservice teachers responded to the course.

This infusion of multicultural content and pedagogical strategies into the courses was based on the following beliefs: (1) the content used in reading methods courses can be made more multicultural through literature that reflects diverse cultures and questions that relate equity issues within topics (Mangano 1988); (2) preservice teachers can be equipped to construct curriculum that reflects ethnic and cultural diversity (Gay 1977); and (3) university teachers should begin to model the behaviors they expect teachers to demonstrate in their classrooms (Gay 1977; Mangano 1988). Based on the above beliefs, this chapter will discuss and demonstrate how the reading methods courses were made multicultural through in-class activities and homework assignments.

IN-CLASS ACTIVITIES

In-class activities included examining culturally responsive instruction, reading and modeling use of multicultural literature, doing cooperative learning and reciprocal teaching, and journal writings.

Culturally Responsive Instruction

It was intended that the students in the reading methods courses develop high expectations for minority students. It is generally believed by the majority culture that minority children do poorly in school because they lack ability or motivation, and their parents and/or cultural backgrounds are to blame (Cuban 1989). The idea that minority students fail because schools ignore their cultures, needs, and abilities while accommodating these same features of the majority cultures was introduced into the course. Minority students, among other things, are asked to relate to material that is not produced in their community or culture, is not presented from their perspective, and tends to ignore their existence (Gordon, Miller, and Rollack 1990); and the material often depicts experiences alien to the children who must use them (Shade and New 1993).

I began by asking, "How many of you have heard of Marva Collins and her work with inner-city youth in Chicago?" Only a few recalled having seen the Marva Collin's story on television and no one knew why she had been successful. I then introduced the term *cultural congruence*, defined it as the relationship between the curriculum and the pupils' cultural experiences outside the school (Hollins 1982), and explained that this is what Ms. Collins did for her students. We discussed how Ms. Collins minimized competition but encouraged cooperative and collaborative learning, noting that cooperative learning works especially well in minority classrooms. Children were allowed to use their home language to help them understand and verbalize concepts but were taught the standard English dialect. After much discussion along these lines, we concluded that students must be invited to succeed and that it is the initial task of the teacher to develop a learning climate that accommodates the diversity of communication and learning styles in the classroom. Pedagogical strategies and experiences used to help teachers develop high expectations and learn to teach in a culturally congruent manner are discussed and demonstrated in the section on homework under the heading of literature-based lesson plans.

Multicultural Literature

The fact that teachers need to know the subject matter to be taught and something about the students they are teaching is well documented (Hollins 1993). One means of working toward this competency was to use multicultural literature that focused on people of color and/or women in the reading methods courses. Multicultural literature was used for several reasons. First, these groups have usually been marginalized, excluded, or stereotyped in literary canons and the curricula. Secondly, the knowledge base of students can be expanded through multicultural literature. Third, culturally conscious literature that reflects the social and cultural traditions of the group depicted (Bishop 1987) can promote respect and appreciation for diverse cultures. And fourth, minority groups can derive pleasure and pride when reading and hearing stories about persons who look and sound as they do. Toward this end, literature about different cultural groups was brought to class and shared by me and my students. This section will discuss some ways multicultural literature was used in teaching the reading methods courses.

Modeling is an important teaching tool to use when working with minority students. These students pay very close attention to the affective factors in the classroom environment, as well as to verbal and nonverbal presentations of the teacher (Delpit 1986, 1988; Pearson 1989; Reyes 1991). What follows is an example of a reading process I modeled using multicultural literature that preservice teachers may use in their classrooms.

At the beginning of class, I read the title *An Enchanted Hair Tale*, as I showed the book to the class and asked, "What is enchanted hair and what do you think this book is about?" (It is a story about being different. Sudan, the main character, was teased because his hair was different, but one day he discovered a way to belong, enchanted hair [dreadlocks] and all).

The students studied the picture of a boy with dreadlocks on the cover before one student hesitantly responded, "dreaded or braided hair," which led to a discussion on the difference between dreaded and braided hair and whether or not they had ever seen a person with dreads. Dreadlocked hair is uncombed, which results in a natural locking of the hair and as the hair grows it appears to be braided, whereas braided hair is a twisting or plaiting of the hair. A few students had heard about dreadlocks and very quickly connected the hair to the late Reggae singer, Bob Marley, and present day Reggae singers. They supposed the story would be about what happened to the boy on the cover because of his hair.

I read the story, showing them the pictures and stopping at regular intervals to ask questions and to get their predictions. At first, they seemed ill at ease and were not sure how to respond, but they eventually relaxed and enjoyed the experience. At the end of the story, we talked about their predictions and discussed the importance of talking about dreadlocks and putting the story in context because most of them did not have the background knowledge to fully appreciate the story without this information. I explained the importance of using as many prereading activities as needed before reading to children, teaching children to read, or teaching them to learn from reading text. It is necessary to activate as well as build the background knowledge of students about a subject in order for them to understand and enjoy text.

The role that culture plays in understanding text was illustrated when I read the same book to minority preserve teachers (nine African Americans, four Hispanics, one Asian American, and one Native American). They (African Americans) immediately knew that the boy's hair was in dreadlocks, and they connected the hair to Jamaica, Rastafarians (a term commonly associated with dreadlocks), Bob Marley, Ethiopia, etc. This reinforces the fact that knowledge is dependent upon culture, and what is considered natural is, in fact, a "way of taking" meaning from our environment (Heath 1985).

Books were read throughout the course; each time a process similar to the reading process above was modeled, and each time the purpose for reading the book was different. For example, *Sarah Plain and Tall* was read in three sessions to model using a literature-based lesson plan (Hennings 1989), as we worked on developing lesson plans in class. It is a story about a strong woman and the fragile beginnings of a family relationship. Sarah answers an ad from a man asking for a wife, and she brings a song, humor, wisdom, and happiness into the lives of two children, Anna and Caleb.

The above reading process was also modeled to read the book, *Brother Eagle, Sister Sky: A Message from Chief Seattle*. It is a story about a Suquamish Indian Chief describing his people's respect and love for the earth and concern for its destruction. The consensus of the class was that the story was well done and the pictures were very colorful and inclusive of the Native American culture. However, a critique of the book written by Ron Hirschi (1991), which considered much of the text and illustrations to be incorrect, was read to demonstrate the importance of researching the history of a cultural group for factual information before writing about that group. The question was explored as to whether authors can accurately write about cultures with which they do not have interactions.

Modeling reading the above literature to the students, not only taught content and pedagogical strategies, but it also proved to be a very powerful motivator to get students to respond to similarities, differences, and strengths in cultural groups. For example, *An Enchanted Hair Tale* was appreciated by all students because of its universal theme (not fitting in because of one's looks), and students unfamiliar with the culture enjoyed the story content, while learning about the culture.

Cooperative Learning

Students were assigned to work in groups, but, since they had been taught how to use cooperative learning in another class, there was no concern for teaching any particular cooperative learning approach in Reading Methods. It was explained to the class that, while cooperative learning is known to work well with minority students, the teacher should be sure to communicate product expectations and to give guidance and appropriate feedback. Lisa Delpit (1991, 1993) relates the necessity of being explicit in communicating the importance of a task when teaching across cultures, i.e., White teachers who are teaching ethnic minority children. Therefore, the cooperative groups used were a combination of cooperative learning (Johnson and Johnson 1987) and reciprocal teaching. The reciprocal teaching approach (Palinscar and David 1991) is for the purpose of understanding text, is guided by a dialogue leader, is based on asking questions, summarizing, clarifying, and predicting, and has been deemed successful in working with diverse groups. Both Delpit (1988, 1991) and Maria de la Luz Reyes (1991) support providing structure and guidelines in a literacy instruction program for ethnic minority students.

Reciprocal teaching was modeled as follows: A transparency on Black English was placed on the overhead projector. Students were directed to read the information silently. I then acted as dialogue leader.

T	What is dialect?
S_1	A variety of a particular language that differs from other varieties in terms of vocabulary, grammar, intonation, stress, etc.
S_2	We all speak a dialect.
T	What do you mean?
S_2	Well, what we call standard English is really a dialect—but a standard English dialect because it is accepted by the majority.
T	What is Black English dialect?
S_3	Well, our text says it is a legitimate linguistic system with rules.
T	What do you mean, rules?

The reciprocal teaching lesson continued in the above fashion through the four activities of questioning, summarizing, clarifying, and predicting.

Preservice teachers were then allowed to practice the reciprocal teaching process by reading text on the topics bicultural, bidialectal, bilingual, learning disabled, hearing impaired, visually impaired, gifted, and talented in cooperative groups. Groups were given a transparency with their topic typed on it. They worked in groups using the reciprocal teaching process and made their reports to the class using the transparency on the overhead projector. Class members asked questions and discussed the material presented. Stereotypes in children's books were also covered in groups. The ten ways in *Ten Quick Ways to Analyze Children's Books for Racism and Sexism* (CIBC 1974) were copied onto a transparency and presented on the overhead to be discussed in groups and later discussed as a class.

Journal Writing

Students kept journals highlighting the events that occurred during class. The following excerpts illustrate the discussion and sharing used to help students begin to develop a multicultural perspective about knowledge and instructional materials and to begin to critique their feelings and attitudes.

> We shared and discussed the book, *A Birthday Basket for Tia* and the lack of children's literature by and about Mexican Americans. This discussion led to another about how one is unable to assimilate when one's appearance is different. We discussed how to detect bias in children's literature....

> Today, K. read a book on Indian poetry entitled *Dancing Tepees: Poems of American Indian Youth*. Professor S. showed us her replica of one of the illustrations from the book. We shared and discussed interpretations of the poetry and illustrations.... We moved on to discuss the children's literature of the African-American group.... The students described a book they selected....

The above excerpts show that the students are beginning to develop an appreciation for the literature of other groups, to respect ethnic diversity, and to evaluate instructional materials.

> Someone brought up the question of whether or not the proper term was Mexican American or Chicano. It was decided that when in doubt it is best to ask persons what they would like to be called. It is as important as getting a person's name correct.... The class discussed different situations about racism they have come across in their schools, jobs, etc. The class discussed what could be done in classrooms to overcome stereotyping and racism.

Again, the students are afforded an opportunity to examine their own attitudes and feelings and discuss ways to make them compatible with multicultural teaching.

HOMEWORK ASSIGNMENTS

Students gained information about multicultural literacy education through homework assignments. They selected and shared a children's book with the class, made a seating chart in their field experience, read and responded to a novel, and developed and taught a multicultural literature based lesson.

Children's Book

The students selected a book (copyright after 1980) about an ethnic minority group and/or about women. They shared this book with the class and told of any bias or stereotypes in the story. I did not recommend books for this assignment because I wanted them to browse and peruse lots of books and make their own choices. Whether or not the book contained bias or stereotypes was not important. We had discussed stereotypes in class, and I wanted to see how adept they were in critiquing story content, pictures, and illustrations for stereotypes.

Seating Chart

In their field experience, students created a seating chart with the ethnic and gender make-up of the class specified and prepared name tags for all their students in order to learn their names. They thought this assignment ridiculous and too easy until I explained to them that getting to know their students and their students' ethnicity is a very basic way of affirming and accepting who their students are. Involving students and interacting with them from the start is one way to gain their respect and cooperation and thus begin to build an inviting academic classroom climate. Several students reported that the assignment forced them to look at the ethnic and gender make-up of the class, the seating arrangement, and to discover that bilingual students and students who did not speak English were also in the classrooms. The consensus was that knowing this kind of information would have an effect on their teaching style.

In some instances it was not easy for students to get this information because some classroom teachers are still operating from the premise of "not seeing color" and told the preservice teachers that they did not know their students' ethnic background. This was discussed in class, and it was decided that as teachers they must recognize and celebrate diversity in their students, and, yes, they would see color!

Novel

Students were asked to read and respond to the novel *Their Eyes Were Watching God* by keeping reaction journals and sharing their reactions in class. This book was chosen because it is rapidly becoming a classic, it is written in Black dialect, the protagonist is a female, and there are well-developed male characters. Additionally, it provides the reader an inside view of Negro life prior to 1940, which helps one to understand the culture and thus begin to understand the African American student. The novel tells the story of Janie Crawford's three marriages, other experiences, and determination in her search for self. I expected that the students would enjoy the book (they did) and would have problems with the dialect (they did). In fact, several responded to the question, "Did reading the first chapter of this novel make you want to read on?" in the negative because of dialect, semantics, and syntax? Some responses were:

> I found it difficult to read at first. The dialect used made me read slower than usual, so that I would not miss anything the people were saying. For example, "Tain't no use in your trying to cloak no ole woman lak Janie Starks,..." I had to read some of the lines over several times just to understand the meaning.

> It took me a while to become familiar with reading and, then, to understand the dialect. I had read about two chapters before I felt comfortable! I also did not feel a connection with Janie. She seemed kind of rude for not stopping and talking with the people sitting on the porch. Who is Tea Cake? I guess I didn't know what to think after the first chapter. There were so many characters.

> At first I was experiencing some problems with understanding the story. For example, "Yessuh! DeGrand Lodge, de big convention of livin' is just where Ah been dis year and a half y'all ain't seen me." After reading the chapter for a second time, I began to understand what was going on. As the story continued, I began to appreciate the language of the book because it helped me to visualize the characters. Janie was coming back from somewhere, and the whole town was talking about it. This did make me want to read on and find out why she was so important.

The discussions about the novel were highly charged sessions. The females defended Janie's actions, and the males thought her actions were less than honorable, thus revealing that the novel is timeless in its impact on both sexes. The literary elements of the novel were discussed, and the students shared their reactions. One male wrote that he learned a lot about male and female perspectives on achieving success because Joe Starks lived the American dream, but the majority of the females liked Tea Cake (a migrant worker) better than Joe. A female student said that she was surprised at how vehemently the males in class defended Joe Starks's honor based only on how he amassed his own fortune and found little fault with how he treated Janie, but they considered Janie's motives and actions to be suspect.

The novel was well received and thoroughly enjoyed by the majority of the students. We discussed how a good novel is able to transcend ethnic background in its appeal to the populace.

Literature-based Lesson Plans

Multicultural literature-based lesson plans were developed as a group and taught using the team approach. The team approach was used so as to have preservice teachers experience and model a cooperative method that they would employ in their own teaching. Students were instructed to select the literature that they would use to teach their classes (Hiebert and Colt 1989), to provide structure and guidelines for minority students (Delpit 1988, 1989; Reyes 1991), and to establish a classroom climate of cooperation, flexibility, and teacher leadership (Hollins 1982).

The following literature was used: a) African American - *The People Could Fly*, b) Asian Pacific American - *The Invisible Thread*, c) Native American - *Dream Catcher, the Legend and the Lady*, d) Puerto Rican - *Going Home*, e) Mexican American - *Abuela*, and f) Caribbean - *Anansi Finds a Fool*.

The groups developed literature-based lesson plans and shared them with me and the class for our approval and feedback before they taught them. Prior to the groups developing literature-based lesson plans, I had modeled literature-based lessons in class, and each individual had developed and shared a lesson with the class. Important pedagogical principles emphasized to develop culturally responsive instruction were: developmentally appropriate literature, high student expectation, and good literacy instruction involving pre-, during-, and postreading activities. Especially emphasized were the use of cooperative groups, extensive prereading activities so as to provide adequate background knowledge, hands-on activities, teacher leadership, and some form of writing based on the content.

An example of one of the lessons developed and taught to sixth grade students is found in Appendix A. The preservice teachers are required to write detailed lesson plans especially for the prereading activities because of the importance of building, as well as activating, the background knowledge of students. Also, novice teachers need detailed information readily available because they do not have the experience of veteran teachers.

PRESERVICE TEACHERS' RESPONSES TO MULTICULTURAL PERSPECTIVE

Students were asked to choose events that they had experienced or observed that may have helped to integrate the course multiculturally and to discuss why they chose these events.

The most often listed critical events were: reading by the classroom teacher, recognizing stereotypes in children's books, selecting and sharing a book, and learning about language differences. Having me bring in books and read to them and their having to choose and share a book about another cultural group were the two top critical events. This was not surprising to me because being read to is a pleasure that appeals to all age groups, and the fact that these books were about cultures different from their own made them more appealing than they would have been otherwise.

Regarding selecting and sharing their books about another culture, one student commented that the assignment "made me look for good literature, analyzing it for tokenism, standard for success, women's roles, and lifestyles." A second student stated, "I came to realize that as a teacher, I am ultimately the one who is responsible for analyzing books I choose to read in my classroom." A third student wrote, "I enjoyed searching, selecting, and perusing the books for bias; a valuable learning experience." Others wrote similar responses about locating books about other cultures, noting that they needed a reason to read some children's literature critically. Several students specifically discussed the books they had chosen and related how the content personally impacted them and how refreshing it was to look at differences among people from another perspective. In regards to the lesson on stereotypes, the majority thought the detailed lesson on what to look for in books would reduce their chances of offending any race or gender, and they would be careful not to misrepresent cultures or heritages.

Some student comments about language differences were:

> "I always wondered how I would deal with it (dialect) once I was a classroom teacher"; "I came to the resolution that simply adding to the original dialect is the best approach…;" "…informed me of my role as a teacher in terms of bilingual and bicultural children."

Most comments expressed the importance of the preceeding lesson and specifically focused on the importance of understanding the history and influence of the Black English dialect and its place in children's homes and communities.

Some students explained teacher input as critical because I related my own teaching experiences with African American students and allowed for spontaneity in class discussions. Although not considered multicultural (beforehand), three students considered in-class journal writing and sharing to be critical. One student aptly summed up their comments by relating the importance of getting the perspectives of people of a different gender, race, and background on how they deal with obstacles we all face. While several students listed the cooperative groups as critical, one student's comment on a group assignment made the entire endeavor worthwhile:

> "I especially enjoyed working on a group project with T. The minority population at our university is low, and I have never had a chance to work with someone of non-European descent before. I still notice some prejudicial tendencies in myself once in a while and any opportunity to help put them to rest is most welcome."

CONCLUDING COMMENTS

The responses from these preservice teachers may inform literacy educators who desire to multiculturally integrate their reading methods courses. First, the students enjoyed experiencing children's literature about diverse groups when shared with them by the instructor in the same manner that one would share stories with children. Second, they enjoyed choosing and sharing books with the class about diverse groups. Third, the information and discussion about bias in children's books were extremely helpful. And fourth, the information gained about language differences was very important to them.

Literacy educators must not wait until they have a well-defined plan as to what it means to multiculturally integrate their methods courses before they begin to do so but must start now with whatever limited knowledge they may have. Also as literacy instructors redesign their courses to better prepare White preservice teachers to teach in diverse classrooms, they need to share this information with others.

Finally, given the predominantly White female teaching force and the growing student diversity in our public schools, we must believe that White teachers can be effective in multicultural classrooms and that a great deal of the responsibility for their effectiveness lies with teacher educators.

APPENDIX A

Topic of Lesson: Children's Literature from the Caribbean
Grade Level: Fifth
Anansi Finds a Fool by Verna Aardema.
Objectives:
The lesson is designed to (1) introduce the students to the children's literature of the Caribbean region of the world via the history and location and the reading of *Anansi Finds a Fool*, and (2) provide a follow-up writing activity based on the lesson.

Proposed Sequence of Activities

Prereading Activities: When I say the word *Caribbean*, tell me what comes to your mind. (List the students' suggestions on the board.) Today, we are going to learn about literature that comes from the Caribbean.

Can someone show me on the map where the Caribbean region of the world is located? Ask if the students can name any of the island territories and countries of the Caribbean.

In order to understand what Caribbean literature is about, it is important to know where the Caribbean is and the history of the people who live there. (With a map, explain in detail where the Caribbean is located and what countries are in this region.) Ask if any of the students know about the history of the islands.

The Caribbean Islands were inhabited by native groups: The Caribs and the Arawaks. When Columbus set out to discover the new world, he landed in the West Indies, in the Caribbean. Soon, other Europeans followed, and within fifty years, the Europeans had exterminated almost all of the native people.

More and more Europeans came to settle in the West Indies and established plantations—to grow sugar cane and other tropical fruits. Plantations are very large farms, and the people who owned these plantations wanted to get people to work for them in the fields. The Europeans made slaves out of the people of Africa. Ships would go from Europe to the west coast of Africa. There, captured African people were put on board the ships. The ships would then sail to the islands of the West Indies, where some of the slaves were sold or traded for sugar and rum. From the West Indies, the ships would sail to the American colonies to trade the remaining slaves, sugar, and/or rum for tobacco and cotton. They then sailed back to Europe.

The slaves brought from Africa represented many different tribes—they were Hausa and Kanuri, Tiv and Fanti, Yoruba, Ashanti, and Congo. The plantation owners came from many different parts of Europe: England, France, Spain, the Netherlands, Denmark, and Portugal. After the English abolished or outlawed slavery in 1834, large numbers of Chinese and Indian (from India) people were brought to the West Indies as indentured servants. Can anyone tell me what an indentured servant is? (They are people who agree to work for a certain amount of time in exchange for paying their way to the new land.)

The Caribbean has people of many cultural backgrounds, but the majority of the population is of African origin. Similar to African American literature, many of the stories are passed from generation to generation by storytelling. One of the most popular characters in Caribbean literature is Anansi. Has anyone ever heard of Anansi or read any Anansi folktales? (Anansi stories originate from the people of Africa, and the story tradition was brought to the Caribbean with the slaves.)

Anansi is a trickster, always trying to fool someone or some character out of money, food, and respect. Anansi can be either a man or a spider. He usually changes into a spider after he has fooled someone, so he can get away.

Today, we are going to read an Anansi story. It is called, *Anansi Finds a Fool*, and it is written by Verna Aardema. (It is an Ashanti tale with a delightful twist, in that instead of being the trickster, Anansi has the trick played on him. He seeks to trick someone into doing the work of laying his fish trap, but, instead, he is fooled into doing the job himself.)

The teacher should introduce *Anansi Finds a Fool* by showing the class the cover of the book, explaining a little about the story background and defining any new vocabulary terms.

During Reading: The teacher can stop and ask the students to predict what might happen next or ask the students if any of the events of the story are similar to their own family events.

After Reading: The students can write a summary of the history of the people of the Caribbean or a summary of the story, *Anansi Finds a Fool.*

The students can write their own Anansi-type trickster tale—describing how they have tried to trick a brother or sister, friend or parent.

The students can create a web—pertaining to the geography or history of the Caribbean or a web of *Anansi Finds a Fool.*

Closing Set: Ask students to describe what they have learned about the Caribbean (teacher will list these on the board). Students will share their summaries, trickster stories, and webs with the rest of the class. (Either the students can read their own, or the teacher can read them to the class.)

Evaluation: The lesson will be successful if the students write a summary, personal trickster story, or web and share/discuss what they have learned about the Caribbean.

Materials: Anansi Finds a Fool, wall map, overhead transparency map, and globe.

Bello, Yahaya (1992) Caribbean children's literature. In *Teaching Multicultural literature in grades K–8*, ed. V. Harris, 245–265. Norwood, MA: Christopher-Gordon.

REFERENCES

Barrera, R. (1992, Feb.). The cultural gap in literature-based literacy instruction. *Education and Urban Society* 24(2):227–43.

Bishop, R. (1987). Extending multicultural understanding through children's books. In *Children's literature in the reading program*, ed. B. E. Cullinan, 60–67. Newark, DE: International Reading Association.

Council on Interracial Books for Children (1974). *10 quick ways to analyze children's books for racism and sexism, Guidelines for Selecting Bias-Free Textbooks*, 1841 Broadway, NY 10023.

Cuban, L. (1989). The "at-risk" label and the problem of urban school reform. *Phi Delta Kappan* 70(10):780–4.

Delpit, L. (1986). Skills and other dilemmas of a progressive Black educator. *Harvard Educational Review* 56(4):379–385.

———. (1988). The silenced dialogue: Power and pedagogy in educating other peoples' children. *Harvard Educational Review* 58(3):280–298.

———. (1991). A conversation with Lisa Delpit. *Language Arts* 68:541–547.

———. (1993). An interview with Lisa Delpit. *Writing Teacher* 7(1):4–11.

Gay, G. (1977). Curriculum for multicultural teacher education. In *Pluralism and the American teacher*, ed. F. Klassen and D. Gollnick, 30–62. Washington, DC: AACTE.

Gordon, E., F. Miller, and D. Rollock. (1990). Coping with communicentric bias in knowledge production in the social sciences. *Educational Researcher* 19:14–19.

Harris, V., ed. (1992). *Teaching multicultural literature in grades K–8*. Norwood, MA: Christopher-Gordon.

Heath, S. B. (1985). What no bedtime story means: Narrative skills at home and school. In *Toward multiculturalism: A reader in multicultural education*, ed. J. S. Wurzel. Yarmouth, ME: Intercultural Press.

Hennings, D. (1990). Children with language differences and difficulties. In *Communication in Action: Teaching the language arts*. Boston: Houghton Mifflin.

Hirschi, R. (1991). A very shallow dance of ink on paper, *The Web* 16(1):31–34. Columbus, OH: The College of Education, The Ohio State University.

Hollins, E. (1982). The Marva Collins story revisited: Implications for regular classroom instruction. *Journal of Teacher Education* 33:37–40.

Hollins, E. (1993). Assessing teacher competence for diverse populations. *Theory into Practice* 32(2):93–99.

Hurston, Z. (1990). *Their eyes were watching God*. New York: Perennial Library, Harper and Row.

Johnson, D., and R. Johnson. (1987). *Learning together and alone*, 2nd ed. Englewood Cliffs, NJ: Prentice-Hall.

Mangano, N. (1988, Winter). Guidelines for integrating nonsexist multicultural education in the university methods class. *Educational Considerations* 15(1):2–5.

Norton, D. (1990, Sept.) Teaching multicultural literature in the reading curriculum. *The Reading Teacher* 44(1):28–40.

Palinscar, A. S., and Y. M. David. (1991). Promoting literacy through classroom dialogue. In *Literacy for a diverse society: Perspectives, practices and policies*, ed. E. H. Hiebert, 122–140. New York: Teachers College Press.

Pearson, P. (1989) Reading the whole language movement. *Elementary School Journal* 90:231–241.

Reyes, M. (1991). A process approach to literacy instruction for Spanish-speaking students: In search of a best fit. In *Literacy for a diverse society: Perspectives, practices, and policies*, ed. E. H. Hiebert, 151–171. New York: Teachers College Press.

Shade, B., and C. New. (1993) Cultural influences on learning: Teaching implications. In *Multicultural Education, Issues and Perspectives*, ed. J. Banks and C. Banks, 2nd ed., 317–331. Boston: Allyn and Bacon.

Children's Books Cited

Aardema, Verna. (1992). *Anansi finds a fool*. New York: Dial Books.

DeVeaux, Alexis. (1987). *An enchanted hair tale*. New York: Harper and Row.

Dorros, Arthur. (1991). *Abuela*. New York: Dutton Children's Books.

Hamilton, Virginia. (1985). *The people could fly*. New York: Alfred A. Knopf.

Hartman, Karen. (1992). *Dream catcher, the legend and the lady*. Campbellsport, WI: Weeping Heart Publications.

Jeffers, Susan. (1991). *Brother Eagle, Sister Sky: A message from Chief Seattle*. New York: Dial Books.

MacLachlan, Patricia. (1985). *Sarah Plain and Tall*. New York: Harper Collins.

Mora, Pat. (1992). *A birthday basket for Tia*. Riverside, NJ: MacMillan.

Mohr, Nicholasa. (1986). *Going home*. New York: Dial Books.

Sneve, Virginia Driving Hawk. (1989). *Dancing Teepees: Poems of American Indian Youth*. New York: Holiday House.

Uchida, Yoshiko. (1991). *The invisible thread*. Englewood Cliffs, NJ: Julian Messner.

9

Charlene Klassen-Endrizzi and Richard Ruiz

Constructing a Multicultural Orientation Through Children's Literature

Numerous teacher educators and researchers have proposed ways to meet the multicultural needs they perceive in classroom teachers (Banks 1986; Gay 1977; Gollnick and Chinn 1990, Grant and Sleeter 1989; Modgil 1986; Murra 1941; Rogers and Muessig 1963). Citing the homogeneous backgrounds of teachers (87 percent of elementary teachers come from European American backgrounds) and the increasingly diverse student population (29 percent of the student population in elementary through high school do not come from European American backgrounds), educators are calling for a diverse teaching force and preservice and in service courses for classroom teachers (Banks 1994; CES 1987; Grant and Secada 1990). Proponents of multicultural education maintain that classroom teachers need occasions to consider the purpose and content of a multicultural perspective. However, simply espousing a multicultural approach to teachers is not adequate. Teachers need opportunities personally to explore and construct a multicultural orientation toward learning.

For the most part, prospective teachers experience "multicultural education" as just one more subject among their university courses and in service workshops. They hear about it, read about it, and occasionally talk about it in a context that requires them to re-present the material to the instructor at the end of the experience. Rarely are they active participants in the construction of a multicultural learning community in their university classrooms. The need is for a teacher education that is multicultural, rather than one where multicultural education is one of the many topics "covered" (Grant 1978). More than presenting lectures or leading class discussions on the purpose and content of multicultural education, teacher educators need to create curricular opportunities for classroom teachers to experience and live the process of an education that is multicultural.

An Education That Is Multicultural Through Children's Literature

In an effort to explore multicultural teacher education, Charlene Klassen (1993) initiated a research study in a required course for preservice teachers at the University of Arizona. She designed the study in an effort to expand preservice teachers' orientation toward multiculturalism through the use of multicultural children's literature. The setting was a children's literature course offered for preservice teachers during the 1992 spring semester. The thirty-two students enrolled in the course represented a range of cultural backgrounds. Twenty-one were proficient in English; eleven were also proficient in either Spanish, German, or American Sign Language. Twenty-five of the students were from European American backgrounds (i.e., Ukrainian, Polish, Italian, Jewish, German); seven were from Mexican American or Latin American backgrounds. Twenty-eight students were from the Southwestern region of the U.S.; one came from Panama. Twenty were between the ages of 20 to 30; the others were in their thirties or forties. All thirty-two preservice teachers were enrolled in the College of Education undergraduate or post-baccalaureate teacher education program for the purpose of acquiring an elementary teaching credential.

The methodological framework of this inquiry with preservice teachers stemmed from a collaborative and naturalistic research perspective (Cousin and Aragon 1990; Hanssen 1987; Harste 1992). Based on the belief that knowledge is socially constructed, the classroom and research experiences created were designed to provide all participants with the opportunity to explore issues of interest collaboratively. Efforts were made to create a methodological and peda-gogical match between theory and practice. Decisions about how to conduct research evolved from the need to create a community that expanded relation-ships, knowledge, and effectiveness, therein educating and transforming all participants (Lieberman 1992).

Research, seen as an occasion to learn deliberately (Boomer 1987), provided the teacher researcher with an opportunity to take on the dual roles of educator and inquirer of learning experiences. While these two roles are traditionally sepa-rated in the inquiry process, a unified "teacher researcher" perspective offered two distinct ways of exploring how people construct new understandings. "Intentional, systematic inquiry" (Cochran-Smith and Lytle 1990) was seen as a natural and necessary part of learning for teachers at the elementary or university level. By uniting the often separate roles of (a) making theory-based instructional choices and (b) observing, documenting, and interpreting responses to students, the complex theoretical and practical realities of classroom learning were acknowledged (Patterson and Stansell 1987).

While students in previous children's literature courses had grown in their awareness and understanding of the central role of books for learning about language, about literature, and about other content area subjects (Short and Klassen 1993), the role literature played in providing a context where teachers and students could expand their social, political, and cultural understanding had not been fully considered. The goal of this particular course was to explore the potential of literary experiences with multicultural literature for creating a critical consciousness of the need for a multicultural orientation toward learning in teachers and students. The overall research question that guided the inquiry process was, "In what ways does the use of multicultural children's literature impact preservice teachers' awareness and understanding of multiculturalism through a children's literature course?"

Literacy experiences with multicultural children's literature were created in order to foster critical reflection in preservice teachers. Klassen collected three sources of data during the semester—literature circles, dialogue journals, and end-of-semester interviews. Literature circles (discussion groups) with four to six students provided an occasion for preservice teachers to share personal connections made through transactions with literature, consider their own perspectives, explore the process of reading, and expand their social, political, and cultural understandings by listening to the responses of others (Harste, Short, and Burke 1988; Peterson and Eeds 1990; Short and Klassen 1993). Dialogue journals that moved among three students and the teacher researcher offered an opportunity for the students to clarify new insights, consider diverse perspectives, and expand their current understandings by reading and responding to written reflections of classmates (Atwell 1985; Gambrell 1985). End-of-semester interviews conducted with each preservice teacher were occasions for students to explore, clarify, and reflect on their current thinking about multicultural literature through five open-ended questions (Hammersley and Atkinson 1983).

In an effort to actualize inquiry as an ongoing process of discovery (Britton 1983), data were briefly analyzed during the course experiences, analyzed collaboratively during the summer months following the course by eight preservice teachers and the teacher researcher, and independently analyzed by the teacher researcher during the winter months after the study. Multiple voices heard through the process of collaborative analysis added a complexity to the research investigation and presented an avenue through which to consider divergent perspectives. Preservice teachers' rigorous course of study at the university did not provide opportunities to continue collaborative analysis beyond the summer. The teacher researcher spent several months reexamining, coding, analyzing, and interpreting data, using a constant comparative method (Glaser and Strauss 1967). Categories created through analysis provided a structure through which to describe emerging patterns.

THE PROCESS OF CHANGE IN PRESERVICE TEACHERS

Examination of data sources revealed the impact of multicultural children's literature on the preservice teachers' awareness and understanding of multiculturalism in several ways. Specifically, end-of-semester interviews provided evidence of the changes in students' orientation toward multiculturalism. Literature circles documented the kinds of talk that promoted greater understanding of multiculturalism. Dialogue journals and end-of-semester interviews offered examples of the multicultural issues and concerns raised by students.

A Changing Orientation Toward Multiculturalism

Findings from the end-of-semester interviews revealed three areas of changing perceptions about education—multicultural education, multicultural literature, and literature circles. As preservice teachers reflected on their new understanding of multicultural education, they showed evidence of an expanding personal perspective on culture and multiculturalism. As students began to view culture not just in ethnic terms but as people's "approaches to life" (Sandy), multicultural education came to be viewed as "a philosophy toward learning" (Sandi), not facts to be taught, but "a way of living" (Marla). The role of multicultural education was not simply to "open up students' minds to differences" (Efren) but also to "bring people together" (Kimberly). From this view, multiculturalism "impacted the entire curriculum" (Marcia), not just the literature curriculum considered throughout the course. Preservice teachers examined the needs of elementary learners, as well as their own multicultural needs as teachers, and recognized how multiculturalism "started with them and their own cultural views" (Vivian).

Preservice teachers also demonstrated growth in their knowledge of multicultural children's literature. As their conceptualization of this form of literature evolved, they were shocked to recognize the "whiteness of most children's books" for the first time (Billie). Students expressed a desire to share a "wide variety of diverse perspectives" through books (Mia) which "presented their own culture as well as other diverse cultures" (Lisa). While the need to share multicultural literature with children became more evident, preservice teachers noted the difficulty in locating these books in local libraries, classrooms, and bookstores. Students also investigated the role of multicultural literature as they discussed how vital it was for all learners to "see their own culture and life-style valued" through books (Lisa). Virginia spoke of how these books offered "insights into various ways of perceiving the world" which helped students and teachers develop a greater "appreciation of others" (Cynthia). Mia described the immense amount of "reflection these texts encouraged" and how her ways of "thinking about multiculturalism" were directly changed through experiences with this kind of literature.

Throughout the end-of-semester interviews, preservice teachers repeatedly referred to literature circles as the single most powerful course experience which promoted change in their multicultural understanding. This third area of growth explored in the interviews was an opportunity for students to examine the impact of literature circles. Jennifer described literature discussions as a "huge awakening" which promoted an explosion of thought and ideas. Cynthia noted that she witnessed a "real give and take" and a "posing of honest questions" among group members. Literature circles were also a central vehicle for helping students consider multicultural issues. Teresa described how these discussions helped her recognize that people from diverse backgrounds provided different perspectives and interpretations on a single book. Literature discussions were instrumental in forcing students to "examine differences" that accompany each person's perspective (Mia).

As preservice teachers explored their changing perceptions of multicultural education, multicultural children's literature, and literature circles through the interviews, various levels of understanding about multiculturalism were evident. At an initial awareness level of understanding, preservice teachers were just beginning to construct knowledge of multiculturalism; at an acceptance level of understanding, students were working to value multiculturalism; and at an appreciation or affirmation level, their attitudes and behavior reflected a more global understanding of multiculturalism (Grant and Sleeter 1989). The teacher researcher began to view multicultural learning as a continuous cycle of expanding one's orientation toward pluralism.

Kinds of Talk That Promote Multicultural Understanding

As noted above, the preservice teachers found the literature circles to provide particularly powerful opportunities for learning. The various kinds of talk that occurred within these collaborative literature experiences were examined in order to clarify how students went about sharing their pluralistic perspectives, thereby creating a context that promoted an expansion of their orientation toward multiculturalism.

Before exploring the literature circles for the types of talk that promoted growth, the discussions were examined for the breadth or narrowness of students' perspectives on culture. While their definition of culture at the beginning of the semester was limited to ethnicity or race, they utilized a broader notion of culture to explore multicultural interests during the literature discussions. Analysis of eight literature circles revealed how students used fourteen perspectives on culture (including ethnicity, race, nationality, social class, gender, family, age, language, religion, exceptionalities, music, ecology, history, socioeconomic status, and education) as they collaboratively explored books. This broader view of culture (Gollnick and Chinn 1990) pointed out the usefulness of multiple perspectives for enlarging preservice teachers' orientation toward multiculturalism. The students' expanding view of culture as reported through the end-of-semester interviews highlighted the power of literature circles for providing a setting where they could hear and consider beliefs from a single culture and across diverse cultural groups.

Examination of the literature discussions revealed how students used various forms of talk to consider multiple perspectives on culture. Three forms of talk (conversation, story, and dialogue) each contributed in different ways to build a community of learners intent on creating new understandings (Henson 1993). Conversational talk, a natural kind of interchange, provided a way for preservice teachers to begin to develop a bond with others. Story talk allowed students to enter into another person's world by listening intently to the experiences shared. Dialogue talk, for the purpose of understanding, disclosing, and constructing meaning with others, included both critique and inquiry as students critically listened and thought with others (Peterson 1992).

One literature discussion on *Tortillitas Para Mama* (Griego et al. 1981) with six preservice teachers provided an example of how students used conversational talk to share prior understandings, explore various topics, and pose questions.

Students' responses to this bilingual Spanish/English picture book of Latin American nursery rhymes during a twenty-minute discussion offered a context for them to dialogue about parent/child relationships in Mexican American and European American families. It also was an opportunity for them to examine the usefulness of translations and other interests through a conversation.

Max: I made a point of reading the whole [book] in Spanish before I read it in English, and I was pretty disappointed with it in English.

Teresa: It doesn't translate...

Max: Sometimes I wonder about the value of translating these things.

Mia: Ya.

Teresa: I could pretty much understand all of it but...like if there's a word I couldn't get, I'd look in English....

Leyda: Which one did you like?

Teresa: I liked the chocolate one [nursery rhyme].

Leyda: Me, too.

Teresa: I thought that was fun. I also liked the little lullaby, the last one....

Mia: I liked that one, too.

Teresa: Do you guys know the tunes to all of these?

Through conversation, Efren, Leyda, Liana, Max, Mia, and Teresa were getting to know each others' bilingual abilities and each others' likes and dislikes of these nursery rhymes. Conversational talk allowed for the discussion to change rapidly as they explored numerous topics of interest. This form of discourse with no specific direction constituted 62 percent of the talk analyzed across literature discussions.

The purpose of story talk was often quite similar to conversational talk. Students usually used stories as a way to reveal their cultural beliefs and under-standings to one another. On rare occasions, preservice teachers came to know one another in extraordinary ways as they heard the events of another person's life (Peterson 1992). One literature discussion about two contemporary fiction books involving grandparents and grandchildren (*Storm in the Night* [Stolz 1988] and *Now One Foot, Now the Other* [dePaola 1980]) showed evidence of five preservice teachers using story talk as a means of getting to know one another better as they shared their childhood experiences with grandparents. In this instance, stories helped to continue their conversation.

Vivian: Well I liked [the book] a lot because I spent a lot of time with my grandparents growing up. I was like my grandfather's favorite, so I was always there on Friday night, or I'd stay the whole weekend....

Candice: Ya, I'm real close to mine. I still am. I used to walk there from kindergarten....

Throughout the remainder of the fifteen-minute literature discussion, Candice, Cynthia, Kimberly, Nora, and Vivian continued to share short vignettes about a favorite or difficult experience with a grandparent. This form of discourse used to build community and revisit prior experiences constituted 23 percent of the talk analyzed across literature discussions.

Dialogue, an unusual form of talk, occurred infrequently throughout literature discussions. A literature circle on *Child of the Owl* (Yep 1977) provided an example of five preservice teachers willing to risk sharing divergent ideas with one another. Students' responses to this contemporary fiction book about a Chinese American teenager struggling to understand her bicultural identity created a context where they chose to listen critically and think together. During the twenty-minute discussion, Bev, Candice, Leyda, Nora, and Shannon repeatedly considered the main character's loss of ethnic identity from various perspectives.

Leyda: I never realized about color until I came to the United States. I never realized that there were different-colored people. I thought everyone was the same. When you come here, people look at you by your color. So I can identify with [Cassie, the main character] and her trying to find her identity. After living here, you lose your identity to some degree.

Shannon: She didn't know any of that. That's what intrigued me, how she gradually transformed and took on the culture of the Chinese.

Leyda: But that's something you never lose. You have it forever. You may adapt to another one but you always...

Candice: I think you can lose it.

Leyda: You think you can?

Candice: I think there were people in this book who were trying to. The older people couldn't forget the old ways....I don't think you can lose who you are on the outside but I think you can lose a culture really easy....

During the remainder of the discussion, several students went on to express their personal struggle to regain lost identity. This twenty-minute literature circle did not lead to singular answers. In fact, unresolved questions were food for thought long after the close of this brief exploration. What appeared to set dialogue apart from other kinds of discourse was the students' willingness to pose authentic dilemmas for consideration. Agreement was not the goal of dialogue; instead, students shared their multiple perspectives on a singular issue like loss of ethnic identity in order to push one another's thinking. New ways of acting and thinking were considered through these dialogic transactions. This unusual form of discourse constituted 15 percent of the talk analyzed across literature discussions.

The change in thinking reflected in these kinds of talks suggests the generative nature of dialogue for expanding students' orientation toward multiculturalism. While conversation and story (the most common kinds of talk) were useful for building community, exploring topics of interests from several perspectives and sharing prior understandings, dialogue (an infrequent form of talk) was oriented toward posing problems for group consideration. Authentic dilemmas, such as loss of ethnic identity, were not issues to be solved in twenty-minute discussions; students entered into a dialogue for the purpose of exploring an issue, not resolving it. These discussions provided a context for the preservice teachers to engage in the complex task of hearing, valuing, and utilizing the multiple voices available from different cultures for the purpose of broadening their multicultural orientation. By singling out this curricular experience, students acknowledged the power of talking with others about critical issues in order to expand their awareness, acceptance, and appreciation of multiculturalism. Preservice teachers also emphasized their professional need to experience personally a curriculum that is multicultural.

Multicultural Issues and Concerns Explored

Preservice teachers' discussions in dialogue journals and end-of-semester interviews were examined in order to explore the multicultural interests and issues considered by the students themselves. The intent was to uncover the problems and needs they saw as central to expanding their understanding of multiculturalism.

Over the course of the semester, preservice teachers explored both personal and educational dilemmas they recognized while analyzing their past, present, and future learning experiences. Personal issues and concerns focused on the usefulness of conceptualizing culture and multiculturalism in broader terms (beyond ethnicity and race) and the need to recognize and respond to intolerance. Students considered actions that would confront prejudice and lead to greater understanding of multiculturalism in their families, communities, and future classrooms.

> [Cassie's experiences in] *Child of the Owl* were basically how I felt when I went to Pueblo High School. I was an outcast. I was Mexican. I didn't speak Spanish. I didn't walk or dress like them. I was called a "pocha" which means American born and raised, an Oreo. I was dark on the outside and White on the inside....I think I've thought about it [trying to live in two distinct ethnic worlds] because I lived it. My mother made sure that we associated with the Whites. She made sure that we weren't just Mexican. I found myself in a predominantly Mexican high school with White friends....
>
> Not until recently during our class did I wake up and think, "Why don't you have Mexican friends?..." Personally when I become a teacher, I want to work with Hispanic children. I want to say to them, "Be proud of it. You are who you are. It's not color but what's inside" (Darlene).

Darlene recognized the need for multicultural education as she reflected on her life experiences. A critical look at prejudice within herself changed her attitudes about her own heritage and empowered her to consider action that could change her future students' understandings of their multicultural world. Other preservice teachers also investigated multicultural issues and concerns through a personal perspective first. Once they began to explore and expand their own orientation toward multiculturalism, new potentials were possible for them as teachers. This cycle of reflecting on personal experiences and considering new ways of acting within their communities and classrooms was evident throughout their change process.

Educational concerns and issues raised by the preservice teachers encompassed a broad look at multicultural education and a more focused look at the specifics of using multicultural children's literature through literature circles. As they considered the need for an education that is multicultural, they explored the purpose for a multicultural education, children who needed this perspective, and the necessity for teachers themselves to acquire this orientation toward learning. Preservice teachers also recognized the need for a multicultural orientation toward all learning experiences, not only literary experiences with multicultural children's literature. Multiple perspectives were to be included throughout the curriculum. Marcia addressed the necessity of including diverse cultures throughout subject areas.

> Now I see multiculturalism in everything. It's in language, in reading, in math, in science; it's all the time. In the math textbook, it's not just having names like Jane and Bobby but having names like Khalid. It's bringing in all cultures…I don't know how to describe it. I didn't think I'd be thinking about it every day in the classroom.

Other students also spoke about the curricular impact of multiculturalism on studies encompassing U.S. history, art, music, and social studies.

Preservice teachers saw a need to heighten children's awareness of the value of multiculturalism. Shannon expressed his goal of working to broaden the orientation of all students toward living in a multicultural society.

> [Multicultural education] has to be in your classroom regardless of your classroom cultural make-up. If you present African American literature and you don't have African American children in your class, your students can acquire an appreciation for a culture other than their own. They can sympathize or empathize or develop a different impression.

These students came to understand that an education that is multicultural was not just for culturally diverse learners or learners from the dominant class; it was for everyone. Preservice teachers like Shannon explored the vital role multicultural children's literature could play in altering stereotypes or intolerance toward other cultural groups.

As students examined the role of multicultural literature, they recognized the basic need for all children to find themselves in books, including children from diverse backgrounds. They acknowledged that it would take a concerted effort by teachers to provide enough of these books, since a majority of the books currently available in classrooms, libraries, and local bookstores were pieces of literature that represented the dominant culture. In order to avoid stereotyping any cultural group of people, students also noted that teachers had a responsibility to share numerous books depicting each culture.

> I think that it's equally important that [children] read lots and lots of books so that they have many different ideas of what that culture is like. I mean it would be great for a student to read about a successful African American lawyer, but if a child reads only this book, then they could think that all African Americans are successful lawyers. This can be just as damaging as a student [who], after reading one book, thinks all African Americans are cotton pickers (Candice).

Preservice teachers also examined a curricular component that provided a context to hear and explore multiple perspectives. Literature circles were a place to explore the value and usefulness of diverse perspectives for the purpose of expanding one's own orientation toward multiculturalism. Mia noted, "It is really easy to think that your own viewpoint covers everything. We really need the input from other individuals to grow beyond our own conceptions." Literature discussions provided an opportunity for preservice teachers to personally engage in the process of learning that is multicultural and reflect on the power of this curricular engagement for children in classrooms.

As students explored both personal and educational issues relating to multiculturalism through their dialogue journals and end-of-semester interviews, they had the opportunity to work toward connecting their beliefs about learning with the selection of materials and curricular experiences. Rooting practice in theoretical understandings proved to be a challenging task for preservice teachers. Beyond having an impact on their transactions with children in classrooms, the multicultural issues they chose to explore also influenced relationships in their families and communities. A multicultural orientation influenced learning in and out of school.

A Cyclical Framework of Learning That Is Multicultural

Examining preservice teachers' changing theory and practice of multicultural education through the analysis of three data sources (end-of-semester interviews, literature circles, and dialogue journals) provided insights into the long-term process of how students grew in their understanding of multiculturalism. Three elements that helped to clarify how students began to expand their multicultural orientation emerged.

First, perspectives from diverse groups beyond students' own experiences were essential for expanding their understanding of pluralism. Literature circles and dialogue journals both offered curricular occasions to hear and explore the multiple perspectives available from various cultural groups. As students listened to others share knowledge gained through their ethnic, racial, social class, gender, family, age, language, or political groups, they encountered a plurality of voices beyond their own cultural views. Alternative ways of thinking and acting in a pluralistic society were considered through these collaborative experiences.

Second, dialogue and tension played a central role in fostering an environment that promoted an expanding multicultural orientation. The notion of dialogue emphasized the presence of diverse perspectives needed for the construction of new understandings. A multiplicity of voices among the preservice teachers fostered an exchange of divergent ideas as they explored multicultural issues of concern (e.g., loss of ethnic identity, learning a second language). Analysis of these transactions provided evidence of the tension present during dialogue. Tension appeared to be useful for promoting reflection and pushing students to consider alternative ways of thinking and acting within their cultural groups long after the literature discussions and journal entries were completed. Dialogue and tension generated a more critical consciousness among students as they began to examine their multicultural concerns.

A third component of learning that is multicultural encompassed expanding levels of awareness, acceptance, and affirmation of cultural pluralism (Grant and Sleeter 1989). For some preservice teachers, course experiences pushed them to become aware of a multicultural orientation toward learning for the first time. For other students who had already begun to examine multiculturalism, they moved toward a greater acceptance of pluralism. And yet, for others, they explored ways to affirm differences across and within cultural groups. These three levels of understanding were not meant to limit and confine beliefs according to a set standard; instead, they were designed to describe a student's ever-expanding orientation toward multiculturalism over time. The cyclical process of learning about multiculturalism was unique for each student. Changing beliefs about one issue influenced prior beliefs about related concerns at various levels of understanding. With each new issue explored during the semester, new ways were found to help preservice teachers expand their current awareness, acceptance, or affirmation of multiculturalism.

The multiple perspectives shared from various cultural groups and the dialogue and tension created through the exploration of complex issues generated a constant force for learning that fostered greater awareness, acceptance, and affirmation of pluralism in preservice teachers (see figure 9.1). An expanding critical consciousness of world experiences altered students' orientation toward multiculturalism and urged them to think and act in a more global manner within their own cultural groups and in schools.

ISSUES EVOLVING FROM THE INQUIRY

The goal of moving students beyond surface level changes in their awareness of diversity toward a deeper knowledge of pluralism emphasized growth as a long-term process. Preservice teachers' literary experiences with multicultural literature initiated a process of change that should continue over many years of

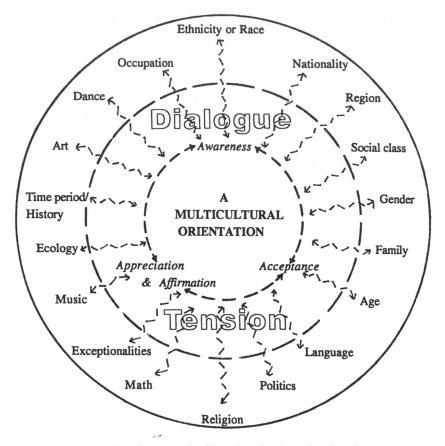

Figure 9.1   A cyclical framework of learning that is multicultural.

learning with students in classrooms. One curricular experience that graphically depicted their efforts to explore pluralism was evident in the dialogic exchanges in literature circles. Through transactions with multicultural literature, students began to clarify their own perspectives, reflect on these understandings, explore divergent perspectives presented by group members, and consider a transformative, multicultural orientation toward learning. These dialogic experiences urged preservice teachers to move beyond their present awareness of diversity toward greater appreciation and affirmation of pluralism. The tension resulting from hearing a multiplicity of voices encouraged reflection on these issues long after the actual literature discussions were done. Dialogue provided students with opportunities to verbalize the possibilities and potentials for change. Reshaping multicultural understanding verbally inside the classroom encouraged them to consider new ways of thinking and acting outside school.

The power of these dialogic experiences with multicultural children's literature to expand students' orientation toward multiculturalism underscores the need for other curricular experiences that transform students' and teachers' understanding of pluralism. Dialogue requires an inclusive stance that invites students, teachers, families, and communities to participate in the process of learning that is multicultural. Dialogue that leads to an affirmation of pluralism, not just awareness of diversity, has the potential to transform one's orientation toward the whole of our multicultural society.

Actualizing an orientation toward learning that embraces pluralism must include a dialogic exchange among schools, families, and communities that transforms everyone's view of multiculturalism. As teachers make efforts to utilize the parental and community resources and value the child's learning environment at home, parents can begin to see how educational experiences do not separate knowledge constructed outside and inside of school. In fact, learning that is truly pluralistic must include and build on knowledge constructed outside the classroom.

During the end-of-semester interviews, one preservice teacher (Marla) discussed how she saw the class, not as an opportunity for the teacher researcher to "teach" multicultural concepts, but as an occasion for the students and teacher to "live" multiculturalism. Her comments point out a major dilemma that faces multicultural teacher education today. The dominant theory of learning that guides classroom practice at the elementary, secondary, and university levels is the transmission view, characterized by Paulo Freire (1970) as the banking concept of education. Instead of allowing students to construct their own understandings, teachers deposit knowledge into the passive minds of students. This view of learning contradicts studies of learning theory over the past fifty years that have pointed out the need for students to construct knowledge within their own social, political, and cultural contexts (Dewey 1938; Smith 1986).

Preservice teachers confirmed this dominant view of learning at the university level through their end-of-semester interviews when they were asked if and when they had considered multiculturalism in other College of Education courses. They provided examples of teacher educators who spent a morning discussing gender bias, assigned a reading on multicultural education, lectured on cultural bias in standardized tests, talked about the need to be aware of students' diverse backgrounds, and provided a definition of multicultural education which they copied off the chalkboard. More than a lecture or a reading, preservice teachers require holistic demonstrations from teacher educators who "live" rather than just "cover" the curriculum (Harste 1989) of multicultural teacher education. Just as children in classrooms need occasions to explore and critically reflect on our pluralistic society, preservice teachers likewise must have opportunities to consider their world experiences in light of global complexities. A global frame of reference prepares teachers to function more effectively in the social, political, and cultural climates of their schools and communities.

One year after the completion of this collaborative inquiry, the thirty-two preservice teachers were invited to reflect on and reconsider the semester of learning in light of their current experiences in schools. The urgent need for teacher education that provides opportunities to live multiculturalism is expressed in the struggles one preservice teacher discussed as she considered learning with students in her own classroom the following school year. Mia's words depict a teacher cognizant of the need to actively confront the harsh realities presented by a society that negatively focuses on differences. As a reflective preservice teacher who recognizes the need to create a critical consciousness in students, she provides one example of the power and potential in teachers whose awareness, acceptance, and affirmation of pluralism transforms their goal of striving to live a curriculum that is multicultural.

> Being at [an inner-city school] this semester has been a real eye-opening experience for me. It is a multicultural environment, yet it is not a truly integrated environment. I am seeing firsthand how difficult it is in the real world to achieve desegregation and a positive celebration of differences.....I have observed such comments by the children as, "I hate you White folk; get out of my face," and "Why do you hug him? He has dirty brown skin..."
>
> I believe that we, as teachers, need to openly discuss these issues with the children more (I know I will) to bring about an awareness that we are all thinking, feeling, caring people, and we may come in different packages, and that's okay. Would we really want to be the same anyway? I believe, now more than ever, that the lack of understanding and acceptance of individual and cultural differences is really at the root of our society's deepest problems.
>
> I guess, for me, it took immersing myself in a situation where people are not so accepting of one another to see how essential it is to openly and aggressively teach multicultural acceptance and celebration (Mia).

Mia's words help clarify the purpose, content, and context of learning that is multicultural. Her experiences point out the need for "a democratic approach to teaching and learning that seeks to foster cultural pluralism within culturally diverse societies and an interdependent world" (Bennett, Niggle, and Stage 1990, 243). Indirectly, she also addresses the dire need for curricular materials such as multicultural children's literature that presents a diversity of perspectives for collaborative exploration. Additionally, she speaks to the need for multicultural learning environments that create a context for a multiplicity of voices to dialogue about critical issues and concerns.

Mia graphically emphasizes the complexities and struggles inherent in attempting to live a multicultural orientation toward learning. Nothing less than aggressively teaching and celebrating pluralism is required. Her words also challenge teacher educators to seek ways to transform our orientation toward multiculturalism. Only after we in our university classrooms have made multiculturalism a part of our theory and practice of learning can we hope to witness a transformed orientation toward learning and living in schools.

References

Atwell, N. (1985). Writing and reading from the inside out. In *Breaking ground: Teachers relate reading and writing in the elementary school*, ed. J. Hansen, T. Newkirk, and D. Graves, 147–168. Portsmouth, NH: Heinemann.

Banks, J. A. (1986). Development, paradigms, and goals of multicultural education. In *Multicultural education in western societies*, ed. J. A. Banks and J. Lynch, 3–30. New York: Praeger.

———. (1994). *Multiethnic education: Theory and practice.* Boston: Allyn and Bacon.

Bennett, C., T. Niggle, and F. Stage. (1990). Preservice multicultural teacher education: Predictors of student readiness. *Teaching and Teacher Education* 6(3):243–254.

Boomer, G. (1987). Addressing the problem of elsewhereness: A case for action research in schools. In *Reclaiming the classroom: Teacher research as an agency for change*, ed. D. Goswami and P. Stillman, 4–12. Portsmouth, NH: Heinemann.

Britton, J. (1983). A quiet form of research. In *Reclaiming the classroom: Teacher research as an agency for change*, ed. D. Goswami and P. Stillman, 13–20. Portsmouth, NH: Heinemann.

Center for Education Statistics (CES). (1987). *Digest of education statistics*. Washington, DC: U.S. Government Printing Office.

Cochran-Smith, M., and S. L. Lytle. (1990). Research on teaching and teacher research: The issues that divide. *Educational Researcher* 19(2):2–11.

Cousins, P. T., and E. Aragon. (1990). *Collaborative research: Considering a new para digm for educational research.* Research report, California State University, San Bernardino, CA.

dePaola, T. (1980). *Now one foot, now the other.* New York: Putnam.

Dewey, J. (1938). *Experience and education.* New York: Macmillan.

Freire, P. (1970). *Pedagogy of the oppressed.* New York: Continuum.

Gambrell, L. B. (1985). Dialogue journals: Reading-writing interaction. *The Reading Teacher* 38(6):512–515.

Gay, G. (1977). Curriculum design for multicultural education. In *Multicultural education: Commitments, issues, and applications*, ed. C. A. Grant, 94–104. Washington: Association for Supervision and Curriculum Development.

Glaser, B., and A. Strauss. (1967). *The discovery of grounded theory.* Chicago: Aldine.

Grant, C. (1978). Education that is multicultural—isn't that what we mean? *Journal of Teacher Education* 29(5):45–48.

Grant, C. A., and C. E. Sleeter. (1989). Race, class, gender, exceptionality, and educa tional reform. In *Multicultural education: issues and perspectives*, ed. J. A. Banks and C. A. M. Banks, 46–65. Needham Heights, MA: Allyn and Bacon.

Grant, C. A., and W. G. Secada. (1990). Preparing teachers for diversity. In *Handbook of research on teacher education*, ed. W. R. Houston, 403–422. New York: Macmillan.

Griego, M. C., B. L. Bucks, S. S. Gilbert, and L. H. Kimball,. (1981). *Tortillitas para mama and other nursery rhymes*. New York: Henry Holt.

Hammersley, M., and P. Atkinson. (1983). *Ethnography: Principles in practice*. New York: Routledge.

Hanssen, E. (1987). The social creation of meaning: Learning as a dialogic process. Dissertation proposal, Indiana University, Bloomington, IN.

Harste, J. C. (1989). The future of whole language. *The Elementary School Journal* 90(2):243–249.

———. (1992, November). Changing views of research. Paper presented at the annual fall meeting of the National Council of Teachers of English, Louisville, KY.

Harste, J. C., and K. G. Short, with C. Burke. (1988). *Creating classrooms for authors: The reading-writing connection*. Portsmouth, NH: Heinemann.

Henson, J. (1993). The tie that binds: The role of talk in defining community. In *Cycles of meaning: Exploring the potential of talk in learning communities*, ed. K. M. Pierce and C. Gilles, 25–40. Portsmouth, NH: Heinemann.

Klassen, C. R. (1993). Teacher education that is multicultural: Expanding preservice teachers' orientation toward learning through children's literature. Ph.D. dissertation, University of Arizona, Tucson, AZ.

Lieberman, A. (1992). The meaning of scholarly activity and the building of community. *Educational Researcher* 21(6):5–12.

Modgil, S., ed. (1986). *Multicultural education: The interminable debate*. Philadelphia: The Falmer Press.

Murra, W. F. (1941). Have you read? *Social Education* 5(2):128–133.

Patterson, L., and J. C. Stansell. (1987). Teachers and researchers: A new mutualism. *Language Arts* 64(7):717–721.

Peterson, R., and M. Eeds. (1990). *Grand conversations: Literature groups in action*. New York: Scholastic.

Peterson, R. (1992). *Life in a crowded place: Making a learning community*. Portsmouth, NH: Heinemann.

Rogers, V. R., and R. H. Muessig. (1963). Needed: A revolution in the textbook industry. *The Social Studies* 54:169.

Short, K. G., and C. Klassen. (1993). Literature circles: Hearing children's voices. In *Children's voices: Talk in classrooms*, ed. B. Cullinan, 57–71. Newark, DE: International Reading Association.

Smith, F. (1986). *Insult to intelligence*. New York: Arbor House.

Stolz, M. (1988). *Storm in the night*. New York: Harper Trophy.

Yep, L. (1977). *Child of the owl*. New York: Harper Trophy.

10

RENÉE J. MARTIN

Multicultural Social Reconstructionism and the Secondary English Classroom

The primary purpose of this chapter will be to investigate the possibilities for teaching from a critical theoretical, and, by extension, multicultural social reconstructionist (MCSR), perspective within the confines of English methods courses. This chapter chronicles my own endeavors as a high school classroom teacher and my work as a multicultural teacher educator and suggests possibilities for the creation of what Peter McLaren has discussed as a "dialectical tension among theory, practice, and experience" (1989, 157). While there can be little doubt that schools of teacher education, and American public schools in general, are in need of massive institutional restructuring relative to diversity, this chapter asserts that the efforts of individual educators can add to a discourse that alters relationships of power and knowledge in order to provide challenging environments to interrogate the status quo thereby replacing what is with what might be. Further, it provides a point of intersection for theoretical constructs, classroom practice, and student and educator experiences.

THE TEACHER EDUCATION CONTEXT

There are numerous forces at work that make teaching from a MCSR perspective a difficult task. Lois Weis has cautioned that "practice in mainstream discourse has often meant the stipulation of workable programs, policies designed for operation within the rules and terms of existing institutional structures. Practice in this mainstream sense at best merely allows for incremental modifications necessary for the maintenance of existing institutional frameworks and power relationships"(1988, 31). For the most part, colleges of teacher education have inadequately addressed issues of diversity, failing to incorporate them within the entire spectrum of the curriculum. When multicultural education is included, it is most likely to be found in a single course often taught by people of color and/or untenured, female faculty members whose efforts are tokenized and marginalized. To complicate matters, teacher education students, most of whom are White, female, and middle class, lack adequate preparation to comprehend the complexities associated with issues of diversity and are therefore unable to unravel the pedagogical dilemmas that teaching about such issues demands. Perhaps nowhere is this dilemma better exemplified than in the English methods arena, where the average student and the average faculty member tend to be White, middle class, and female.

Teacher educators wage a two-front battle against ideological constraints and institutional constrictions. The lack of articulation of multicultural issues throughout the curriculum, the limited time frame in which we are forced to address "everything you always wanted to know about race, class, and gender but were afraid to ask," to paraphrase the pop culture saying, while simultaneously incorporating the basics of secondary English education present nearly insurmountable challenges. In addition, questions about diversity abound and have become fodder for speculation in the popular media as well as in educational circles. The general disdain for higher education coupled with misunderstanding and ignorance of multicultural issues promulgated by right wing ideologues and cult figures such as Rush Limbaugh and Phyllis Schlafley intervene and compete with our efforts. The advocacy of single sex schools for African American males, promotion of voucher systems in low income neighborhoods, debates over bilingual education, and sarcasm about political correctness divert attention from substantive issues and thwart multicultural education at all levels. It is not difficult to commiserate with bell hooks as she notes that "struggling to educate for liberation in the corporate university is a process…(that is) enormously stressful (1989, 102).

Most methods instructors and, in fact, most university professors are unacquainted with multicultural, nonsexist approaches to education. As noted earlier, English educators, because of their backgrounds, rely on a framework that teaches prospective educators to prepare their students for "appropriate participation in the political order…through the promotion of myths, history, and stories" that underscore and assure…"order, public civility, and conformity to laws" (Bennett and LeCompte 1990, 8).

Methods courses purportedly exist to bridge the roles of preservice and inservice teaching. Unfortunately, they tend to reinforce the role of the teacher as authoritarian and the role of the student as passive recipient. For the most part, they promote notions of noncollaborative, rugged individualism, leaving entry level teachers vulnerable to the same pitfalls as those of their predecessors. Most such courses rob the neophyte educator of the "dignity to risk" (Wolfensberger 1972) and thrust them into a polarized state where they are told their word is law, that there are a finite number of approaches or answers to any question, and in which their histories and those of their predecessors as educators are obliterated. Prospective teachers are seldom exposed to compelling accounts of classroom life; instead, they are introduced to a narrow range of "methods" that fail to scrutinize inherent complexities and conflicts present in contemporary classrooms. Students in methods courses are taught to circumnavigate the rough waters of alternative ideological paradigms and controversial educational issues. Remaining on course means sticking to a prescribed curriculum, employing standardized tests, maintaining order in the classroom, teaching the "classics," and perpetuating the exclusive use of standard English.

GREAT EXPECTATIONS

This work is informed by my practice as a first year secondary English teacher in a small rural/suburban, mostly middle-class, White community in Wisconsin. Christine Sleeter and Carl Grant (1993) have noted the importance of linking the biographies of students and teachers to the teaching and learning process. This portrait expands upon that notion by integrating biographical anecdotal incidents of my teaching with possibilities for transformative pedagogy in secondary English and, by extension, English methods classrooms.

My experiences were not unlike those of the dozens of student teachers whom I have supervised in all content areas. While my own undergraduate teacher preparation exposed me to some human relations and multicultural issues which opened a new range of possibilities, I was unprepared for the extent to which my efforts would be hampered by the ideological constraints of the public schools in which I taught. My own dilemmas are recounted here in order to exemplify ways in which teacher educators might confront pedagogical issues related to diversity, thereby calling into question dominant ideology and methodology. Susan Adler and Jesse Goodman have noted that the potential to relate methods courses that are thought provoking and challenging "can be realized only if educators develop courses from a sound theoretical understanding of schooling and society that takes into full account the complexity of teaching, and describe their efforts to develop substantive methods courses so that our knowledge of this complement within teacher education can be enriched" (1986, 2).

My initial high school teaching experiences might have been subtitled *Great Expectations*. On the opening day of school, a student whom I had never seen, entered my first hour class, tossed a book on his desk, and announced "I hate English." This student's attitude, I was later to learn, was not atypical. He bluntly informed me that he had never read a book in his life, did not intend to, and that he had no use for all that "punctuation and spelling stuff." It became apparent to me that what was happening in most secondary English classrooms occurred in isolation from students' lives and that not much had been done to capitalize upon their interests, biographies, or diversity. The secondary English curriculum in the school in which I taught had been in place for twenty or more years and had experienced only minor alterations. Opportunities to experiment with alternative forms of pedagogy such as MCSR or to transform the curriculum were few, and those who sought to challenge the existing paradigm were often marginalized.

The prevailing structural functionalist atmosphere was typified by several early encounters I had with the chairperson of my department. For example, I chose to teach *Macbeth* rather than *Julius Caesar* to my sophomore classes. Although *Macbeth* was not being taught in any other courses, the chairperson informed me that *Julius Caesar* was the play chosen for sophomores. I explained that I wanted my students to read a play that included strong roles for women as well as men, one which I felt would have wider appeal, at which point she commented emphatically that "Julius Caesar is *the* sophomore play." With a smiling, I responded that I must have missed the part in the play's introduction where Shakespeare acknowledged that he had written the play for sophomores. She followed my comment with an admonition that she certainly hoped that I was capable of taking my teaching seriously. It was indeed my impression that I was the one who understood the impact of my work on the learning and lives of my students. While this confrontation may appear minor, it raised several issues for me. It illustrated the rigidity and inflexibility within the established paradigm, it called into question the relationships of power between me and more senior faculty, and it served as a basis for me to question my goals relative to issues of diversity. It was merely a precursor to the pedagogical dilemmas which I would regularly encounter.

Not long after the aforementioned incident, I discovered several boxes of unopened books in an office adjacent to my classroom. They contained copies of novels by Richard Wright and James Baldwin. When I asked the chairperson of the department in which courses the books were being used, she simply said, "None, we don't have any minorities here and our kids really aren't interested in that sort of thing." Her comment foreshadowed the later work by Grant and Sleeter (1993) regarding the five most common approaches to teaching about race, class, and gender. The scenario supported their premise (when they discuss the approach Teaching to the Exceptional or Culturally Different) that exposure to racial and ethnic groups other than those represented in the school system is often viewed as unnecessary or conflictive. My advocacy of literature, drama, and poetry by women and people of color was a radical departure from the teaching of my predecessor, a woman who had held the position for thirty years and who was well-liked by students, parents, and grandparents whom she had taught in our community.

STUDENT RESISTANCE

The ideological battles I encountered in my high school teaching were not limited to contestations with other department members. I was underprepared for the resistance from students who had heavily invested in the dominant paradigm's conventional roles for students and teachers. Hooks has written, "when one provides an experience of learning that is challenging, possibly threatening, it is not entertainment, or necessarily a fun experience, though it can be" (1989, 103). Students dislike the unpredictable and find alternative paradigms threatening. When confronted with racism, sexism, classism, and homophobia, many rely upon their individual experiences and assume that they, as individuals, are being blamed or held up to ridicule. The classroom is a dynamic and constantly changing environment, where the challenge is to maintain the unpredictable nature of knowledge reflective of life in contemporary society, while offering students options for meaningful social action in which they can come to an understanding of systemic, institutionalized oppression. Preparing students for the real world is not a task that can be prescribed or codified. Doing so often means fragmenting existing pedagogical practices and upsetting business as usual. This may take the form of minor pedagogical strategies such as "interior decorating," creating nontraditional seating arrangements, designed to facilitate discourse and interaction among students from a variety of races, ethnic backgrounds, lifestyles, and genders; allowing students to move freely about the classroom; ameliorating power differentials by encouraging them to speak without raising their hands to ask for permission; or simply displaying nontraditional materials representative of the cultural diversity in American society. It may mean altering student and teacher relationships by offering a wider range of choices for how to do assignments, how to take exams, and how to evaluate performance. For example, I sometimes gave traditional exams; however, as an option I formulated cooperative groups that included students of both genders and a range of abilities who were able to discuss and engender numerous responses to essay questions, dilemmas, or problems posed in the exam. Written papers were an integral part of assigned work; however, students often edited, reflected upon, and reacted to each other's work.

Engaging in alternative pedagogical strategies sometimes provoked resistance. Those most vehemently opposed to such changes were students in college-bound or "honors" classes who had been indoctrinated and rewarded for their participation in dominant ideology. Challenging the dominant paradigm had implications for their success, and it was difficult for them to admit that they had benefited from an inequitable or unjust system. Most students learn to be actively passive, to dismiss the experiences of peers as unimportant, and to rely on individualistic, competitive strategies for success. To ameliorate these behaviors students need numerous exemplars and time to practice being democratic in the classroom, just as they had been given years of practice in dominant discourse.

There was ample resistance to learning anything that had not been included in the curriculum by my colleagues or my predecessor. In order to diminish resistance, I blended two approaches to curriculum construction, one which organized the year by literary genre and one that organized it around issues of diversity. The former approach was explicit and satisfied the demands of the school hierarchy (a department chairperson who advocated a prescribed curriculum and the principal who required weekly detailed lesson plans). Embedded in each of the activities pertaining to literary genre, grammar, and the technical elements of English were issues of diversity in American society.

INCORPORATING ISSUES OF DIVERSITY: ANECDOTAL ILLUSTRATIONS

It is my belief that students tend to be most receptive to issues for which they feel some affinity; therefore, in my high school English classes I began with a unit on ableism. In our district special education students were mainstreamed, some of them had been harassed in our high school, and the topic was one that had been addressed in the student newspaper. It helped that the textbook for the course contained stories about Helen Keller and a young man with disabilities who had learned to type with his feet.

There was also a short story about two boys who had recently acquired their drivers' licenses. In it, the boys arrive at a local mall during a rainstorm and decide to park in a space designated for people with disabilities which is located near the mall entrance. Students were told to read the story as homework and to reflect upon whether they agreed or disagreed with the decision that the boys had made. When they arrived in my class the next day, I asked them to take a "pop quiz" about the story, stipulating that they should all write the answers with their left hands. After their initial looks of incredulity, I began to read a list of questions. As they wrote the responses to the questions, I wandered throughout the room commenting on their writing ability, the inordinate amount of time that some of them were taking to write the answers, and their neatness or the lack thereof. Several people became upset and noted that some students were already left-handed and that writing with their left hands was not fair. Some felt that left-handed students should be required to switch hands also. After a few minutes, we discarded the quiz (having agreed that the members of the class would gain the quiz points through discussion), and I asked them how they felt about what had happened. In one class, an argument broke out between two boys, one left-handed and the other right-handed. The left-handed student recalled other times in his life when he had been teased because of his perceived lack of ability as a right-handed writer. Students recollected that teachers in early elementary grades had forced them to use their right hands, and one even remembered being punished for writing with her left hand. We discussed ways in which they felt that society advantages right-handed individuals. The next day students brought examples of how right-handed implements, appliances, automobiles, and numerous other tools functioned to favor "righties." We brainstormed possible projects and activities regarding ableism, and each student chose, from among the list, one that she or he wished to research, write about, and present to the class. Some students investigated opportunities for physically challenged persons to negotiate our school building, others wrote letters to businesses that did not have facilities for physically challenged people, while some assessed the role of media in the perpetuation of physical and mental handicaps. Another group wrote a positive short story about a teen with a disability.

One of the most valuable aspects of that particular unit was the way in which students gained confidence to draw upon their own experiences and to make inferences from what we had read and researched for their own lives. In their journals, students spoke of their fears regarding the impact of drug use on their futures as parents who might produce children with birth defects. A student who had lost his arm in a farm machinery accident at the age of four discussed his struggles and told me privately that he felt much more a part of the class than he ever had because no one had ever given him the opportunity to discuss the accident with his peers. This student later became the first student with a disability to play basketball on our high school team. Another student brought her five-year-old Downs Syndrome brother along with her citizen activist parents to school, and they spent the day with my classes enlightening us about the syndrome and debunking myths about mental handicaps.

In a later activity, we read *Johnny Got His Gun* (Trumbo 1970), a story about a young soldier in World War I who lost his limbs, his eyesight, and his ability to communicate verbally. His struggles became ours. We investigated what it would mean to someone his age to be motionless, unable to communicate for several months. In order to get students to comprehend his struggle, I moved all of the desks to the sides of the room and asked students to lie on their backs with their eyes closed for five minutes. When they thought that five minutes had elapsed they were to quietly return to their seats. Most only lasted about a minute; however, they wrote about what they thought it might mean to be isolated in the society and discussed how they had taken such basic concepts as the passage of time, relationships with family and friends, and their own physical capabilities for granted. We also invited a paraplegic veteran of the then recent Vietnam War to discuss his experiences with our classes. In preparation, we read poetry written by and about soldiers and victims of World War II, and students wrote about their concerns over going to war and its possible outcomes. They questioned the draft, whether or not wealthy people had been able to buy their way out of military service, and the roles of women and people of color in the military. Today numerous topics such as the Tailhook incident, the harassment of a female Annapolis cadet who was tied to a urinal, the battle over whether or not to comply with Title IX and admit women to The Citadel in South Carolina, and the general lack of other than token people of color at the upper echelons of the military are topics that could easily be incorporated into a similar lesson.

NOVEL APPROACHES

A unit which began with the basic elements of the novel almost turned the classroom into a combat zone. As I wrote three basic types of plot on the board, person versus person, person versus nature, person versus the self, I listened to my sophomore students grumble. "Hey, Miss Martin," one of them volunteered. (Despite my repeated and obvious use of the title Ms., none of them was willing to engage in the use of what they considered to be a liberated designation.) "That's not right," the gangly sophomore continued. "It's s'posed to be man versus man, man versus nature, and man versus himself." I replied that I thought that it would be best to use words that were nonsexist and more inclusive. With that, several of the female students began to balk. As I later learned, "feminist" teachers were not highly regarded by teenage women in that high school. I then asked the class if they would be more comfortable with descriptors that more fully represented the population, and the response was a resounding "Yes". I erased the writing on the board and replaced it with woman versus woman, woman versus nature, and woman versus the self, explaining that these descriptions would be more appropriate, since 53 percent of the population is female. It immediately drew comments from the male students such as "I don't want to be called a girl," and "I ain't no sissy!" This provided a natural entré into a discussion of sexist language which was to permeate our work throughout the remainder of the year. We discussed how the boys felt about being referred to with feminine descriptors, and we discussed the fact that much of the misogyny predicated in the culture is homophobic. While they were clearly uncomfortable with a discussion of homophobia, a topic which I was aware was risky in a school district in which fundamentalist religious groups had removed books from the school's library, I observed that they were willing to engage in the discussion, perhaps because, as one student later put it, "I've never talked about any of this stuff in school, and it's kind of interesting."

The girls in the class noted that they did not mind being referred to via the use of masculine descriptors as long as they were accorded traditional feminine privileges (having the boy pay for a date, having someone open doors for them, etc.) However, as they became aware of statistics about jobs and wages, much of their skepticism about nonsexist language turned into anger and frustration with the injustices perpetuated by a culture that honors the lives and accomplishments of men more than women.

We discussed the gutter-pedestal syndrome (Tavris and Wade 1984) and the ways in which it is reflected in the roles of women in literature. We began with a discussion of favorite fairy tales and of the roles ascribed to women and men, moved to a discussion of contemporary soap operas, and later to women in novels. Students rewrote contemporary soap operas and fairy tales retaining the meaning and plot but revising sexist roles and language. One group portrayed a cleverly written twist on *Cinderella* which they titled Cinderfella, while another group converted the Erica Kane character of the soap opera *All My Children* into a man.

Thematic, social issues overlapped in numerous ways with our reading throughout the year. Once we had defined ableism as an issue of oppression, students better understood sexism, classism, and racism. For example, in one of the fairy tales that students wrote they included a physically challenged character and an African American. There is not enough space in this chapter to discuss the full evolution of the course; however, a few more examples are pertinent.

Among the novels we read was *To Kill A Mockingbird*, which is frequently used to portray racism in the culture. Harper Lee's writing is rich in sexist metaphors which students can be encouraged to locate and deconstruct. Both racism and sexism surface as issues in the book, which serves as an ideal vehicle for a discussion of the interconnectedness of issues of oppression. Further, it is a book frequently read in high schools and one with which young women as well as young men can identify. One of the problems that remains largely unaddressed in secondary English classes is the proliferation of literature that students read written by men about their lives and experiences. Novels by or about women, it is feared, will not hold the interest of teenage boys, so women authors are frequently disregarded. Developing an appreciation and understanding of the oppression of women and their work can be achieved if male students become aware of the ways in which sexism (as well as racism, classism, etc.) negatively affect their lives.

In *To Kill A Mockingbird* students were able to identify with Atticus Finch and the moral and ethical imperatives that were part of his struggle. In addition, they questioned the stereotypic demands made upon Scout and other female characters, and they empathized with Tom, the African American, who was unjustly accused of a crime. Students read newspaper accounts of trials and compared and contrasted them with the one in the book. Today, students might compare and contrast cases such as Rodney King's and Reginald Denny's or those of William Kennedy Smith and Mike Tyson. The book provided an interesting segue for the reading of the previously mentioned works by Baldwin and Wright and later led us into a discussion about social class structure, at which point we read F. Scott Fitzgerald's *The Great Gatsby*.

The vapid, meaningless lives of the elite Daisy Buchanan and Jay Gatsby and the objectification of women provide myriad opportunities for discussions of poverty, wealth, and status. Today, in conjunction with the novel, teachers might use the film *Roger and Me* which provides a contemporary look at the auto industry and its impact upon the lives of working-class citizens in the city of Flint, Michigan, as it continues to be embroiled in economic and class struggles. In the film, several auto industry magnates attend a Gatsby party, and the arrogance with which they address the struggles of the workers who have been responsible for their largesse is significant. Students whose families have been affected by runaway factories, or, in our case, students whose family farms had been swallowed up by large agribusinesses, readily embrace the issues in the novel and are able to understand the intersection of power and culture that produces and stratifies various social conditions.

Finally, the novel *Grapes of Wrath* can also be used to address issues that plague low-income, migrant workers. The struggles of John Steinbeck's characters parallel conditions that Mexican-American migrant workers encounter in contemporary society. Since a large number of the high school students whom I taught were from rural families, the book struck a personal chord. Numerous innovative projects such as one student's description of the process of a vegetable grown, picked by migrant workers, and marketed, a story he entitled *My Life as a Tomato*, emerged. Others read and wrote poetry about farm life and interviewed grandparents and parents about their farms' histories. The book led us to work by the late Cesar Chavez and other contemporary Hispanic American authors.

IMPLICATIONS FOR ENGLISH METHODS COURSES

Elizabeth Ellsworth has written that "critical pedagogues are always implicated in the very structures that they are trying to change" (1989, 3). Implicit in this discussion of how to make a complex theoretical position such as multicultural social reconstructionism meaningful is the assumption that teacher educators must first come to understand the ways in which they are raced, classed, and gendered subjects who have internalized and acted out oppressive pedagogy. As Audre Lorde reminds us "the true focus of revolutionary change is never merely the oppressive situations which we seek to escape, but that piece of the oppressor which is planted deep within each of us" (1984, 123).

Restructuring of English methods pedagogy therefore implies that we deconstruct how we have incorporated cultural norms, standards, and values into the choices that we make. We must investigate the messages that we send to prospective educators about what is and what is not a "classic" piece of literature and the purported values of such works, what types of language we revere as appropriate or inappropriate, and the styles of writing that we value.

Knowledge and practice must be reconfigured to represent the complexities of intervening ideologies and power relationships. All sites of domination, and schools in particular, are shaped by the contours of the experiences of people as individuals and as members of numerous microcultural groups in the society. Teacher education students must be taught how to cultivate an appreciation for the diversity of experience and knowledge that is to be gained from reading novels, poetry, and other literature by and about women and people of color. We ought not to be intimidated by cultural or irresponsible pedagogical practice that causes us to select works by male authors because "that's all that high school boys will read." Doing so underestimates their potential to think critically and to become agents for significant social change and robs them of the dimensions of a representative curriculum.

Deborah Britzman has written that "knowledge and practice are presented as dualism. This separation tends to mystify the actual and potential relations between 'how' and 'what' and limits pedagogy to mechanical transmission" (1991, 37). We cannot continue to permit teacher education students to think of themselves as rugged individuals who may sink or swim with every stroke of their teaching performance. Nor can we permit them to continue to be mesmerized by the glare of the obvious mechanistic models of teaching and learning that have prevailed in the past.

Examples such as the ones discussed in this chapter can be used in methods courses to illustrate that the cultural context in which students live provides valuable pedagogical opportunities. In addition, teacher education students must be taught the relevance of the intersection of knowledge, culture, power, and ideology. Using work by Kathleen Bennett and Margaret LeCompte (1990) and Sleeter and Grant (1993) can lay the theoretical groundwork for theories of social transmission and social transformation and comprehending the potential impact each can have upon teaching and learning. The use of teaching anecdotes helps students deconstruct pedagogical dilemmas that they and their predecessors will or have faced and enables prospective educators to contextualize theoretical positions that may impair or enable them to become effective.

Methods instructors must continue to research and theorize about educational practice. Ethnographic studies, analyses of students' journals about their experiences in the student teaching and field experience classrooms, and research by and about entry level educators in the area of English education must be incorporated into methods courses if the field is to begin to accommodate the diversity in American public schools.

Understanding the intersection of theory, practice, and experience enables us to move beyond reification of the traditional into the realm of meaningful pedagogy that will hold greater promise for learner involvement and academic success.

REFERENCES

Adler, S., and J. Goodman. (1986). Critical theory as a foundation for methods courses. *Journal of Teacher Education* 35(4):2–5

Bennett, K., and M. LeCompte. (1990). *How schools work.* New York: Longman.

Britzman, D. (1991). *Practice makes practice.* Albany, NY: SUNY Press.

Ellsworth, E. (1989). Why doesn't this feel empowering? *Harvard Educational Review* 59(3):297–324.

Fitzgerald, F. S. (1925). *The Great Gatsby.* New York: Scribner & Sons.

Lee, H. (1960). *To kill a mockingbird.* Philadelphia: Lippencott.

hooks, b. (1989). *Talking back: Thinking feminist thinking Black.* Boston: South End Press.

Lorde, A. (1984). *Sister outsider.* Trumansberg, NY: The Crossing Press.

McLaren, P. (1989). *Life in schools.* New York: Longman.

Shapiro, S. S., and D. E. Purpel. (1993). *Critical social issues in American education.* New York: Longman.

Sleeter, C. E., and C. A. Grant. (1993). *Making choices for multicultural education: Five approaches to race, class, and gender.* Columbus: Merrill.

Tavris, C., and C. Wade. (1984). *The longest war: Sexism in perspective.* San Diego: Harcourt Brace Jovanovich.

Trumbo, D. (1970). *Johnny got his gun.* New York: Bantam Books.

Weis, L. (1988). *Class, race, and gender in American education.* Albany, NY: SUNY Press.

Wolfensberger, W. (1972). *Normalization: The principle of normalization in human services.* Canada: The National Institute on Mental Retardation.

11

MARILYNNE BOYLE-BAISE _____

Teaching Social Studies Methods
from a Multicultural Perspective

I am a multicultural educator first and a social studies professor second; I specialize in curriculum and instruction from a multicultural perspective, but I teach social studies methods as well. There are several reasons for this. I teach in a regional, state university where the education faculty is small and we tend to do a little of everything. This means we teach several of the required methods courses that are central to our program. My background in multicultural studies was considered a "natural" fit with, and an important perspective for, social studies teaching and learning. As a result, my teaching assignment includes a social studies methods course for the K–9 level, and I have spent the last four years learning to be a multicultural social studies educator.

Our teacher education program defines reflective teaching as a program goal. To me, reflection means thinking about one's actions in terms of long-term goals for equality, equity, and social justice (Zeichner 1981–1982). To stimulate this type of reflection within my social studies methods course, I work toward building critical consciousness about issues related to race, ethnicity, social class, and gender.

In addition, program faculty are committed to including multicultural information in all of their courses; however, a course specifically oriented to multicultural education is not required. Students, for the most part, have limited experience with a multicultural orientation when they begin methods courses. To integrate multicultural and social study, I work toward building a multicultural social studies perspective about issues related to citizenship in a pluralistic, democratic society.

A critical and multicultural orientation toward citizenship form two over-arching "ways of thinking" that are emphasized in my methods course. I assume that the readers of this chapter will be well-versed within the social studies but unfamiliar with a critical multicultural perspective. The objective of this chapter is to provide insight into the integration of this perspective within the social studies by focusing on the curriculum-in-use in my social studies methods course. First, foundations for critical multicultural social study are described. Second, strategies infused with a critical multicultural perspective are delineated. The reader is encouraged to consider my teaching as I do—as unfinished learning experiences—and engage with these experiences as struggles to reconsider social studies teaching.

LAYING FOUNDATIONS FOR MULTICULTURAL SOCIAL STUDIES

The students in my methods course are mostly white women who bring to class certain expectations for teaching and learning. With few exceptions, they expect the professor to be the primary source of information, determine what and how they learn, and serve as sole evaluator for their work. They have not had much experience questioning authors and consider the written word truth rather than opinion. They are quiet and passive and sit in the same seats for each class.

These students personify the effects of a "banking education" (Friere 1970) in which teachers make deposits of predetermined information into the supposedly empty vaults of students' minds. Frances Maher (1989) argues that women students are especially harmed by banking education because knowledge is dominated by information about men and instruction is oriented toward masculine styles of learning. Banking education is antithetical to multicultural education, which is based on reconsideration of what counts as valid knowledge and appropriate instruction.

In order to counteract banking education and model multicultural education, I use critical teaching methods to motivate a questioning posture among students (e.g., Friere 1970; Shor 1980; Giroux 1983; Gordon 1985; Maher 1989). Maher provides a clear description of critical teaching for women students that she calls "interactive pedagogy" (1989, 496). This approach centers around interactions among teacher and students which foster diverse points of view and connect student experience to subject matter. This approach depends upon establishing a safe space in which discussion may blossom and alternative views may be heard.

It is a continual challenge to jar students from norms of passivity. I set and discuss standards for the class which include interactive pedagogy, safe space, "self-as-subject" (Maher 1989, 498) and critical posture. In addition, experiences are provided (e.g., interviewing each other, sharing snacks for break-time, and assigning break-groups) that acquaint students and begin to build collegiality. Also, I introduce techniques for participating in discussions, for example, listening actively and encouraging group members to speak.

One of the major stumbling blocks for interactive teaching is traditional norms for grading. Students are not willing to participate in novel teaching processes and yet be graded traditionally. I have taken the following steps away from traditional norms: a take-home midterm exam includes a selection of essay questions, mini-inquiries (field research) are not graded but credited according to certain standards, and the development of units of study may be completed with a partner for a shared grade. It would be desirable to consider additional strategies for giving authority to students for grading.

After establishing instructional parameters, students are challenged to consider their ideological stances toward social studies teaching. Discussing the following questions helps them to outline their perspectives and begin to realize their positions are not value-free.

1. What does it mean to be a good citizen in a pluralistic, democratic society?
2. What does it mean to teach citizenship for U.S. society?
3. What knowledge is important to teach in elementary social studies?
4. What skills are important to teach in elementary social studies?
5. What do you think about teaching values in social studies?
6. What do you think about including controversy in social studies?

Working in small groups, students analyze and report common and variant responses to these questions. The emergence of belief sets the stage for the intro-duction of paradigmatic thinking (Kuhn 1970) related to the social studies. I describe two varying camps in simplistic terms: "Essential and Mainstream Thinking" and "Critical and Multicultural Thinking." The first is characterized as the transmission of traditional knowledge and values through banking education; the second is described as the promotion of multiple points of view through inter-active pedagogy.

For delineating the critical multicultural paradigm in a manner particularly suited to the social studies, I have found Walter Parker and John Jarolimek's monograph on citizenship education extremely useful. Parker and Jarolimek define citizenship education as "the special assignment of social studies educa-tion" (1984, 3). According to their definition, citizenship education is based on "three fundamental perspectives: a pluralist perspective, a global perspective, and a constructive perspective" (2). The pluralistic perspective is based on "disciplined respect for human differences—differences of all sorts but particularly of opinion and preference, of race, and religion, of ethnicity, and in general, of culture...as a desirable quality of democratic group life" (2). The global perspective "involves the willingness and ability...to think globally and act locally" (2). And, the constructivist perspective "involves competent participation in social, political, and economic processes as well as an ongoing critique of those processes" (2).

The development of such citizens is clearly aligned with the mission of multicultural education and links multicultural and social studies in a meaningful and powerful way. Two of the three concepts defined above, pluralism and constructivism, fit easily with critical and multicultural study. Global studies actually introduces international issues which differ in some ways from the concerns usually embraced by multicultural education. However, the considera-tion of local and global citizenship allows these differences and similarities to be introduced.

Another technique that helps students develop critical regard for social studies teaching is to present the curricular history of the social studies and examine each curricular period for evidence of the paradigms described above. For example, students usually find little regard for pluralism and constructivism within the traditional transmission-oriented social studies model. I consider the article by James Banks (in press) very helpful for this type of presentation. Banks describes the following four curricular periods and examines each one from a multicultural perspective: the traditional period, the social studies revolution of the 1960s and 1970s, the public issues and social participation period of the 1970s and 1980s, and the current emphasis on history-centered or multicultural curriculum. Locating their own schooling experiences within these periods helps students understand the roots of their perceptions about social studies teaching.

A helpful teaching tool for delineating the multicultural social studies perspective is the *Curriculum Guidelines for Multicultural Education* prepared by the National Council for the Social Studies (J. Banks 1992). This document presents a clear rationale for the promotion of pluralism through social studies education and provides numerous curricular guidelines. However, the guidelines are not easily understood without previous discussion of concepts such as cultural diversity and pluralism. Also, they are prescriptive and difficult to view with objectivity. For these reasons, I prefer to use them after laying the foundational groundwork detailed above.

PROVIDING STRATEGIES FOR MULTICULTURAL SOCIAL STUDIES

As students learn about the critical multicultural perspective and think about issues related to racism, classism, or sexism, they often feel overwhelmed and distressed by what they do not know. They worry about pluralizing content and developing interactive teaching techniques. They raise questions such as: what kind of bias is most important to eliminate, how can I make lessons pluralistic when I only know one side of the story, or how can I encourage student participation when I only remember memorizing facts? Teaching strategies that respond to these questions include: diversifying content, oral history, literature-based study, social issues study, and mini-inquiries.

Diversifying Content

Diversifying social studies content depends on the inclusion of multiple perspectives within the curriculum. While I have presented the notion of inclusion in numerous ways, the use of feminist standpoint theory provides a conceptual schema grasped easily by students. According to standpoint theory, there is no one stance that fully explains the "truth" of social reality, rather there are varying standpoints or social positions from which reality is perceived (e.g., Code 1991; Harding 1991; Riley 1992). The search for truth requires consideration of many standpoints, including minority and majority points of view.

Glenda Riley (1992) describes standpoint theory as a circle of perspectives on social reality. The way in which one defines reality depends on where one stands on the edge of the circle. To see reality more pluralistically requires understanding one's own position and trying to comprehend the position of another on the circle. While one's position may be grossly considered, such as a majority or minority point of view, points on the circle are indefinite and can be more finitely considered, such as a white, female, middle-class standpoint.

The students and I experiment with the circle metaphor in unit planning. We work together to plan units that present at least two standpoints. Most often this means investigating one minority view and comparing it to a majority standpoint. Examples of units of study that evolve from this planning include: investigating homelessness by visiting homeless centers and interviewing staff and occupants, researching information about the Chinese contribution to the Union Pacific Railroad, considering alternative definitions of the family, and examining Illinois history from the standpoint of John Deere's impact on Illinois agriculture.

Collecting Oral/Social History

Most students do not think about the standpoint from which they know history. To encourage students to consider their historical standpoint, a listing is made of their knowledge about a certain time period. Students find their knowledge centers around history about majority group men, military and political events, and extraordinary feats. Also, discussion of the notion of "his-story" emphasizes that history is someone's story, and use of "her-story" spurs realization that a fund of stories has been omitted from social studies texts. This realization is extended to include stories of people of color and common folk meeting the challenges of ordinary life.

One method for seeking a fuller and more accurate historical account is to use oral history techniques to collect social history information. This means interviewing people about the routines, leisure activities, and trials and tribulations of everyday life. An easy and accessible way to begin this type of investigation is to develop a recipe story.

Recipe stories capture the daily or special events centered around the making of a traditional family recipe. To complete a recipe story, students ask the oldest person in their immediate families to tell them about a recipe that has been a family favorite, describe how it was passed down to him or her, recall family occasions on which it was served, and share directions for making the dish. The stories are written up in first person narrative, which gives it the distinctive flavor of original speech.

Reading the stories aloud provides evidence of the wealth and diversity of family knowledge that can be gleaned from a fairly simple exercise. Students display interest and pride in their family stories, and these feelings are discussed. Also, time is spent considering extension activities for interesting leads in the recipe stories. Many students are surprised at the ease with which curriculum is made meaningful and pluralistic.

To capture the multicultural essence of the stories, probing questions, such as the following, are raised. What was the role of men and women in passing down this piece of family history? In what ways did race, ethnicity, and social class impact upon the dishes that became favorites? In telling about domestic life, whose story was told?

Developing Literature-based Social Studies

The increased availability of quality multicultural children's literature is a boon to the social studies. It may be used to reduce prejudice and stereotyping and increase self-esteem, overcome the biases and omissions in textbooks, and add relevance to the curriculum (C. M. Banks 1992; Pang et al. 1992). In addition, research shows that children learn history best when historical information is placed within meaningful contexts (Levstik 1986). Historical narratives provide such contexts by helping children imagine "being there" in history (Levstik 1989).

There are a number of ways to integrate multicultural literature and social studies. I have experimented with several strategies which include hosting multicultural literary societies, creating thematic booklists, and developing biographic studies.

To participate in a multicultural literary society, students are asked to read trade books for children or young adults, which include topics or themes related to cultural diversity. For this exercise the working definition of cultural diversity includes differences related to race, ethnicity, social class, gender, mental or physical ability, religion, first-language, and sexual orientation. Students are encouraged to look for literature written by and about people of color or members of the group referenced in the story.

The agenda for the society includes: discussing the books, hearing book presentations, sharing and exchanging books, and engaging in general literary conversations. The literary society provides a natural forum for the discussion of multicultural literacy and models a method for encouraging this form of literacy.

Thematic booklists are assigned as part of the field experience component of the course. For this project, students develop a thematic booklist around a social studies theme under study within their field placement classroom. They use the list to develop and teach a literature-based social studies lesson. An example of a thematic booklist for the theme "Pioneering" includes: *Wagon Wheels* by Barbara Brenner, *Justin and the Best Biscuits in the World* by Mildred Pitts Walter, and *Sarah Plain and Tall* by Patricia MacLachlan (Boyle-Baise, Gillette, and Grant 1991).

Some difficulties that students have experienced with this assignment may be instructive. In selecting books to represent multiple standpoints, students tend to focus on one form of difference in storylines and characters. For example, the central character is described as female, and her experience is seen through the lens of gender. The race, social class, and region of the character are usually overlooked. By reducing characters to one form of difference, students miss opportunities to consider the story in powerful ways. This problem is often aggravated by the literature itself; singular forms of difference are emphasized, while others stay in the background—part of the scene, but not central to the story.

I work with students to grapple with this type of reductionism in the following ways. I use the circle metaphor to show students that one's position is complicated by factors such as race, class, and gender. Also, I read literature selections aloud to the class and discuss varying aspects of diversity represented in the story.

A form of thematic study that is easily adapted to a multicultural perspective is biographic study. Research shows that elementary age children learn history by connecting with the lives of people who lived in the past (Levstik 1986). In addition, there is evidence that children's views of politics and government are highly personalized—they see leaders as particular people before coming to understand the abstract functions of leadership (Parker and Kaltsounis 1986). These findings point to the importance of introducing children to a pluralistic array of people who have contributed to U.S. society.

Biographical study usually centers around various themes of accomplishment, such as leaders, explorers, inventors, teachers, heroes, and heroines (Parker and Jarolimek 1984). To complete a biographical study, students select a manageable number of candidates for particular themes. To complete the study from a multicultural perspective, students search for candidates who are male, female, people of color, and the like.

The process of developing biographical studies can be used as another opportunity to encourage students to consider the impact of multiple group membership on a person's life. For example, candidates for the theme "Political Activists" may include Susan B. Anthony, Elizabeth Cady Stanton, Ida B. Wells Barnett, and Mary Church Terrell. Queries for students about these activists can include: what difference did it make that Susan B. Anthony was a White woman activist and Ida B. Wells was a Black woman activist, and what did these women have in common?

Social Issues Study

Many of the students I work with are not "socially engaged" or vitally interested in social issues. When I ask them, "What's in the news that relates to social studies?" I get limited responses. Yet, the social issues of today contain the quandries and controversies that should be at the heart of social studies as citizenship preparation (Longstreet 1993). From a multicultural perspective, social issues within current events are more likely to contain multiple viewpoints than stories rehashed in textbooks.

A first step in studying current issues is to motivate student awareness of the news. I encourage students to listen to National Public Radio or television news shows, such as McNeil and Lehrer, which present multiple points of view. Print media is acceptable, but without reading several sources it is difficult to glean more than one perspective. Students are asked to listen and watch for issues, information, and contributions that show evidence of attention to pluralistic concerns.

A second step is routinely including current events in methods classes. As mentioned above, I regularly pose the question "What's in the news?" at the beginning of class. This is followed by brainstorming ways in which news issues relate to citizenship preparation for elementary students.

The value/inquiry process provides a framework for the consideration of controversial issues. One useful model of the value/inquiry process is detailed in J. Banks' 1990 book and includes nine specific steps for examining issues and declaring preferences. A briefer framework found in the work of Jarolimek and Parker (1993) also provides workable guidelines for identifying the facts and issues of a case and considering and choosing possible solutions. To promote a multicultural focus for this exercise, current issues in which diversity plays a key role are used. For example, controversy about the separation of church and state between the state school board of New York and a Jewish community stimulated fertile class discussion.

Another strategy for addressing social issues is to hear personal accounts from people actively involved in them (Totten 1989). I organized a monthly Issues Forum for a multicultural seminar and invited social studies students to attend. Each month a team of students worked with me to select a current local issue, invite guests representing different viewpoints, and develop interview questions. As examples, one forum focused on the viability of a constitutional amendment about school funding and included state representatives from differing political parties. Another forum addressed the notion of inclusion with regard to special education and included special education teachers and a reform leader.

Using the forum permitted access to people as "living curricular resources" (Totten 1989, 114) and allowed in-depth questioning of those vitally concerned about a local issue. However, the organization of the forum was extensive and should be considered as a special event for a methods course.

Museum Study

Museums are often perceived as institutions that serve educated, middle- to upper-class people. In fact, familiarity with museums, like acquaintance with the fine arts and literature, is considered "cultural capital" or valued cultural knowledge (Bourdieu, cited in Giroux 1983). Also, museum displays have tended to be biased toward the views of the dominant group, for example, displaying the bones of Native people as curiosities but not doing the same with European Americans. However, museums are trying to change this image, become educational sites for general populations, and revise displays to represent a more diverse notion of the "truth" (Boyd 1993). For these reasons, museums are becoming a welcoming site for multicultural social studies.

A recently built museum in my locale chronicles the history of the Mississippi mound-building tribes and uses dioramas to give the visitor a sense of "being there" in history. I use this site for museum study and direct students to the benefits of realistic displays and accurate information about Native society in pre-Columbian times. A major limitation of such an exhibit is that it compounds commonly held student views that the culture of Native people is an artifact of the past. This is a partial portrait which should be balanced by information about the current lives and issues of Native people.

A new exhibit at our state museum promises to be an exciting site for museum study. The exhibit, *At Home In the Heartland*, features three centuries of Illinois family life. Material culture, such as oral histories, newspaper and magazine advertisements, and photographs provides clues to the past, and interactive computerized displays portray real-life families and simulate everyday decision making (Wass 1992).

I plan to use this exhibit for museum study and ask the following types of questions. To what extent do families represent the cultural mix of Illinois? What type of treatment is given to the complexities of diverse peoples living side by side? In what ways is family history relevant for children? In what ways can techniques used in this exhibit transfer to historical study in the classroom?

Mini-Inquiries

Our teacher education program integrates clinical experiences within methods courses to fulfill state requirements and provide opportunities to combine theory and practice. Often, activities are assigned that allow students some practice with techniques, such as teaching a small group or developing a display. I emphasize inquiry-based field research tasks that I call mini-inquiries. I use several types of inquiries, including neighborhood walks, bulletin board reviews, textbook analysis, teacher interviews, and curriculum-in-use studies. Textbook analysis and curriculum studies are described here.

Prior to the inquiry experience, the nature of field research is described. Terms like firsthand research, data collection, participant observation, and key-informant interviewing are defined and discussed. Data analysis is considered as a process of categorizing and collating information. A debriefing session is scheduled for the class following the field experience; the data students collect are analyzed and interpreted during this session.

To analyze social studies textbooks, students examine the rationale, text components (e.g., illustrations and chapter titles), and storyline. To study the rationale, students read this section in the teacher's manual and report the objectives for the text. The content of the text is reviewed by completing the following tallies:

1. count people in illustrations according to race, ethnicity, social class, and gender;
2. describe in detail two outstanding illustrations;
3. name chapter titles and concepts emphasized in each;
4. describe the nature of supplemental information;
5. read one chapter for examples of controversy; and
6. provide examples of assessment.

In addition, students read several chapters (depending on the length and level of the text) and ascertain the standpoint most fully presented within the storyline.

The data collected by students are collated by the questions assigned. Data are interpreted according to considerations such as the following: attention given to cultural groups, contrasts between primary and supplemental content, inclusion of conflict or controversy, level of thinking reflected in assessment, and standpoint emphasized in the storyline. In light of the findings of this exercise, textbooks are assessed as sources for multicultural social study.

To describe and analyze social studies curriculum-in-use, students interview their practicum teacher, asking questions such as: What are the main themes and concepts you are teaching this year? what instructional techniques do you prefer, and why? and what lesson did you enjoy teaching most this year, and why? Students observe and draw bulletin board displays and describe one lesson in detail. As part of this observation assignment, students are asked to provide evidence of attention to pluralism in the displays and lesson. Students then write an analysis of their observation in which they compare curriculum-in-use to curriculum proposed in methods class and consider the extent to which the teaching they observed promoted citizenship education.

The interview data collected by students are discussed in a question-by-question manner during the debriefing session. The observation data are grouped by school location, according to inner city, suburbs, or small towns. It is then analyzed for attention to cultural diversity, use of participatory teaching methods, and level of thinking required of students. Differences among each group are noted and discussed. This type of differentiation initiates consideration of the social context of learning.

SUMMARY AND CONCLUSIONS

This chapter is an examination of one professor's struggle with the implementation of multicultural social studies within a traditional teacher education program. The comments included here are written as a stimulus for conversation, certainly not as a definitive plan. A plan is not needed, rather we need to reconsider our definition of what counts in the social studies.

Teaching social studies from a multicultural perspective may require challenging the status quo. It is not sufficient to prepare students to teach social studies in a noncritical manner. Rather, students must learn to question business-as-usual and look, particularly, for biases, omissions, and stereotypes in traditional curriculum and instruction.

Reorienting social studies teaching in this manner is hindered by referring to the course primarily as "methods," which presupposes emphasis on how-tos. Students wonder why so much time is spent thinking about social studies teaching rather than learning to do it. It may be helpful to retitle the course, Multicultural Social Studies: Ideology and Practice.

It is very difficult to teach social studies from a multicultural perspective when students have minimal prior experience with the concepts and issues central to multicultural education. However, there are several ideas and ideals that can serve as heuristic tools for redefining social studies to include a multicultural agenda. The notion of paradigmatic thinking can be used to establish the existence of a value-loaded social studies teaching agenda. The concept of critique can be used to question normative social studies curricula. The ideal of pluralistic, constructive citizenship can be used to reconsider the purpose of teaching social studies. The theoretical posture of standpoint theory can be used to examine and revise cultural bias in historical, geographic, and civic accounting. The notion of interactive strategies can be used to motivate teaching grounded in discussing, inquiring, investigating, and analyzing.

It is important to infuse every aspect of the social studies with a multicultural orientation. This means taking a critical look at the foundations, curriculum, and instruction presented in methods courses. Foundations must be built around concepts of pluralism, equality, and equity. Curriculum must reflect the cultural diversity of society. Instruction must encourage participation for all students and teach activism and critique.

This type of orientation may "upset the applecart" of students' thinking. It has certainly challenged me to rethink what it means to teach "methods." It has required some willingness to take risks to grapple with the trials of a new approach for multicultural and social study.

REFERENCES

Banks, C. M. (1992). Shattering stereotypes and reducing prejudice with multiethnic literature. *Social Studies and the Young Learner* 5(2):6–8.

Banks, J. (1990). *Teaching strategies for the social studies: Inquiry, valuing, and decision-making.* New York: Longman.

———. (1992). Curriculum guidelines for multicultural education. *Social Education* 56(5):274–294.

———. (in press). Teaching social studies for decision-making and action. In *Campus and classroom: Making schooling multicultural,* ed. C. A. Grant and M. L. Gomez. Columbus, OH: Merrill.

Boyd, W. L. (1993). Museums as centers of learning. *Teachers College Record* 94(4): 761–770.

Boyle-Baise, M., M. Gillette, and C. A. Grant. (1991). *Multicultural education, The Leadership Letters.* New York: Silver, Burdett, and Ginn.

Code, L. (1991). *What can she know? Feminist theory and the construction of knowledge.* London: Cornell University Press.

Friere, P. (1970). *Pedagogy of the oppressed.* New York: Seabury Press.

Giroux, H. (1983). *Theory and resistance in education.* South Hadley, MA: Bergin and Garvey Publishers.

Gordon, B. (1985). Teaching teachers: "Nation at Risk" and the issue of knowledge in teacher education. *The Urban Review* 17(1):33–46.

Harding, S. (1991). *Whose science? Whose knowledge? Thinking from women's lives.* New York: Cornell University Press.

Jarolimek, J., and W. Parker. (1993). *Social Studies in elementary education.* New York: Macmillan.

Kuhn, T. S. (1970). *The structure of scientific revolutions.* Chicago: University of Chicago Press.

Levstik, L. S. (1986). Teaching history: A definitional and developmental dilemma. In *Elementary school social studies: Research as a guide to practice*, ed. V. Atwood, 68–84. Washington, DC: National Council for Social Studies.

————. (1989). Once upon a time past—History in the elementary classroom. *Social Studies and the Young Learner* 2(2):3–5.

Longstreet, W. S. (1993, November). Teaching strategies for a lesson which emphasizes decision making over merely remembering. Presentation at the annual meeting for the National Council for the Social Studies, Nashville, TN.

Maher, F. (1989). Women students in the classroom. In *Rereading America: Cultural contexts for critical thinking and writing*, ed. G. Colombo, R. Cullen, and B. Lisle, 493–504. New York: St. Martin's Press.

Pang, V. O., C. Colvin, M. Tran, and R. H. Barba. (1992). Beyond chopsticks and dragons: Selecting Asian-American literature for children. *The Reading Teacher* 46(3):216–224.

Parker, W., and J. Jarolimek. (1984). *Citizenship and the critical role of the social studies.* Washington, DC: National Council for the Social Studies.

Parker, W., and T. Kaltsounis. (1986). Citizenship and law-related education. In *Elementary school social studies: Research as a guide to practice*, ed. V. Atwood, 14–33. Washington, DC: National Council for the Social Studies.

Riley, G. (1992). *A place to grow: Women in the American West.* Prospect Heights, IL: Harlan Davidson.

Shor, I. (1980). *Critical teaching and everyday life.* Boston: South End Press.

Totten, S. (1989). Using oral histories to address social issues in the social studies classroom. *Social Education* 53(2):114–116 and 125.

Wass, J. T. (1992). At home in the heartland is an exhibit about...*The Living Museum* 54(4):52–53.

Zeichner, K. (1981–1982). Reflective teaching and field-based experience in teacher education. *Interchange* 12(4):1–22.

12

MOZELL P. LANG

Preparing Teachers For Multicultural Science Integration

.

A high incidence of low achievement exists among groups who are underrepresented in science. These groups include African Americans, Hispanics, Native Americans and females. The phenomenon of low achievement proliferates in classrooms throughout the nation and is one of the reasons why there is a need for exemplary multicultural science teacher education courses (Clewell, Anderson, and Thorpe 1992). The premise for the need is based upon the following factors: (1) negative attitude toward low achievers in science; (2) traditional approaches to science instruction, including rigid teaching strategies and uncreative techniques; (3) a view of science as an elitist discipline for only a few; (4) the image of science as the domain of white males; (5) role models, contributions, and perspectives in science without representation from diverse groups; and (6) context in science detached from cultural relevance.

Curriculum design and instructional strategies must visibly promote multicultural instruction for all students. Much effort should be directed toward the development of materials that will allow students to learn more about their culture and its contribution to the scientific enterprise. Emphasis on multicultural instruction promotes a more accepting and positive attitude toward other cultural groups and helps to reduce negative stereotypes and misconceptions. To achieve this goal, the curriculum must be carefully examined and redesigned to reflect the culturally diverse nature of science and effective teaching practices that support the diversity in the classroom. But this kind of integration is time-intensive and requires dedication to conducting research, finding resources, and gathering materials. This kind of effort is necessary, however, to produce a balanced curriculum and rich instruction.

Teacher educators often wonder how, or if it is even relevant, to consider preparing teachers to integrate multicultural concepts with science. This chapter will show how such integration can occur, by providing a model for multicultural science integration and illustrating that model with a unit. Each component of the model can serve as a focus for instruction in a science methods course, with a culminating activity being the requirement that students apply the model to the development of a science unit, like the unit presented in this chapter.

MULTICULTURAL INSTRUCTIONAL DESIGN COMPONENTS

The approach that follows delineates a curriculum and instructional design model that can be used in any content area. The model provides strategies for multicultural integration focusing on five major components that can be used as organizers for integrating multicultural science concepts. These categories are: (1) cultural perspectives, (2) sensitivity awareness, (3) context, (4) role models, and (5) motivational extensions.

Cultural perspectives document science through a group's traditions, characteristics, and scientific view of the world. Sensitivity awareness demonstrates an appreciation for other cultures and their disposition toward science, and for the strengths and difficulties of one's own students regarding science learning. Contexts feature science activities related to real world experience and cultural relevance. Role models feature significant contributions made by nontraditional scientists. And, finally, motivational extensions provide opportunities to reinforce pluralism, beyond the classroom, through empowerment toward sustained multicultural teaching and learning practices. This instructional design will empower teacher educators with a tool that will promote a more equitable teaching and learning classroom environment. At the heart of this effort is the goal of scientific literacy for all students.

This model is illustrated in figure 12.1. The right-hand column in figure 12.1 provides a space for applying each component to a particular science unit. Use of this model will be illustrated later in the chapter, after the model is explained in more detail.

Cultural Perspectives

Multicultural science education integration provides an opportunity to enrich the curriculum with science-related experiences and perspectives of diverse groups. It affirms the value of different cultures, fosters appreciation, improves self-esteem and academic achievement, and it is an important component in achieving the goal of literacy for all students. Multicultural science education serves to reduce prejudice and enhance cultural appreciation in the service of improved academic achievement of all students. Cultural perspectives should naturally permeate the curriculum in a variety of ways. These include experiences, traditions, and characteristics related to scientific endeavors seen through the eyes of those who reflect the spirit of a particular culture. Teacher educators can help preservice teachers explore cultural perspectives by starting with questions such as, How have people of African descent (or indigenous Americans, or people of Asian decent, etc.) approached the understanding of a particular natural phenomenon? As the example in this chapter illustrates, a great deal of material exists that can answer such a question, if one begins to look for it.

Sensitivity Awareness

Sensitive educators assume that science literacy is within reach of all students and that the responsibility for getting students to that point is at the heart of their role. Each student's scientific performance is evaluated on the basis of their opportunity to learn, their prior knowledge, their preparation, their economic background, and individual needs.

Figure 12.1

A Curriculum Design Model For Multicultural Science Integration

Category	Objective	Science
1. Cultural Perspectives	Convey science experiences through integrating cultural traditions, characteristics, and scientific view of the world.	
2. Sensitivity Awareness	Recognize strengths and deficiencies in students' performance and provide strategies on the basis of their opportunity to learn.	
3. Context	Anchor science activities in real world experiences based upon ethnic and cultural practices, attitudes, and traditions.	
4. Role Models	Showcase significant achievements made by women, minorities, and cultural groups.	
5. Motivational Extensions	Empower students by employing effective instructional strategies such as hands-on science, extended investigation, and cooperative learning. Apply science concepts to out-of-classroom learning opportunities to affirm multicultural connections.	

In designing curriculum and instruction, sensitivity awareness considerations are encouraged relative to diversity in the science classroom. This means recognizing the strengths and positive characteristics of each ethnic group and its importance to the scientific enterprise. Such recognition fosters mutual respect for all students and the cultures they represent. Preservice teachers can begin to develop sensitivity awareness by interviewing students to explore their interests, strengths, and experiences with science and to learn about strengths and resources in students' communities.

Context

Throughout history, underrepresented groups have found solutions to problems related to medicine, the environment, agriculture, architecture, the arts, sports, music, and philosophy. Science curriculum and instruction can recognize these discoveries through the context of real life experiences.

Instruction can include topics that have natural relevance to specific cultural mores. For example, Native Americans have a tradition of success in agriculture, stewardship to nature, astronomy, and food preservation. African Americans have a keen understanding of agriculture and have excelled in many areas of science through contributions and inventions. Hispanics have a rich history through storytelling and the asset of bilingual learning.

Role Models

Students are influenced by cues and stereotypes they view in the media, textbooks, and other learning materials. Positive role modeling can openly affirm pride in one's own culture and convey images that counteract the historical omission and underrepresentation of various ethnic groups in science.

Students and teachers can use the accomplishments of role models as a basis and reference point to motivate successful performance. For example, tracing the history of African Americans in science or the role of Native American environmental stewardship provides a balanced perspective and dispels notions of noncontribution. Integrating multicultural models into the curriculum helps all students to understand and appreciate various cultures and their accurate and appropriate representation in instructional materials.

Motivational Extensions

Research shows that learning can be more effective with hands-on approaches within and beyond the classroom (Froschl and Sprung 1991). Students should engage in investigative science regularly and actively. Much learning occurs beyond the classroom, as students can be encouraged to seek out information in their communities. Appropriate extension and application activities can support classroom multicultural instruction and take advantage of natural and cultural opportunities that are available in the students' environment. Students can gain information from local experts and written material as well. Some examples include interviewing the elderly about their farming practices, medical treatment, storytelling, and weather predictions and shadowing minority role models in scientific professions.

Another effective motivational tool is the use of interactive study groups and cultural support groups. The collaborative learning process can promote understanding and appreciation for individuals and their perspectives. The beneficial outcomes include cooperatively working together, sharing ideas, focusing on a goal, and improving achievement. Finally and most importantly, motivational extensions help students develop empowerment and decision-making and problem-solving skills to become effective agents of change in today's technological and multicultural society.

Following is a unit on weather, which demonstrates for preservice teacher educators ways to facilitate each component. To learn to use this design, preservice teachers can be organized into teams based on their interest to explore one of the multicultural components. They may decide to (1) expand weather examples in each of the components, (2) develop component strategies for another unit, or (3) create a new model that will achieve similar results—namely, a systematic approach to multicultural integration. Once an instructional design is in place, such as the model discussed in this chapter, and preservice teachers have learned to use it, multicultural science integration can become a systemic process.

OUTLINE OF A WEATHER UNIT WITH MULTICULTURAL INTEGRATION

Weather plays an important role in students' daily lives. It can have a severe impact on human activities, including food production, transportation, water supplies, and recreation. An understanding of weather and its impact on human activities is an important component of scientific literacy. It allows preparation for extreme weather conditions and, to some extent, diminishes the harshest consequences of severe weather.

Descriptions of weather are heard or read almost daily in the media. While the specifics of weather vary from season to season in most of the United States, daily weather reports typically contain several key components, including temperature, wind speed and direction, cloud cover and precipitation, humidity, and barometric pressure. These components are used to describe the existing weather, to describe typical changes in weather as the seasons progress, and to predict the development of storms and other hazardous weather conditions.

A scientific understanding of weather rests on an image of the atmosphere as a dynamic blanket of air completely covering an extremely large, spherical earth. This dynamic expanse of air has regions of various temperatures and humidities that are constantly moving and interacting (Michigan State Board of Education, 1991).

Objectives

The focus of this unit is: What causes different types of weather? The objectives of the unit will differ from one level of education to the next. After outlining objectives for each level, this chapter will develop the unit, using the model described above.

Elementary. At this level, the main objective of a unit on weather is for students to learn to describe weather conditions and climates. As students' understanding of the atmosphere develops, their descriptions of weather can become increasingly more complex. In the elementary grades, students' descriptions of weather and climates should include at least its visible aspects—temperature, wind speed and direction, cloud cover, and precipitation. They should be able to use a thermometer and a wind vane to observe and record outdoor conditions. Their descriptions of seasonal changes should also include these components.

Middle School. At the middle-school level, the main objective for students is to describe patterns of changing weather and how these patterns are measured. By middle school, as students come to understand the molecular nature of the atmosphere, their descriptions of weather should begin to include the unseen components of humidity and pressure. As they describe changing patterns of weather—sudden temperature changes, changes in cloud cover, and the development of storms—they begin to think in terms of the movements of air masses, cold fronts, and warm fronts. They can begin to use several common weather instruments, as well as interpret satellite images and weather maps.

High School. At this level, the main objectives are to have students describe patterns of air movement in the atmosphere and how they affect weather conditions as well as explain and predict general weather patterns and storms. By high school, students should develop a view of the atmosphere that includes prevailing winds and the jet stream. They begin to use these phenomena in their descriptions of daily weather changes and their interpretations of daily weather reports.

Content Area Integration

The weather unit that follows is interdisciplinary, although the main discipline is science. Preservice teachers should be helped to see connections among disciplines and to develop units that integrate content areas. Mathematical skills can be integrated throughout the study of weather. A few examples include accurate measurement of wind direction and speed, precipitation, humidity and pressure, data collection from maps, graphs, charts, and satellites. The study of weather and climate related to latitude, longitude, and geographical areas are anchored in mathematical concepts. Children's literature is also integrated into this unit, in the forms of children's books about weather and books about famous scientists.

Multicultural Integration

Students at all levels should begin to conceptualize that different cultures often respond to weather conditions in different ways due to geographical location, access to technology, and customs. A comprehensive study of the weather would include cultural perspectives related to prediction, measurement, and weather data collection instruments. Instruction would encourage sensitivity awareness, context, role models, and motivational extensions to affirm the value of different cultural experiences, contributions, and achievements. Preservice teachers may have very little background for integrating multicultural content into a science unit. After they have worked through a unit such as the following, they will have a grasp of what can be done with a science unit and will have learned some multi-cultural content about weather.

Column three in figure 12.2 suggests teaching strategies for implementing each component of the model. The following activities are illustrations of each multicultural component of the weather unit.

COMPONENT #1—CULTURAL PERSPECTIVES

CULTURAL WEATHER PREDICTION PRACTICES

The main objective of activities in Component #1 is for students to learn about weather prediction practices from the scientific views of the world of different cultural groups. Before the development of modern weather instruments and equipment, many elders in the early African American cultures were known for their ability to predict the weather. Many were careful observers of the atmosphere. They paid close attention to natural signs such as the behavior of animals and birds, the color of the sky, and cloud formations. Suggested activities for this component build on the knowledge of such elders and include:

- Have students identify and study selected cultural weather predictions and conduct the following investigations for scientific accuracy. Conduct interviews with historians, meteorologists, and older family members of various ethnic groups to determine accurate weather predictions related to body aches and pains, the body's reaction to low air pressure, squirrels hiding acorns, and the sound and pitch of blowing wind.
- Visit the local museum to observe and record information about early weather instruments and early weather prediction practices.
- Observe flight direction of birds to determine the relationship of flight pattern to weather changes.
- Record weather data throughout the winter to establish accuracy of the ground hog seeing its shadow as a prediction of a severe winter.

COMPONENT #2—SENSITIVITY AWARENESS

CULTURAL APPRECIATION THROUGH BOOKS

The second component supports the kind of teaching that recognizes students' strengths and deficiencies and teaches concepts that they may not have had an

Figure 12.2
A Curriculum Design Model For Multicultural Science Integration

Category	Objective	Science
1. Cultural Perspectives	Convey science experiences through integrating cultural traditions, characteristics, and scientific view of the world.	African Americans making weather predictions based upon the cloud formation and animal behavior.
2. Sensitivity Awareness	Recognize strengths and deficiencies in students' performance and provide strategies on the basis of their opportunity to learn.	Interview students to find out about their knowledge, disposition, and exposure to weather-related concepts and activities.
3. Context	Anchor science activities in real world experiences based upon ethnic and cultural practices, attitudes, and traditions.	Make a wind vane similar to those used by Native Americans. Record over a two-week period wind direction data and show connections with weather conditions.
4. Role Models	Showcase significant achievements made by women, minorities, and cultural groups.	Have students study Matthew Henson's successful exploration to the North Pole resulting mostly from his ability to interpret data from weather instruments and predict weather conditions in the Arctic.
5. Motivational Extensions	Empower students by employing effective instructional strategies such as hands-on science, extended investigation, and cooperative learning. Apply science concepts to out-of-classroom learning opportunities to affirm multicultural connections.	Have teams of students focus on a career in meteorology. Identify a meteorologist from a particular ethnic group and learn about their work and interests. Encourage students to design extended investigations operationalizing what meteorologists do.

opportunity to learn. Sensitive science instruction builds on students' knowledge, disposition, and exposure to weather-related concepts. Many books are now available at local book stores and libraries that provide culturally diverse views on this topic. Listed below are titles and descriptions of weather-related books that promote multicultural sensitivity awareness. Use some of them or others of your choice to enhance cultural integration. Students find books such as these interesting and relevant to their own understandings of weather. The books may be used in ways such as the following:

- Have students select a multicultural weather book and share their ideas about the culture through role playing, a class skit, weather report, or a class story book to reflect sensitivity to cultural weather perspectives.
- Provide opportunities for students to investigate a concept or idea presented in a book they have read. One example might be: How accurate were the early Native American-made wind vanes compared to more modern versions?

Multiculturally-Oriented Books About Weather

Branley, Franklyn. *Flash, Crash, Rumble and Roll.* Harper Collins Publishers, 1985. (Nonfiction) $4.50

Explanation of thunderstorms—why they occur, how they work, and safety precautions that should be taken. Illustrations show children of several ethnic backgrounds. Grades 3–6.

Branley, Franklyn. *Hurricane Watch.* Harper Collins Publishers, 1987. (Nonfiction) $4.50

Explanation of how hurricanes occur and safety measures to take. Illustrations show children of several different ethnic backgrounds. Grades 3–6.

DeWitt, Lynda. *What Will the Weather Be?* Harper Collins Publishers, 1991. (Nonfiction) $4.50

Basic weather lessons—temperature, wind, etc. Also explains work that meteorologists do. Meteorologists portrayed are African-American and Caucasian men and women. TV newscaster shown throughout is African American woman. Grades 1–6.

Ets, Marie Hall. *Gilberto and the Wind.* Puffin Books, 1963. (Fiction) $3.99

Hispanic boy discovers wind and the many things it can do. Grades K–4.

Gibbons, Gail. *Weather Forecasting.* Macmillan Publishing Company, 1987. (Nonfiction) $13.95

Detailed description of seasons, weather conditions of each, instruments meteorologists use to predict weather, and how weather affects people in different work settings. Illustrations throughout are people of different ethnicities. Grades 3–6.

Gilman, Michael. *Matthew Henson: Black Explorer.* Chelsea House Publishers, 1988. (Nonfiction) $7.95

The story of Matthew Henson, an African American explorer who, as a member of Admiral Perry's team, was one of the first men to reach the North Pole. Grades middle school–adult.

Keats, Ezra Jack. *The Snowy Day.* Puffin Books, 1962. (Fiction) $4.99

African American boy enjoys a day in the snow with his mother. Grades K–3.

Stoly, Mary. *Storm In the Night.* Harper Collins Publishers, 1988. (Fiction) $4.95

African American boy spends the night with his grandparents. Through a conversation with his grandfather, the boy learns about storms and overcomes his fear of them. Grades 3–6.

COMPONENT #3—CONTEXT

REAL WORLD WEATHER EXPERIENCES

The main objective of the third component is to help students anchor science activities in real-world experiences based upon ethnic and cultural practices, attitudes and traditions. Casual observation tells us that it is fall when the leaves drop off the trees, it is about to rain when it is overcast and windy, or the temperature has reached freezing when ice forms on the windshields. In other cultures and other times, the connection between people and their physical environment was closer, and the observations they made often preceded dramatic weather changes. Not many modern day observers take time to note that ants are piling the dirt higher around the openings into their homes, bees are flying slower before the geese head south overhead, or count the number of strands a spider is weaving. But when these activities are linked to food production, safety, or family life, the message can signal urgency and the need for a quick response.

Students can learn to make observations about weather, using insights and instruments that have been used in other cultural contexts. Many cultures have customs and traditions that influence their reaction to natural phenomena. Understanding the basic differences and similarities of these customs and beliefs confirms the validity of other cultures' ways of knowing. Suggested activities include:

• Study Native American rain dance rituals to learn more about this cultural practice. Research the Native American weather stick as an example of an early weather instrument. Weather sticks are available at Nature Company stores for about $5.00. A natural barometer indicates weather change by responding to changes in air moisture. It was attached in a fixed position outside of a dwelling and pointed up or down depending on weather conditions. Variations were used by American Indians throughout the U.S.

- Observe spider webs and orb-weaving spiders such as the garden spider. These spiders may spend an hour constructing their familiar web with spiral. However, orb-weaving spiders will string single strands of silk to catch food because they don't have time for an orb before the expected weather change. American Indians and Polynesians made these observations and used them to predict weather changes. In African stories, spiders were often referred to as the messengers of the gods—and weather change may be one example of a message delivered by them. Students can practice observing spiders and attempt to predict weather changes in this manner.

- Far north of the Arctic, in "the land of the midnight sun," inhabitants must contend with ice, snow, high winds, and severe cold weather. The arctic north is covered with snow for more than half the year. This situation poses many challenges for humans, plants, and animals, as they seek to survive and carry out everyday living activities, such as traveling, hunting, and eating in an ice and snow environment. Inhabitants require special clothing, transportation devices, food, and other considerations. Imagine the level of planning and preparation undertaken by Matthew Henson and Robert Perry to endure the severe weather conditions on their many journeys to the North Pole! Study the Arctic biome and design a project to convey life in the land of the midnight sun.

    1. Students can work in groups or teams to design a project to demonstrate living in the Arctic as it relates to: food, transportation, clothing, animal adaptation, or plant adaptation.

    2. Compare variety and distribution of plants and animals and ways in which they have adapted.

    3. Identify type of plants, soil type, diversity, and competition.

COMPONENT #4—ROLE MODELS

SIGNIFICANT ACHIEVEMENTS

The main objective of the fourth component is that students will learn significant achievements made by women and diverse cultural groups. One such achiever was Matthew A. Henson (polar explorer and cofounder of the North Pole, 1867–1955).

Matthew A. Henson was the first person to place the American flag at the North Pole and was widely regarded as a courageous world explorer. Henson and Perry surveyed Nicaragua and made several trips to Greenland preparing for their ultimate trip to the North Pole. They traveled together for many years and spent nineteen years learning about travel and survival in the Arctic before they reached the North Pole. The final expedition began in February of 1908 and seemed doomed from the outset. Soon the other members of the team had to fall back, leaving only Henson and Perry. Finally, on April 6, 1908, Perry took a reading using his sextant. All of the data were correct; they had reached their destination. Perry then asked his friend and coworker to plant the American flag on the North Pole. It was a very proud moment (Path Finders 4 1989). Matthew Henson became one of the world's leading authorities on the Arctic. His early training as a sailor and his ability to interpret data from weather instruments made the accomplishments of the entire Perry expedition possible. Henson later received a silver medal from the United States Navy for his leadership role (Dolan 1992).

Students can work with this kind of information in ways such as the following:

- Compare how scientists traveled in the past to today's transportation technology. For example, what type of sled would be used by Henson and Perry now to travel to the North Pole?
- Role play two teams traveling to the North Pole, one historical and one modern. Portray each member of the team and their interactions (e.g., social behavior, weather instruments, and travel patterns).
- How would people from each continent view the North Pole? What kind of weather conditions would each continent experience?

COMPONENT #5—MOTIVATIONAL EXTENSIONS

METEOROLOGIST—A CAREER PROFILE

The main objective of the fifth component is for students to apply science concepts outside the classroom. In this sample unit, students will develop an appreciation for weather-related careers and learn about the work performed by meteorologists.

Meteorologists are scientists who study the atmosphere and how it behaves; they try to understand and predict the weather. Meteorologists gather information about the atmosphere at hundreds of different places and at many altitudes. They also study changing global weather conditions and the effects of air pollution on the weather. Modern day meteorologists use many tools and instruments to compile weather statistics, including weather satellites and computers. As the atmosphere can rapidly change, forecasting weather is not a simple process. Meteorologists study data and reports on the amount of precipitation in an area, the pressure of the atmosphere, wind speeds, and cloud formation. They also gather weather information about wind patterns and ocean currents. Weather information and data are used by the United States Weather Bureau to produce daily weather maps to show the nation's weather.

Meteorologists are employed by the National Weather Service, airlines and airports, news bureaus, and groups of farmers. The weather forecaster on the evening news is a meteorologist. Some meteorologists are employed by the military. Weather forecasting is only one part of being a meteorologist. Many of these professionals work at weather stations, where they record data and make observations.

A career in meteorology requires a good background in mathematics and science and the ability to be a careful observer. A career as a meteorologist requires technical school or community college training. More advanced jobs in meteorology require a four-year college education, or more.

When studying careers in meteorology, students can learn about diverse people who occupy such careers. For example, Dr. Warren M. Washington is an excellent role model. In 1972, Warren Washington, a famous African American meteorologist, was appointed by President Carter to serve on the National Advisory Committee on Oceans and Atmosphere. This committee guided the Executive Branch of the government and Congress on issues that related to the atmosphere and the oceans. Warren Washington is currently the director of the Climate and Global Dynamics Division at the National Center for Atmospheric Research in Boulder, Colorado. He has built computer models of the atmosphere and oceans in order to study the changes they have undergone and predict what might happen in the future. He is interested in the effects of pollution and the cutting down of forests on the earth and its atmosphere (Lang 1992).

Students can explore careers in meteorology through activities such as the following:

- Have students work in teams or groups to gather information from various individuals (such as Warren Washington) about a career in meteorology. Suggest exploratory strategies such as interviews, audio-visuals, readings, or library research.
- Interview a local meteorologist to find out more about modern weather prediction techniques.
- Conduct an investigation to study how gardening is affected by various climates and by different weather conditions.

CONCLUSION

Teacher education programs are important in promoting the integration of multi-cultural science instruction. If pre- and in-service teachers are equipped with multicultural integration tools and strategies, they will better serve the needs of all students in their classrooms. Some of these tools and strategies include: (1) careful adherence to multicultural integration practices that become a permanent component of curriculum instruction and lesson design; (2) routine cooperative and interactive group learning; (3) authentic integration of multicultural images and perspectives in curriculum, instruction. and the physical environment; and

(4) development of continued professional development opportunities. The appendix provides a list of suggested resource materials that can be used to assist providers in strengthening their teacher education programs.

APPENDIX

SUGGESTED LIST OF RESOURCE MATERIALS

Atwater, M. A. (1993). *Multicultural Science Education: Assumptions and Alternative Views*. Athens, GA: University of Georgia, Science Education Department.

Black Achievers In Science (1988). Chicago: Museum of Science and Industry.

Clark Grevious, S. (1993). *Ready-to-Use Multicultural Activities for Primary Children*. New York: The Center for Applied Research in Education.

Carter Cooper, E. (1990). *ABCD For Teachers Project, Training Manual*, Volume I and II. Lansing, MI: Michigan Department of Education.

Densmore, F. (1974). *How Indians Use Wild Plants for Food, Medicine, and Crafts*. New York: Dover.

Derman-Sparks, L. (1989). *Anti-bias Curriculum: Tools for Empowering Young Children*. Washington, DC: National Association for the Education of Young Children.

Dommen, A. J. (1988). *Innovation in African Agriculture*. Boulder, CO: Westview.

Duschi, R. A. (1990). *Restructuring Science Education*. New York: Teachers College Press.

Estes, J. W. (1989). *The Medical Skills of Ancient Egypt*. Canton, MA: Science History.

Ezeabasili, N. (1977). *African Science: Myth or Reality?* New York: Vantage.

Goldstein, T. (1988). *Dawn of Modern Science*. Boston: Houghton Mifflin.

Howard, J., et. al. (1988). *Efficacy: The Elementary School Curriculum*. Arlington, MA: The Efficacy Institute Incorporated.

Jegede, O. J. (1989). Toward a philosophical basis for science education of the 1990s: An African view-point. In *The History and Philosophy of Science in Science Teaching*, ed. D. E. Herget, 185–198. Tallahassee, FL: Science Education and Department of Philosophy, Florida State University.

Jegede, O. J., and P. A. Okebukola. (1991). The effect of instruction on sociocultural beliefs hindering the learning of science. *Journal of Research in Science Teaching* 28(3).

Kreinberg, N. (1989). The practice of equity. *Peabody Journal of Education* 66(2): 127–146.

Nabhan, G. P. (1989). *Endunng Seeds: Native American and Wild Plant Conservation*. San Francisco, CA: North Point Press.

Noone, P. Portland State University, Northwest Equals Program, P. O. Box 1491, Portland, Oregon 97207.

Oakes, J., and T. Ormseth. (1990). *Multiplying Inequalities: The Effects of Race, Social Class and Tracking on Opportunities to Learn Mathematics and Science.* Santa Monica, CA: Rand Corporation.

Oakes, J., A. Gamoran, and R. N. Page. (1992). Curriculum differentiation: Opportunities, outcomes and meanings. In *Handbook of Research on Curriculum*, ed. P. W. Jackson, 570–608. New York: Macmillan.

Ogbu, J. U. (1990). Minority status and literacy in comparative perspective. *Deadalus* 119:141–168.

Reiss, M. J. (1993). *Science Education for a Pluralist Society.* Philadelphia: Open University Press.

Weatherford, J. M. (1988). *Indian Givers: How the Indians of the Americas Transformed the World.* New York: Crown.

Wong-Filmore, L. (1992). The curriculum and linguistic minorities. In *Handbook of Research on Curriculum*, ed. P. W. Jackson, 626–658. New York: Macmillan.

REFERENCES

Addison-Wesley Publishing Company. (1993). *Multiculturalism in Mathematics, Science, and Technology: Readings and Activities.* New York: Addison-Wesley Publishing Company.

Clewell, B. C., B. T. Anderson, and M. E. Thorpe (1992). *Breaking The Barriers: Helping Female and Minority Students Succeed in Math and Science.* San Francisco: Jossey-Bass.

Dolan, Sean. (1992). *Matthew Henson: Arctic Explorer. Junior World Biographies.* Ottawa, Ontario: Chelsea House Publishers.

Froschl, M., and B. Sprung. (1991). *Hands on to Science.* New York: Educational Equity Concepts, Inc.

Lang, Mozell P. (1992). *Cultural and Gender Perspectives In Science.* Lansing, MI: Michigan Department of Education.

Michigan State Board of Education. (1991). *Michigan Essential Goals and Objectives For Science Education (K–12).* Lansing, MI: Michigan Department of Education.

Path Finders 4. (1989). *Minority Scientists and Inventors.* MICHCON, 500 Griswold Street, Detroit, Michigan 48226.

13

MIAN M. YUSUF_____

Mathematics and Multiculturalism

INTRODUCTION

There is much evidence that equity in the treatment of diverse students does not exist in most mathematics classrooms (Fennema 1990; Leder 1990). Albert Villasenor summarized the performance in mathematics by the various groups as follows:

> Statistics show that those who study mathematics are most often white males. Women, African Americans, Hispanics, and Native Americans study less mathematics and are seriously under represented in careers in the mathematics, engineering, technology, and sciences....In urban schools serving economically disadvantaged populations, less than half of the students take mathematics beyond one year of algebra and one in five do not take any algebra at all. In fact four out of five students attending high school in the largest urban districts take no mathematics at all beyond the minimum required for graduation. (1992a, 6)

According to the National Research Council (NRC), since 1975 the percentage of top high school seniors who expressed an interest in majoring in mathematics or statistics has declined by over 50 percent (NRC 1989, 17). Inadequate preparation in mathematics imposes a special economic handicap on minorities. Gender differences in mathematics performance are predominantly due to the accumulated effects of sex-role stereotypes in family, school, and society.

Due to demographic, economic, and social changes, there is a demand for change of the mathematics curriculum (NCTM 1989, 2). Justice in mathematics will not be achieved until the National Council of Teachers of Mathematics (NCTM) Standards are met equally by each group as called for under the heading "New Social Goals" (NCTM 1989, 3). Mathematics is a "critical filter" for many math/science-related occupations and careers in areas such as banking, accounting, and engineering (Fennema 1990, 2). By raising expectations for performance in mathematics by diverse groups, we can enhance both equity and excellence. Equity for all requires excellence for all; both thrive when expectations are high (NRC 1989, 29).

Educators are very important change agents. They can help each group of the diverse population to achieve equity in mathematics. Educators are expected to

187

take up their responsibility for changing mathematics curriculum and for developing new methods and techniques to provide justice to all students. The NCTM Standards provide a framework for considering how to improve instruction in mathematics for all students. The introductory chapters of both Standards (NCTM 1989, 1–11 and NCTM 1991, 1–7) make the following recommendations:

1. Math problems/exercises must be connected to the students' real life situations including their cultures.
2. Math and science should be integrated. Other subjects should also be integrated with math/science.
3. The computer and the calculator should be integrated into the math/science curriculum and also into the curriculum of the other subjects.
4. Students should be guided to construct math in the classroom.
5. Students should be involved actively in math for constructing problems/exercises and for solving problems.
6. Students should be encouraged to solve the same problem in different ways.

The major goal of this chapter is to help teacher educators provide opportunities to preservice mathematics teachers for attaining the knowledge, skills, and attitudes needed to be effective in multicultural and urban classrooms. The first half of the chapter reviews some areas of knowledge and skill to be used in the mathematics classroom: the use of multiculture literature and introduction of cultural contributions; the significance of variation of teaching methods and learning styles; use of technology and, particularly, integration of the computer; and use of problems that relate to cultural practices and everyday life. The second half of the chapter describes how I involve my own students in learning these skills in mathematics methods courses.

CULTURAL CONTRIBUTIONS TO MATHEMATICS

Multicultural diversity plays a fundamental role in the affairs of both mathematics instruction and assessment, and such recognition is a necessary starting point for strategies to raise levels of students' mathematics achievement (Bailey and Shan 1991). Multicultural diversity can be a blessing if we integrate it into the mathematics curriculum and appreciate the contributions of different racial, ethnic, and cultural groups. Schools rarely emphasize cultural or historical aspects of mathematics. Raising students' awareness of the contributions to mathematics by men and women from a variety of cultural and ethnic backgrounds provides them with an appreciation for the discipline which can motivate for further study of mathematics (Villasenor 1992b, 7).

For instance, preservice teachers could be engaged to find out the contributions of their own culture in addition to that of two other cultural groups in transformation of the society using mathematics. The students could be asked to find names of five persons from different cultures who used mathematics and contributed to building the United States highway system or the Sears Tower in Chicago. They may be expected to analyze and express their own contributions in the future as mathematics teachers for the transformation of society.

Math teachers build the foundation of future scientists, engineers, doctors, mathematicians, architects, and other professionals. Many people used math for the benefit of the future generations. For instance, the person who designed Kenosha's city street numbering system used a coordinate system of mathematics with its origin at the north-east corner of the city area which is at the banks of Lake Michigan. Avenues run north-south (the numbers increase if you go west just as X increases if you go right from the Y-axis), and streets run east-west (the numbers increase if you go south just as Y increases as you go up from the X-axis). Unit and tenth place digits show the order and the side of the house/building on the avenue/street, while the remaining digit(s) show the avenue/street number. If one knows the number of the house/building and the number of the avenue/street, then it is very easy to find it. For example, say you want to go to Whittier Elementary School at 8542 51st Avenue. From this address, we know that the gate of the building is on 51st Avenue after crossing the 85th street. The number 42, which is even (even numbers are located on the west side of the avenues), shows the building is on the west side of 51st Avenue. The system is so useful that there is no need to consult a map or to ask anybody for directions.

Educators can use multicultural literature to teach how diverse cultures have contributed towards the development of mathematics, so that young people can relate mathematics to the work of real people, including people like themselves. Preservice teachers can be guided in the study and use of such literature as *Multiculturalism in Mathematics, Science, and Technology: Readings and Activities* (Addison-Wesley 1993). For example, a multicultural mathematics curriculum can highlight the roles played by diverse groups, such as the Egyptians and Aztecs, in the development of theory and practice in mathematics (Banks 1991, 38). The following types of questions could be included about number system in the curriculum:

> What is the relationship between the number system used within a society and its culture [counting by 2s, 5s, 10s, 15s, and 20s, etc.]? What do the symbol systems within a culture reveal about it [1, I, 0, & . etc.]? Historically, what contributions have different ethnic groups made to our number system [Egyptians, Greeks, Arabians, and Indians, etc.]? (Banks 1991, 36)

The students in our schools would like to see teachers as role models of their groups. Unfortunately, we are short of such role models (King 1993). The profession is failing to attract and retain a proportionate supply of teachers of color to meet the needs of an increasingly diverse student population. In the absence of sufficient role models for diverse groups, I would suggest inviting guest speakers.

A committee of preservice teachers, charged to invite guest speakers from diverse groups, could be formed with the following guidelines: (1) In addition to an African American guest speaker, at least one guest speaker should be selected from the culture represented by the students. Another minority guest speaker should be selected according to the local demographic situation (e. g., a female African, Hispanic, Asian, or Native American math teacher/educator/social worker/politician). (2) The speakers should be successful professionals. (3) The guest speakers should be given the following questions in advance so that they could help make the mathematics curriculum multicultural:

a)   We want to hear stories of their lives, specifically considering math effects on their lives as a child, a student, and an employee. How has math affected their social and cultural lives and their contribution to society?

b)   What type of math could be included in the curriculum to make it multicultural?

c)   What steps should be taken by the teachers to make the math multi-cultural?

d)   What can a mathematics teacher do to make all students successful in mathematics?

e)   How can we work together for attaining equity in mathematics education?

ACCOMMODATION OF DIFFERENT LEARNING STYLES

Each individual is different from others and learns differently. Similarly, cultural patterns often influence an individual's learning-style preferences and strengths. The preservice teachers should know how to investigate the learning styles of various individuals and groups so that they could teach effectively in the multi-cultural classroom. For example, instructors in math methods should provide models and examples of excellent lesson plans and math activities to accommo-date a variety of learning style. Some students tend to learn best by observation and modeling of the activity, not by being told (Heath 1983). They may have a high energy level and need a variety of tasks and much movement (Boykin 1982). Such students should be provided various math activities and options. Other students prefer process material and learn through kinesthetic activities (writing of math problems, physical activities such as measurement of floor for carpeting, role playing of a cashier); visual images (video math games, photographs of mathematicians, charts of math history); auditory input (records, music); interac-tive participation (group discussion); haptic strategies (drawing of geometric maps, painting, sculpturing). Still others prefer print oriented approaches such as reading assignments (Shade 1990).

    For the improvement of girls' performance in math and science and to help girls develop the skills and self-confidence to pursue a full range of interests and careers in math and science, prospective teachers should be guided to study *Strategies for Parents and Educators: How to Encourage Girls in Math & Science* (Skolnick, Langbort, and Day 1982). The prospective teachers should be encouraged to make presentations selecting some strategies and activities from this book for making math enjoyable and reducing math anxiety. For example, this book points out that girls tend to score behind boys in spacial visualization skills and offers many hands-on activities and projects to help children develop spacial skills.

Preservice teachers need to learn multiple instructional strategies which stress active hands-on problem-solving activities. They could be actively engaged in creating a book of multicultural math activities. They should be guided to study the following books for the construction of multicultural mathematics activities using different learning styles: *Math Instruction Using Media and Modality Strengths* (Carson and Bostick 1988), and *Culture, Style, and the Educative Process* (Shade 1989).

Use of Technology in Teaching Mathematics

Instructional technology like calculators and computers provide a powerful means of expanding teachers' repertoire of mathematics instructional strategies and strengthen their ability to meet the need in urban multicultural classrooms for a range of active, engaging, and problem-solving learning opportunities. For example, South Carolina requires that prospective teachers pass an Education Entrance Examination. A study was conducted to find out the effects of computer-assisted instruction (CAI) on basic skills mathematics achievement and locus of control of minority students seeking admission to teacher education programs. The results of statistical analysis showed that CAI increased the students' mathematics scores and that they developed a more internal orientation through its use (Reglin 1987). Both calculators and computers are equally essential to mathematics education and have equal potential for wise use or for abuse (NRC 1989, 61). Work with the microcomputer should be included in the preservice teacher education programs for broadening students' horizons by making them aware of its scope and diversity (Schroeder 1984).

Computers have the capability of raising student achievement, particularly in multicultural and urban schools. For example, the low performance in geometry at the national level (Carpenter et al. 1981; Lindquist and Kouba 1989) suggests that the teaching of geometry at the middle and secondary levels could use some new approaches. One approach to introducing new teaching strategies is to show teachers and students how to use computers as effective instructional tools for teaching and learning geometry. Logo Based Instruction (LBI) is a new approach (a different method) for teaching geometry by integrating Logo computer language into the geometry curriculum. The aim of LBI is to enable teachers and students to investigate and explore Logo integration in the geometry curriculum. Several research studies showed that the use of turtle graphics had a positive effect on students' confidence and motivation (Papert 1988; Silver 1988; Ernest 1988; Battista and Clements 1988a, 1988b). Logo computer language could be used in three different ways, focusing on students' confidence, motivation, creativity, problem solving, and excitement as follows:

1. *Tutorials:* Tutorial programs can be developed for teaching geometry. The students would follow the instruction on the screen for effective learning. The teachers can write programs in Logo to make the multicultural math problems simple or complex.
2. *Programming:* Logo activities can be developed to program the computer. The students can be taught Logo for programming the machine to draw geometric figures on the screen and to solve the multicultural math problems.
3. *Developing Software:* Logo tutorials and exercises can be developed by the teachers for whole class and individual instruction using Logo computer language. For example, Logo Mathematics Tutorial 1 (LMT1) was developed for teaching points, rays, lines, and line segments to minority students using the Apple IIe machine. A total of 206 Logo programs were developed integrating Logo into the geometry curriculum (Yusuf 1990). Logo Mathematics Tutorial 2 (LMT2) is in progress for teaching polygons to minority students using the Macintosh machine.

I conducted a research study to determine whether the middle-school students taught the geometry concepts of points, rays, lines, and line segments with LBI would score significantly higher, would have a more positive attitude towards learning geometry, learning Logo, learning through LBI, and would have a better conceptualization of points, rays, lines, and line segments than the students taught the same concepts by the teacher through lecture and paper and pencil activities (Yusuf 1990 and 1994). The sample consisted of sixty-seven (76 percent African American, 24 percent white) seventh and eighth graders. Most ANCOVA and t-tests were significant at 0.05 level in favor of the experimental group. Audio taped interviews of thirty-two (78 percent African American, 22 percent white) were analyzed. The results indicated that the students in the experimental group had a deeper conceptualization of the four geometry concepts after the LBI. The results also indicated that the students in the experimental group had significant increases in their van Hiele levels in comparison to the students in the control group. (There are five van Hiele levels used to assess understanding of geometric concepts.) The researcher observed that the black students, males and females, were motivated and actively involved in Logo activities. They clapped when they saw the results of their Logo activities on the screen. Some of them were so excited that they called their teacher to show him their achievements on the computer screen.

Microcomputers provide a tool for illustrating and manipulating mathematical concepts that can be both motivating and beneficial to students who become bored with paper and textbooks. Preservice teachers should be instructed in how to use microcomputers and other kinds of technology as alternatives or supplements to more traditional instruction.

MULTICULTURAL MATHEMATICS PROBLEMS

Activities and games can bring the vitality of ethnic and cultural diversity into the mathematics curriculum, can enhance the background of the ethnically different child, and can expose children to the ethnic heritage of others (Krause 1983). Mathematics problems can be developed that relate to the everyday life of diverse children. The reader is directed to the activities presented by Marina Krause (1983) in *Multicultural Mathematics Materials* for classroom use.

We should involve students in the development of multicultural math problems, connecting mathematics with diverse traditions and cultures. The community can also be involved in writing real-life mathematics problems (Barnes 1993). Here are a few examples.

Example 1 Some religious groups don't drink. Suppose an average American drinks $0.50 beer each day. How much money would s/he have saved in 10 years if s/he would not have been drinking beer? How could the saved money have been spent in a better way? Why do you think so?

Example 2 Some Indians like to eat fresh bread prepared at home from wheat flour every day. We can construct simple and complex wheat flour problems as follows:

Simple: An Indian family of 4 members want to buy flour for 10 days. Each member eats one pound of flour every day. A 20-pound bag of flour costs $6.00. How many bags of flour are needed? How much will they cost?

Complex: An Indian family of 5 members want to buy flour for 7 days. Each member eats one and a half pounds of flour every day. A 20-pound bag of flour costs $5.50. How many bags of flour are needed? How much will they cost?

By changing the numbers only, we can make the problem simpler or more complex. At this juncture, the instructor can integrate the computer by motivating preservice teachers to write a program in BASIC or Logo that can make these problems simpler or more complex for students. We can further change the problem for a shopkeeper who sells flour, or for a supplier of flour for a city, or we can change it for national-level production of wheat, or for production of machinery for the farmers, etc. Preservice teachers could be guided to construct similar problems for diverse groups to make the math curriculum multicultural.

Example 3 An African American girl needs 100 beads of 5 different colors for the decoration of her hair. A bag of 100 beads of 3 different colors costs $1.00. A family has two such girls. How many bags of beads should be bought for these girls? How much will they cost? Why do you think so?

This problem can be made simpler or more complex. It could also be extended from the perspectives of a shopkeeper, a supplier, and a producer.

Example 4 Answer the following questions:

(1) What is the ratio of the circumference (C) to the diameter (D) of a circle? Can you find it out yourself? If yes, how?

(C/D = π = 3.1415. The ratio C/D was denoted by π in the 18th century A.D. π is the 16th letter in the Greek alphabet.)

(2) Why is the ratio C/D called π? Can we call it K because it is a constant? Can we name it with any letter such as P, etc.? Why do you think so?

(P is the 16th letter in the English alphabet)

(3) Write a paragraph on the history of π (Pi) explaining its different values used at different times and the contributions of various cultures.

(e.g., Babylonians π = 3 1/8 and Egyptians π = 4(8/9)2 about 2,000 B.C.)

(4) Write the following program in Logo, and use it for drawing three circles of different sizes on the screen. Find out the ratio C/D for each circle. Write your own conclusion using the Logo investigations. What name would you like to give to this ratio? Write your comments providing reasons.

TO POLY :N :S

REPEAT :N [FD :S RT 360 / :N]

END

(You may type POLY 22 5 to draw circle 1, POLY 44 5 to draw circle 2, and POLY 88 5 to draw circle 3)

Example 5 Assign a question to each group for presentation in the class from the following (students may be guided to collect the information needed from various sources such as dictionaries, encyclopedias, etc.):

(1) Find out five calendars of five different cultures in use. Where are they being used? Compare their characteristics (e.g., Gregorian, Hebrew, Muslim, Chinese, and Hindu calendars).

(2) Compare two calendars, including your own calendar, commenting on their merits and demerits. Can you develop a procedure for finding out the day of your birth according to each calendar? If yes, how? If no, why not? (e.g., solar and lunar calendars)

(3) Find the days of birth of five leaders of different cultures such as George Washington, Martin Luther King Jr., Ada Deer, Gloria Molina, Black Hawk, Muhammad Ali Jinnah, and Mohandas Karamchand Gandhi.

Example 6 I have used this examination of calendars to explore everyday dates. I have provided the following information and used the questioning and answering technique for developing a procedure for finding out the day of birth.

The solar year (the time the earth takes to orbit from one vernal equinox to the next) is 365 days 5 hours 48 minutes and 46 seconds (365.24). The fraction of a day was taken up in a 366-day leap year every four years. But, by 1582, it was more than 10 days behind the seasons because the time difference between 365.24 and 365.25 days (11 minutes 14 seconds) amounts to 7–8 days over 1,000 years. Pope Gregory XIII therefore deleted 10 days in 1582, and, to reduce future error, he decreed that centennial years should be leap years if divisible by 400 (so 1900, for example, was not a leap year, but 2000 will be). The Gregorian calendar was adopted in Britain and the American colonies in 1752. (DeVinne 1987, 256)

We decided that the first day of the week is Monday and the last day of the week is Sunday. According to Gregorian calendar, there are 12 months in a year and 7 days in a week. In January there are 31 days; if we divide 31 by 7 to find complete weeks, then we get the remainder 3. If the first of January was Monday, then the last day will be Wednesday because the remainder is three and the third day of the week is Wednesday. In February, there are 28 days; if we divide by 7, then the remainder is zero. If the first day of February was Monday, then the last day will be Sunday because the remainder is zero and the last day of the week is Sunday. Hence, if we can calculate the complete weeks from the beginning of Gregorian calendar, particularly the remainder, then we can find out any day of the week for a particular date. So, we created table 13.1 to find out the day of the week when we knew the remainder by consulting column numbers 1 and 2. If we added various remainders, then we called the sum extra days and divided it again by 7 to find out the last remainder. To find the extra days for the months, we consulted column numbers 3–6, and to find the extra day for the complete years we consulted column numbers 7–8.

Students may be asked to find out the days of birth of three persons they like from three different cultures from the local community and to write a paragraph on each person explaining why they like them.

Here is an example following the ten-step procedure to find out the day of one's birth using table 13.1.

Zubaidah was born on March 17, 1960. Find the day of her birth.

1. No. of complete years 1960 - 1	=	1959	
2. No. of Extra days in 1900 years	=	01 from column 7 and 8	
3. " " " " " 59 "	=	59 " " " "	
4. " " " " " 59 leap years	=	14 (59/4 = 14)	
5. Complete month = February 1960 1960 is a leap year			
6. No. of Extra days against February in the leap year column No. 6	=	04 from column 6	
7. No of days in March 1960 taking all days in the birth month	=	17	
8. Total	=	95	
9. Remainder	=	95/7 = 4	
10. Hence Zubaidah's birth day	=	THURSDAY from column 1 and 2	

Table 13.1
Using the Gregorian Calendar

1 Remainder	2 Day of the Week	3 Month	4 No. of Days	5 Extra Days	6 Extra Days in a Leap Year	7 No. of Years	8 Extra Days
0	Sunday	January	31	3	3	1	1
1	Monday	February	28/29	3	4	100	5
2	Tuesday	March	31	6	7	200	10
3	Wednesday	April	30	8	9	300	1
4	Thursday	May	31	11	12	400	0
5	Friday	June	30	13	14	1600	0
6	Saturday	July	31	16	17	1900	1
		August	31	19	20	2000	0
		September	30	21	22		
		October	31	24	25		
		November	30	26	27		
		December	31	—	—		

ENGAGING PRESERVICE TEACHERS IN INVESTIGATION AND PLANNING

Multicultural mathematics is a relatively new field. We can involve preservice teachers in the development of goals and curricula for the multicultural methods course. I have used cooperative group projects as a means of engaging them in the investigation and development of various areas. I organized my students into the following committees in the first class session so that they would be prepared mentally to perform their duties effectively during the semester: (1) Objectives Committee, (2) Computer Application Committee, (3) NCTM Standards Implementation Committee, (4) Multicultural Mathematics Activities Book Committee, (5) Mathematics Exhibition Committee, and (6) Invitation/Publicity Committee. Each committee was responsible for creating a product to be presented in the Mathematics Exhibition towards the end of the semester.

The work of the following three groups was very important for developing the multicultural math curriculum. The Objectives Committee was responsible for developing an answer to the following question and for presenting it to the class and in the mathematics exhibition: What are the objectives of teaching mathematics to a diverse population, particularly considering students of color, poor families, and females?

The NCTM Standards Implementation Committee developed guidelines for providing equity in math for implementing the NCTM Standards. The group arranged presentations by the preservice teachers for integrating multicultural hands-on activities on specific mathematics topics. Each preservice teacher was required to present hands-on activities involving all students in the class. Selected activities were presented in the mathematics exhibition.

The Multicultural Mathematics Activities Book Committee developed and collected (from each classmate) activities to make the mathematics curriculum multicultural and to relate math to the real-life experiences of diverse students. The group produced a booklet containing about fifty multicultural mathematics activities similar to those in the previous section of this chapter. A survey could be conducted to find out mathematical procedures needed in different cultural situations and at different jobs to help in developing activities for mathematics classrooms and computer applications.

The reports of the committees on planning and organizing the activities for the whole semester were discussed in the second class session. The students were allowed to express their views, criticisms, and comments freely. They were permitted to decide for themselves what to do for the achievement of the committee goals. As an instructor, I worked as a facilitator. I did not try to impose my views. In one of the semesters, the committee for exhibition decided not to arrange any exhibition; I accepted their decision.

The exhibition committee plans the exhibition, and the Invitation/Publicity committee takes care of all publicity. So far, students have completed the mathematics exhibition twice. The project involves putting on a one-day fair, showing how to integrate math and science methods for teaching elementary, middle-, and secondary school students. In the most recent exhibition, the preservice teachers in my math and science methods classes chose a central theme, "A Whale of a Tale," around which they developed hands-on activities in math and science, connecting them with the real-life situations and integrating the computer. The preservice teachers were encouraged to create various activities to present math/science concepts in different ways. For example, to find one's day of birth, preservice teachers included the following different procedures: (1) a simple math procedure was presented on a chart and a handout was given to the visitors so that they could try it with their relatives and friends, (2) student visitors were provided practice to find out the day of their birth following the ten-step procedure using table 13.1, (3) a computer program in Logo was presented to find out the day of the birth on an Apple IIe machine, and (4) another computer program in Terrapin Logo was presented to find out the day of the birth on a Macintosh machine. Children from a nearby elementary school attended the exhibition and tried out the activities.

The Journal Times of Racine published a front-page article titled, "A whale of a tale: UW-P exhibit makes learning fun," with colored photographs of the Math and Science Exhibit on December 7, 1993. Selected parts of the article are presented below:

> That's why a class of college students constructed a life-size whale to show that math and science can be fun, especially if teachers use hands-on projects.... They built a 12-foot-high, 60-foot-long and 32-foot-wide whale made out of plastic sheets....The large room was filled with children's laughter and giggles as they crawled into the big creature. "It's neat. It's fun to do instead of the boring old paper work and stuff," said [name], a sixth-grader at Whittier Elementary School in Kenosha. Hands-on exhibits—some with oceanographic themes—let children become little scientists and mathematicians as they discovered what the ocean tastes like, what days they were born and how other cultures count....The secret to teaching is not to just tell the information but to let them figure it out themselves, said [preservice teacher]....As a part of a college course, students organized the fair, created hands-on lessons and published them in a workbook....Yusuf said when teachers learn to be facilitators instead of lecturers, children can learn and retain so much more...."By listening we forget; by seeing we can learn," he said. Yusuf not only wants math and science to be interesting, but he also wants the subjects to include multiculturalism. Students did this by teaching the children how people from around the world count and measure. With popcorn kernels and pasta shells, [preservice teacher] showed a different number system called Maya math while a crowd of students hovered over her exhibit. "I had kids fighting to do math," she said. (Velasco 1993, 1A, 11A)

I used the exhibition project as a means of motivating my students in their development of multicultural and active strategies and as a mean of promoting this approach to mathematics more broadly on the campus and the community. The students in my math/science methods classes were encouraged to plan and organize excellent activities in their major areas for inclusion in their portfolios for when they interview later for jobs. The students were so motivated and excited that they persuaded the University of Wisconsin-Parkside chancellor to fund the exhibition project.

CONCLUSION

The improved mathematics achievement among racial minority, female, and low-income students is an important part of the broader agenda of insuring equal educational opportunities, as well as life opportunities, for all groups in society. Accomplishing this will demand new approaches to mathematics instruction. I believe that the strategies I have described in this chapter can help to prepare beginning teachers with the skills to undertake a more effective and culturally responsive approach to mathematics instruction.

REFERENCES

Addison-Wesley Publishing Company, (1993). *Multiculturalism in mathematics, science, and technology: Readings and activities.* Menlo Park, CA: Author.

Bailey, P., and S. J. Shan. (1991). Mathematics for a multicultural society, under-achievement and the national curriculum. *Mathematics in School* 20(2):20–21.

Banks, J. A. (1991). *Teaching strategies for ethnic studies*, 5th ed. Boston, MA: Allyn and Bacon.

Barnes, S. J. (1993). Involve the community. *Mathematics Teacher* 86(6):442–448.

Battista, M. T., and D. H. Clements. (1988a). A case for Logo-based elementary school geometry curriculum. *Arithmetic Teacher* 36(3):11–17.

Battista, M. T., and D. H. Clements. (1988b). Using Logo pseudoprimitives for geometric investigations. *Mathematics Teacher* 81:166–174.

Boykin, A. W. (1982). Task variety and the performance of Black and White school children. Vervistic explorations. *Journal of Black Studies* 12:469–485.

Carpenter, T. P., M. K. Corbitt, H. S. Kepner Jr., M. M. Lindquist, and R. E. Reys. (1981). *Results from the second mathematics assessment of the national assessment of educational progress.* Reston, VA: NCTM.

Carson, J. C., and R. N. Bostick. (1988). *Mathematics instruction using media and modality strengths: How...it figures.* Springfield, IL: Charles C. Thomas.

DeVinne, P. B., ed. (1987). *The American heritage illustrated encyclopedic dictionary.* Boston, MA: Houghton Mifflin.

Ernest, P. (1988). What's the use of Logo? *Mathematics in School* 17(1):16–20.

Fennema, E. (1990). Justice, equity, and mathematics education. In *Mathematics and gender*, ed. E. Fennema and G. C. Leder, 1–9. New York: Teachers College Press.

Heath, S. B. (1983). *Ways with words*. New York: Cambridge University Press.

Krause, M. C. (1983). *Multicultural mathematics materials*. Reston, VA: NCTM.

King, S. H. (1993). The limited presence of African American teachers. *Review of Educational Research* 63(2):115–149.

Leder, G. C. (1990). Gender difference in mathematics: An overview. In *Mathematics and gender*, ed. E. Fennema and G. C. Leder, 10-26. New York: Teachers College Press.

Lindquist, M. M., and V. L. Kouba. (1989). Geometry. In *Results from the fourth mathematics assessment of the national assessment of educational progress*, ed. M. M. Lindquist, 44–54. Reston, VA: NCTM.

National Council of Teachers of Mathematics (NCTM). (1989). *Curriculum and evaluation standards for school mathematics*. Reston, VA: NCTM.

———. (1991). *Professional standards for teaching mathematics*. Reston, VA: NCTM.

National Research Council (NRC). (1989). *Everybody counts: A report to the nation on the future of mathematics education*. Washington, DC: National Academy Press.

Papert, S. (1988). *Mindstorms: Children, computers, and powerful ideas*. New York: Basic Books.

Reglin, G. L. (1987). *The effects of computer assisted instruction on mathematics and locus of control*. Washington, DC: ERIC Document Reproduction Service No. ED 310919.

Schroeder, T. L. (1984). Teacher education: Using microcomputers with pre-service teachers. *Arithmetic Teacher* 31(5):4–5.

Shade, B. J. (1990). *African American perceptual style: Implications for future research*. Paper presented at the annual meeting of the American Psychological Association, Boston, MA.

Shade, B. J., ed. (1989). *Culture, style and the educative process*. Springfield, IL: Charles C. Thomas.

Silver, S. B. (1988). Creativity through play and Logo. *Childhood Education* 64: 220–240.

Skolnick, J., C. Langbort, and L. Day. (1982). *Strategies for parents and educators: How to encourage girls in math and science*. Palo Alto, CA: Dale Seymour Publications.

Velasco, C. A. (1993). A whale of a tale: UW-P exhibit makes learning fun. *The Journal Times* 1A, 11A.

Villasenor, A. (1992a). Equity: An important goal in mathematics reform efforts. *Education Forward* 9(10):6.

———. (1992b). Schools re-examine the basics in mathematics. *Education Forward* 9(10):7.

Washington, V., and W. Harvey. (1989). *Affirmative rhetoric, negative action: African American and Hispanic faculty at predominantly White institutions*, Report No. 2. Washington, DC: School of Education and Human Development, The George Washington University.

Yusuf, M. M. (1990). Effects of Logo based instruction on the learning of selected geometric concepts at the secondary school level, Ph.D. Dissertation, University of Cincinnati.

———. (1994). Cognition of fundamental concepts in geometry. *Journal of Educational Computing Research* 10(4):349–371.

14

THERESA MICKEY MCCORMICK_____

Technology and Multicultural Nonsexist Teaching

> In this age of massive manipulation
> and disinformation, criticism is the
> only way we have of taking something
> seriously. The greatest patriots of our
> time will be those who explore our
> ideology critically, with particular
> attention to the gaps between myth-
> ology and practice.
>
> (Scholes 1991, 89)

I am a teacher educator who specializes in multicultural nonsexist education (MCNSE), not a professor of educational technology; however, I work in a university that has "of Science and Technology" appended to its name and in a department that reflects this orientation in its mission of infusing technology into all phases of undergraduate and graduate teacher education. In our teacher education program, students seeking Iowa licensure are required to take, among other professional education courses, a three credit-hour course in instructional technology (which includes media and computer skills and applications). As a part of the professional requirement, our students also take a two credit-hour course in multicultural nonsexist education and select an additional human relations course from a long list of approved courses, such as African American history or Women's Studies. Although a separate course in multicultural nonsexist education is required, we who instruct the course and the department chair support infusion of multicultural nonsexist concepts and materials in all phases of teacher education, but this is not yet a reality in all courses.

As the opening quote intimates, I will bring a critical eye to the topic of technology in teacher education in this paper. First, I will examine some problematics of technology in society which will ground the second part, that is on problematics of technology in education from the perspective of a multicultural nonsexist educator whose focus is on race, class, and gender issues. Third, I will consider some perspectives on knowledge and curriculum relative to MCNSE, teacher education, and technology and discuss the implications for instructional technology. Finally, I will suggest some positive uses of technology that are empowering to students and teachers.

PROBLEMATICS OF TECHNOLOGY IN SOCIETY

In recent years, the din of researchers' and social critics' voices has been resounding in their warnings against equating technological progress with human progress and the wedding of the computer business/industry with educational technology. As Colleen Cordes notes,

> Technology has become a religion, some scientists and scholars argue, that is devouring American culture and exacerbating environmental and social problems. A glib focus on technical challenges, they say, is distracting governments, businesses, educators, and ordinary citizens from the real causes of many problems—and the toll of such technological bias to date. (1994, A10)

Author of *The Virtual Community: Homesteading On The Electronic Frontier*, Howard Rheingold says, "Most people...remain unaware of how profoundly the social, political, and scientific experiments under way today via computer networks could change all our lives in the near future" (1993, 28). Rheingold believes, as I do, that technology has the potential to provide a tremendous social, intellectual, political, and commercial leverage to ordinary people, but we "must learn about that leverage and learn to use it, while we still have the freedom to do so, if it is to live up to its potential" (1993, 29). Rheingold gives us cause for reflection via these questions:

> In this age of information, will a few select corporations end up controlling the flow? Will we become obsessed with trivia when so much of it is at hand? Will all our communication be monitored and recorded? Could we even end up in the era of Orwell—and never really notice? (1993, 28)

William Howell (1994), Executive Director for Science of the American Psychological Association, reflects on the recent push by the Clinton administration to install an "information superhighway" and argues for the discussion of "people issues" from the beginning stages and for the inclusion of social and behavioral scientists in the planning process. Having similar concerns as Howell, Langdon Winner, Professor of Political Science at Rensselaer Polytechnic Institute, believes that "substantial technical innovations [such as the interstate highway system and the information superhighway] involve a reweaving of the fabric of society," and he urges "more focused attention on the social and cultural aspects of technological development" (1993, B1). Very little attention is given to the needs of the ultimate user, other than marketing strategies. This happens over and over again "because the people who are given responsibility for developing technological systems aren't inclined to think about social and behavioral consequences" (Howell 1994, A40). Howell warns, "Without some major changes now in our approach to the information revolution, we'll pay heavily again [in reference to the greed, corruption, and political favoritism and the side effects of air pollution and traffic deaths that accompanied the installation of the interstate highway system during the Eisenhower administration] and on a much grander scale" (1994, A40).

Already existing high tech networks, with electronic fingers that know no boundaries, enable computer-mediated communications (CMC) among corporations, organizations, and institutions, and of course, among individuals. Rheingold (1993) says that CMC has the potential to effect change in our lives on three different, but strongly interrelated, levels:

1. On the individual human level—the person's personality, perceptions, and thoughts; the way they use the medium and the way it uses them; their physical, intellectual, and emotional needs. Rheingold (1993) emphasizes the point by citing the change in vocabulary of young people around the world that reflects the effect of MTV, cellular telephones, and CMC in the age of media saturation.

2. On the person-to-person interaction level—where "many-to-many" communication may occur; where friendships, relationships, and communities may happen. Social scientists agree that there is a need for rebuilding a sense of community in the United States, but whether CMC will help bring people together or further isolate them is still being debated.

3. On the political level—where politics is a combination of communications and physical power; where the role of communications media is especially relevant to citizens involved in the politics of democratic societies. Rheingold reminds us that "the idea of modern representative democracy as it was first conceived by Enlightenment philosophers included a recognition of a living web of citizen-to-citizen communication known as civil society or the public sphere" (1993, 34). I remind Mr. Rheingold that this sphere was not intended for, nor open to, women and people of color when representative democracy was established in the United States (McCormick 1994).

Cordes summarizes the main themes of critics of technology as follows:

- The lack of democratic participation in the design and use of technologies that profoundly alter ordinary citizens' lives here and around the world.
- The threat of global and local ecological crises fueled by technological advances with unforeseen consequences.
- The increasing isolation of human beings from the rest of the living world, and a technological vision that would make most of the natural living world—including most of the human body—obsolete.

- The weakening of family and local community ties, even as individuals plug themselves into machines that encourage long-distance relationships—and a false sense of power over distant events.
- The tendency for new technologies and the global economy they promote to centralize political and economic power and to homogenize and impoverish cultures. (Cordes 1994, A10)

PROBLEMATICS OF TECHNOLOGY IN EDUCATION

Issues of Access, Participation, and Bias

The prevailing view of technology in the United States as an autonomous process and as an economic and pedagogical savior along with an uncritical embrace of computers and anything that is "high tech" (Bornet 1992) strongly influence and color the attitudes of educators toward technology in schools, too many of whom seem to view technology as a quick fix for educational problems.

While many voices since the 1960s have proclaimed the wonders and possibilities of advancing technologies in education, *relatively few* voices have devoted attention to issues of equity in the field. In the frenzied push to keep up with what is new in technology (see the April 1994 issue of *Educational Leadership* for an update), educators gave little thought to the differential effects of computer-assisted instruction on different cultural groups and female students (McCormick and McCoy 1990). However, by the mid-1980s some researchers began to voice concern about computer equity for students of color and female students (DeVillar and Faltis 1991: Kramarae 1988: Women's Action Alliance 1987; Sanders and Stone 1986: Lockheed 1985). Enrollment and participation data show that the typical computer user is a relatively affluent white male. Voicing concern over this situation, the Iowa State Department of Education stated, "Students who have historically benefited least from schooling—minorities, the disabled, the poor and female—are the same students who are in danger of becoming technologically disadvantaged" (1986, 1).

Specific equity issues to attend to when computers and students converge in classrooms are: issues of equal access to software and hardware; concerns about equal participation and the caliber of computer usage in the classroom; concerns about the perpetuation of race and sex biases and stereotypes via computer software; the issue of socioeconomic equity and opportunity; and teacher-student and student-student interactions. Other equity concerns include "hidden curriculum" issues which will be explored in a latter part of this chapter.

A basic principle of multicultural nonsexist education (MCNSE) is the provision of educational equity for all students. It seeks to eliminate the inequity and discrimination that result from a student's race, sex, religion, exceptionality, language, or class. All students need to see themselves reflected in instructional materials, such as computer software, in an authentic, accurate manner for them to gain the most from the learning experience.

Ruth Perry and Lisa Greber (1990) are one research team among many who concur about the problem of differential access to computer-assisted instruction based on race and sex. Patricia Frenette and Karen Harrington (1993) found these areas of disparity between males and females—of four different age/grade levels (from elementary school to college) in three different school districts and one college—in computer usage: (1) Women are depicted neither in popular computer magazines nor in computer textbooks. (2) Males have greater access to computer use in the home. Males are more likely to use computers and are given more help during usage by role models. (3) Female students tend to prefer word processing programs, while males prefer games. (4) Females usually view computers as tools, while males tend to use computers additionally for recreation and exploration. In summary, Frenette and Harrington (1993) found the following perception among the respondents at all levels and created an equation to illustrate it: Males + Technology + Computers = Normal Gender Skill. Here we see the power of traditional sex-role socialization that, in effect, pushes female students to convince themselves that computer usage is a male domain. No doubt, other factors—such as differential treatment of male and female students by teachers and software that focuses on themes and actions that are males-oriented—are at play here, but rigid sex-typing is the main culprit, I believe.

Critical Perspectives on Knowledge and Curriculum

Most critics of education have recognized for some time that school curriculum is not neutral knowledge. Increasingly, critical theorists such as Bowers and Apple are warning that technology in the curriculum is not neutral, that we must look at how technology alters the learning process, and "that the microcomputer, along with software programs, is part of the much more complex symbolic world that makes up our culture" (Bowers 1988, 24). Apple argues against a perspective of technology that "is set apart and viewed as if it had a life of its own, independent of social intentions, power, and privilege" (1991, 59). Bowers continues this line of thought by stating,

> When we think that expertise in the area of computers involves only a technical form of knowledge for using and improving computers, we are in fact, under the influence of the conceptual guidance system of our culture. In terms of the cultural bias built into our way of thinking, new ideas and technologies are understood as progressive by their very nature. But what is not as clearly recognized is that the new forms of knowledge and technologies often lead to unanticipated consequences whose disruptions may outweigh any gains from the innovations....A knowledge of the educational uses of computers...should also involve an understanding of how this new technology alters the cultural ecology of the classroom as well as influences the larger culture. (1988, 2)

Our love affair with computers and technical knowledge is rooted in what curriculum theorist, William Doll (1993), calls the "technical rationality" model that swept the country during the early years of the Industrial Revolution up through World War II. Specificity and quantification, the twin "scientific" aspects of the model, undergirded U.S. industrialists' goal of efficient production, which eventually became the hallmark of U.S. industrialism and a major influence on U.S. life and schools. Technical efficiency, assured by measurement and quantification (modeled after the factory), became the guiding paradigm of U.S. education by midcentury and still wields major influence on schools today. Doll concludes, "So began the pattern of devising curricula in small, measured units"(1993, 43). Out of this paradigm also grew the view of teachers as dispensers of bits of knowledge and students as passive receivers of quantifiable knowledge. The canon of knowledge to be dispensed in U.S. schools was created and approved by middle- to upper-class White men and reflected their experience and value system. This hegemonic control of knowledge in schools has been a major force in subordinating women and people of color in the United States because their various experiences, histories, contributions, values, and perspectives have been omitted or distorted.

The Hidden Curriculum

The "hidden curriculum" refers to the values, assumptions, and norms that form the foundation of the formal, "overt" curriculum. Interlaced with these elements are subtexts of power and control that significantly impact most classrooms. These aspects of a student's education are not written down nor formally taught, yet they have a tremendous influence on classroom dynamics and equity. For example, whether or not the teacher provides equal help and opportunity to ask questions to students of color as compared to the White students in the computer lab is a hidden dimension of the curriculum that may mean the difference between success and failure for the student. Quality, quantity, and type of teacher-student and student-student interaction and structural aspects (e.g., patterns of class scheduling that negatively affect a particular group of students) of the computer lab and of school programs are also important hidden dimensions that affect student achievement and participation.

The canon of knowledge (i.e., the knowledge that is valued by the dominant, elite, White male culture, then codified and taught), as well as the way it is taught, and other hidden dimensions in a school day (e.g., those examples given above, as well as requirements for neatness and punctuality) serve the needs of our industrial society by training "good workers" (see Joel Spring [1975] for an elaboration about the purpose of mass schooling being to train workers for the industrial state).

IMPLICATIONS FOR THE INTERFACE OF TECHNOLOGY AND MCNSE

You might be wondering, "What do all these perspectives about "knowledge" and "curriculum" have to do with MCNSE and educational technology?" Here are some of my interpretations and some corroborations by other researchers.

Computers, being a product of mathematics and engineering (both male-dominant fields), came to be characterized by a mechanistic ("how-to-do-it"), male-centric paradigm of learning and knowledge. In her book, *Machina Ex Dea*, Joan Rothschild shows "how use of male language forms reflected an exclusively male view of technology, the 'prototype'—the inventor, the user, the thinker about and reactor to technology—is male" (1983, xix, cited in Rothschild 1988, 58).

Computer education and instructional technology are natural outgrowths of the technical rationality/efficiency paradigm of knowledge and education discussed earlier, and this paradigm is not compatible with a multicultural, feminist view of knowledge.

Scientifically developed knowledge that is decontextualized is valued in instructional technology over practically developed knowledge or tacit knowing. Instructional technology is most commonly based on instructional design theory that has its roots in behavioristic stimulus-response-reinforcement learning theory (Sunwood 1994)—which, not surprisingly, fits well with factory-model schools. Sunwood says,

> ...superiority of theory over practice is amplified in instructional design models which consider knowledge as objective and decontextualized, and not related to any particular value orientation....Theory should be tested using the methods of science, excluding personal values. The goal is to develop objective knowledge which is generalizable to many contexts. In order to find such knowledge, they say theorists should be distanced from practice to ensure "value free" knowledge and theory. This, of course, is the opposite of a multicultural, non-sexist way of looking at knowledge and knowing. (1994, 8)

Peter McLaren, critical theorist, forcefully argues,

> Today, technocratic consciousness is looked upon as the new educational mechanism for generating classroom health....As teachers, we need collectively to demythologize the infallibility of educational programmers and so-called experts, who often do nothing more than zealously impose their epistemological assumptions on unassuming teachers under the guise of efficiency and procedural smoothness. What we are left with is an emphasis on practical and technical forms of knowledge as opposed to productive or transformative knowledge.
>
> A particularly serious problem with the technocratic mentality is its appearance of objectivity and value-neutrality. What its adherents don't tell you is that a hidden political agenda often times informs new policy and program directives. (1989, 222–223)

The critiques of technology given above are important because multicultural nonsexist education (MCNSE) requires that educators weigh the social consequences of all kinds of innovations, including Computer-Assisted Learning (CAL), Distance Education, and Computer-Mediated Communication (CMC). Who has access to computers? Who is using them in schools? Who is being left out or left behind?

These critiques raise questions about power and control and about the sociocultural, political, and economic contexts of technology in education. Those are the same issues and contexts that ground most inquiries in multicultural nonsexist education. For example, I, as a multicultural nonsexist educator, question why conservative business and scientific groups have jumped on the bandwagon of "equity." Framing a response to this question in a socioeconomic context, Suzammne Damarin, professor at The Ohio State University, contends that these groups

> ...see in the demand for equal educational outcomes an opportunity to capitalize upon "human resources" from a larger pool of individuals. Today, the idea of educational equity is totally confounded with ideas of scientific progress, national economic interest, and technological supremacy. In this context the idea that all naive learners will have equal opportunity to gain access to power through knowledge is eclipsed by the idea that already powerful institutions will gain access to knowledgeable persons from all societal subgroups. (1994, 34)

Critiques of technology from a MCNSE perspective are important to hear because of the ongoing hegemonic control of knowledge and the continuing imbalance of power held by White elite males in society, education, and in technology which maintain the oppression and marginalization of women and people of color. Judy Wajcman says, "Over the last two decades feminists have identified men's monopoly of technology as an important source of their power; women's lack of technological skills as an important element in our dependence on men" (1991, iix). Mary Herring concurs with Wajcman and brings into the discussion the issue of class when she says,

> ...know-how has become a central player in the class politics of technological work. Technical competence is seen as a key source of men's power over women, providing them with the capacity to command higher incomes and attain scarce jobs....Women may have knowledge about the technology, but the key to power is flexible, transferable skills that remain the property of men. (1994, 8)

Muffoletto reminds us that, "Technology...is part of discourse grounded in logical positivism, social control, and system management. It is a powerful discourse which has positioned technology behind the neutral facade of hardware, software, and science" (1994, 24). This reminds me of a connection with Sandra Harding's book, *The Racial Economy of Science*, in which she and other authors in the book "try to locate the broader social projects of Western cultures that have appropriated the resources of the sciences and to identify the features of Western sciences that have made them particularly attractive and susceptible to appropriation for *racist and imperialist agendas* (emphasis added) (1993, ix). Robert Johnson argues "that without examining and being aware of these various developments [scientific breakthroughs and technological development], Black Americans risk being subjugated to the vicissitudes of scientific and technological forces which are as oppressive, demeaning and domineering as are the socioeconomic and political forces of racism and exploitation" (1993, 458). Harding's and Johnson's comments point to two concerns of MCNSE educators. One is the hegemonic control by White males of scientific and technological knowledge and history and, thus, control of the curriculum. The second concern is about the historic tendency to misuse science and technology for racist purposes.

PARADIGMS AND PROMISES FOR AN EQUITABLE USE OF TECHNOLOGY VIEWED THROUGH A MCNSE LENSE

An ongoing concern is how to prepare a predominantly White female group of preservice teachers (who have been socialized through home and school to be passive, powerless, silent, and nice) to be both technologically literate and prepared to teach an ethnically diverse student population. As discussed earlier in the paper, the former (technology) is perceived to be a male domain by many women students, and the latter is resisted because of a clash between their cultural norms and unconscious values and those of a course with a different set of values and assumptions and a goal of preparing them to be agents of social change (McCormick 1993).

Nurturing Critical Perspectives and Liberatory Pedagogy

In order to empower preservice teachers (75 percent female) to engage in a meaningful way with technology and multicultural nonsexist education, we in teacher education must first have a clear vision of the political context of their lives today and of the depths of oppression that they have internalized and still experience because of the misogyny that is inherent in the male-centric education system. We must recognize that many women students resist liberatory education because it is perceived to be "unsafe" for their survival in a White dominant patriarchy (Lewis 1990). I speculate that the dynamics for women students who resist science, math, and technology may be similar—they fear these male-dominated fields and have internalized the sexist messages from society that they do not belong and are not wanted in math, science, and technology.

Revisioning Knowledge and Knowing

Christine Sleeter (in press) says that women entering teaching do not need to be taught what they already know (i.e., oppression, sex stratification), rather, they need help in how to reconstruct and use that knowledge for their own growth and liberation, not how to fit into the male model of technologized education. This requires a reconceptualization of knowledge that shifts from a Western androcentric perspective to a more holistic view that includes females and males and people of all cultures.

A perspective on knowledge and knowing that is counter-hegemonic is needed to enable technology to meet the needs of all learners—students of color and White females—not just White males. *Constructivism* fits the demands of multicultural nonsexist education that learners need to be actively engaged rather than passively accepting and feeding back tidbits of knowledge. The students' various learning styles are honored by the constructivist view of knowledge because, as Renee Campoy says,

> ...knowing is seen as a process of constructing a personal reality through discussion and exploration. The role of the teacher then becomes one of a facilitator and organizer of problems for students to study, discuss, and solve; and technology supports this philosophy by providing rich resources for students to use as they construct their personal knowledge bases. (1992, 21)

This perspective on knowledge and knowing encourages the student to weave webs of meaning, to incorporate personal experience into webs of connected knowing, to connect inner tacit knowledge with external knowledge. This perspective enhances reflectivity, critical thinking, and problem solving in the knower. Here, the focus is on the student, not on a body of knowledge. This view of knowledge envisions a circular flow of interactions between teacher and student, rather than a linear, one-way flow of interaction from teacher to student.

For technology to incorporate a multicultural, nonsexist perspective on curriculum, the static view of knowledge and behavioristic orientation to learning need to exit the same door that the objective-driven curriculum exits. In its place, an experientialist orientation to curriculum (Schubert 1993) and a constructivist approach (Doll 1993) would be compatible with James Banks (1991) and Donna Gollnick and Phillip Chinn's (1994) goals for multicultural curricula. William Schubert says that an experientialist orientation to curriculum has its foundation in ideas of John Dewey and integrates diverse people and ideas. He posits that it is concerned with

> everyday dilemmas...[that] surely relate to today's increased consciousness of persons who are oppressed or silenced because of race, class, gender, health, age, place....The central assumption is that curriculum reform is enhanced by grass roots participation of those who will be affected most directly by the reform. (1993, 84)

Doll explains constructivism in this manner:

> From Piaget, Prigogine, Dewey, and Bruner come the ideas of construction— with all but Piaget, and he, in part, favoring open-ended, nondeterminist construction. Hence, a constructive curriculum is one that emerges through the action and interaction of the participants; it is not set in advance (except in broad and general terms). (1993, 162)

Promising Practices

As mentioned at the beginning of this chapter, technology holds great potential to assist learning if it is used wisely, with care and reflectivity. Following are some examples of applications of technology that are compatible with multicultural nonsexist education concepts and principles.

Robert DeVillar and Christian Faltis (1991) offer an alternative conceptual framework for incorporating computer use within a heterogeneous classroom. Their model integrates the ideas of L. S. Vygotsky on social learning theory with Gordon Allport's contact theory and the principles of cooperative learning. The computer is used to enhance discovery-oriented learning and to enhance communication for pupils collaborating in small work groups.

Campoy (1992) describes recent improvements in software that truly engage the students in problem solving, problem producing, and decision making. Some examples are HOTS (Higher Order Thinking Skills), a remedial program that is intended to teach thinking skills to at-risk students and "Decisions, Decisions," a simulation that requires cooperative learning and group skills.

Jo Sanders, director of the Computer Equity Project during the last two-and-a-half years, showed two hundred math and computer-science teachers from grades 6 through 12 how to recognize and eliminate gender bias in their classrooms. She encouraged the teachers to involve more girls in the computer world by organizing mentor programs with older students and by having girls-only days at the computer labs at school (Hafner 1994).

During the past two years, Mary Herring, an instructor of a multicultural nonsexist education class in my college, had been dealt the same kind of resistance from students that I mentioned earlier in this chapter. This past semester, she decided to tackle the "resistance and silence" problem by making a journaling-via-E-mail assignment:

- E-mail assignment: E-mail a journal entry every other week to the instructor. Suggested topics you may wish to reflect upon are: class discussions and presentations, questions developed from your readings, questions that you personally wish to have a response given from the teacher.
- In addition, the instructor asked for feedback on specific topics as was timely and appropriate (e.g., the students' comfort level with the class or a classroom presentation).
- The instructor responded personally to each entry and included the original letter in the response for the student's reference.

Student E-mail Message, Example 1: On Content of the Course
From John Moore (fictional names, original messages)

Hello again.
I thought the lecture about gays, lesbians, and bisexuals was very interesting the other day. It is easy to see just how uncomfortable the issue really is. When you were talking about it, there were many questions, but when a known lesbian got up to speak about the issue, there were very few questions. There was only one question asked by a woman in the class other than yourself. It is amazing that this can be

seen, even in a class that deals totally with multiculturalism and nonsexism. The speaker seemed a little uncomfortable, but I can see why this might be so. She expected to answer a lot of questions and got very few, instead. I am glad you asked her to speak to us; I have had very little known contact with gays, lesbians, and bisexuals and learned some things I had not known before.

Instructor E-mail Response, Example 1:

Yes John. I was amazed by the female's reaction also! I guess it shows how strong our socialization about the stereotype of gays, lesbians, and bisexuals is. Females that have responded have mainly said they were afraid that if they asked questions they would be typecast as a lesbian by classmates. If they feel that way in our class, imagine the oppression outside of class!! Most respondents echoed your sentiment in regards to the contact activity experience. Glad you found the class period a learning experience! Have a good weekend. MCH

Student E-mail Message, Example 2: On the Process of Journaling
From Susan

The whole journaling experience has been extremely helpful for me as a student. Not only did it give me the opportunity to communicate with you when I wasn't able to meet with you in person, but it also gave me an outlet for ideas and thoughts about the subject matter in our class. It was one way for you to become familiar with my personality besides the one you knew from class and also for me to become familiar with yours. Often, your journal responses were a nice supplement to the material we were covering in class. It offered a deeper insight into the subject matter and the perspective from which we have been studying.

Student E-mail Message, Example 3: On the Technology
From Joe

This E-mail thing is a good way of talking about issues that we don't have time to talk about in class. I think you should keep doing it. I am a very reflective, nonimpulsive learner, so I don't feel comfortable about contributing to discussions until I have thought out my opinions, and by that time we have usually moved on to something else. E-mail gives me all the time I need to think about things first.

• Instructor's personal assessment of the assignment: The students were able to question constructs of lessons, direction of the course, and their own personal questions that arose as a part of the coursework. Of particular importance, was the ability to deal immediately with their personal disequilibrium on a one-on-one basis; so often, this disequilibrium caused the students to shut down and turn off from the class. The ability to offer them immediate personal feedback greatly facilitated the process.

Next semester, in my multicultural nonsexist education class, the preservice teachers will be connected twice each month with an urban multicultural school system via Distance Education, a system of two-way interactive television. Various formats (panels, presentations, interviews, etc.) will evolve, according to the interests of the university students and the people at the remote site. The purpose of this activity is to connect my students (all White women, mostly from small rural, all-White communities) with teachers, counselors, and administrators who work with multicultural populations in the schools; to connect them with students who go to school in a multicultural urban setting; and to connect them with parents of children in the inner city. This Distance Education experience is part of the students' field experience attached to the regular lecture class.

SUMMARY

In this chapter, I examined technology with a critical perspective, starting with the problematics of technology in society. Secondly, I looked at the problematics of technology in education, using the lens of a multicultural nonsexist educator to examine issues of access, participation, and bias. Next, critical perspectives on knowledge and curriculum were examined, and then aspects of the "hidden curriculum" were discussed. Some implications for the interface of technology and multicultural nonsexist education were drawn. The final section, paradigms and promises for an equitable use of technology, included the topics of nurturing critical perspectives and liberatory pedagogy, revisioning knowledge and knowing, revisioning curriculum, and promising innovative practices, including two that are occurring in my college—journaling between instructor and students via E-mail, and Distance Education via two-way interactive television.

REFERENCES

Apple, M. (1991). The new technology: Is it part of the solution or part of the problem in education? *Computers in the Schools* 8(1/2/3):59–77.

Banks, J. (1991). *Teaching strategies for ethnic studies.* Needham Heights, MA: Allyn and Bacon.

Bornet, B. (1992). Challenging the dominant computer culture: Pluralism in PC pedagogy. Paper presented at the American Educational Research Association meeting, San Francisco.

Bowers, C. (1988). *The cultural dimensions of educational computing.* New York: Teachers College Press.

Campoy, R. (1992, August). The role of technology in the school reform movement. *Educational Technology*, 17–22.

Cordes, C. (1994, April 27). Technology as religion? *The Chronicle of Higher Education*, A10, A15.

Damarin, S. (1994, February). Equity, caring, and beyond: Can feminist ethics inform educational technology? *Educational Technology*, 34–39.

DeVillar, R., and C. Faltis. (1991). *Computers and cultural diversity*. Albany, NY: SUNY Press.

Doll Jr., W. (1993). *A post-modern perspective on curriculum*. New York: Teachers College Press.

Frenette, P., and K. Harrington. (1993, November 4). Gender inequity in computer use. Paper presented at Research on Women in Education meeting, Toledo, OH.

Gollnick, D., and P. Chinn. (1994). *Multicultural education in a pluralistic society*. New York: Merrill.

Hafner, K. (1994, April). Getting girls on-line. *Working Woman*, 60–61.

Harding, S., ed. (1993). *The racial economy of science*. Bloomington, IN: Indiana University Press.

Herring, M. (1994, June 16). Progressing toward praxis: A personal journey. Paper presented at the National Women's Studies Association meeting, Ames, IA.

Howell, W. (1994, June 8). How social scientists can contribute to the information revolution. *The Chronicle of Higher Education* 40(40):A40.

Iowa State Department of Education. (1986). Multicultural, non-sexist education. Des Moines: Author.

Johnson, R. (1993). Science technology and Black community development. In *The racial economy of science*, ed. S. Harding, 459–471. Bloomington, IN: Indian University Press.

Kramarae, C. (1988). *Technology and women's voices: Keeping in touch*. New York: Routledge and Kegan Paul.

Lewis, M. (1990, November). Interrupting patriarchy: Politics, resistance, and transformation in the feminist classroom. *Harvard Educational Review* 60(4):467–488.

Lockheed, M. (1985). Women, girls and computers. *Sex Roles* 13(3/4):115–121.

McCormick, T. (1993, November 6). Learning from patterns of student resistance to a course on multicultural nonsexist education awareness. Paper presented at the Research on Women in Education meeting, Toledo, OH.

McCormick, T. (1994). *Creating the nonsexist classroom—A multicultural approach*. New York: Teachers College Press.

McCormick, T., and S. McCoy. (1990). Computer-assisted instruction and multicultural education: A caveat for those who select and design software. *Computers in the Schools* 7(4):105–124.

McLaren, P. (1989). *Life in schools: An introduction to critical pedagogy in the foundations of education.* White Plains, NY: Longman.

Muffoletto, R. (1994, February). Technology and restructuring education: Constructing a context. *Educational Technology* 34(2):24–28.

Perry, R., and L. Greber. (1990). Women and computers: An introduction. *Signs* 16(1):74–101.

Realizing the promise of technology. (1994, April). *Educational Leadership,* Special issue, 51(7):3–93.

Rheingold, H. (1993, November 29). Redefining community. *Informationweek,* 28–34.

Rothschild, J., ed. (1983). *Machina ex dea: Feminist perspectives on technology.* New York: Pergamon Press.

Rothschild, J. (1988). *Teaching technology from a feminist perspective.* New York: Teachers College Press/Athene.

Sanders, J., and A. Stone. (1986). *The neuter computer: Computers for girls and boys.* New York: Neal-Schuman.

Scholes, R. (1991). Power and pleasure in video texts. In *Video icons & values,* ed. A. Olson, C. Parr, and D. Parr, 81–95. Albany, NY: SUNY Press.

Schubert, W. (1993). Curriculum reform. In *Challenges and achievements of American education,* ed. G. Cawelti, 80–115. Alexandria, VA: Association for Supervision and Curriculum Development.

Sleeter, C. (in press). Teaching Whites about racism. In *Practicing what we teach,* ed. R. Martin. Albany, NY: SUNY Press.

Spring, J. (1975). *A primer of libertarian education.* New York: Free Life Editions.

Sunwood, K. (1994, June 18). Different ways of knowing—Different ways of showing: Teaching instructional design and media production multiculturally. Paper presented at National Women's Studies Association meeting, Ames, IA.

Wajcman, J. (1991). *Feminism confronts technology.* University Park, PA: Pennsylvania State University Press.

Winner, L. (1993, August 4). How technology reweaves the fabric of society. *The Chronicle of Higher Education* 39(48):B1–B3.

Women's Action Alliance. (1987). *Do your female students say 'no thanks' to computers?* New York, NY: Author.

15

NEDRA COBB

Preparing Music Teachers for Multicultural Challenges

Multicultural education expands knowledge, affects value systems and beliefs, and influences ways of looking at almost every facet of life. Incorporating a variety of cultural experiences in music will have an influence on the general level of well-being of teachers and students. However, the music instructor must possess the discipline and desire to research and do field work on various cultures.

Music teachers today are confronted with numerous problems as they strive to instruct student bodies with wide variations in nationalities, ethnicities, and economic backgrounds. They are faced with the challenge of relating to children who perceive and react differently to stimuli in the same environment.

In light of cultural challenges, music teachers need to put more emphasis on multicultural teaching strategies in music education courses. In doing so, future educators would become more prepared to face diverse cultural encounters in the classroom and skillfully use different materials and/or instructional approaches to cater to the needs of culturally different children. This chapter will explore reforms necessary to successfully implement multicultural concepts in music courses.

BACKGROUND

Historically, the purpose of music education was based solely upon aesthetic rather than social/cultural principles. These aesthetic principles inadvertently overshadowed the importance of including and advocating music of various cultures. Music instruction was constricted in scope. Non-Western music and certain forms of jazz, popular, and folk music were almost altogether neglected (Campbell 1991).

In retrospect, culture must first be understood as an essential part of what music is, in order for music education to make continued progress in the realm of multicultural education. When teachers realize that music education is first and foremost cultural education, they will seek to increase their knowledge and understanding of various musical cultures. Warrick Carter states that "music is not a universal language, but rather a product of each culture, subculture or social class within our complex society" (1993, 41). The perception of music being something separate and apart from daily living tends to divorce music and music behavior from life. As a result, teachers having no other musical experiences or understanding of other cultures would find difficulty in effectively teaching and relating to music of other cultures and, most importantly, to their students.

Teaching methodologies designed to change or diminish the acceptability of other cultural influences obstruct and deprive culturally different students from essential materials and different instructional approaches conducive to their musical growth. Such lessons more than likely turn out sterile and alienating to the students. Since music plays an increasingly prominent role as a significant transmitter of society's artistic and sociocultural heritage, method courses need to be further assessed (Anderson and Lawrence 1991).

If multicultural trends are to progress in music education, the music methods taught in universities and colleges must include non-Western, jazz, and folk music from all cultures and periods. In acknowledging diverse cultural standards, music teachers take a stronger stand in upholding the integrity of each ethnic group by demonstrating their appreciation of other music, language, ethnicity, history, and heritage.

TEACHING STRATEGIES

Two basic areas covered in my methods class are philosophy of music and lesson planning. I begin my course by discussing the philosophy of music education, analyzing why music should be taught, what music should be taught, and how music should be taught from a multicultural perspective. Students are later expected to apply multicultural strategies to the basic concepts and objectives of their lesson plans.

Philosophy: Why Teach

Most students have a general idea as to why they want to teach music and a basic understanding of its importance in education. Comments such as "I like music," "I like kids," or "I was inspired by my music teacher" are common responses. Teacher burnout in music education usually derives from not having a strong or clear conviction of purpose for teaching music.

I guide the discourse into a broader spectrum using multicultural concepts that allow the student to see music as a part of the world about us, as part of our heritage, and as a means of personal expression. Students are expected to research, examine, and discuss various opinions regarding these issues and formulate their own philosophies which are strengthened throughout the course.

For example, I tape two large sheets of paper on the chalkboard. The first sheet of paper has headings and columns on which each student is to identify her or his ethnic/social background, musical interests, and collections of recordings, books, and so forth. It is interesting to observe how the students identify themselves culturally. Comments are made regarding the wide variety of musical interests and tastes in the class and the glimpses they reveal of personality.

Then they focus on the second large sheet of paper having similar headings but apply it to their interaction with other cultures. Here, they identify their experiences and interests in cultures other than their own. We discuss the significance of their multicultural experiences and note the impact their cultural background has on their musical taste.

Finally, they analyze the various types of music associated with the other students on the chart and observe the similarities and differences on the chart. Then we look at various music textbooks locating song material that represents the various categories listed on the chart and note uses of the music among each group, for example holidays, patriotic occasions, and so forth.

This exercise illustrates why multiculturalism is such a vital and essential component in music education. Music is viewed as being a powerful life force that can connect one with a broad range of people. However, the ultimate goal of multicultural education is, not only to have students simply tolerate or understand the extreme degrees of diversity among people and their music, but to appreciate them as well.

Philosophy: What to Teach

I explain to my students that, as teachers, they will begin to understand more clearly what to teach when they deal more effectively with culturally different children. They will take a stronger stand in upholding the integrity of each ethnic group and teach others how to appreciate and value others' music, language, ethnicity, history, and heritage. They will teach how to relate to who and what people are and not to what they would like them to become (Fillmore 1993).

Classes become most enjoyable and rewarding in teaching multiculturalism in music when concepts are related to the happenings in the real world. So, we look at pictures of children reacting to music in different social environments such as households and religious communities. We discuss the effect that these various situations possibly could have on a child's cultural identity. We note the manner in which the diverse environments provide stimulation and development in cultural cognizance and artistic taste.

For example, although the public has mixed feelings regarding the merit of rap music as an art form, it is an extremely popular phenomenon among many young people. Therefore, we desire to reach students enamored with this style of music by constructively implementing it into a lesson, rather than completely disregarding it as an art form.

Due to the limited amount of class time, I suggest that the students, on their own time, experience a variety of cultural activities such as ethnic festivals, churches of various denominations, powwows, synagogues, MTV, rap and rock concerts, and all other popular media today. I encourage them to incorporate these multicultural experiences in teaching basic music concepts as well as songs in the text. These experiences help students, not only to understand and to tolerate individual differences, but to appreciate them as well.

The Silver Burdett Music Series I used in general music instruction from 1982 to 1986 contained wonderful material on diverse cultures. At the fifth-grade level, units on Polynesia, Africa, and Asia specifically addressed these cultures showing pictures of the people, maps, instruments, and providing appropriate recordings to represent the music of these cultures.

In 1990, I was invited to give a presentation at an elementary school on African American music, and I thought to incorporate some of the material I used in the Silver Burdett Series. But to my dismay, all of the cultural units I recalled from earlier editions had been extracted from the current text. After reviewing several other music texts, I discovered that music education was changing in its philosophy. Rather than promoting students to accept and respect the diversity of Americans, the series focused on promoting and defining the dominant American culture.

I felt that it was most unfortunate that music education was attempting to eliminate and ignore cultural diversity in its music texts. Educators that go along with such a policy fail to realize the intrinsic value in teaching music of diverse cultures and do not exhibit empathy toward the culturally different. In essence, they support the notion that the music of other cultures is "trite," "vulgar," and "lacking in musical substance," especially when compared with "classical music." The value of diverse music must not be overlooked, particularly if used as the starting point in the music education of culturally different students.

I inform my students that, in order to make up for the cultural deficiencies in such texts, they need to get involved and invite visiting musicians, composers, and scholars to their classroom or assemblies. They should consider artists-in-residence programs to cultivate the musical interests in the school and community. All cultural resources in the community should be called upon to expand and enrich their schools and music programs.

However, it is the classroom teacher's responsibility to personally develop knowledge and accumulate instructural materials which supplement the school's standard curriculum with more culturally diverse materials. As future teachers, they are encouraged to design insightful and practical lessons by drawing upon their personal experiences. Later, we try some of the ideas outlined in specialized multicultural sources, such as *Teaching The Music Of Six Different Cultures* by Luvenia A. George (1987) and *Integrating Music Into The Classroom* by William M. Anderson and Joy E. Lawrence (1991).

Philosophy: How to Teach

Students are required to visit as many varied teaching situations as possible to observe different school environments and teaching styles. In addition, I invite other music teachers from various areas, such as the inner-city, suburban, rural, private, and public school systems to speak to my students regarding their experiences in the classroom. Some teachers bring students with them for further input. I assign video tapes on teaching episodes and perform in-class simulations so students can recognize the importance of establishing better human relations with their pupils. Video tapings of the students' own teaching draws attention to their enthusiasm, eye contact, and physical interaction with pupils.

Students note that some teachers, in their observations, appear to be uncomfortable with children of various backgrounds. They describe the teacher as being robotic, having glazed over smiles or deadpan expressions, giving nonemotional compliments, and exhibiting no real enjoyment in teaching the subject or teaching the subject to the children. Students are advised to keep in mind that children not only react to what is being said but also to how it is being said, which can either embrace or isolate the child. I explain to my class that children encounter situations of overt and subtle forms of racism. As teachers, they need to make the children feel good about themselves, their accomplishments, race, and culture. Positive images of their lives, histories, and cultures through books, magazines, and cultural places of interest are important and should be displayed in the class.

Students are reminded that they are not just music educators who primarily teach music but overall teachers who teach children. They must go beyond how to teach music to work more broadly with culturally diverse groups of students. We simulate situations in class pertaining to racial bias and discipline. Derogatory remarks from classmates and biased attitudes from authorities are discussed. I inform the students to address these immediately. Let the children know that, when someone says something demeaning about another race, it is not a reflection of the children's worth or their people. It may mean that the person who made the comment is ignorant about the culture and contributions of that race or that the person who exhibits this racism is one who cannot deal with his or her own inadequacies or inabilities and so, instead, demeans others. Or, the child may be repeating what had been taught at home. The music students are advised to attempt to resolve the situation by talking to the children involved and, if necessary, contacting the parents (Friedman 1980).

After several observations of other teachers and various teaching situations, students are more aware of the importance of teaching ethics and values. They conclude that teachers need to possess a sense of self-worth and maturity in order to generate a genuine warmth and response to and from students.

Multicultural Concepts in Lesson Planning

The ultimate goal in my music methods course is to help students to successfully implement multiculturalism in teaching basic music concepts, which are melody, rhythm, texture, dynamics, timbre, and form. These six concepts are used as the basic conceptional framework in music education, and the students in methods class are encouraged to illustrate how these individual components can vary and combine in different forms from one cultural group to another. The elements of music remain constant factors, but they can be expressed and combined in a variety of ways to reflect the variations in culture.

The following examples illustrate some of the ways that students in my elementary and secondary methods classes have described how they integrated multiculturalism into lessons they taught in their field experiences.

Example 1: Native American The student used a Native American song entitled "Indian Dance" from a music text out of print. The objective was to introduce the song to kindergarten students and reinforce the basic concepts of rhythm (steady beat) and timbre (tone colors). The procedure went as follows:

1) Drew class attention to the pictures of the Native Americans illustrated on the music. Discussed the pictures, particularly the attire.
2) Taught lyrics of song by rote.
3) Placed bells around the ankles of the children.
4) Played music on recording or chord on piano as children walked/ danced in circle to the rhythm (steady beat).

Example 2: African American The student's objective was to teach the rhythm (accent on off beat or beat 2) and introduce syncopation to a third grade. The procedure went as follows:

1) Performed review song "All Night All Day" having pupils clap on the beat.
2) Showed accented rhythms on chalkboard.
3) Showed picture of an African American Gospel Choir.
4) Illustrated movement of gospel choirs' accentuation of the second beat.
5) Teacher functioned as a gospel choir director having the class stand and sway side to side clapping on the second beat of the music.
6) Repeated step 5 with another selection (O Happy Day) and incorporated a syncopated clap (or double clap).
7) Instructor requested that a few volunteers bring more gospel selections next time.

Example 3: Jewish The student's objective was to introduce a kindergarten class to the "Dreydel Song," and play the game which is practiced during the Jewish holiday "Hannukah." The procedure went as follows:

1) Student Instructor discussed Hannukah with the class and made a dreydel beforehand to show the class.
2) Instructor had class clap and rock to the steady beat while singing the song.
3) Taught the lyrics by rote.
4) Class sang and clapped along with recording.
5) Played the game while singing without recording.

Example 4: Polynesian The student's objective was to teach a third-grade class melody, form (phrasing), and timbre (tone colors) using the song "Hawaiian Rainbow." The procedure went as follows:

1) Student Instructor showed and discussed picture of Hawaii, referring to its location on the map, the climate, and so forth.
2) Student Instructor played "Hawaiian Rainbow" and permitted students to move to music spontaneously.
3) Class identified the various sounds in the recording.
4) Taught lyrics and phrase movements to song by rote.
5) Pupils then performed movements and sang with recording.

Example 5: Polynesian The student's objective was to teach a fifth-grade class rhythm (the beat in three) using tini-kling, which is a Polynesian dance. The dancers hop between two bamboo poles as the pole bearers keep the steady beat, lightly tapping the poles on the floor twice and striking them together once or vice versa. The procedure went as follows:

1) Instructor provided two or four long poles (mop handles would be appropriate) and demonstrated rhythmic technique with another student. Pupils clapped along using patschen (pat, pat, clap).
2) Another student took the instructor's place and repeated the exercise.
3) The instructor then hopped between the poles demonstrating the dance.
4) Another group of students set up to perform the dance.

Example 6: African Student's objectives were to define and teach rhythm (polyrhythm) to a sixth-grade class, identify the timbre of various instruments of Africa, and create polyrhythmic compositions. The procedure went as follows:

1) Instructor showed map and had a student volunteer point out Africa.
2) Pupils looked at pictures of people in the book and discussed the location, climate, and so forth.
3) Instructor first played a familiar song from Africa called "Che Che Koolay."
4) Students listened to other music from Africa and discussed the various sounds in the recording. Students acknowledged voices and instruments and identified string, percussion, brass, or woodwinds.
5) Students looked at various pictures of the instruments and made parallels to instruments that were more familiar to them.
6) Instructor taught polyrhythmic patterns and had a few students at a time take turns in performing the rhythms in front of the class on various orff instruments.
7) Pupils were allowed to create their own rhythmic patterns.

Example 7: Hispanic The student's objective was to teach a fourth-grade class timbre (tone colors) and melody (up/down direction of melodic line) using the song, "A La Nanita." The instructor developed an interdisciplinary activity with the art department by having the class make piñatas for the holiday (same with the dreydels). The procedure went as follows:

1) Student Instructor played the recording and discussed origin of the song. Students were able to identify the sound of the guitar and voices.
2) Instructor taught song by rote.
3) Pupils identified when the melody line was moving up or down by drawing contour of the melody line on the chalkboard.
4) Instructor strummed on the guitar or autoharp while singing.
5) Instructor gave more information about the significance of the guitar in Hispanic culture.

Example 8: Hispanic The student's objective was to teach a middle-school class rhythm, melodic movement, and timbre (tone colors) using a Spanish song entitled "De Colores. " The procedure went as follows.

1) Played recording of song.
2) Asked class to identify the language. Explained the meaning of the lyrics and music.
3) Taught the Spanish lyrics by rote (clapped rhythm while speaking words.)
4) Sang the melody by rote and discussed the stepwise movement of the melody.
5) Sang song through without, and then with, instruments.

Example 9: Carribean/Latin American The student's objective was to enable a high school class to create an original percussion part to be played with a song of Latin American style.

1) Played recording "Planet Drum."
2) Discussed the origin of the music. (Mickey Hart, the drummer for the Grateful Dead, composed "Planet Drum" by compiling percussive music heard throughout the world.
3) Showed, named, and demonstrated the hand held instruments.
4) Passed instruments out to the students.
5) Performed call and response. Instructor played a rhythm, and they repeated the pattern on their instruments.
6) Practiced individual rhythms by assigning each student a different rhythm to play.
7) Played rhythms simultaneously.
8) Traded instruments and played new rhythms.
9) Performed instruments and sang with a familiar song, "Banana Boat Song."

These lesson plans could be revised to focus on different concepts, as in the case of Example 7. Pupils could identify ABA form in "A La Nanita, " by making soft/loud dynamic contrasts or distinguishing between thin and thick textures, instead of melodic direction. The lessons may also be adapted to other grade levels with minor revisions.

Here we have seen a few examples of how basic concepts can be uniquely taught through cultural diversity. What better way to reinforce concepts than with songs that are unique or related to the cultural background of the pupil.

The students can plan a lesson by (1) starting with one of the six concepts; (2) picking a particular behavior that can be expressed by verbalizing, visualizing, drawing, or creating music of their own improvisation or composition; (3) associating the concept with a topic which could be seasonal or part of a broader interdisciplinary unit; (4) starting with a music selection such as jazz, blues, rock, classical, and so forth; or (5) taking relevant questions or inquiries from their pupils.

I advise students to consider their pupils as being their greatest resource in formulating lessons because they come to music class with a multitude of songs from their social/cultural backgrounds. I recommend that they incorporate this type of activity in their lesson planning as much as possible. For example, in the African American culture, some children learn how to sing gospel songs and play complicated rhythms on the tambourine proficiently at a very young age. These pupils could contribute a new skill and greater musical insight in the class.

Teachers tapping into such knowledge turn commonplace encounters into interesting experiences and focus more on motivational techniques than classroom management and discipline. When general music methods students try to relate the music material to their pupils' knowledge and experiences, they can expect to create more meaningful lessons in which students would find it easier to retain and understand musical concepts. Learning about other music cultures in this manner would enrich the lives of the teacher and the students. Music classes thus taught are sure to become both interesting and exciting and become an enjoyable experience for teacher and pupil rather than a grind.

REFERENCES

Anderson, W. M., and J. E. Lawrence. (1991). *Integrating music into the classroom*, 2nd edition. Belmont: Wadsworth.

Campbell, P. (1991). *Lessons from the world*. New York: Schirmer Books.

Carter, W. L. (1983). Music education for the culturally different student: Myths vs. reality. In *Methods and perspectives in urban music education*, ed. C. E. Hicks, J. A. Standifer and W. L. Carter, 32–59. Washington, DC: University Press of America.

Fillmore, L. W. (1993). Educating citizens for a multicultural 21st century. *Multicultural Education* 1(1):10–12.

Friedman, D. L. (1980). *Education handbook for Black families*. Garden City, NY: Anchor Press.

George, L. A. (1987). *Teaching the music of six different cultures*. Danbury, CT: World Music Press.

16

VERONICA M. ACOSTA-DEPREZ_____

Approaches to Making the Comprehensive School Health Education Curriculum Multicultural

In many ways, the characteristic goals and approaches of health education parallel those of multicultural education. One overlapping goal of these two areas, for example, is to enhance the attitudes and behaviors of students so that they can survive and live healthily and happily in this culturally diverse society. Both areas confront people's habits, assumptions, and prejudices. Both link new methods of instruction to resulting behavioral changes. It is in these two areas that teachers encourage students to become powerful agents of change so they can accomplish their highest ideals and dreams. Both areas engage students in critical thinking and modes of reflection about themselves and others so that they can think and challenge themselves in new ways. When health teachers instill multi-cultural views into their teaching, they undoubtedly influence the physiological, social, psychological, and cultural health of their students, as well as their ways of knowing and thinking about health. In teaching health, they influence their students' multicultural views especially as this pertains to the health of others. In this regard, when multiculturalism is integrated into health education, the impact of this education on the health, knowledge, attitudes, and behaviors of students will be more profound.

In affirming the multicultural view, I infuse multiculturalism into all of my health education and teacher preparation courses, including a course entitled "Methods of Health Instruction," which will be the focus of this chapter. To enable students to think multiculturally, I use various approaches that target enhancing the multicultural viewpoint. The primary purpose of these approaches is to broaden students' views about the world and to raise awareness on the various ways of thinking about health, people, the environment, and society. In this chapter, I will provide a basic description of the central philosophical foun-dation of the course, followed by a more detailed explanation of the activities and approaches which I utilized to enhance the multicultural viewpoint. These approaches will be described in light of the Comprehensive School Health Education (CSHE) program. The CSHE program is "an organized set of policies, procedures, and activities designed to protect and promote the health and well-being of students and staff which has included health services, healthful school environment, and health education" (Meeks and Heit 1992, 11). In its expanded concept, it has also included five other components, which are school food services, school-site health promotion programs for faculty and staff, school counseling and psychology programs, school physical education, and integrated community and school health promotion efforts (Allensworth and Kolbe 1987). In this chapter, I delve into strategies that infuse multiculturalism into each of the first three components of the Comprehensive School Health Education (CSHE) program, namely health instruction, healthful school environment, and health services; most of these strategies, with a little modification, may also be applied to the other components. I then explore some methodological as well as conceptual issues which may be confronted by teacher educators in attempting to fulfill their multicultural health education purposes. In addition, I provide a few suggestions on how to implement these approaches more successfully.

PHILOSOPHICAL FOUNDATION OF THE COURSE

The teaching challenge in this course is to enable each student to develop a multicultural philosophy that will evolve from the knowledge and application of various multicultural concepts, theories, or paradigms. One such concept is the adaptation of certain multicultural characteristics, skills, and ways of looking at the world as exemplified by Peter Adler (1977, 10) in his definition of the multicultural person:

> Multicultural (man)[woman] is the person who is intellectually and emotionally committed to the fundamental unity of all human beings while at the same time he [she] recognizes, legitimizes, accepts, and appreciates the fundamental differences that lie between people from different cultures.

Another concept is that portrayed by Christine Sleeter and Carl Grant who described an approach to education that is multicultural and social reconstructionist which

> deals more directly...with oppression and social structural inequality based on race, social class, gender, and disability...the approach prepares future citizens to reconstruct society so that it better serves the interest of all groups of people and especially those who are of color, poor, female, gay, and/or disabled" (209–210).

This concept transcends education to include the use of approaches that teach students to become critical thinkers and that cultivate social action skills, thus enabling them to actively participate in and control their own health and destiny.

These two concepts undergird the goals for the course, which are to develop a multicultural orientation toward looking at issues and the commitment to act on that orientation. The evolvement of a multicultural philosophy depends much on the processes that enable students to think, experience, and relate these thoughts and experiences to their own lives. Hence, approaches that focus on social critique and critical thinking (Shor 1980), experiential learning (Kolb 1984), empowerment (Freire 1970), and reflective practice (Schon 1987) are emphasized and repeatedly implemented in the course. It is hoped that students will eventually develop a multicultural health education perspective that moves beyond the intention of merely transmitting information or solving today's problems to the embarkation on some altruistic endeavor reflecting a personal health education mission.

MULTICULTURAL COMPREHENSIVE SCHOOL HEALTH EDUCATION

In making the CSHE program multicultural, my attempt is to engage students in modes that will evoke individual forms of communication, comprehension, and interest. Primarily, I stress approaches that engage students in exploring and understanding: (1) the goals and purposes of health education; (2) the concept of school as a social system and how this concept parallels the comprehensive school health education program perspective; and (3) individual knowledge and experiences in relationship to those of others. In the following sections, activities that relate to these approaches will be described.

Understanding Others' Goals and Purposes and Developing One's Own

The success of health education is based on clearly defining one's personal purpose for teaching and, in effect, for educating for and about health. Without a personal purpose, the notion of teaching will be no more than just a job (Borich 1993). A purpose must reflect an intent, or a sense of mission, and must also reveal one's personal character, identity, or soul. This purpose must be clearly defined and uniquely one's own, although the purposes of others when integrated into one's own intensifies its meaning. In his book entitled *Clearly Outstanding*, Gary Borich states, "...the real reason we are teachers can only be known to us, and the techniques needed to fulfill our purpose can only be discovered by us" (1993, 57). In the following activities, students examine various health education purposes and perspectives and, in the process, revise, formulate, and/or adapt their own personal purposes for health education.

In the first activity, students are to read the first chapter of their text and research various perspectives and purposes of health education found in health resources other than their text. Providing a list of resources which include several health textbooks, journal articles, promotional magazines, organizational newsletters, etc., is helpful. Students write several definitions or perspectives and purposes of health education explicated from their resource list. Complete references for the articles from which these perspectives and purposes were derived are also included. Students are then asked to describe who the authors are, what their personal and professional backgrounds were (if available), and to speculate on how their authors' definitions and purposes were formulated. The objective of this discussion is twofold. First, this provides basic information regarding the different health education goals and objectives. And second, in examining how these purposes have been formulated, students may discover ways of developing their own personal purposes. In small groups, students share their assignments with each other.

A follow-up writing activity permits students to discover their own purposes and rationale for health education based on linking others' with their own. Borich's (1993) approach to developing educational purposes and objectives by "finding the person inside" was employed in this exercise. This reflective and critical thinking activity may work best as homework, since it requires more than classroom time for a sound response. In order to more clearly illustrate the activity, I have included the assignment directions and an example of one student's assignment. The directions are as follows:

1. After reading several definitions and purposes of health education, quote at least five purposes for health education that you have researched (provide complete references to these definitions, if applicable).
2. On another page, write a paragraph or two about the social, economic, cultural, racial, or religious influences on your health and life. These are the factors that have been a part of you without your knowing it, yet are very important and should not be hidden in the classroom. Particular attention is to be placed on those factors or experiences that have had a strong impact on your health and life. Reflect on how these experiences, concerns, or factors could be integrated into what you hope you can contribute and make a difference in the field of health education and to the enhancement of the health of your students.
3. And on the third page, in relation to your reflection, develop ten good or real purposes based on these influences and life experiences. Be prepared to share at least one purpose with the class, and explain what type of influence (social, economic, cultural, etc.) had an impact on your interest to develop such a purpose.

The following is a short example of one student's assignment: (The student's real name has been withheld for confidentiality, and a fictitious name has been provided)

Mull T. National
Methods of Health Instruction

I.   Purposes, definitions, and descriptions of health education.
    A.   Professional Preparation in Health Education in Schools of Public Health. A Report prepared for the 1965 Annual Meeting of the Association of Schools, *Health Education Monographs*, 21. Describes health education as a "process which affects changes in the health practices of people and in the knowledge and attitudes to such changes. Education is an internal process of the individual

concerned....Education thus places responsibility on the individual and is essentially different from a compliance approach. It involves motivation, communication, and decision-making."

B.   Galli, Nicholas. (1978). *Foundations and Principles of Health Education*. New York: Wiley and Sons, Inc.

"The goal of health education is to provide information that individuals can use to enhance health status...the person who is educated about health is not only well-informed, but uses this information in daily life ideally resulting in higher levels of well-being."

C.   Fruedenberg, N. (1928). Shaping the future of health education: From behavior change to social change. *Health Education Monographs* 6 (4):372–377.

Describes health education in terms of social change: "Health education for social change identifies the health-damaging elements in our society. Its goal is to involve people in collective action to create health-promoting environments and lifestyles...."

D.   Dwore, R., and J. Matarazzo. (1981). The behavioral sciences and health education. *Health Education* 12(4):4–8.

Suggests that "the behavioral sciences and health education have many common means and ends, strengths and weaknesses. Both are oriented toward studying human behavior and improving the quality of life for the individual, family and society, through teaching, research, and service...."

E.   Grant, C., and C. Sleeter. (1989). Race, class, gender, exceptionality, and educational reform. In *Multicultural education: issues and perspectives*, ed. J. Banks and C. McGee Banks. Boston/London/Sydney/Toronto: Allyn and Bacon.

Describes multicultural education from a social reconstructionist perspective. This perspective relates to health education in many ways. They state, "this approach teaches students how to use social action skills to participate in shaping and controlling their own destiny....Social reconstructionism seeks to reform society toward greater equity in race, class, gender, and handicap."

II.   Social, cultural, environmental, economic, political factors that influenced my health and life:

I grew up in a neighborhood where religious or racial prejudice existed, and I have a special understanding of its effects on people. I have learned how to deal with these effects. My neighborhood was also environmentally and socially unsafe. There was trash everywhere, gangs existed on street corners and the mall, and there was a high incidence of child abuse. Given this background, I have some special desire to make this or my future environment better so as to decrease my and my future children's health risk for disease or death. I am also concerned with my lack of assertiveness because I grew up in a country and society that treated passivity especially among women with high respect; they disdained assertiveness. And now I live in a society that regards assertiveness as important, and I believe I may have a special understanding and experience on how people manage or cope in this present society in order to survive. From a more positive light, I came from a family that encouraged a strong sense of cooperation and sharing and thus do realize the benefits derived from these in my life.

III. Given these various influences, strengths, knowledge, and experiences, and in reading others' purposes, I have developed the following good purposes which are personally meaningful to me, with the belief that I bring into these purposes the knowledge, experiences, and strengths that may benefit my health education students.

A. To teach my health education class the importance of a clean and safe environment and suggest things to do in order to keep it clean and safe.

B. To help make the environment safe for children in my class by actively participating in the development of curricula that put a strong focus on environmental health and, upon careful examination of government regulations on environmental health concerns, will make every effort to influence legislators regarding environmental policies.

C. To teach my elementary health class ways in which they can be assertive in making decisions regarding their health knowledge, attitudes, and behaviors such as in saying "no" to alcohol or unsafe sex.

D. To teach my elementary health class that each of us must take responsibility for sharing our thoughts and feelings with others.

Understanding the School as a Social System and the Components of CSHE

Comprehensive School Health Education has been taught largely on the basis of the three (or more) roles of teachers—providing health instruction, promoting a healthful school environment, and providing health care services. For the comprehensive school health program to be successful in fostering a high level of health and well-being among children, teachers must consider their responsibilities in these three roles as equally important rather than placing more value on only one role. What transpires often is that preservice teachers treat and understand these roles as separate and not connected. Additionally, a big question remains about how to help students understand and consider these roles not as teacher "tasks" but acts of consciousness and responsibility in the hope of facilitating healthy lives among children. In this regard, it is essential to help preservice teachers understand the connections among these roles—that each role supports, promotes, and strengthens the others.

To provide a basis for viewing these connections, the concept of "school as a social system" is introduced to the students. Students are assigned to read James Banks's (1989) chapter, *"Multicultural Education: Characteristics and Goals"* which describes his concept of the school as a social system. This chapter portrays the different components/areas within the school that must be considered if a school intends to implement reform for multicultural education. Additionally, the author discusses how all these components are highly interrelated and that the whole system would function best and carry out its goals to the fullest if all, and not just one, of these components were strengthened and/or reformed (Banks 1989). It was fitting to equate this notion with the CSHE program wherein focusing on and strengthening solely one component (i.e., health instruction) without consideration for the other components (healthful school environment or health services) will not facilitate full achievement of the health education purpose. Linking the teacher roles in CSHE to the concept of the school as a social system enables students to ponder ways to instill equity and multiculturalism. This linkage may be reflected in approaches where teachers: teach in ways that each child can relate his or her health knowledge and experiences to the concepts being taught (health instruction); in conjunction with staff, faculty, and other students in the school, create a school environment that promotes the health and well-being of each child (healthful school environment); and work towards providing health services so that each child benefits from and has access to these services fully and equitably (health services).

Understanding Individual Knowledge and Experiences and Those of Others

In describing a multicultural education project for teacher trainees, G. William McDiarmid reports that "the more people know about others who are different from themselves, the less likely they are to view these others negatively" (1992, 89). To promote learning, the diversity of knowledge and experiences among students must be considered. Additionally, health educators can "bring a health topic to life" (Poris 1989, 20) when they capitalize on the wealth of culture, tradition, and community identification present among students. In the following sections, I describe some classroom approaches which have been utilized in teaching about the three health educator roles. These approaches capitalize on human diversity and employ strategies such as critical thinking, empowerment, group interaction, reflection, and experiential learning.

Role I: Providing Health Education/Instruction   The acquisition of knowledge about school health education consists of learning the basic foundations for health instruction, including the different health content areas as well as planning, implementing, and evaluating learning activities. To enable students to think about school health education in multicultural ways, I first help them to become aware of the influence of cultural worldviews on what they consider to be "health," as well as on their own health practices and behaviors. In the process of understanding their own perspectives, they also think about how they define health issues, decide what and how to teach about health, and examine how the decisions stem from their own cultural assumptions about what health is. They become aware that, each time they select instructional materials or information to teach their students, they are also selecting assumptions about health and about groups of people, rooted in somebody's worldview. Students are encouraged to extend their thinking (Dwyer 1993) as they explore different cultural beliefs, values, and practices that relate to health. They reflect on their own cultural beliefs and values and examine how these influence their health care practices and health care seeking (e.g., treatment) patterns (Spector 1985). They are also introduced to the idea that we are all bound by the limitations of our personal knowledge and experiences and that there are other ways of thinking about and experiencing health knowledge, attitudes, and behaviors. According to Fahlberg et al., "....health is both individual and contextual; the determination of what is healthy is based on unique characteristics of people and also on unique characteristics of their worlds" (1991, 189).

To help students explore diversity in health cultures, I have them interact and engage in dialogues on discussion topics such as Western science-based health philosophy, as well as alternative health philosophies such as Christian Science beliefs, the theory of the Ch'i on which acupuncture is based, and the different ways of thinking about how the mind and body are linked. For example, an excellent television documentary that has challenged many students' thinking is Bill Moyer's special documentary entitled *The Power of Ch'i*. In this documentary of Chinese medicine, the marriage between alternative health care treatments and practices and those which are Western science-based is brought to life. Several illness situations which were subjected to Ch'i-based and Western science-based treatments simultaneously are portrayed. Additionally, scenes from a Western science-based hospital wherein patients were readily treated with both herbal medications and pharmaceutical drugs are shown. Western-trained medical doctors who practiced both science-based and Ch'i-based philosophies are also interviewed regarding their perceptions and experiences. This documentary provides a venue through which students discuss their reactions to health care practices that are uncommon and unusual to them and share their ideas and experiences on various health care practices they experience, including those that have not been readily acceptable from a Western-science viewpoint such as reflexology, naturopathy, holistic medicine, acupuncture, iridology (e.g., Cornacchia and Barrett 1993). In addition, other topics and questions may be raised in relation to their readings and to the film: What social, cultural, economic, educational, physiological, etc., factors affect our experience of certain health-related phenomena or situations? How does language (e.g., science-based or foreign) affect the way we perceive or deal with situations? In what ways can language limit us in our perceptions and experiences? What other limitations and barriers exist that may hamper our discovery and limit our multicultural perspectives? How can we eliminate, or at least lessen, these limitations or barriers?

It is important to note that the primary focus of interaction and dialogue within the classroom is to critically examine these instructional materials in light of the diversity of information, theories, knowledge, and experiences they offer. Every effort at decreasing students' attention to bias is made. For example, questions such as "How are different population groups depicted?" or "Does the material portray any bias in terms of the population groups being portrayed?" are not emphasized during interaction and dialogue. Instead, the emphasis is on the knowledge, experiences, and information that are provided by different cultural contexts. As Betty Ch'maj (1993, xxviii) states, "The challenge to cope with theory will mean looking at book lists and assignments not with an eye to determining whose 'bias' prevails, which form of 'discourse' is being used, but for ways to open up dialogue and increase possibilities for bridging across the borders."

The critical examination of health-related instructional materials provides a wholesome venue through which the rational powers of students are explored. Instructional materials such as books, magazines, lesson plans, teaching techniques, and educational media are reviewed, and dialogues and discussions are encouraged as to how these materials have infused cultural diversity. As students become familiar with their cultural resources, they ponder reasons why particular materials have been chosen by them or other teachers, why these materials interest them—for example, what specific characteristics of a book prompt teachers to utilize or choose it, or what type of information might teachers look for in an instructional material. Also, how does the choice of instructional material affect students—their learning outcomes, their health knowledge, attitudes, and behaviors now and in the future? What are the implications of instructional material choice for health education? If instructional material was generally useful for you, but some of its contents, parts, or units you disagree with, would you utilize it? If you decide to utilize it, would you make any adjustments or changes? If so, what types of adjustments or changes would these be? And how would you go about implementing these changes?

We also critically examine theoretical and methodological research articles that directly or indirectly link cultural variables to health. Research articles from refereed journals, books, and other publications such as the Mortality and Morbidity Reports are collected and summarized. Students arrange these articles according to emerging themes that tend to emanate from the collection. These themes are studied in light of multiculturalism and analyzed in terms of their implications for health education. In a majority of articles, students have found that particular groups of people were described in terms of their illnesses and diseases (e.g., incidence of alcoholism among Mexican Americans). While the information may be very valuable, it may simultaneously delineate a particular group as possessing "illnesses" or "diseases," terms which may easily pose serious negative implications for that group. So, it is essential to spend time ascertaining myths, clarifying misconceptions, and verifying information that is implied in statements which unintentionally render sweeping generalizations.

Students also evaluate culture-related health articles in terms of their scientific merit, although the objective of this type of evaluation is more to help students understand the limitations posed by research studies than to teach students that the scientific method is the only method that will enable them to make sense out of the world. The following questions are thereby discussed: What is the purpose of the study? What does the review of literature illustrate? How was the population sample chosen by the researcher? Who funded the research? Does the researcher/funding organization have any stake in the study? What was the central problem/illness/situation being studied in this population? What impact do our readings of research have in our perception of the "real" or present situation? Are there other research methods that may be applied? Would you do this study yourself? How would you approach this study if you had an opportunity to do it? What recommendations will you make? What processes will you apply? What other research questions might be posed by the study? What other culture-based health-related research studies could/must be done in the area of cultural diversity and health now and in the future? Can you provide examples of topics that could be potentially studied?

Additionally, we discuss how almost everything that is perceived is based on science and that this science-based view may limit us in our perceptions of the world. So, we further explore other ways of viewing the world and discuss the following questions: What other philosophies, theories, or ideologies have influenced a person's health practices, beliefs, and health care seeking patterns? Provide examples wherein these philosophies when applied provided the intended results even without "scientific" basis. What types of research could be done in these areas? How could these research studies be approached?

Typically, in numerous research studies the focus is placed on describing the racial breakdown of results (e.g., adolescents' knowledge and attitudes about violence: a racial breakdown). In this example, a health topic is the primary focus of the study, and, in addition, differences in results among ethnic or other population group categories are described. It is evident in titles such as this that numerous research titles are catchy, providing the impression that the study's main purpose was to find differences among diverse groups. Upon reading the articles in depth, however, one may find that (a) the breakdown was due to convenience—from the sample, certain percentages were inadvertently drawn; and, thus, (b) sampling techniques may have been poor, and the groups were not representative of the population. Because research contains a myriad of limitations and biases, it is important for students to become involved in careful scrutiny and critical analysis of various research findings, look for consistencies between the purpose and findings, and identify any fallacies in question framing.

Students additionally examine teaching ideas that focus on culturally appropriate or culture-based teaching techniques. These are abundantly found in health education journals as well as textbooks and have been helpful in providing teachers with information about new ways to teach various health topics. In examining ideas on various teaching strategies, preservice teachers engage in the processes of deconstructing and reconstructing the titles and objectives of selected published teaching strategies, ponder the cultural assumptions being made or that have been brought to bear, and reflect on how their understanding impacts on how these materials and subsequent strategies will be utilized in the classroom.

The evolution of numerous teaching strategies related to health has stemmed from a challenge for health teachers to make teaching fun and enjoyable, especially in an area where their students have prior knowledge and experiences. It is a widely accepted assumption that, when a sense of enjoyment is felt about what is being learned, the motivation to participate and become further involved in learning is increased. Since enjoyment is usually influenced by successfully understanding and accomplishing a learning task, preservice teachers learn about strategies that focus on empowering their audience to understand and accomplish a learning task, as well as on helping them to relate what is being learned to their own lives, in addition to how effectively they (audience) may be amused or entertained. For example, to empower students to think about culturally diverse group health practices, a fun and enjoyable role-play strategy could be utilized. While students may have fun in role-playing, the activity does not end in the role-play itself, but opportunities are provided for students to relate the content to their own health practices. For example, students share their own reactions, feelings, or experiences in responding to questions such as: What are your positive and negative ideas about the health practices of the particular population described? How have your conceptions about these ideas evolved? What factors influenced your notions or perceptions about these ideas?

Another meaningful experience for preservice teachers is for them to make recommendations as to how these ideas, techniques, or methods could be improved so that the information reflects a broadened multicultural perspective. Since numerous well-intended, seemingly infallible, but conflicting teaching strategies exist, preservice teachers need to practice the process of critically examining the strategies they learn and adapt in light of their overall multicultural health education purpose. Students present their health lesson plans to the class and provide suggestions to each other on approaches to developing their lessons from multicultural perspectives. In conclusion, their presentations should provide, not a culmination, but a new beginning towards pursuing, rethinking, reexamining, refocusing, and reevaluating their past, present, and future health knowledge and experiences.

Role II: Promoting a Healthful School Environment Another important role that health teachers assume in participating in a Comprehensive School Health Education (CSHE) program is promoting an environment that is conducive to the health of children. A healthful school environment is that part of a "comprehensive school health program that focuses on the school day, school building and surrounding area, and specific school activities, procedures, and policies that protect the health and safety of faculty, staff, and students" (Meeks and Heit 1992, 13). Further, an environment that is favorable to health is fostered when students' physiological, social, psychological, cultural, and spiritual well-being is enhanced and respected. Approaches that emphasize wholesome communication techniques and respect for individual differences, values, beliefs, and practices while, at the same time, emphasize regard for the global society in which we live are integrated into learning about how to promote a school environment conducive to health. Preservice teachers are assigned to read Carol Anne Dwyer's (1993) article, "Teaching and Diversity: Meeting the Challenges for Innovative Teacher Assessments," in which the author presents a set of criteria for assessing beginning teachers in four areas. These areas include: (1) organizing content knowledge for student learning; (2) creating an environment for student learning; (3) teaching for student learning; and (4) teacher professionalism. These areas provide a basis through which students could examine the goals of their teacher preparation program and relate this to their health education practice.

Dwyer (1993, 125) suggests that teachers should model fair behaviors and "value the ways in which diverse students express themselves." In our class, we analyze various talk shows such as Geraldo or the Oprah Winfrey Show, MacNeill Lehrer News Hour or excerpts from C-Span and relate these shows to classroom situations. Students analyze and evaluate these shows using questions related to Dwyer's criteria for assessor reflection (1993, 125): In what ways does the talk show host (teacher) help the audience (students) to have access to learning? Are there patterns of either exclusion or overattention in audience (student) – host (teacher) interactions? Do the audience members (students) treat each other fairly? Does the talk show host (teacher) respond appropriately to stereotype-based, demeaning, or other unfair comments by audience (students)? Students are then asked to relate their responses to different classroom scenarios and situations.

In small groups (through either role-play or discussion situations), students practice diversity-affirming communication skills. According to Kathryn Kavanagh and Patricia Kennedy (1992), diversity affirming communication skills, based on Paul Pedersen's (1981, 1988) approach, are those that "facilitate mutual understanding and prevention of unanalyzed and inappropriate cultural or subcultural imposition" (Pedersen 1981, 42). These skills include: the ability to articulate and present an issue or problem as perceived from another's perspective, knowing how to recognize and reduce resistance and defensiveness during communication, and acknowledging that we are subject to mistakes and that it is preferable to communicate and risk error than to play it safe and not communicate at all (Pedersen 1981, 42). Additionally, a skilled communicator learns how to distinguish stereotypes from the reality of situations and is able to modify interactions according to what is manifested. In their book on *Promoting Cultural Diversity*, Kavanagh and Kennedy (1992) provide several scenarios on how these communication techniques may be practiced, learned, and developed.

Fundamental to creating an environment that enhances health and learning is the notion of empowerment (Freire 1970; Wallerstein and Bernstein 1988). Empowerment is a liberating process that enables individuals, groups, and communities to experience growth and change in ties as well as within the organizational, economic, cultural, political, sociological, and spiritual contexts (Fahlberg et al. 1991). Various situations or examples in which health educators may facilitate empowerment among their students are discussed. According to Larry Fahlberg (1991), health educators can facilitate empowerment by: (a) being aware of and able to reflect critically about the greater social context, as well as about his or her own ego needs; (b) realizing that the most successful programs that are oriented towards empowerment are those where people are running their own programs as a way of life; and (c) relinquishing "power over" others and respecting the contexts and realities in which their students/participants live.

Role III: Providing School Health Services Some of the most widely suggested roles of teachers in providing school health services emphasize the biological and psychological domains of health, such as careful observation of physiological and psychological changes, referral to appropriate sources, control of diseases, and providing emergency care (Meeks and Heit 1992). A teacher with a multicultural perspective views his or her role in school health services as one that goes beyond mere observation and referral to integrating concepts such as empowerment into his or her work. In describing empowerment in health education, Fahlberg et al. (1992, 186) suggests,

> Rather than treat symptoms, arrest movement towards a negative end, or merely assist participants in adapting to the environment, empowerment approaches are intended to enable people to increase their capacity to enhance their own health as they define it, both individually and collectively...focus is on the process of growth and elimination of social structural barriers that restrict it such as poverty....

A multicultural perspective encourages teachers to explore the historical, cultural, social, economic, and political dimensions of health and examine how these dimensions influence their roles in school health services. Thus, it is important that students not only view health as a multidimensional concept (physiological, psychological, spiritual, intellectual, social, and cultural) but also view their teaching role as multidimensional—instructing in the classroom as well as working towards eliminating or decreasing the barriers that hinder the achievement of health and well-being among students.

To facilitate students' understanding of their varied roles in school health services, I engage them in numerous activities that stimulate critical thinking, reflection, and experiential learning to emphasize the concept of empowerment. For example, utilizing examples from several books, students analyze and examine case studies, ethical situations, and hypothetical scenarios requiring them to make decisions and judgments based on their own knowledge and experiences. They actively explore the consequences that may prevail relative to their decisions or judgments. Kavanagh and Kennedy's book, *Promoting Cultural Diversity* (1992), provides practice situations on various themes such as race, health conditions, ethnicity, socioeconomic status, age, sex role, and gender, etc., which "increases familiarity with cultural patterns and social processes, while decreasing fear of the unfamiliar and different..."(p. 8). Rachel Spector's (1985) *Cultural Diversity in Health and Illness* provide case study scenarios for health practitioners and educators working in diverse settings. Kenneth Cushner, Averil McClelland, and Philip Safford's (1992) book on *Human Diversity* presents discussion questions and activities at the end of each chapter that stimulate thinking and reflection.

Students further examine health care services from a broader national context and discuss various health care issues such as the pros and cons of government-controlled and competitive health care systems. We evaluate President Bill Clinton's health care reform plan as well as the health service plans of other countries such as Canada and Sweden. We analyze how certain aspects of these plans facilitate or discourage the achievement of the nation's goal of Healthy People 2000 (U.S. Dept of Health and Human Services 1992) which include increasing life span, reducing disparities in health status, and providing access to health care services. In conjunction with these discussions, students relate their perspectives about these issues to what their roles would be in providing health care services to their own students.

As a supplementary activity, students reflect on the slogan, "Think globally and act locally" and attempt to make connections between the slogan and their own multicultural health education perspectives. In a brainstorming session, students provide various examples of how the slogan links individual diversity to global health, and vice versa. For example, they may contribute their individual unique strengths but may also enhance their awareness of different positions, as well as study and learn experientially by collaborating with other alliances (anthropology, sociology, economics) in the achievement of global health. To expand the existing international health perspective, I have utilized Mohammed Forouzesh's (1990) questionnaire on international health issues with students both as a pre-assessment knowledge tool and as a basis for discussion on various international health issues. The questionnaire is composed of both knowledge and attitude questions which challenge students to resolve global issues and reflect on themselves as citizens of the world. In the words of Forouzesh, "the urgency to act, the spirit of global harmony and the commitment to respect our differences, view most issues globally, and learn the world around us could be instilled in our classrooms" (1990, 56).

REDEFINING ONE'S PURPOSE IN THE CONTEXT OF MULTICULTURALISM

Towards the end of the course, a follow-up activity to the development of purpose is assigned whereby students are to analyze their previously developed personal purposes and then restate these so that the consideration of human diversity and multiculturalism is reflected in their meaning. Students are provided with the opportunity to share their redefined multicultural health education perspectives with their classmates. In the final analysis, students integrated multicultural concepts into health education when their experiences were positive and their knowledge increased as a result of actively participating in the activities in the course.

THE CHALLENGE:

Before multicultural approaches can be effectively implemented in the classroom, teachers will need to prepare themselves to decrease or eliminate the barriers they may encounter that curtail successful implementation. For example, the diverse views of their students regarding what the multicultural challenge means to them may hinder their learning and openness towards multicultural approaches. A great deal of skepticism has been exhibited by those who perceive multicultural education as something that is separate from other teaching challenges or adding to other teaching challenges and/or problems. This skepticism may be reflected in the following statement of one teacher, "There is too much work to do in preparing for class, grading assignments and tests, catering to the needs of students, and maintaining a well-disciplined classroom—and in addition, I now have to learn about different cultures?" Given the diversity of views regarding multiculturalism and students' lack of professional preparation regarding multicultural approaches, it is important that teachers provide students with a firm foundation from which they will draw their perspectives and which will provide them with the basis for applying the skills (such as critical thinking, reflection, decision making, etc.) needed for thinking multiculturally and encountering multicultural experiences.

Another barrier that may impede successful implementation is the expectations of the students regarding the course itself. The title imposes certain limitations as to what to expect. As a methods course, most students expect to be taught different techniques and strategies for teaching health. They may expect activities for making teaching health fun. They anticipate movement and action, excitement and entertainment, interesting and motivating information, and, most of all, effortless ways to fulfill the necessary requirements of the course. The infusion of a multicultural perspective into a health education methods course poses a tremendous challenge for teachers. The first step is for teachers to deconstruct the very notion of "methods" and help students move as delicately and creatively as possible from their narrow "expectations" (e.g., fulfilling requirements) of the course to experiencing the processes of critical thinking, empowerment, reflection, and decision making in positive ways. An important guideline is to provide students with the foundation as well as structure that they expect, as in describing the steps in their assignments and activities in detail, while, at the same time, encouraging them to explore the topics to the extent that they see interconnections and in ways that makes sense to them.

Dividing students into smaller groups during discussion periods provides them with the opportunity to interact closely and readily with others. It is usually very helpful in the beginning (and throughout the course) to provide some articles for them to read in their groups and spend classroom time in discussing these. Primarily, the focus should be on the experience of interaction and dialogue and not on fulfilling requirements. A grading system that allows flexibility and the opportunity to improve helps students focus on the learning processes and experiences rather than on the grade.

There is a mixture of perspectives among students about the nature of the course and its value or usefulness in their future work. This mixture is considered because health education has not been mandated in all U.S. states. Depending on the state where one may be teaching, some students will be assuming roles in a comprehensive school health education program wherein health may taught as a separate subject; others may teach health by integrating it into other subjects such as math, science, or family life; and still others may never have to teach it at all. In light of varied expectations and added contradictory awareness, teachers may concentrate on the usefulness of the multicultural approach not in terms of satisfying their teaching "competencies" and/or responsibilities but in light of broadening their perspectives about life and health. Teachers cannot expect that their students' knowledge, attitudes, and skills will change overnight; nor could they expect all their students to change. Teachers can, however, experience triumph in their efforts if they can only modestly make a small difference in the lives of a few students.

CONCLUSION

Integrating multiculturalism into comprehensive school health education poses a tremendous challenge for teachers. There are barriers that may impede the successful implementation of the most ideal approaches. However, once these barriers are recognized and solutions are found to overcome these barriers, the health teacher will experience success and gain a sense of fulfillment in his or her work. As health teachers, our goal is to help our students live healthily and happily. This could be accomplished by contributing to their knowledge and skills, as well as to the enhancement of their attitudes, so that they could live readily and productively as members of the culturally diverse society in which they live. Meanwhile, we need to strengthen our knowledge and experiences, as Margaret Wilkerson (1992, p. 63) challenges us teachers to "think how we want our students to think and do what we ask our students to do—to continue learning."

REFERENCES

Adler, P. (1977). Beyond cultural identity: Reflections upon cultural and multicultural man. *Topics in cultural learning: Concepts, application and research*, ed. R. Brislin. Honolulu: University of Hawaii Press.

Allensworth, D., and L. Kolbe. (1987). The comprehensive school health program: Exploring an expanded concept. *Journal of School Health* 57(10):409–412.

Banks, J. (1989). Multicultural education: Characteristics and goals. *Multicultural education: Issues and perspectives*, ed. J. Banks and C. Banks. Boston: Allyn and Bacon.

Borich, G. (1993). *Clearly outstanding: Making each day count in your classroom.* Boston: Allyn and Bacon.

Ch'maj, B. (1933). Multicultural America and the PC debate. *Multicultural America: A Resource for teachers of humanities and American studies*, ed. B. Ch'maj. New York: University Press of America.

Cornacchia, H., and S. Barrett. (1993). *Consumer health: A guide to intelligent decisions.* St. Louis: Mosby-Yearbook, Inc.

Cushner, K., A. McClelland, and P. Safford. (1992). *Human diversity in education: An integrative approach.* New York: McGraw-Hill, Inc.

Dwyer, C. A. (1993). Teaching and diversity: Meeting the challenges for innovative teacher assessments. *Journal of Teacher Education* 44(2):119–129.

Fahlberg, L., A. Poulin, D. Girdano, and D. Dusek. (1991). Empowerment as an emerging approach in health education. *Journal of Health Education* 22(3):185–193.

Forouzesh, M. (1990). Student knowledge and attitudes toward international health issues: Applications to teaching. *Phi Beta Delta International Review*. Austin, TX: University of Texas Publications.

Freire, P. (1970). *Pedagogy of the oppressed.* New York: Continuum.

Grant, C., and C. Sleeter. (1989). Race, class, gender, exceptionality, and educational reform. *Multicultural Education: Issues and Perspectives*, ed. J. Banks and C. Banks. Boston: Allyn and Bacon.

Kavanagh, K., and P. Kennedy. (1992). *Promoting cultural diversity: Strategies for health care professionals*, Newberry Park: Sage Publications.

Kolb, D. (1984). *Experiential learning: Experience as the source of learning and development.* Englewood Cliffs, NJ: Prentice-Hall.

McDiarmid, G. W. (1992). What to do about differences? A study of multicultural education for teacher trainees in the Los Angeles school district. *Journal of Teacher Education* 43(43):83–93.

Meeks, L., and P. Heit. (1992). *Comprehensive school health education: Totally awesome strategies for teaching health*. Blacklick, OH: Meeks-Heit Publishing Company.

Pederson, P. (1981). The cultural inclusiveness of counseling. In *Counseling across cultures*, ed. P. Pedersen, J. Draguns, W. Lonner, and J. Trimble, 22–58. Honolulu: University Press of Hawaii.

Pederson, P. (1988). The three stages of multicultural development: Awareness, knowledge, and skill. In *A handbook for developing multicultural awareness*, ed. P. Pederson, 3–18. Alexandria, VA: American Association for Counseling and Development.

Poris, B. (1989). Student multi-ethnicity: The untapped health education resource. *Health Education* 20(7):20–22.

Shor, I. (1980). *Critical teaching and everyday life*. Boston: South End Press.

Sleeter, C., and C. Grant. (1994). *Making Choices for Multicultural Education*, 2nd edition. New York: Macmillan.

Schon, D. (1987). *Educating the reflective practitioner*, San Francisco, CA: Jossey-Bass.

Spector, R. (1985). *Cultural diversity in health and illness*, 2nd ed. Norwalk, CT: Appleton-Century-Crofts.

U.S. Dept. of Health and Human Services. (1992). *Healthy people 2000: A summary report*. Boston: Jones and Bartlett Publishers.

Wallerstein, N., and E. Bernstein. (1988). Empowerment education: Freire's ideas adapted to health education. *Health Education Quarterly* 14(4):379–394.

Wilkerson, M. (1992). Beyond the graveyard: Engaging faculty involvement. *Change* 24(1):59–63.

Wurzel, J. (1988). *Towards multiculturalism*, ed. J. Wurzel. Yarmouth, ME: Intercultural Press.

17

OLGA M. WELCH _____

Exceptional Children from Diverse Cultures:
An Overlooked Population
in the Movement Toward Inclusion

When the three status distinctions of poverty, minority, and exceptionality intersect, the children involved and their families are uniquely vulnerable to systematic discrimination (Herman 1983, as cited in Harry 1992). This poses important questions and issues for educators who prepare special education teachers. There is little doubt that those charged with implementation of The Education for All Handicapped Children Act (P.L. 94–142, 1975), amendments to it (e.g., P.L. 98–199 and D.L. 99–457), and subsequent legislation have failed to confront the problematic issues surrounding special education services in culturally diverse contexts. These issues include the disproportionate numbers of Black and Latino children found in classrooms for the mentally retarded, behavior disordered, and learning disabled and the inequities in access, assessment, and follow-up of special-needs children from culturally and linguistically diverse backgrounds (Heward and Orlansky 1993). That these inequities exist illustrates in yet another context the central problems of race, class, and gender found in the larger society. As Beth Harry notes:

> It is essential that professionals in the United States understand the tension that exists between an outsider's and an insider's view of minority people's experience: the dimensions of power/powerlessness, traditional/atraditional, cultural pride/culture shame are intertwined in a dynamic process through which the cultural consciousness of minority peoples evolves. The pride that most minority peoples feel in their traditional culture has continued to thrive despite the widespread promotion of images of cultural deficiency, pathology, and hopelessness. Thus, more important than knowing particular features of any one cultural group is the recognition by American (special) educators of the cultural base of their own belief system.
>
> Indeed, the very mandate of The Education for All Handicapped Children Act is couched in concepts that are uniquely Western, both in terms of a medical model of disability and of a framework of services derived from a technological culture. (1992, 23)

Harry's study (1992) of culturally diverse families who were receiving special education services illustrates the reification of categories which bore little resemblance or relevance to reality. Despite that, these categories became the instructional parameters which delineated both expectation and performance for professionals. Not surprisingly, Harry found that, for the families, the meanings of disability differed along cultural lines, with the boundaries of normalcy much broader than those used by the educational system. Moreover, the different designations of disability led to confusion among parents, with the result that terms like handicap and retarded became attached to extreme forms of impairment. No less important was that these designations sometimes carried particular moral meanings, most notably the (idea) that characteristics ascribed to one family member reflected the character and health of the entire family unit. As powerfully as Erving Goffman's (1963) "tribal stigma," these designations guided the responses of some professionals to both the children and their families. More significantly, they occurred even as parents had developed their own hypotheses about the origins of their children's difficulties, hypotheses which never became a part of their dialogue with special educators.

None of this ambiguity is reflected in the legislation which establishes special education services nor in the preparation of the teachers who will serve an increasingly diverse population. As Bruce Ramirez notes, "By the turn of the century, it is estimated that 40% of public school students will be from ethnically diverse backgrounds (1988, 45). Despite this statistic, however, teacher preparation programs in special education continue to view issues of cultural diversity as peripheral to the "real business" of educating exceptional children. Even as they stress individualization of instruction and holistic approaches, they fail to prepare preservice teachers to engage in the kind of inclusive special education practice which empowers children and families from diverse cultures. Yet, it is precisely this kind of practice which is needed to address the systemic inequities discussed earlier. But where to begin?

In the preceding chapters, my colleagues have stressed the importance of placing issues related to diversity and multiculturalism at the center of the dialogue in teacher preparation. They suggest that existing practices have evolved from inherently flawed philosophical underpinnings and assumptions which marginalize discourse on issues of race, class, and gender. Their arguments parallel those advanced by advocates of the Regular Education Initiative. In brief, they suggest that mere access to the current general education mainstream, which they view as unable to respond effectively to individual student diversity and difference, is insufficient. Rather, they contend that general education requires a major reconstitution if it is to meet the needs of handicapped and other special needs students (Edgar 1987, 1988; Reynolds, Wang, and Walberg 1987; Skrtic 1987, 1988; Stainback and Stainback 1984, as cited in Davis 1989). Bolstered by the passage of Public Law 99–457 (Education of the Handicapped Act Amendments, 1986) and, more recently, the Americans with Disabilities Act (1990) and the Individuals with Disabilities Education Act (1990), this movement is receiving growing scrutiny, particularly in school systems already attempting to include a variety of students. While widespread adoption has not occurred, more university teacher preparation programs have begun experimental classes with kindergarten children in which preservice teachers are provided with practicum experiences in classrooms employing inclusive curriculum models. Despite these efforts, the core special education classes offered in universities continue to focus on categorical descriptions of disability while marginalizing issues related to cultural diversity and exceptionality.

DESCRIPTION OF SPECIAL EDUCATION CORE COURSES

Generally, core courses in special education involve students in discussions of the history of special education, including the legislation and litigation surrounding it, the nature of various exceptionalities, and appropriate intervention and educational practices with each. Most also contain information on early intervention and working with parents and educators in public school classrooms. Currently, many of the texts used in these courses have added sections on transition issues, including career development training and postsecondary education. Not a few have also begun to offer overviews of cultural diversity in special education with attention given to information on individual racial and ethnic groups.

While such efforts are a good beginning, they represent just that...a beginning. Although students do obtain a better understanding of the nature of individual disabilities, as well as strategies for identifying and referring students with special educational needs, they learn little about the relationship between disability and the systemic discrimination to which Harry (1992) referred. Indeed, the fact that issues related to diversity are presented at the end of most introductory courses suggest to some students that they are of peripheral importance in the education of children with disabilities. Further, as few preservice programs require practicum experiences in settings which educate children with or without disabilities in some classes, education majors rarely receive demonstrations of appropriate strategies. Such demonstrations as well as opportunities to participate in planning for instruction in these classes could assist preservice teachers to think about teaching in terms of individual, rather than group, learning. With few of these experiences, however, they often leave the special education classes with little more than a surface awareness of some of the issues related to exceptionality and cultural diversity.

REPERTOIRE OF STRATEGIES

In addition to an inadequate special education foundation, preservice preparation does not provide students with adequate strategies to fit the variety of learning styles and behaviors encountered in any classroom. Equally troubling is the assumption held by too many teacher trainees that educational practice can be applied like a template to all students, without considering individual learning differences.

Indeed, Asa Hilliard (1989, 67) argues that learning style is the one aspect of social culture which most affects learning. He further contends that teachers must recognize that these styles are not innate but rather learned approaches which can be changed. Thus, multiple styles can be taught to students, which they, in turn, can alter according to the context.

In a similar vein, Henry Giroux and Peter McLaren (1986) argue for preservice preparation which allows students to become "transformative intellectuals" whose pedagogy reflects the ideals of democracy and social justice. Such preparation would link student experience and voice to critical study of the interrelationship between power, language, culture, and history. For Giroux and McLaren, transformative intellectuals serve as "bearers of dangerous memory" whose instruction "makes clear that people are called to struggle, that political alternatives do in fact exist, and that the buried knowledge found in the subjugated histories, experiences, stories and accounts of oppressed persons needs to be appropriated in the interest of creating more democratic societies" (1986, 227).

However, such preparation assumes the presence of teacher candidates with the interest and background to participate in such a process, as well as school systems which invite as well as encourage such an approach to education. Instead, partly, or, some would say, mainly, schools have not been an instrument of positive social change; they function largely as vehicles for the reproduction of society in its own image, not as conduits for the production of a new global society (Katz 1975; Bowles and Gintis 1976, as cited in Zimpher and Ashburn 1993).

Moreover, the parochialism found in some teacher candidates insulates them from the very diversity they will confront in their classrooms. This limited cultural milieu and frequently conservative orientation reflects what Howey and Zimpher (1989) refer to as the "closed loop" problem in the majority of teacher training institutions. What makes the consequences of such an approach to teacher education problematic is its reinforcement of the already narrowed view of schooling held by some students. As John Goodlad (1986) notes: "To derive one's world view from (this kind of parochial perspective) almost always emerging from limited participation in the human conversation is dangerous...for oneself and for those who live just beyond one's experiential neighborhood" (424)

For those who teach in classrooms containing students with diverse needs and cultures, it can lead one to "ignore those who are 'strangers' (and there are many) as well as the issues related to moral equality which their presence raises" (Greene 1986, 84). If public education is to help all students achieve their fullest potential, those who prepare teachers in special education classes must begin to question the content of those classes and the theories about normalcy and deviance which are presented.

INTRODUCTION TO THE EXCEPTIONAL CHILD

This was certainly the case when a colleague and I team-taught Introduction to the Exceptional Child, the College's introductory course in Special Education. According to the catalogue, the purpose of the course is to provide information about various disabling conditions that teachers encounter in public school classes. Typically, education majors take this course during their third year in the teacher preparation program. This means that they have completed courses in history and philosophy of education, child development, their own areas of specialization in elementary or secondary education, and practicum experiences in the public school. The majority of the students are undergraduates, but several are reentry students. Required by the state to gain teacher certification, the class has an average size of between sixty and eighty students. Although the course focused mainly on issues related to the inclusion of children with disabilities, we were interested in having students carefully examine the historical, political, and social structures which influence educational practice.

In the process, we hoped they would come to question these structures, as well as the assumption that special education categories do describe the reality of "different" children. Like many of our colleagues, we believe that the reluctance of nonspecial educators to write about or even talk about children with disabilities lies in the supposition that there is all this technical knowledge about these children which they really do not understand. We wanted our students to begin to challenge this notion, as well as to begin to view all their students as individuals, rather than as "instances of a set of general characteristics attributed to the group of which they are a part" (McDiarmid 1990, 18).

We also wanted to address the artificial dichotomy which we saw developing between the "regular" and "special" preservice teachers, a dichotomy which, we believe, hampers the working relationship needed to insure the effective inclusion of children with disabilities. To do this, we had to recognize some of the issues discussed earlier in this chapter, the content of most courses in special education, the backgrounds of our students, and the requirements of the school systems in which they would practice. It was not our intention to create revolutionaries, but rather, students whose heightened sense of the oppressive nature of schooling for ALL children would lead them to focus on teaching in ways which assured that genuine learning occurred for every child.

In taking this approach, we recognized that our students, like readers of this chapter, may have supposed that the existence of a special education class reaffirmed the existence of "exceptional" children who needed to be considered in a separate way. Yet, we believed that, unless preservice teachers began to see children with disabilities as students whose learning they facilitated through appropriate accommodations, they would continue to view these children, particularly those with mild disabling conditions, as too deviant or exotic for their classrooms. In addition, when disabled children are from a different culture, the potential for inappropriate instruction based on biased assumptions can be even greater.

Sara Lawrence Lightfoot believes that the "one thing all good teachers have in common is that they regard themselves as thinkers, as existing in the world of ideas" (Moyers 1989, 159). Ultimately, this is what we hoped would occur with our students even as they learned about the categories of exceptionality.

With these ideas in mind, my colleague and I selected the text, outlined the requirements, chose guest speakers, and planned field trips. In addition, we assigned books and readings upon which we jointly decided. Students also viewed and wrote short papers on commercial films related to exceptionality (e.g., "Rainman," "My Left Foot"), and they were tested on their general knowledge of each exceptionality studied. These activities, along with guest speakers and the field trips to programs serving special needs populations, were intended to develop in our students an understanding of and a positive, rather than patronizing, attitude toward diversity. Further, we encouraged them to imagine and plan adaptations they would make in their own classrooms and/or programs to actively facilitate equality of opportunity.

Using scenarios, we also sought to assist students to examine questions related to why people learn information or skills, why environmental context influences learning, and why teacher and student bias have subtle and often unconscious influences on every phase of instruction. These questions and the scenarios focused on the consequences of a lack of tolerance for differences in people and *why* the actor in the scenario held his/her opinions. Initially, the scenario was presented, followed by related questions posed by the professors to which the students provided answers. To illustrate, I've offered the following sample scenario:

SAMPLE SCENARIO: Using a milestone in scientific theory as her rationale, a legislator announces her intention to oppose a piece of social legislation because "...if these people (people for whom the legislation is proposed) really *wanted* a good education and a way to earn a good living, they would do it in spite of the grinding poverty in which they live because nature decrees that the 'fittest' survive."

PROFESSOR'S QUESTIONS:

1. What scientific theory is the legislator basing her political stance on?
    Students' answer: Darwin's Theory of Evolution.
2. Having named the theory, is this legislator's stance a correct interpretation of the theory?
    Students' answer: Some say "No." Some say "Yes." Here we pursue with follow-up questions about why students answered the way they did.
3. Do you find yourself saying to students in your classes, "Anyone who wants to learn, can learn?"
    Students' answers: Some say "No." Some say "Yes." Again, follow-up questions.
4. How would you characterize a person who holds an opinion like the legislator's?
    Students' answer: Student responses range from radical Republican to radical Democrat, to fascist, to biological determinist, to "The legislator is absolutely correct."

In the course of the discussion, we hope that students would become aware that: scientific theories can be misinterpreted and result in an excuse for no social conscience; and that Social Darwinism, a corruption of Darwin's Theory of Evolution, was used in the early 1900s to justify deliberately lax governmental policy, one which has continued to influence our political and social practice. We also want students to understand that philosophies such as Social Darwinism influence our thinking as well as the assumptions upon which that thinking is based. This scenario and the activity I describe next encouraged students to critique the oppressive system of education and to relate these criticisms to the practice of teaching in their own classrooms.

HISTORY, RESEARCH, AND RACISM

The second activity involved the historical fact that racism has been supported by "science" (albeit questionable) and that the influence of this science, though unacknowledged and unconscious, can be an excuse for racist behavior (cf. Gould 1981).

Students read undated excerpts from scientific journals written at various points in American history. The journal excerpts were paired with first person accounts from diaries, newspaper articles, and speeches written by members of various oppressed racial and ethnic groups (e.g., Irish and Italian immigrants, Blacks, Native Americans, Latinos, and Asian Americans). The pairing of an article with a diary excerpt allowed the students first to read the research, then read a first person account of how the findings had affected a real individual. By participating in this activity, we hoped students would come to realize that biased belief couched in the cachet of research can become a powerful influence on public policy and perception. Moreover, these "scientific" beliefs, if embraced by the general public as true, can become the rationale for discrimination in education, housing, and employment. Afterwards, the students discussed the ideas presented in the journal articles, including a recurring theme which supported the genetic inferiority of a particular racial or ethnic group. At this point, the students learned when the articles were written and the social, political, economic, and historical events which surrounded them. Here, the discussion centered on how these ideas, based on "flawed" science, tangentially influenced educational, economic, and social opportunities for the ethnic or racial group involved.

THE HISTORY OF SPECIAL EDUCATION

The above activity was followed by an overview of the history of special education, again including first person accounts of people with disabilities or those, like Dorethea Dix or Anne Sullivan, who worked with them. Again, students focused on the oppressive outcomes of interventions which, in general, were intended to be beneficial and/or benevolent. During this activity, students also examined the relationship between societal perceptions of a variety of disabilities (e.g., mental retardation and emotional disturbance) and the educational opportunities available to persons with these disabilities.

Invariably, after these simulations and activities, some students questioned their relationship to teaching, asserting that they dealt with history, not special education. For us, the students' responses were troubling, particularly the comments which showed them unable to discern the relevance of the discussion. As professors interested in fostering a climate in which reflective discourse could occur, we struggled, not only to understand what was occurring with the students, but also how what we were doing or not doing might be contributing to it. After a time, we came to realize that the responses might be a reflection of the students' previous experiences and the emphasis in that preparation on skill-building connected with the particular disciplines or levels they would teach. For example, if the students' previous training had focused on instructional techniques, then our students were experts on "how" to teach Math or Science or English but had little understanding of "why" and in what ways their biases influenced their teaching and the learning environment. Further, despite several discussions and demonstrations of general instructional strategies which could be used with ALL children, they appeared ill-prepared to address what Goodlad (1990) and his colleagues term "the moral issues of teaching." Nor were they prepared to instruct students with disabilities and/or those from diverse cultural backgrounds. Our concern then was not that our students challenged our points or failed to embrace our view of the world, but rather, that they seemed unable or unwilling to examine critically their ideas about education, in general, or special education, in particular. Instead, they appeared annoyed at our insistence that they engage in this activity.

As teacher educators, we needed to find a way to tackle the problem. As professors, we needed to clarify for ourselves what our own philosophies were, make them clear to our students, identify the biases which existed within them, and encourage those in our classes to challenge both our and their own ideas. This decision also required us to admit our culpability in the existing problem. If aspiring teachers are to become engaged in the world of ideas, those who prepare them must rethink the way they design their courses. We chose to examine the following questions and the issues which arose from them to guide our thinking:

1. What is the course really for?
2. Where does it "fit" in the preparation of teachers for working with diverse populations, in general, and children with special needs, in particular?
3. What other course(s) or practicum(s) experience could it be aligned with to make it more effective?
4. How do we make the information personally meaningful?

At the center of these questions was our larger concern that our selection of course activities with our focus on "exceptional" children, inadvertently, had resulted in students defining difference as deviance. Some of their written work suggested a parochialism discussed earlier, coupled with a paternalism when they discussed children with disabilities. More than once, we read reaction papers to the film, "Rainman," in which students excused the less desirable aspects of autism in favor of the "redemptive" nature of the one brother's disability on the character of the other. We found this especially troubling, since it was never our intention to leave the students with the impression that a disability made one somehow better or worse than others.

Our in service experiences also implied that teachers perceive their inability to work with exceptional children as a failing in themselves. Rarely do these teachers avoid teaching exceptional students because those students were "too much work." Instead, their reluctance appeared to represent an inexperience with teaching as an interactive process, rather than a collection of strategies. As mentioned earlier, few preservice teachers participate in classes in which interactive teaching models are used. Therefore, they encounter difficulty situating their own teaching practice within a conceptual framework flexible enough to accommodate differences of any kind. Were such a framework to exist, it might help them better appreciate the critical importance of education which fosters intellectual curiosity even as it helps students develop the moral imperative required to address equity issues. A general education curriculum which stresses surface encounters with the historical, philosophical, and sociological perspectives which give meaning to a democratic society will not accomplish this. Rather, such encounters must become personal and occur in an academy where "true pluralism exists and many stories can be told and heard in concert" (Palmer 1990, 3). Further, it is teachers who must themselves become active proponents of intellectual discourse in the pursuit of knowledge, rather than promoters of "education as a spectator sport, in which students observe while pros [teachers] engage" (Palmer 1990, 2). As Goodlad and colleagues (1990) note:

> The human dialogue is too rich for teachers or students to remain unaware of the ways humankind structures experiences, experiences that are embedded in the subject matter of the school curriculum. (1990, 21)

This is no less the case for special educators who must construct ways to think about teaching which create opportunities for preservice teachers to "live the question" (Palmer 1990, 11).

LIVING THE QUESTION

In a recent article, Parker Palmer (1990) described good teaching as both an act of generosity and a risky business in which learning becomes a matter of "living the question." (p. 11) Through examples from his own experiences, he provides illustrations of knowledge as a transaction between the teacher and learner which encourages both internal and external conversation, the use of critical episodes or autobiographical accounts (microcosms) as "critical grains of sand within which a world is revealed," the intersection of autobiography and knowledge, and classrooms in which conflict and competition become the means through which students evolve a consensual climate. Above all, for Palmer, "living the question" involves the "courage" to take risks, to expose oneself to contradictions, and to relinquish control in order to empower the group. He describes courageous teachers as those willing to "profess their faith (disciplines) in the midst of a dangerous world" (p. 16).

INTRODUCTION TO EXCEPTIONAL CHILDREN: REVISING THE APPROACH

Recently, my colleague and I were discussing Palmer's ideas as we began revising the introductory course discussed earlier. The revised course would take common concepts or disciplines (such as measurement, time, reading, writing) which *all* children are expected to master and which produce the same outcome (regardless of the culture) to examine educational process and meaning across cultures. Our goal would be to help students better understand if a concept (e.g., measurement) has a different meaning in different cultures, what those differences are, and how children learn that concept in different cultures. In the process, students may come to understand how the same outcomes may have different meanings to individuals from diverse backgrounds. For example, in some Native American cultures, children watch an adult make baskets. Afterwards, they gather the materials and, in private, construct their own baskets, neither soliciting nor receiving adult approval. The children then return to look at the baskets produced by the adults, comparing their baskets to those of the adults and making adaptations. When each child feels his/her basket is ready, it is taken to the adult, who either confirms the child's judgment or offers advice about needed changes or materials. This differs from schooling in a society in which each stage of the process must be sanctioned by an authority (either a teacher or boss) before the next step can be undertaken. The cultural difference is embedded in the process.

In special education, what results in poor practice with culturally diverse populations is that process and meaning may be different from those of the teacher. While those preparing to become special educators *hear* this frequently, many have not analyzed their own learning processes in their college classes. Behind the safety of syllabi, clearly stated objectives and activities, and lectures, they have been insulated from the need to explore actively their own learning protocols and the meanings which guide them.

Thus, at first, our revised introductory class would feature no syllabus, list of activities, or textbook. Instead, students and teachers would create the issues around which the course would be designed. These issues, in turn, would guide the selection of initial reading, field trips, speakers, and activities in which the students and professors would engage. Together, they would explore how different cultures learn the concepts or disciplines required in American elementary and secondary classrooms. In learning teams, students would work out the questions and/or issues related to these concepts and, in concert with the professors, set out to find the answers. Classes would be held in the library, with each succession of questions resulting in new ones.

From these shared experiences of learning and the issues and questions generated through them, students and professors would then examine the particular accommodations and adaptations required to meet the individual learning styles of children with disabilities, as well as the role of cultural perspectives, their own and the children's, in the construction of effective instruction.

By forcing students to examine their own learning behaviors more closely, we hoped to lessen their tendency to deny the individuality of children with disabilities by applying general teaching strategies indiscriminately. Thus, for example, with the concept of measurement, students and professors would not only explore how children from different cultures viewed this concept but how they might use the views of a child with special needs to design instruction about measurement consistent with that child's unique learning style.

What students and professors learn in this process is that each brings cultural perspectives and experiences to the transaction of knowing. Together, this autobiographical material as well as the Western concept of schooling affect teaching and learning and the way all involved view the outcomes. The cognitive dissonance created by having to learn this initially, without the safety of such known accoutrements as a syllabus, quizzes, and lecture notes forces both students and professors to begin to understand the ambiguous nature of the "truths" they seek to impart to children, as well as the central role of culture in education. In a real sense, these activities make professors and students inept copartners in the construction of knowledge and, through that process, reinforce the tenuous nature of absolute truth. To encourage constant reflection, both teachers and students keep journals throughout the course which, in concert with the library work, form the basis for determining how to approach instruction for *all learners*.

As Jacqueline Jordan Irvine notes:

> Effective teachers of culturally diverse students use their students' everyday experiences in an effort to link concepts with prior knowledge. This is a process of finding the gap between the known (the students' personal cultural knowledge) and the unknown (materials and concepts to be mastered).
>
> (Such) teachers understand that the twenty-first century will demand that citizens be critical thinkers and problem-solvers, (therefore), the practices of "drill and kill" and "chalk and talk" are not elements of these effective teachers' repertories. (1993, 82–83)

Thus, "living the question" for both professors and learners in this class on exceptionality centers on the realization that children, like ideas, are not "cut flowers uprooted from their earthly origins," (Palmer 1990, 16) nor categories of deficits, but products of diverse cultures which prepare them to be authentic copartners in their own learning.

REFERENCES

Davis, W. E. (1989). The regular education initiative debate: Its promises and problems. In *Educating exceptional children*, ed. K. L. Freilberg, 13–19, 5th ed. Guilford, CT: The Dushkin Publishing Group.

Giroux, H. A., and P. McLaren. (August 1986). Teacher education and the politics of engagement: The case for democratic schooling. *Harvard Educational Review* 56(3):213–238.

Goffman, E. (1963). *Stigma: Notes on the management of spoiled identity*. New York: Simon and Schuster.

Goodlad, J. I. (1986). The learner in the world's center. *Social Education* 50(6):424–438.

Goodlad, J. I., R. Soder, and K. A. Sirotnik, eds. (1990). *The moral dimensions of teaching*. San Francisco, CA: Jossey-Bass.

Gould, S. J. (1981). *The mismeasure of man*. New York: W. W. Morton & Company.

Greene, M. (1993). Openings to possibility: The common world and the public school. In *Bad times, good schools*, J. Grymier, ed. West Lafayette, IN: Kappa Delta Pi.

Harry, B. (1992). *Cultural diversity, families, and the special education system: Communication and empowerment*. New York: Teachers College Press.

Hilliard, A. G. (1989). Teachers and cultural styles in a pluralistic society. *NEA Today* 7(6):65–69.

Heward, W. L., and M. D. Orlansky. (1992). *Teaching Exceptional children*. New York: Macmillan.

Howey, K. R., and N. L. Zimpher. (1989). *Profiles of preservice teacher education: Inquiry into the nature of programs*. Buffalo, NY: SUNY Press.

Irvine, J. J. (1993). Making teacher education culturally responsive. In *Diversity in teacher education: New directions*, ed. M. Dilworth, 79–92. San Francisco, CA: Jossey-Bass.

McDiarmid, G. W. (1990). *What to do about differences? A study of multicultural education for teacher trainees in Los Angeles Unified School District*. Research Rep. No. 90–II. East Lansing, MI: National Center for Research on Teacher Education, Michigan State University.

Moyers, B. (1989). *A world of ideas*. New York: Doubleday.

Palmer, P. J. (1990, January/February). Good teaching: A matter of living the mystery. *Change* 22(1):11–16.

Ramirez, B. A. (1988). Culturally and linguistically diverse children. *Teaching Exceptional Children* 20(4):45.

Warden, K., and O. Welch. (1992, Winter). Disturb the Inertia—Exist in a world of ideas: Preparing thinking teachers. *Tennessee Education* 21(3):26–29.

Zimpher, N. L., and E. A. Ashburn. (1993). Countering parochialism in teacher candidates. In *Diversity in teacher education: New directions*, ed. M. Dilworth, 40–62. San Francisco, CA: Jossey-Bass.

18

CARL A. GRANT AND CATHY A. ZOZAKIEWICZ

Student Teachers, Cooperating Teachers, and Supervisors: Interrupting the Multicultural Silences of Student Teaching

> And of course I am afraid, because the transformation of silence into language and action is an act of self-revelation, and that always seems fraught with danger. But my daughter, when I told her our topic and my difficulty with it, said, "Tell them about how you're never really a whole person if you remain silent, because there's always that one little piece inside you that wants to be spoken out...."
>
> In the cause of silence, each of us draws the face of her own fear—fear of contempt, of censure, or some judgment, or recognition, of challenge, of annihilation. But most of all, I think, we fear the visibility without which we cannot truly live.
>
> (Audre Lorde 1984, 42)

As we walk through schools where student teaching is taking place, we hear many silences. Some of these silences are of great concern to us. We are not hearing about issues of diversity and equity. We are not hearing discussions about racism, sexism, heterosexism, or classism. We are not hearing questions about present policies and structures that may be inequitable. Such silences in student teaching about such issues of multicultural education are rarely being broken, nor

259

is there much discussion about why the silences exist. What are the reasons for them? This chapter will identify the silences, illuminate why they exist, and offer strategies to challenge the silences.

We begin with a literature review of the three major stakeholders in the full-time student teaching experience: the student teacher, the cooperating teacher, and the university supervisor. Methods and procedures of our investigation are then discussed. A presentation of the silences follows next, leading to a discussion of the silences and their causes. Finally, strategies for challenging the silences are presented.

LITERATURE REVIEW

The literature in preservice teacher education often focuses on the triad—student teacher, cooperating teacher, and university supervisor. We located over three hundred articles and other printed materials written within the last ten years dealing with each of these triad members. The material covers a wide range of topics important to the student teaching experience. We organize this review to inform the reader about the many topics included within the student teaching literature.[1]

Student Teachers

The student teaching literature published over the last decade can be divided into nine categories: (1) descriptions of ongoing student teaching programs (e.g., Heller 1992; Vacc and Russell 1992); (2) research studies of the effects of programs on the student teachers (e.g., Kleinfeld 1991; Shapiro 1991; Verloop 1984; Williams 1991; Yon and Passe 1990); (3) models and methods of supervision (e.g., Fraenkel 1992; Henry 1981; Rikard 1982); (4) student teaching guidelines and handbooks (e.g., Alessia and Owens 1983; Liebert 1992; Priebe 1986; Wentz and Yarling 1982); (5) descriptive reviews and analyses of student teaching literature (e.g., Griffin 1981; Grumley 1989; Ralph 1989); (6) problems (for example, stress, causes of failures) within student teaching (e.g., Hourcade 1988; Jelineck 1986; Knowles and Hoefler 1989); (7) comparison of teaching perspectives between and among the members of the triad (e.g., Griffin 1983; Kalekin-Fishman and Kornfeld 1991); (8) analyses of different teaching methods—e.g., microteaching, reflective teaching—(Peters and Moore 1983); and (9) student teaching and multicultural education (e.g., Cooper, Beare, and Thorman 1990; Dana 1992; Grant and Koskela 1986; Mahan 1982a). The central theme of the majority of the literature is how to better understand the student teaching experience in order to foster improvement (e.g., Griffin 1983; Hourcade 1988; Kleinfeld 1991). A few studies investigated the necessity of the student teaching experience itself (e.g., Bennie 1982; Clark 1985).

Twenty-seven of the studies discussed or made mention of multicultural education issues in some manner, ranging from minimal to substantive discussions. Some examples of studies that took action to disrupt multicultural education silences of the student teaching experiences follow.

Arnold Cooper, Paul Beare, and Joseph Thorman (1990), Nancy Dana (1992), and James Mahan (1982a) interrupted the multicultural silences by immersing students in settings with culturally different student populations. Cooper, Beare, and Thorman disrupted the silences by studying the effects of placing some student teachers from the student teaching cohort in a Hispanic school district in South Texas, while the remaining members of the cohort student taught in Northern Minnesota, where students and student teachers shared the same culture. Cooper, Beare, and Thorman stated, "The Student Teaching in the Texas program was conceived as a way to redirect teaching practice from the vantage point of a different cultural setting" (1990, 2). Similarly, Dana (1992) placed White female intern teachers in low socioeconomic, all African American schools. Mahan interrupted multicultural silences by placing student teachers on American Indian reservations, in Hispanic communities, or within urban communities. Beyond student teaching, the students were also required to take a course focusing on the cultural group(s) with whom they were working. Additionally, they were required to work in a nonteaching capacity within their school community weekly in order to "meet and work directly with people from various walks of life and become acquainted with 'how a living is made'" (1982a, 1).

Carl Grant and Ruth Koskela (1986) interrupted multicultural silences by providing students with a baseline knowledge of multicultural education as part of their first teacher education course. During their methods courses, practica, and full-time student teaching, they were interviewed, and their lesson plans were examined for evidence of multicultural education. In these interviews, students explained what they were doing with multicultural education and why.

Cooperating Teachers

The literature discussing cooperating teachers over the last decade covers eight major categories: (1) the role of the cooperating teacher (Balch and Balch, 1987; Cusimano 1988); (2) supervision methods and/or procedures (Balch and Balch 1987; Martin and Yoder 1985; Rikard 1990; Shapiro and Sheehan 1986); (3) the relationships between and among the cooperating teacher, student teacher, and supervisor (Bean and Zulich 1991; Moon 1988; Ryan 1982; Scholl 1990; Vogt 1988); (4) descriptions of ongoing programs (Butler 1989; Wedman 1985); (5) reviews of cooperating teacher preparation (Abel 1987; Morehead and Waters 1987; Polacheck 1992); (6) comparisons of the beliefs and perspectives of the cooperating teacher, student teacher, and supervisor (Barnes and Edwards 1984; DeBolt 1988; Moon 1988; Tanner 1987); (7) literature reviews on the roles and/or history of the cooperating teacher (Griffin 1981; Grippin 1991; Vogt 1988, Zerr 1988); and, finally, of particular importance to this chapter, (8) multicultural education and the cooperating teacher (Campos 1983; Haberman and Post 1990; Mahan 1982b).

Of these studies, only three discussed the cooperating teacher and multicultural issues. Frank Campos (1983) revealed that cooperating teachers and their student teachers have negative attitudes and low expectations for their Mexican American students. Martin Haberman and Linda Post (1990) reported that 80 percent of cooperating teachers believe that the goals of multicultural education (at best) should be tolerance and cooperation. Mahan (1982b) discovered that when Native Americans serve in key training roles within the student teaching cultural immersion project, the student teachers become more culturally relevant educators and have greater success acquiring employment teaching Native American students.

A prevailing finding within the cooperating teacher literature is that the cooperating teacher has the most significant impact on the development of the student teacher during the student teaching experience. This literature provides general recommendations for cooperating teachers, such as the importance of developing a relationship with the student teacher. It does not address the complexity of the student teaching experience or the relational aspects that are a part of small group interaction. Deeper issues, such as the power dynamic involved, differences in teaching philosophies, or communication styles, are rarely addressed directly. Similarly, little is presented that explores issues of multicultural education, such as inequities in school systems, biases in textbooks and materials, student demographics, home-school relations, community culture, and plans of action to meet the needs of diverse learners.

Supervisors

The literature on supervision has focused on supervisory models to improve instruction (Blumberg 1980; Eisner 1979; Glickman 1981; Glickman and Bey 1990; Goldhammer 1966; Mosher and Purpel 1972; Sergiovanni and Starratt 1979; Smyth 1984). More recently, the literature on supervision has included attention to the preservice experience and student teaching as it relates to the triad members: the student teacher, cooperating teacher, and university supervisor (Clark et al. 1984; Koehler 1984; Rothman 1981). However, practically all of this literature is silent on issues of multicultural education and particularly about the university supervisor's role and responsibility for helping the student teacher teach from a multicultural perspective.

Maureen Gillette, in a review of the supervision literature concludes, "there is a paucity of research related to the role of student teaching in facilitating the development of multicultural perspective with student teachers....we currently know almost nothing about what techniques, methodologies or curricula facilitate or impede the development and maintenance of multicultural perspective in student teachers" (1990, 83). We located only three documents dealing with supervision and multicultural education: Gillette (1990), C. A. Bowers and David Flinders (1991), and Patricia Davidman (1990).

Gillette (1990) studied a teacher-supervisor in a program designed to prepare student teachers for diversity. It was found that this teacher-supervisor focused her attention on immediate classroom routines and the technical aspects of teaching. She gave little ongoing encouragement for the student teacher to examine practice in terms of multicultural education.

Bowers and Flinders have produced a monograph, "Culturally Responsive Teaching and Supervision," that is written in response to the cultural and demographic changes in society and the schools. They posit:

> The act of observing teachers (or student teachers) and providing them with feedback about their interactions with students cannot be separated from the larger questions surrounding the purposes of education. (1991, 3)

More specifically Bowers and Flinders argue:

> Supervision, like classroom teaching, is embedded within a cultural milieu. This connection between supervision and relevancy of what happens in the classroom to the political priorities of the larger society is a subtle yet vitally important one to grasp.
>
> To suggest that the supervisor can guide and evaluate a teacher's performance solely on the basis of objective data is both naive and irresponsible. On the other hand, to argue that the supervisor must evaluate teacher and student interactions strictly in terms of political priorities (even "progressive ones") is equally wrong. (1991, 4)

Bowers and Flinders advocate a model of supervision that takes into account the political and social contexts within which schools exist. They believe that supervisors should begin to question the policies and structures in place, and the activities and language that teachers and student teachers utilize, to uncover inherent assumptions and biases.

Davidman (1992) presents the need for multicultural teacher education and supervision. She reports that, within her program at California Polytechnic State University, supervisors and student teachers use a classroom demographic profile inventory and a typology of multicultural education to better enable them to teach from a multicultural perspective. It is also recommended that the supervisors in this program encourage their student teachers to develop a letter of context for lessons to be observed. Davidman states, "This letter provides information about the lesson and bulletin boards, includes requests for specific feedback, and a section which centers on the cross-cultural observations made by the candidate" (p. 49).

The overriding theme within all of the literature about student teaching and each of the triad members is to discover how to improve the student teaching experience. Almost entirely neglected within this literature is how to improve the student teaching experience in terms of developing teachers who understand and practice multicultural education and aspire to address social justice issues within their teaching. The literature that does discuss multicultural education does so generally, often focusing on a particular issue (e.g., stereotypes) or a single concept (e.g., teacher attitudes toward Mexican American students) that falls under multicultural education as a broad category, not acknowledging the overall philosophy and process of multicultural education. This literature fails to present multicultural education as an overall orientation to the whole schooling process: the structures, policies, curricula, staff, and practices of education. Such a limited interpretation of the concept of multicultural education squelches the opportunity to empower educators and students to build a nation that is more equitable and truly democratic in nature.

METHODS AND PROCEDURES

Background

Our investigation took place at a large research institution in the Midwest. The fundamental goals of the teacher education program are the preparation of teachers who are (1) reflective and (2) responsive to diversity. The study occurred over three semesters, from the Fall of 1992 through the Fall of 1993, during the student teaching experience which follows the public school calendar. The methods included classroom observations of student teachers during their final teaching experience, discussions during supervisory conferences and seminar meetings, and information from some interviews and written seminar assignments.

Participants

Of the thirty-two student teachers involved, twenty-six were White and female, three were White males, two females were biracial, and one was a female of color. The student teaching classrooms ranged in student population from predominantly White to forty percent children of color. Nine classrooms were predominantly White, including zero to two students of color, and the remaining twenty-four classrooms were more racially diversified, ranging from three to eight students of color. The children of color were African American, Asian American, Hispanic, Native American, and Southeast Asian (Hmong and Vietnamese).

All the cooperating teachers were White, except one who was Asian American. Twenty-one of the cooperating teachers were female and four were male. Also, most of the school staff were White and female, except for two principals who were female and African American, and four White male principals.

The supervisor/researcher is a White, female graduate student, whose area of study is multicultural education and social justice. The program director/researcher is an African American male whose research interest includes multicultural education.

DESCRIBING THE SILENCES

When student teachers begin the full-time student teaching phase of this program, a central goal of this experience is to allow them to further develop their personal teaching philosophy and to develop and implement methods and practices that they have studied in their preservice courses. Once in the classrooms, this goal is difficult to attain. Often, student teachers' planning and teaching adhere to the policies and practices of the school and the particular classroom, limiting the implementation of alternative methods and practices and the development of their own personal educational philosophy; and so the multicultural silences begin.

To us, these "silences" are absences of attention and/or discussion or the superficial and limited attention and/or discussion about issues of multicultural education within the student teaching experience. In the classroom, there is a lack of or limited discussion about multicultural education in practice, or there is an apprehension to openly address such issues among members of the triad. Beyond such discussions, there is a silence of action: the implementation of multicultural education is limited, sporadic, or rarely present.

Absences and/or Superficial and Limited Attention and Discussion

Silences occur many places throughout the student teaching experience, and are especially notable in lesson plans, classroom activities, and in conferences among members of the triad.

Lesson Plans and Classroom Activities. The majority of planning done by student teachers emphasized instructional routines and procedures, and the curriculum content was seldom multicultural. For example, the daily plans included what to do with the students, problems to solve, materials to be used, and content themes or titles. Unit plans generated by the student teachers and taught during lead teaching were where most multicultural teaching occurred. The range and depth of the multicultural teaching in these units varied widely. Some incorporated multicultural education throughout the unit, e.g., plans about the history, culture, and contributions of an ethnic or racial group. Others included multicultural issues minimally, e.g., using literature written by authors of different gender and racial groups without a discussion of race or gender. Nevertheless, in these units issues of social justice, for example, how cultural groups have been oppressed, how sexism affects women, or how differently abled people are discriminated against, were rarely addressed.

Since plans alone do not entirely explain the organizational and management characteristics nor the teacher-student interactions, it is necessary to look directly at teaching and the classroom activities. The classroom teaching and activities were consistent with the planning in the limited attention given to multicultural education. Most student teachers did not change or modify curriculum content to demonstrate a variety of multicultural perspectives, nor did they integrate multicultural perspectives into their class practices. Some students did, on occasion, incorporate multicultural literature into the content of the curriculum. Several others made multicultural literature a consistent part of their teaching content. A few were working to develop a more comprehensive practice of multicultural education.

We noticed that the inclusion of multicultural education in both areas, lesson planning and classroom activities, were affected by the diversity of the student population and by the cooperating teacher's and student teacher's knowledge and commitment to multicultural education. In schools that were predominantly White, many student teachers did not incorporate multicultural materials into their plans or integrate multicultural perspectives into activities. When they did, it was mainly to list or incorporate multicultural literature and resource materials (a film on Martin Luther King Jr. or a book written by or about Native Americans). In schools where there were more diverse populations and the cooperating teachers and student teachers were knowledgeable and committed to multicultural education, there was broader incorporation of multicultural materials, perspectives, and activities to foster an awareness and appreciation of diversity. However, many of these activities centered upon facts, fairs, foods, and festivals and heroes and heroines. They neglected to inculcate a multicultural orientation and address social justice issues. On some occasions in diverse settings, attempts were made to incorporate such activities and multicultural perspectives on a regular basis. We observed that such practice was rare, and still, for the most part, issues of social justice were silent.

Conferences. The attention to multicultural education issues during triad conferences was also affected by the diversity of the student population and the knowledge and commitment of the cooperating teacher, student teacher, and the university supervisor to multicultural education. During triad conferences in predominately White schools, discussions of race, gender, and class rarely took place. Instead, attention focused upon classroom management, instructional methodology, and pupil-teacher interaction. In schools where there were more diverse populations, discussions of race, gender, and class occurred on more occasions. These discussions, however, were usually about at-risk students and often did not include multicultural perspectives and social justice issues. Conferences where issues of multicultural education were embedded as a natural part of the discussion occurred in diverse classrooms where the cooperating teacher, student teacher, and/or university supervisor had a multicultural orientation to education. This did not happen in many conferences, however. Usually, when multicultural education and social justice issues were raised in conferences, such discussion was initiated by a member of the triad who was an advocate of multicultural and social justice education (due to their conscious awareness and personal commitment). Though such issues were raised in a number of conferences, multicultural education was seldom the focal point of the student teaching conversations.

How Multicultural Education Is Being Discussed

Our definition of multicultural silences includes superficial and/or limited discussion of multicultural education. When asked to describe or define what multicultural education is or consists of, many of the student teachers' responses were within the human relations realm. They used phrases and words such as: "I treat all students the same," "we all need to learn to get along," "unity," and "acceptance of diversity." These student teachers often believed that this understanding of multicultural education is all that is needed for their teaching. These phrases and terms were used fairly often by those working in both predominately White schools and schools with more diverse student populations.

All of our students reflected upon their classroom practice and performance. Journal writings and discussions about day-to-day teaching, school policies, and practices were evidence of their reflectiveness. Some journal entries and verbal comments tended to be descriptive, focusing on areas such as classroom routines, student teacher-cooperating teacher interactions, pupil-teacher interactions, and other critical concerns. However, these often had a human relations or technical perspective. Commonly missing from these reflections were critical inquiry into multicultural concerns and issues of equity. Critical inquiries by student teachers on multicultural education occurred mainly when they were specifically initiated, encouraged, or required by a member(s) of the triad who was knowledgeable or concerned about multicultural education. When student teachers did inquire critically in a multicultural manner, they were often apprehensive about bringing up their concerns because of their perceived lack of power. Inquiries seemed to seldom develop into consistent in-depth multicultural examination or multicultural teaching practice.

CAUSES OF SILENCES

Why was there an absence of, or limited discussion of, multicultural education within the student teaching experience? Why, so often, when there was some discussion of multicultural education, was it superficial and/or limited? Why was there a lack of critical inquiry regarding multicultural education, including social justice issues? Why was there a silence of action? In this section we will explore these "whys."

When preservice students begin their full-time student teaching experience, often they have not acquired enough multicultural education knowledge and experience to have a solid, working understanding of it. Also, most student teachers have not had the opportunity to observe multicultural education being consistently practiced in the field, nor have they had the chance to test and apply the knowledge they have acquired. The lack of knowledge and practical understanding about multicultural education among student teachers and other triad members often seems to be one of the major reasons for not attending to multicultural education within the student teaching experience.

Members having limited knowledge of multicultural education often leads to various interpretations of its meaning, which also works to complicate the extent to which this educational orientation is addressed and applied within the student teaching experience. For example, some triad members may believe they are doing multicultural education when they incorporate a piece or pieces of multicultural curriculum into their teaching. In addition, the prevalence of student teachers' identification with the human relations view limits their teaching expectations and practices to one of acceptance and learning to get along, neglecting the pursuit of such goals as cultural pluralism, equity, and social justice. These goals may also be neglected due to some members of the triad perceiving multicultural education as controversial and uncomfortable. Some might even believe that multicultural education is not relevant to their student population or important to their curriculum and, therefore, see little need to deal with issues of equity and diversity.

The differing philosophies, personal backgrounds, educational experiences, and commitment to issues of diversity by the triad members contributes to the extent of reflection and inquiry about multicultural education and issues of equity within the student teaching experience. Members may be more concerned with improving other areas of practice and curriculum that they are more committed to and/or interested in. Also, differences in adherence to institutional expectations, standards, and constraints between the employed cooperating teacher and the visiting student teacher and university supervisor contributes to multicultural silences, inhibiting the student teacher's understanding and development of multicultural education.

Few take the risk to verbalize or point out existing inequities and biases in society and in school policy and practice. There are many probable causes for these social justice silences. Some members of the triad may be consciously unaware of the existing inequities or hesitant to introspect and examine their school's or their own positions, beliefs, biases, and assumptions. Some may fear that making critical noise will be damaging or detrimental to their position or reputation. Others may feel they have little power to challenge existing policies and practices. And those that do reflect in such a critical manner may simply not know how to move such inquiries to action, or, if they do attempt action, their efforts may be ineffective due to lack of support from other members or colleagues. The school atmosphere may be such that pushing and challenging policies and structures leads to alienation. Student teachers especially feel a sense of helplessness in this area because they are visitors/students in another "real" teacher's classroom, being mentored by both the cooperating teacher and supervisor. Challenging and changing policies and practices from such a position is often an intimidating risk.

Finally, the most popular reason for multicultural education and social justice silences seems simply to be a perceived lack of time. This is especially so for student teachers, who are frequently so overwhelmed by the amount of responsibility they face during student teaching that applying multicultural education practices may seem secondary to simply learning how to survive and thrive during a regular school day schedule.

In sum, there are many probable causes for these multicultural education silences during the student teaching experience, in and among the triad members.

Reasons such as limited knowledge, background, and commitment of triad members, lack of time, and apprehensiveness to openly challenging the present policies and practices of schools, impact all of the silences we have discussed; none is mutually exclusive. All the causes play a part in the totality of the multicultural silences present within the student teaching experience. Without acknowledging the power and far-reaching influence of all the causes, multicultural education and social justice actions will remain silent as well.

STRATEGIES TO CHALLENGE THE SILENCES

We have so far concentrated on presenting what is and is not happening with multicultural education in the full-time student teaching experience, without explicitly and directly describing our own beliefs and positions. Important to presenting our strategies is explaining our vision of multicultural education within the student teaching experience. It is the framework from which these strategies are derived.

We see multicultural education as a philosophy of education, an orientation to education and living, and a process of learning that is continual and evolving. The philosophy encompasses democratic principles such as equality, justice, and equity. Cultural pluralism and the recognition and affirmation of cultural groups (i.e., race, ethnicity, gender, class, ability, sexual orientation) are key components of multicultural education. Other key components are the promotion of social justice and the development of social structural equality.

Multicultural education is an all-encompassing orientation to education, living, and life. It includes every aspect of school policy and practice: curricula, content, pedagogy, structures, language and communication, relationships between and among colleagues, staff members, and students, and staffing patterns. It is manifested in the daily ongoing high expectations and respectful, nondiscriminatory, nonoppressive treatment that takes place between teacher and student, student and student, school and home, and among all members of the school community.

Multicultural education is not static; it is a lifelong journey of learning, changing, adapting, and restructuring. It is not silent or silencing; it encourages the voicing of different perspectives and groups. It advocates voices that challenge and disrupt what is believed to be the norm or universal truth without marginalizing or dehumanizing others' views. It encourages and affirms differences and the right to be different, providing the space and forum that welcomes a myriad of voices, positions, and beliefs. In conclusion, multicultural education is about helping schools become marketplaces for ideas and learning to critically examine ideas.

A necessary strategy to interrupt the multicultural silences existing in the student teaching experience is to begin to extend the meaning and vision of multicultural education, learning to conceptualize it in a more comprehensive manner. In order for multicultural education to become a more natural part of the planning, teaching, organization, activities, and conferences within the student teaching experience, it must become a more conscious part of everyone's thinking. The entire teacher training program must address multicultural education in a more systemic way than is usually the case; multicultural education must permeate the university structures, policies, and practices. The school of education and its instructors should not only teach the methods and procedures of critical inquiry, but they should also examine their own institutional structures, policies, and practices, ascertaining the extent to which multicultural education is being modeled. To this end, the school of education must encourage, support, and invite students' and teachers' voices and ideas.

Student teachers should have experiences within classrooms and with cooperating teachers who interrupt silences and/or teach from a multicultural perspective. For those cooperating teachers who have not formally studied multicultural education, but are willing and committed to its ideals and the process of learning, accepting, and affirming, graduate courses need to be available and required in order for them to work with student teachers.

The screening and interviewing in the field placement process needs to become more critical of the settings and location where students are placed. If students participate in the placement process, they should be prepared to critically examine the placement, making certain that they would be allowed to develop their multicultural philosophy and practices. Student teachers must feel comfortable trying different strategies and questioning policies and practices, understanding that these efforts will not affect their grades or job recommendations.

University supervisors, in turn, should be knowledgeable and committed to encouraging and guiding student teachers to become more critical and multicultural in all aspects of their practice. Hiring policies should encourage the employment of individuals who have multicultural awareness and sensitivity. They should also possess the self confidence and professionalism needed to advocate multicultural education and to encourage their student teachers to do the same. Seminars and observations should include continuous and in-depth discussions of multicultural issues. They should encourage an open analysis of the policies and practices in the schools and the beliefs, positions, and practices of themselves and the student teachers within the classrooms.

An atmosphere of trust and mutual respect should be fostered amongst triad members, when working all together or when working in dyads, so that pushing and challenging is accepted in a constructive manner. Cooperating teachers and supervisors must realize that the student teacher has the least power in the triad and will need continual support to deal with multicultural issues. This support should include modeling of multicultural instruction by the teacher and supervisor and encouragement and help with resources and methods for multicultural teaching.

Schools at the K–12 level and institutions of higher education must develop and openly declare a mutual vision of multicultural student teacher preparation. They must continually assess the effectiveness of the program to prepare teachers to be multicultural educators. This effectiveness should be measured using both short-term and longitudinal research methods. One important program factor is that the university support and encourage the efforts of the supervisors who interrupt the multicultural education silences.

There are no more than twenty-four hours in each day. For most people, including educators, there is never enough time. However, many find time or make time to do that which is important to them. Doing multicultural education is more about a *commitment* to a philosophy and its accompanying educational practice, than it is an issue of *real* time. Nevertheless, it is important to provide student teachers and other educators with the professional development time to foster their awareness, acceptance, and affirmation of multicultural education. For time must not be allowed to be the excuse teachers use for not doing multicultural education.

Finally, we acknowledge that some student teachers have begun developing and practicing multicultural education and are becoming committed to being multicultural educators. They are working to develop ways to interrupt the silences, along with some of their cooperating teachers and supervisors. We applaud and encourage these efforts. Yet, they are too few. There needs to be more multicultural education and social justice noise.

SUGGESTIONS FOR SUPERVISION: MAKING MULTICULTURAL NOISE WITHIN STUDENT TEACHING

Developing a multicultural education orientation begins with understanding oneself. This calls for some retrospective reflecting and introspective self-examination, for both the supervisor and the student teachers. Explicitly, this involves exploring through a variety of media how racism, sexism, classism, heterosexism, and other oppressive and discriminatory constructs have impacted our lives and thinking. For White teachers and supervisors, it is especially important to explore the concept of being White; whiteness and the privileges afforded by it are often silences within discussions of culture. Going a step further involves exploring how one's race, gender, ability, sexual orientation, and class affect the diverse group of children in schools today.

Modeling and teaching with a multicultural education orientation is essential to interrupting and causing interruptions of multicultural and social justice silences within the student teaching experience. Supervisors should continually reflect upon their own practice in a variety of ways. One way would be to hold multicultural dialogues with other supervisors, the student teachers, and other members of the program. This could include inviting a colleague to observe your practice and meet for a discussion.

Within seminars and classroom observations, supervisors should work and relate to their student teachers according to how they expect these teachers to work and relate within their classrooms. They should listen and support their work, while challenging students to think, grow, and act as multicultural educators. As with children in schools, supervisors need to accept and get to know each student teacher and their cultural background, educational knowledge, and unique experiences.

Another idea involves discovering what multicultural education means to the student teachers in practice. Comparing their beliefs to theoretical literature on multicultural education uncovers many silences within these meanings. This illuminates where and how to guide their multicultural development. It is essential that student teachers come to conceive of multicultural education as an integral and embedded part of teaching and schools; every decision, action, assignment, organizational structure, and communicative act works either toward or against the goals of multicultural education. The idea that multicultural education is mainly content, or a method to learn and use on occasion, must be rethought; multicultural education must be reconceived as a comprehensive way of thinking about teaching and living. Even the simple task of sending someone to move furniture in the auditorium is embedded with multicultural opportunities: sending boys only works against; sending both genders works toward.

An important role of the supervisor is devising ways for student teachers to move multicultural education to action within the classrooms where the cooperating teacher does not have a strong commitment to or understanding of multicultural education. One way of doing this is to make an expectation for student teachers from the beginning, in their teaching, planning, and written assignments for seminar.

Taking seminar time to help student teachers develop units, activities, and pedagogy that is culturally relevant is a hands-on way to create multicultural curriculum. It is important during classroom visits that the supervisor identify opportunities where issues of social justice and multicultural education could be extended and/or included. This is an effective and relevant way to interrupt silences, helping students see that multicultural issues are embedded within their teaching.

CONCLUSION

We know that student teachers are only a college semester away from teaching in the real world. Society often socializes us to ignore what we have learned, especially when much of society is not convinced that it is important or believes it would take away some of their privileges. Nevertheless, our responsibility is to prepare teachers who can participate in a systemic change effort to help schools become the "great equalizer" and proponent of equity for all students. Ignoring the societal structures and policies that hinder and threaten such growth and progress would disillusion or unrealistically serve to minimize the extent to which the multicultural education vision can be attained; ignoring these factors would overlook the overall historical and political context within which we all live and work. Yet, change must begin, and educators are important and essential to the change. The silences must be interrupted. As Audre Lorde explains in *Sister Outsider*:

We can learn to work and speak when we are afraid in the same way we have learned to work and speak when we are tired. For we have been socialized to respect fear more than our own needs for language and definition, and while we wait in silence for that final luxury of fearlessness, the weight of silence will choke us.

The fact that we are here and that I speak these words is an attempt to break that silence and bridge some of those differences between us, for it is not difference which immobilizes us, but silence. And there are so many silences to be broken. (1984, 44)

NOTES

1. The categories listed in the review were created from patterns found within the descriptions of the purpose and focus of the research studies, in order to present the information in a manageable and time efficient manner.

REFERENCES

Abel, F. (1987, February). Enhancing the effectiveness of cooperating teachers. Paper presented at the annual meeting of the Association of Teacher Educators, Houston, TX. (ERIC Document Reproduction Service No. ED 278 641)

Alessia, M., and K. Owens. (1983). Handbook for the student teaching semester. (ERIC Document Reproduction Service No. ED 235 122)

Balch, P., and P. Balch. (1987). *The cooperating teacher: A practical approach for the supervision of student teachers.* Lanham, MD: University Press of America.

Barnes, S., and S. Edwards. (1984). Effective student teaching experience: A qualitative-quantitative study. Report no. 9060. Austin, TX: University of Texas, R & D Center for Teacher Education. (ERIC Document Reproduction Service No. ED 251 441)

Bean, T., and J. Zulich. (1991, December). A case study of three preservice teachers' beliefs about content area reading through the window of student-professor dialogue journals. Paper presented at the annual meeting of the National Reading Conference, Palm Springs, CA. (ERIC Document Reproduction Service No. ED 344 201)

Bennie, W. (1982). Field-based teacher education—A reconsideration? *Teacher Educator* 17(4):19–24.

Blumberg, A. (1980). *Supervisor & teachers: A private cold war,* 2nd ed. Berkeley, CA: McCutchan.

Bowers, C., and D. Flinders. (1991). *Culturally responsive teaching and supervision.* New York: Teachers College Press

Butler, D. (1989, March). Empowering teachers through collaborative mentoring designs: An empirical assessment. Paper presented at the annual meeting of the American Educational Research Association, San Francisco. (ERIC Document Reproduction Service No. ED 307 258)

Campos, F. (1983, April). The attitudes and expectations of student teachers and cooperating teachers toward students in predominantly Mexican American schools: A qualitative data perspective. Paper presented at the annual meeting of the American Educational Research Association, Montreal. (ERIC Document Reproduction Service No. ED 234 026)

Clark, D. (1985). *Field experience in teacher education. A model for industrial arts/technology education.* National Center for Research in Vocational Education. Special publication series no. 52. Ohio State University, Columbus, OH.

Clark, D. C., R. B. Smith, R. A. Thurman, and J. E. Baird. (1984). Supervisors' feedback to student teachers. (ERIC Document Reproduction Service No. ED 257 794)

Cooper, A., P. Beare, and J. Thorman. (1990). Preparing teachers for diversity: A comparison of student teaching experiences in Minnesota and South Texas. *Action in Teacher Education* 12(3):1–4.

Cusimano, B. (1988). Guidelines for cooperating teachers. *Strategies* 1(3):26.

Dana-Fichtman, Nancy. (1992, February). Towards preparing the monocultural teacher for the multicultural classroom. Paper presented at the annual meeting of the Association of Teacher Educators, Orlando, FL. (ERIC Document Reproductive Service No. ED 350 272)

Davidman, P. T. (1990). Multicultural teacher education and supervision: A new approach to professional development. *Teacher Education Quarterly* 17(3):37–52.

Debolt, G. (1988, April). The social system in social studies lessons: Little girl lost vs. work in the real world. Paper presented at the annual meeting of the American Educational Research Association, New Orleans, LA. (ERIC Document Reproduction Service No. ED 296 966)

Eisner, E. (1979). *The educational imagination.* New York: Macmillan.

Fraenkel, J. R. (1992, April). Joint vs. single supervision. Paper presented at the annual meeting of the American Educational Research Association, San Francisco. (ERIC Document Reproduction Service No. ED 346 051)

Gillette, M. (1990). Making them multicultural: A case study of the clinical teacher-supervisor in preservice education. Ph.D. dissertation, University of Wisconsin-Madison, Madison, WI.

Glickman, C. (1981). *Developmental supervision: Alternative practices for helping teachers improve instruction.* Alexandria, VA: Association for Supervision and Curriculum Development.

Glickman, C. and T. Bey. (1990). Supervision. In *Handbook of Research on Teacher Education,* ed. W. R. Houston (549–566). New York: Macmillan.

Goldhammer, R. (1966). *Clinical supervision: Special methods for the supervision of teachers.* New York: Holt, Rinehart & Winston.

Grant, C., and R. Koskela. (1986). Education that is multicultural and the relationship between preservice campus learning and field experiences. *Journal of Educational Research* 79:197–203.

Griffin, G. (1981). Student Teaching: A review. (ERIC Document Reproduction Service No. ED 223 565)

————. (1983). Expectations for student teaching: What are they and are they realized? Austin, TX: University of Texas, R & D Center for Teacher Education. (ERIC Document Reproduction Service No. ED 234 023)

Grippin, P. (1991, October). Intern Mentors: Is this an idea worth pursuing? Paper presented at the annual conference of the Northeastern Educational Research Association, Ellenville, NY. (ERIC Document Reproduction Service No. ED 344 838)

Grumley, F. (1989). A comprehensive bibliography of periodical literature, dissertations, theses, and ERIC documents related to student teaching in music. (ERIC Document Reproduction Service No. ED 312 183)

Haberman, M., and L. Post. (1990). Cooperating teachers' perceptions of the goals of multicultural education. *Action in Teacher Education* 12(3):31–35.

Heller, H. W. (1992). Meeting the needs of students with handicaps: Helping regular teachers meet the challenge. *Action in Teacher Education* 13(4):44–54.

Henry, J. (1981). Evaluation of teaching skills. *South Pacific Journal of Teacher Education* 9(1):61–65.

Hourcade, J. J. (1988). Stress sources among student teachers. *Clearing House* 61(8):347–350.

Jelinek, C. A. (1986). Stress factors and the pre-service teacher. *Teacher Educator* 22(1):2–8.

Kalekin-Fishman, D., and G. Kornfeld. (1991) Construing roles: Cooperating teachers and student teachers in TEFL: An Israeli Study. *Journal of Education for Teaching* 17(2):151–163.

Kleinfeld, J. (1991, April). Wrestling with the angel: What student teachers learn from writing cases. Paper presented at the annual meeting of the American Educational Research Association, Chicago. (ERIC Document Reproduction Service No. ED 347 123)

Knowles, G., and V. B. Hoefler. (1989). The student teacher who wouldn't go away: Learning from failure. *Journal of Experiential Education* 12(2):14–21.

Koehler, V. (1984, April). University supervision of student teaching. National Institute of Education Report No. 9061. University of Texas, R & D Center for Teacher Education, Austin, TX. (ERIC Document Reproduction Service No. ED 270 349)

Liebert, D. K. (1992). Becoming a teacher: Practical guidelines for student teachers, cooperating teachers, principals, college supervisors. (ERIC Document Reproduction Service No. ED 354 227)

Lorde, A. (1984). The transformation of silence into language and action. In *Sister Outsider*, ed. A. Lorde. Freedom, CA: Crossing Press.

Mahan, J. (1982a, February). Community involvement components in culturally oriented teacher preparation. Paper presented at the annual meeting of the Association of Teacher Educators, Phoenix, AZ. (ERIC Document Reproduction Service No. ED 216 004)

Mahan, J. (1982b). Native Americans as teacher trainers: Anatomy and outcomes of a cultural immersion project. *Journal of Educational Equity and Leadership* 2(2): 100–110.

Martin, R., and E. Yoder. (1985). Clinical teaching analysis: A process for supervising. *Journal of American Association of Teacher Educators in Agriculture* 26(4):16–21.

Moon, A. (1988, April). Three perspectives on the language of supervision: How well do the university supervisor, cooperating teacher, and student teacher understand each other? Paper presented at the annual meeting of the American Educational Research Association, New Orleans, LA. (ERIC Document Reproduction Service No. ED 293 806)

Morehead, M., and S. Waters. (1987). Enhancing Collegiality: A model for training cooperating teachers. *Teacher Educator* 23(2):28–31.

Mosher, R., and D. Purpel. (1972). *Supervision: The reluctant profession*. New York: Houghton Mifflin.

Peters, J. L., and G. E. Moore. (1983). Providing on-campus teaching experience for student teachers in agricultural education: A comparison of two techniques. *Journal of the American Association of Teacher Educators* 24(3):32–37.

Polacheck, D. (1992, February). Professional awareness of cooperating teachers. Paper presented at the annual meeting of the American Association of Colleges for Teacher Education, San Antonio, TX. (ERIC Document Reproduction Service No. ED 346 070)

Priebe, D. (1986). A handbook for student teachers and supervising teachers in vocational agriculture. (ERIC Document Reproduction Service No. ED 275 897)

Ralph, E. G. (1989). Developing professional attributes among student teachers during field experience programs. *Education Canada* 29(1):32–40.

Rikard, L. (1982). The student teaching practicum: Preparing supervisors and cooperating teachers. *Journal of Physical Education, Recreation, and Dance* 53(9):60–61.

Rikard, L. (1990). Student teaching supervision—a dyadic approach. *Journal of Physical Education, Recreation and Dance* 61(4):85–87.

Rothman, L. (1981). Effective and ineffective supervisory behavior of college supervisors as perceived by secondary school cooperating teachers. Ph.D. dissertation, University of Florida, Gainesville, FL. Dissertation Abstracts International, 42, 2086A.

Ryan, K. (1982, January). The cooperating teacher: Who? what? why? when? how? and whither? In *Student teaching: Problems and promising practices*, ed. G. Griffin and S. Edwards, 57–68. University of Texas, R & D Center for Teacher Education, Austin, TX. (ERIC Document Reproduction Service No. ED 223 574)

Scholl, R. (1990, February). University supervisor: Circuit rider or teacher educator. Paper presented at the annual meeting of the Association of Teacher Educators, Las Vegas, NV. (ERIC Document Reproduction Service No. ED 317 506)

Seriovanni, T., and R. Starratt. (1979). *Supervision: Human perspectives*. New York: McGraw-Hill Inc.

Shapiro, B. (1991). A collaborative approach to help novice science teachers reflect in the construction of the role of the science teacher. *Alberta Journal of Educational Research* 37(2):119–132.

Shapiro, P., and A. Sheehan. (1986). The supervision of student teachers: A new diagnostic tool. *Journal of Teacher Education* 37(6):35–39.

Smyth, W. John. (1984). *Clinical supervision-collaborative learning about teaching*. Victoria, Australia: Deakin University Press.

Tanner, D. (1987). The theory/practice "double bind" in student teaching. *Teacher Education and Practice* 4(1):45–49.

Vacc, N., and D. Russell. (1992). Summer student teaching: Evaluation of a pilot program. *Action in Teacher Education* 13(4):24–30.

Verloop, N. (1984, April). The effects of video materials on student teachers' cognition during their interactive teaching. Paper presented at the annual meeting of the American Educational Research Association, New Orleans, LA. (ERIC Document Reproduction Service No. ED 243 840)

Vogt, M. (1988, May) The preservice teacher-cooperating teacher relationship: An historical perspective. Paper presented at the annual meeting of the International Reading Association, Toronto. (ERIC Document Reproduction Service No. ED 301 563)

Wedman, J. (1985, February). Reconceptualizing student teaching programs: A synthesis. Paper presented at the annual meeting of the Association of Teacher Educators, Las Vegas, NV. (ERIC Document Reproduction Service No. ED 258 960)

Wentz, P, and J. R. Yarling (1982). Student teaching survival kit. (ERIC Document Reproduction Service No. ED 221 484)

Williams, D. (1991, April). Student teachers as naturalistic inquirers. Paper presented at the annual meeting of the American Educational Research Association, Chicago. (ERIC Document Reproduction Service No. ED 334 178)

Yon, M., and J. Passe. The relationship between the elementary social studies methods course and student teacher's beliefs and practices. *Journal of Social Studies Research* 14(1):13–24.

Zerr, R. (1988, February). What supervisors of student teaching and student teachers tell us about student teaching. Paper presented at the annual meeting of the American Association of Colleges for Teacher Education, New Orleans, LA. (ERIC Document Reproduction Service No. ED 300 362)

NOTES ON CONTRIBUTORS

Veronica M. Acosta-Deprez is an Assistant Professor of health education in Health and Human Performance, Auburn University. Her major professional fields of interest include school health, class, race, and gender issues in health and health education, international health issues, and multicultural health education. She has had experience in several areas of nursing as well as community health in the Philippines and in the United States. She has made presentations and has contributed articles on AIDS education for middle school children, and on preservice and in-service education for multicultural health education. Much of her time has been devoted to studying theoretical and methodological approaches to infusing multicultural perspectives into health education.

William D. Armaline is an Associate Professor of Educational Theory and Social Foundations at The University of Toledo. He teaches courses in sociology and history of education and in teacher education. His areas of scholarly interest include using foundations of education to inform pedagogy across the teacher education curriculum and exploring the intersections of culture and schooling.

Marilynne Boyle-Baise is an Assistant Professor at Indiana University-Bloomington. She is especially interested in preparing in-service teachers for multicultural education. She is the founder of a grass-roots advocacy group, the Coalition for Education that is Multicultural. Boyle-Baise teaches social studies methods and is active in establishing the concept of multicultural social studies.

Nedra Cobb has been an Assistant Professor of music at the University of Wisconsin-Parkside since 1991. Her performance credits range from jazz to classical repertoire. She has presented research papers on multicultural education in music education at the 1993 National Conference of Black Studies in Ghana, Africa, and at the 1994 NAME Conference in Detroit, Michigan. She has served as a regional representative for the Wisconsin Black Artist Guild and, in 1994, founded the vocal ensemble "Voices of Ethnicity," which is a quartet composed of vocalists of diverse ethnic backgrounds that performs throughout the Midwest.

Myrna Cohen is Visiting Assistant Professor and Placement Coordinator at the University of Houston. She received her doctorate from the University of Houston. Her research interests include teacher education and second language acquisition, and she has published an article on multicultural teacher education forthcoming in *The Teacher Educator*.

279

Kathleen S. Farber is an Associate Professor of Educational Foundations and Inquiry at Bowling Green State University. She teaches courses in pedagogy, educational psychology, human growth and development, and gender stereotyping and discrimination in education. Her scholarly interests include using feminist and poststructural lenses to understand the complex interplay between culture and pedagogy.

Gerardo M. Gonzalez is an Assistant Professor in the Psychology Program at California State University, San Marcos. Dr. Gonzalez obtained his doctorate in clinical psychology at the California School of Professional Psychology, Fresno. He completed predoctoral and postdoctoral internships at the University of California, Berkeley and a postdoctoral clinical-research fellowship at the University of California, San Francisco. Among his teaching and research interests are multicultural mental health issues (particularly for the Spanish-speaking population), computerized psychological assessment, and the cognitive prevention and treatment of clinical depression. He is also a licensed psychologist in California.

Carl A. Grant is a Hoefs-Bascom Professor of Teacher Education in the Department of Curriculum and Instruction and a Professor in the Department of Afro-American Studies at the University of Wisconsin-Madison. He has written or edited fifteen books or monographs in multicultural education and/or teacher education. These include *Research and Multicultural Education*, 1993; *Making Choices for Multicultural Education* (with Christine E. Sleeter), 1994; *After the School Bell Rings* (with Christine Sleeter), 1986; *Bringing Teaching to Life*, 1983; and *Community Participation in Education*, 1979. He has also written more than one hundred articles, chapters in books, and reviews. Several of his writings and programs that he directed have received awards. Professor Grant was a Fulbright Scholar in England in 1982–1983 researching and studying multicultural education, and in 1990 the Association of Teacher Educators selected him as one of the seventy leaders nationally in Teacher Education. In 1993 Professor Grant became President of the National Association for Multicultural Education (NAME).

Peter S. Hlebowitsh is Assistant Professor in the College of Education at the University of Iowa. He received his doctorate from Rutgers University. Formerly of the University of Houston, his research interests include curriculum theory, educational policy, and teacher education. He has published in journals such as *Educational Theory*. His recent book, *Radical Curriculum History Reconsidered*, is published by Teachers College Press.

Sandra Jackson is an Assistant Professor, Secondary Education and Curriculum at DePaul University, Chicago. She teaches courses in comparative education and women's studies. Her work has been published in *Harvard Educational Review*, the journal *National Women's Studies Association*, *Curriculum and Teaching*, and *Visual Sociology*.

Charlene Klassen-Endrizzi is an Assistant Professor in the Department of Education at Westminster College, PA. She teaches graduate and undergraduate classes in children's literature, language arts, and reading. She has also taught intermediate grades in Fresno, CA., for ten years. Recently she completed her dissertation entitled *Teacher Education That is Multicultural: Expanding Preservice Teachers' Orientation Toward Learning*

Through Multicultural Children's Literature. Other recent publications include a chapter in *Cycles of Meaning: Exploring the Potential of Talk in Learning Communities*, edited by K. Pierce and C. Gilles (1993) entitled, "Content Area Literature Discussions: Exploring the 'Color of Peace.'" Her research interests include multicultural education, children's literature, teacher education, whole language, and teacher study groups.

Mozell P. Lang is the Science Education Specialist in the School Quality Services program for the Michigan Department of Education. She provides technical assistance in science to schools, organizations, and educators at the local, regional, state, and national levels. She previously served as a program coordinator for the American Chemical Society (ACS) in Washington, DC, where she coordinated Project SEED, Chemistry Olympiad, Chemistry Careers, and the Pre-High School Science program. She is a board member of the Council of State Science Supervisors (CS3), the International Atlanta Science Curriculum Project (ASCP), the New Standards Project (NSP) science assessment advisory committee, and the State Collaborative on Assessment in Science (SCASS). She works actively with the MEAP Science Assessment Program, the Michigan Statewide Systemic Initiative, the Michigan Science Teachers Association, Middle Cities, the Teaching, Learning, and Curriculum (TLC) Leadership Program, and the Multicultural Science Committee. She is codirector of a National Science Foundation-funded, three-year summer science camp program for mathematics and science for middle school minority students. Also, she has served as an author and an advisor on the development of three major science textbooks.

Joseph M. Larkin is Assistant Director for Research and Staff Development with the Compact for Educational Opportunity, an organization which monitors and supports the metropolitan school desegregation program in the Milwaukee area. As a school teacher, a community worker, and a university professor, he has spent twenty-five years working in the field of urban education. Until recently, he was a member of the faculty and chair of the Teacher Education department at the University of Wisconsin-Parkside.

Renée J. Martin is an Associate Professor of Education Foundations at The University of Toledo. Dr. Martin's scholarly work focuses upon issues of diversity in teacher education. She is the editor of a book entitled *Practicing What We Teach: Confronting Diversity in Teacher Education*, the editor of a monograph entitled *Power and the Academy: The Hidden Discourse of Tenure, Promotion and Struggle*, and has written numerous scholarly articles in educational journals which address liberatory pedagogy and its implications for classrooms of the future. She is a past chairperson of the national organization, Women Educators, and an active member of numerous professional organizations such as the American Educational Research Association, the National Association for Multicultural Education, the Association for Supervision and Curriculum and Development, and the National Coalition for Sex Equity in Education.

Theresa Mickey McCormick is a teacher, writer, and artist. She is a Professor of Curriculum and Instruction at Iowa State University who specializes in multicultural, nonsexist teacher education. She has written, edited, and designed a variety of curriculum materials for classroom use, has written and published many journal articles and research reports, contributed chapters to edited books, and made numerous conference presentations on multicultural, nonsexist education topics throughout the United States and in Taiwan. She has written a book, *Creating the Nonsexist Classroom—A Multicultural Approach*, that was published in July 1994 by Teachers College Press.

Clara A. New is Assistant Professor of Teacher Education at the University of Wisconsin-Parkside, where she teaches methods in language arts and coordinates the early childhood program. Her research interests include the influence of teacher (and preteacher) perceptions and thinking on the academic achievement of African American males in the classroom.

Pamela Norwood is a doctoral student in the College of Education at the University of Houston. Her research interests include multicultural education, bilingual education, and teacher education. Her dissertation examines teaching process in bilingual classrooms.

Francisco A. Ríos is an Assistant Professor in the College of Education at California State University-San Marcos. He received his doctorate in educational psychology from the University of Wisconsin-Madison where he developed his interests in teacher cognition in multicultural contexts. He has taught courses in Learning and Instruction, Cultural Diversity in Schooling, Theories and Methods of Bilingual and Multicultural Education, Foundations of Teaching, and Hispanics in Education. He has been teaching for over sixteen years.

Richard Ruiz is Associate Professor in and Head of the Department of Language, Reading, and Culture in the College of Education of the University of Arizona. His teaching and research are in the areas of language planning and policy development and minority group education. He has been a consultant to the governments of Mexico, Australia, the Northern Marianas, the Federated States of Micronesia, Aruba, and native communities in the United States and Canada. He is on the editorial boards of *Urban Education* and *Teaching Education* and has recently been named the new editor of the *Bilingual Research Journal*. He is Chair-elect of the Committee on the Status of Minorities in Educational Research and Development of the American Educational Research Association and a member of the English as a New Language Standards Committee of the National Board of Professional Teaching Standards. He was a member of the Stanford Working Group on the Education of Language Minority Students and was recognized for his expertise in educational policy studies by being named to the Clinton-Gore Education Transition Team.

Rose Mary Scott received her Ph.D. from the Ohio State University. She has been an elementary classroom teacher and reading teacher and is currently an Assistant Professor in the School of Education at the University of Wisconsin-Parkside. Her research interests include literature-based literacy instruction, multicultural education, and preparing effective teachers from a multicultural perspective through literacy education.

Christine E. Sleeter is Professor at California State University, Monterey Bay. She formerly was a high school learning disabilities teacher in Seattle, and a Professor at the University of Wisconsin-Parkside. She teaches both graduate and undergraduate courses in multicultural education and consults nationally in this area. On the basis of her active record of publication, she was awarded the 1993 University of Wisconsin-Parkside annual award for Excellence in Research and Creative Activity and the 1994 Research Award of the National Association for Multicultural Education. She has published articles about multicultural education in numerous journals. Her most recent books include *Empowerment through Multicultural Education, Keepers of the American Dream*, and *Making Choices for Multicultural Education* (with Carl Grant). She also edits a series of books for SUNY Press entitled, "The Social Context of Education."

Kip Tellez is Assistant Professor in the College of Education at the University of Houston. He received his doctorate from the The Claremont Graduate School. His research interests include teacher education issues in the education of language-minority youth, second language acquisition, and pragmatism. He has published in journals such as the *Journal of Teacher Education* and the *Journal of Education for Teaching* and has a forthcoming chapter in the *Handbook of Research on Teacher Education* (with J. Gary Knowles).

Olga M. Welch is a Professor in the Rehabilitation and Deafness Unit of the College of Education at the University of Tennessee. She received her doctoral degrees in deaf education and in educational administration from the University of Tennessee. Dr. Welch is well-known as a researcher, teacher, and administrator in the education of persons who are deaf. She has authored numerous articles, monographs, and book chapters, most recently editing the text, *Research and Practice in Deafness*. She has presented her research widely at national and international conferences. Her editorial responsibilities include service as a reviewer for *Perspectives in Education of the Hearing Impaired* and the *Journal of Childhood Communication Disorders*. Dr. Welch has received several research awards, including the departmental E. C. Merrill Distinguished Research Award and four Faculty Research Awards from the University. Most recently, she was the recipient of the University of Tennessee Alumni Association's Outstanding Teaching Award.

Mian M. Yusuf is Assistant Professor of Mathematics/Computer Science Education, Teacher Education Department, University of Wisconsin-Parkside. He received his Ed.D. from the University of Cincinnati. He has taught math to diverse populations in Pakistan, Nigeria, and United States of America. He received the 1993 Distinguished Alumni Award from the University of Cincinnati and was appointed Wisconsin Teaching Fellow for 1992–93 by the University of Wisconsin System. He has conducted several research projects and workshops for teaching math and involved his students in arranging math exhibits. He has presented several research papers at regional, national, and international conferences. He has developed customized software using Logo computer language for teaching geometry to grades 7 through 10.

Cathy Zozakiewicz is a graduate student in Curriculum and Instruction at the University of Wisconsin-Madison. She presently works as a university supervisor in the elementary education student teaching program. Her teaching and research interests include multicultural education and multicultural teacher education. Previously, she taught elementary school for six years.

INDEX